ELIZABETHAN~
JACOBEAN
DRAMA

·The Theatre in Its Time·

T0109015

ELIZABETHAN~ JACOBEAN DRAMA

· The Theatre in Its Time ·

Edited by
G. Blakemore Evans

Cabot Professor of English Literature, Emeritus
Harvard University

NEW AMSTERDAM
New York

Paperback edition published in 1990

First American edition published in 1988 by
NEW AMSTERDAM BOOKS
171 Madison Avenue
New York, N.Y. 10016

Published by arrangement with
A & C Black (Publishers) Limited, London

© 1988 A & C Black (Publishers) Limited

ISBN 0-941533-13-1 (cloth)
ISBN 0-941533-70-0 (paper)

Library of Congress
Cataloging in Publication Data
is available

Printed in Great Britain

Contents

Illustrations and acknowledgements

(appearing between pages 110 and 111)

1 Miniature of a Young Man amongst the roses, by Nicholas Hilliard (1547–1619) (by courtesy of the trustees of the Victoria & Albert Museum, London).

2 Map of Elizabethan London, drawn by John Flower and based on that in *Literary Landscapes of the British Isles*, published by Bell & Hyman.

3 Panorama of London, engraving by J.C. Visscher, *c.* 1616 (reproduced by courtesy of the trustees of the British Museum).

4 The Swan Theatre, sketch by Johannes de Witt, *c.* 1596 (by courtesy of the University Library, Utrecht).

5 Characters in *Titus Andronicus*, pen sketch possibly by Henry Peacham, 1594–5 (*Longleat Portland Papers*, vol. I, folio 159v, reproduced by courtesy of the Marquess of Bath, Longleat House, Warminster, Wiltshire, England).

6 Portrait of Richard Burbage (by permission of the Governors of Dulwich Picture Gallery).

7 William Kemp on his morris dance to Norwich, drawing from his *Nine Daies Wonder*, 1600 (by courtesy of the Folger Shakespeare Library, Washington D.C.).

8 Morris dance, engraving from Edmund Malone's edition of Shakespeare's *Works*, vol. V, 1790.

9 Characters performing drolls, engraving from frontispiece to Francis Kirkman's *The Wits, or, Sport upon Sport*, 1672 (by courtesy of the Folger Shakespeare Library, Washington D C)

10 A wedding masque, detail from a painting recording the career of Sir Henry Unton, *c.* 1596 (by courtesy of the National Portrait Gallery, London).

11 Costume for Zenobia, Queen of Palmyra, designed by Inigo Jones for *The Masque of Queens*, 1609 (engraving in the Devonshire Collection, Chatsworth, reproduced by permission of the Chatsworth Settlement Trustees. Photo: Courtauld Institute of Art).

12 Stage setting for the House of Fame, designed by Inigo Jones for *The Masque of Queens*, 1609 (engraving in the Devonshire Collection, Chatsworth, reproduced by permission of the Chatsworth Settlement Trustees. Photo: Courtauld Institute of Art).

13 The East Front of Montacute House, Somerset (by permission of A. F. Kersting).

14 Tudor house, the home of John Arden in Abbey Street, Faversham, Kent (by permission of A. F. Kersting).

15 Falconry, woodcut from title page of George Turbervile's *Booke of Faulconrie or Hauking*, 1575 (by courtesy of the Folger Shakespeare Library, Washington D.C.).

Prefatory Note

The general focus of the present anthology is, I believe, adequately explained by the title (*Elizabethan–Jacobean Drama: A Background Book*) and its organization by the two-part division: Part I: 'The Theatre and the World', which, through excerpts from contemporary opinion and official documents, etc., treats various aspects of the 'little world' of the theatre in the immediate context of Elizabethan–Jacobean life and times; and Part II: 'The World and the Theatre', which, again through selections from a wide variety of contemporary writers, illustrates how the many problems of everyday living, complicated as they were by moral, religious, social, political and economic issues, provided an ever fruitful source of real-life materials to the dramatists who practised their craft during this extraordinarily creative period.

Within each part, the several sections (or subsections) are prefaced by introductory notes that attempt to set the selections which follow into historical context (with quotations from, or references to, other contemporary writers and modern authorities), to offer short comments on each selection, and to link, wherever possible, the topic of the particular section to specific examples in the drama.

The body of the anthology, the selections, is drawn from the whole spectrum of Elizabethan–Jacobean writing (including letters and diaries). They have been newly edited and are given in modern spelling, except for the retention of a very few characteristically Elizabethan forms that markedly affect pronunciation. Explanatory notes, dealing with the special problems raised by Elizabethan idiom and language or by local, topical and literary allusions, are appended to each selection. Formal selections from Shakespeare have not been included for two reasons: most readers have their own copy of Shakespeare's works and would, for the most part, already be familiar with such selections; and their inclusion would have necessitated the omission of many less well-known but worthwhile witnesses not otherwise easily available. Aside from this, however, Shakespeare is widely represented by frequent quotations and references in the introductory and explanatory notes (the text quoted being that of *The Riverside Shakespeare*, ed. G. B. Evans, 1974).

Although a substantial number of the selections appear in a collection of this kind for the first time, many were brought to my attention by earlier anthologies like John Dover Wilson's *Life in Shakespeare's England* (1911), a pioneer work, G. B. Harrison's *Elizabethan* (1928–33) and *Jacobean* (1941) *Journals* and *England in Shakespeare's Day* (1928), and M. Harrison and C. M. Royston's *How They Lived*, vol. II, 1963; as well as by such works as *Shakespeare's England* (1916, 2 vols., ed. Sir Sidney Lee and C. T. Onions), M. St. Clare Byrne's *Elizabethan Life in Town and Country* (1925; rev. edn 1946), *Shakespeare in His Own Age* (1976; ed. Allardyce Nicoll; originally vol. XVII of *Shakespeare Survey*,

1964), L. C. Knight's *Drama and Society in the Age of Jonson* (1937), Brian Gibbons' *Jacobean City Comedy: A Study of Satiric Plays by Jonson, Marston, and Middleton* (1968), and Edward H. Sugden's ever useful *Topographical Dictionary to the Works of Shakespeare and His Fellow Dramatists* (1925). The dates of composition cited for plays are usually drawn from *Annals of English Drama, 975-1700*, ed. Alfred Harbage and rev. by S. Schoenbaum (1964), and occasional reference is made to the *Oxford English Dictionary (OED)*, E. A. Abbott's *A Shakespearian Grammar* (3rd edn, 1872), and M. P. Tilley's *A Dictionary of the Proverbs in England in the Sixteenth and Seventeenth Centuries* (1950). My various other debts are legion and are acknowledged, so far as possible, in the introductory and explanatory notes.

I have received generous help from many quarters. Two of the General Editors of the New Mermaid series, Professors Brian Gibbons (who first suggested the idea of the present volume to me) and Brian Morris, contributed much timely advice and helpful criticism, and my good friends and colleagues, Professors John Klause and John Tobin, spent many hours reading the manuscript and correcting my errors (those that remain are, poor things, mine own). The reference librarians of the Widener and Houghton Libraries (Harvard University), particularly Mr Henri Bourneuff, came to my rescue on numerous occasions.

I would also like to thank my editors, Mr Tom Neville and Miss Anne Watts at A & C Black, and Miss Margaret Baker, for their good offices and patience in converting a difficult and not very tidy manuscript into publishable shape.

The sources of the illustrations are acknowledged elsewhere, but I owe a special acknowledgement to the Houghton Mifflin Company of Boston, Massachusetts, for allowing A & C Black to use negatives of a number of illustrations from *The Riverside Shakespeare* (1974) originally chosen by me for that volume. Mr Kenneth Carpenter, Editor of the *Harvard Library Bulletin*, kindly gave permission to make use of parts of an article of mine published in vol. XXI (1973, pp. 254-70).

As ever, my greatest personal debt is to my wife, who, for more than forty years, has been my closest collaborator and staunchest stay. This little book is dedicated to her with my profound and loving gratitude.

G.B.E.

Part I

The Theatre and the World

What is our life? a play of passion;
Our mirth? the music of division.
Our mothers' wombs the tiring-houses be,
Where we are dress'd for this short comedy;
Heaven the judicious sharp spectator is
That sits and marks still who doth act amiss;
Our graves, that hide us from the searching sun,
Are like drawn curtains when the play is done;
Thus march we playing to our latest rest,
Only we die in earnest – that's no jest.

> From Orlando Gibbons, *The First Set of Madrigals and Mottets* (1612). Usually ascribed to Sir Walter Raleigh.

The concept of the world as a theatre is a very old one and the Elizabethans and Jacobeans were fond of such Latin tags as *theatrum orbis terrarum, theatrum mundi,* and *Totus mundus agit histrionem* (All the world plays the actor), reflected in the name of Shakespeare's theatre, the Globe, and glossed by the Melancholy Jaques as 'All the world's a stage/And all the men and women merely players' (*As You Like It,* II.vii.139–40). And it was an easy transition from this view of the world as 'a great stage of fools' (*Lear,* IV.vi.183) to seeing the theatre as a microcosm or 'little world', the proper business of which was 'to hold as 'twere the mirror up to nature; to show virtue her feature, scorn her own image, and the very age and body of the time his form and pressure [image]' (*Hamlet,* III.ii.22–4). Or, as Roger Ascham had earlier put it: 'The whole doctrine of comedies and tragedies is a perfit [perfect] *imitation,* or fair lively painted picture, of the life of every degree of man' (*The Scholemaster,* 1570, ed. W. A. Wright in *English Works,* 1904, p. 266).

1 Attitudes toward the drama in Elizabethan–Jacobean England

Although the age of Elizabeth and James is usually considered as synonymous with the greatest age of English drama, it was also a period when the very idea of poetry and drama was most vocally under attack as morally and politically subversive. Fortunately for us, the attacks were limited basically to two groups: those who objected to plays as incitements to vice of all kinds and who found their voice in a number of Puritan extremists (men like John Northbrooke (*c.*1579), Stephen Gosson (1579), Philip Stubbes (1583), and William Rankins (1587)); and those, like the City Fathers (the Lord Mayor and Aldermen of London and other towns), who saw plays and playhouses as the breeding grounds of civil riots and disease. But neither group could seriously dampen the natural enthusiasm of most Englishmen, in city and country alike, for 'shows' of all kinds, particularly plays. City officials, with the help of neighbouring justices in Middlesex and Surrey, might manage to close the theatres for short periods (because of plague or some unusual civil disorder) and the Puritan factions might fulminate, but the drama flourished under the direct or indirect patronage of the Court, which saw to it that, though some might be too 'virtuous', Sir Toby and his thousands of fellow souls had their 'cakes and ale'. The Puritans, of course, finally achieved their goal when Parliament closed the theatres in 1642 for a period of about eighteen years. Even so, however, surreptitious performances were occasionally given. Something of the catastrophic impact of the new ordinance on the profession may be gathered from a curiously facetious little pamphlet called *The Actors Remonstrance* (1643) (see Dover Wilson's *Life in Shakespeare's England*, 1911, pp. 185–9).

The first three of the following selections present the case against plays and players (see also the later section on 'The actors', pp. 92–100): (i) the Lord Mayor's letter (1597) to the Queen's Privy Council; (ii) William Fleetwood's letter to Lord Burghley (1584) on the relation between street brawls and the theatres, in which he makes clear that in his view it is the existence of theatres that generates much of the civil disorder with which, in his position as Recorder of London, he is forced to deal, week in and week out (as he remarks, somewhat wistfully, in an earlier part of the letter: 'by reason no plays were the same day [Whit Sunday], all the City was quiet'); (iii) a typical Puritan view of the drama from Philip Stubbes's *The Anatomie of Abuses* (1583).

The fourth selection (iv), from Thomas Nashe's *Pierce Penilesse* (1592), offers a spirited defence of plays on more or less conventional lines (compare Thomas Lodge's untitled answer (*c.*1580) to Gosson's *The Schoole of Abuse* (1597), Henry Chettle's *Kind-Harts Dreame* (1593), a partly ironic apology for plays and actors put into the mouth of the famous comedian, Richard Tarlton (died 1588), and Thomas Heywood's

3

Apology for Actors (1612)). All the same arguments in defence of drama and the acting profession are repeated and given a dramatic setting in Philip Massinger's *The Roman Actor* (1626) through the title-character, Paris (I.iii).

The fifth selection (v), a letter (1612) from Sir Thomas Bodley to Thomas James, first Keeper of the Bodleian Library, reflects the low literary regard in which most contemporary English plays (equated with almanacs and other ephemera, 'riffraff books' as he dubs them in another letter) were held by some among the more serious-minded members of society. Playbooks in the Bodleian, indeed!

Stubbes and his fellow moralists saw plays as a microcosm of all the evils of the world. 'Plays were first invented by the Devil', leading mankind to damnation: 'For so often as they go to those houses [theatres] where players frequent, they go to Venus' Pallace and Satan's Synagogue to worship devils and betray Christ Jesus' (*The Anatomie*, ed. F. J. Furnivall, p. 143); or, as a certain I. G. put it: 'Plays are the fruit of vintage and drunkenness, consisting of sundry impieties, comprehending evil and damnable things, wherein is taught how in our lives and manners we may follow all kind of vice with art' (*A Refutation of the Apology for Actors* (1615), p. 39).

One special bone of contention with the Puritan opposition, and one which was peculiarly English, was the regular use of boy actors to play all the women's roles, a practice that flew in the face of the biblical injunction in Deuteronomy 22.5: 'The woman shall not wear that which pertaineth unto the man, neither shall a man put on woman's raiment: for all that do so are abomination unto the Lord thy God' (Geneva version (1560), with sidenote: 'For that were to alter the order of nature and to despise God'). Ben Jonson offers a comic refutation of the Puritan position in *Bartholomew Fair* (1614; V.v), when Zeal-of-the-Land Busy is talked down and made to recant by one of the puppets.

i

Official letter from the Lord Mayor of London and the Aldermen to the Privy Council, 28 July 1597 (from Malone Society *Collections*, Part I, i (1907), pp. 78–80).

To the Lords against Stage-Plays.
Our humble duties remembered to your good Lordships and the rest. We have signified to your Honours many times heretofore the great inconvenience which we find to grow by the common exercise of stage-plays. We presumed to do, as well in respect of   5
the duty we bear towards her Highness for the good government of this her City, as for conscience sake, being persuaded (under correction of your Honours' judgment) that neither in polity nor in religion they are to be suffered in a Christian commonwealth, specially being of that frame and matter as usually they are,   10
containing nothing but profane fables, lascivious matters, cozen-ing devices, and scurrilous behaviours, which are so set forth as that they move wholly to imitation and not to the avoiding of those faults and vices which they represent. Among other inconveniences it is not the least that they give opportunity to the   15
refuse sort of evil-disposed and ungodly people that are within and about this City to assemble themselves and to make their matches for all their lewd and ungodly practices; being as heretofore we have found by th'examination of divers apprentices and other servants who have confessed unto us that the said stage-plays were   20
the very places of their rendezvous, appointed by them to meet with such other as were to join with them in their designs and mutinous attempts, being also the ordinary places for masterless men to come together and to recreate themselves. For avoiding whereof we are now again most humble and earnest suitors to your   25
Honours to direct your letters as well to ourselves as to the justices of peace of Surrey and Middlesex for the present stay and final suppressing of the said stage-plays, as well at the Theatre, Curtain, and Bankside as in all other places in and about the City; whereby we doubt not but th'opportunity and the very cause of many   30
disorders being taken away, we shall be more able to keep the worse sort of such evil and disordered people in better order than heretofore we have been. And so most humbly we take our leaves. From London the 28th of July 1597.
Your Honours' most humble.   35

The inconveniences that grow by stage-plays about the City of London.
    1. They are a special cause of corrupting their youth, containing nothing but unchaste matters, lascivious devices, shifts

of cozenage, and other lewd and ungodly practices, being so as   40
that they impress the very quality and corruption of manners
which they represent, contrary to the rules and art prescribed for
the making of comedies even among the heathen, who used them
seldom and at certain set times, and not all the year long as our
manner is. Whereby such as frequent them, being of the base and   45
refuse sort of people, or such young gentlemen as have small
regard of credit or conscience, draw the same into imitation and
not to the avoiding the like vices which they represent.

2.   They are the ordinary places for vagrant persons, masterless men, thieves, horse-stealers, whoremongers, cozeners, coney-   50
catchers, contrivers of treason, and other idle and dangerous
persons to meet together and to make their matches to the great
displeasure of Almighty God and the hurt and annoyance of her
Majesty's people; which cannot be prevented nor discovered by the
governors of the City for that they are out of the City's   55
jurisdiction.

3.   They maintain idleness in such persons as have no
vocation, and draw apprentices and other servants from their
ordinary works and all sorts of people from the resort unto
sermons and other Christian exercises to the great hindrance of   60
trades and profanation of religion established by her Highness
within this realm.

4.   In the time of sickness it is found by experience that many,
having sores and yet not heart-sick, take occasion hereby to walk
abroad and to recreate themselves by hearing a play. Whereby   65
others are infected, and themselves also many things miscarry.

NOTES

5   *to do* i.e. to do so.
8   *polity* civil government.
11   *profane fables* worldly or pagan fictions.
11–12 *cozening devices* tricks aimed at cheating the unwary, particularly visiting
       country folk.
16   *refuse sort* worthless scum.
17   *make their matches* co-ordinate their schemes.
18   *lewd* evil, wicked.
26–9 *justices . . . . . . City* The Theatre and Curtain playhouses were located in
       Shoreditch in Middlesex, not strictly within the jurisdiction of the Lord
       Mayor and Aldermen of London (i.e. the City); the Bankside (in Surrey)
       was also outside their jurisdiction.
36–66 Against the 'inconveniences' here listed, we may note Thomas
       Heywood's 'advantages' accruing from plays (*An Apology for Actors*, 1612,
       sig. F3r, v): the theatres of London are an ornament, earning the
       admiration of all foreigners; the writing of plays has refined the English
       language to such an 'excellency . . . . . . that in these days we are ashamed

of that euphony and eloquence, which, within these sixty years, the best tongues in the land were proud to pronounce'; plays have instructed the unlearned in 'all our English Chronicles . . . . . . and what man have you now . . . . . . that cannot discourse of any notable thing recorded even from William the Conqueror, nay from the landing of Brute, until this day'; plays teach obedience to the king by showing the 'untimely ends of such as have moved tumults, commotions, and insurrections', hence 'exhorting' the people 'to all allegiance'.

39–40 *shifts of cozenage* the same as 'cozening devices', l. 11–12.
41 *impress* imprint (in the minds of the audience).
43 *heathen* Greeks and Romans.
47 *credit* reputation.
50 *cozeners* cheaters, confidence men.
50–1 *coney-catchers* those who prey upon 'conies' (=dupes or 'gulls'), cheaters.
54 *prevented* foreseen, anticipated.
63 *sickness* specifically, the plague.
64 *heart-sick* 'sick to the core', depressed, despondent.
66 *themselves . . . . . . miscarry* i.e. they also injure themselves; 'things' is probably a slip for 'times'.

ii

London street brawls and the theatres

From a letter (18 June 1584) of William Fleetwood (Recorder of London) to Lord Burghley, Lord Treasurer (in Malone Society *Collections*, Part I, ii (1908), pp. 164–6.

That night [Tuesday] I returned to London and found all the wards full of watchers, the cause thereof was for that very near the Theatre or Curtain at the time of the plays there lay a prentice sleeping upon the grass and one Challes *alias* Grostock did turn upon the toe upon the belly of the same prentice, whereupon the apprentice start up and after words they fell to plain blows. The company increased of both sides to the number of five hundred at the least. This Challes exclaimed and said that he was a gentleman and that the apprentice was but a rascal, and some there were little better than rogues that took upon them the name of gentlemen, and said the prentices were but the scum of the world. Upon these troubles the prentices began the next day, being Tuesday, to make mutinies and assemblies, and did conspire to have broken the prisons and to have taken forth the prentices that were imprisoned, but my lord and I having intelligence thereof apprensed four or five of the chief conspirators, who are in Newgate and stand indicted of their lewd demeanours.

Upon Wednesday one Browne, a serving-man in a blue coat, a shifting fellow, having a perilous wit of his own, intending a spoi[l] if he could have brought it to pass, did at Theatre door quarrel with certain poor boys, handicraft prentices, and struck some of them; and lastly he with his sword wounded and maimed one of the boys upon the left hand, whereupon there assembled near a thousand people. This Browne did very cunningly convey himself away, but by chance he was taken after and brought to Master Humphrey Smith, and because no man was able to charge him he dismissed him. And after this Browne was brought before Master Young, where he used himself so cunningly and subtly, no man being there to charge him, that there also he was dismissed. And after I sent a warrant for him, and the constables with the deputy at the Bell in Holborn found him in a parlour fast locked in; and he would not obey the warrant, but by the mean of the host he was conveyed away; and then I sent for the host and caused him to appear at Newgate at the sessions of oyer and determiner, where he was committed until he brought forth his guest. The next day after he brought him forth and so we indicted him for his misdemeanour. This Browne is a common cozener, a thief, and a horse stealer, and coloureth all his doings here about this town

5

10

15

20

25

30

35

with a suit that he hath in the law against a brother of his in
Staffordshire. He resteth now in Newgate.   40

Upon the same Wednesday at night two companions, one
being a tailor and the other a clerk of the common pleas, both of
the duchy and both very lewd fellows, fell out about an harlot, and
the tailor raised the prentices and other light persons and,
thinking that the clerk was run into Lyon's Inn, came to the house   45
with three hundred at the least, brake down the windows of the
house, and struck at the gentlemen, during which broil one
Raynolds, a baker's son, came into Fleet street and there made
solemn proclamation for 'clubs'. The street rose and took and
brought him unto me and the next day we indicted him also for   50
this misdemeanour with many other more.

Upon Wednesday, Thursday, Friday, and Saturday we did
nothing else but sit in commission and examine these misdemean-
ours: we had good help of my Lord Anderson and Master
Sackforth.   55

Upon Sunday my lord sent two aldermen to the Court for the
suppressing and pulling down of the Theatre and Curtain. All the
lords agreed thereunto saving my Lord Chamberlain and Master
Vice-Chamberlain, but we obtained a letter to suppress them all.
Upon the same night I sent for the Queen's players and my Lord   60
of Arundel his players, and they all willingly obeyed the lords'
letters. The chiefest of her highness' players advised me to send for
the owner of the Theatre who was a stubborn fellow and to bind
him. I did so. He sent me word that he was my Lord of Hunsdon's
man and that he would not come at me but he would in the   65
morning ride to my lord. Then I sent the undersheriff for him and
he brought him to me, and at his coming he stouted me out very
hasty, and in the end I shewed him my lord his master's hand and
then he was more quiet, but to die for it he would not be bound.
And then I minding to send him to prison, he made suit that he   70
might be bound to appear at the oyer and determiner the which is
to-morrow, where he said that he was sure the court would not
bind him being a councillor's man. And so I have granted his
request, where he shall be sure to be bound or else is like to do
worse.   75

NOTES

2 *wards* divisions (twenty-six in all) of the City, each under the jurisdiction
   of an alderman.
   watchers guards, watchmen.
3 *Theatre or Curtain* The Theatre was built by James Burbage in 1576; the
   Curtain, in 1577; both were located in Shoreditch (northern suburbs).
   time......plays Plays usually began about two or three o'clock.

6   *start* jumped.
13   *broken* i.e. broken open.
15   *my lord* i.e. the Lord Mayor of London, Sir Thomas Pullison, draper.
16   *apprensed* apprehended (contracted form).
17   *Newgate* the chief prison for felons and debtors, originally one of the gates of old London.
18   *blue coat* the regular dress of servants.
19   *shifting fellow* rascal given to criminal devices.
      perilous wit dangerous mind.
20   *spoi[l]* act of plunder, theft.
21   *handicraft prentices* boys apprenticed to such trades as carpentry, bricklaying, etc.
27   *after* afterwards; cf. l. 30.
31   *the Bell in Holborn* inn located in Holborn, one of the main thoroughfares of London.
      parlour probably here used for 'bedchamber'.
34   *sessions......determiner* sitting of the Queen's Bench, commissioned to hear and determine (=oyer and determiner) indictments for treason, felonies, etc.
37   *cozener* As a horse stealer, Browne would have belonged to the fraternity of the 'prigging law' (see Robert Greene, *The Second Part of Conny-Catching* (1592), ed. G. B. Harrison, 1923, pp. 13–19).
38   *coloureth* disguiseth, cloaketh.
41   *companions* base fellows.
42   *clerk......pleas* minor officer of the Court of Common Pleas, which judged civil suits.
43   *duchy* district between London and Westminster forming the precincts of the Duchy House of Lancaster.
45   *Lyon's Inn* Inn of Chancery, belonging to the Inner Temple.
48   *Fleet street* ran from Ludgate Hill to Temple Bar.
49   *'clubs'* the rallying cry of London apprentices, who armed themselves with clubs.
      street rose i.e. in opposition.
57   *suppressing* i.e. prohibiting performances at.
58   *lords* i.e. the members of the Queen's Privy Council.
      Lord Chamberlain Charles, Lord Howard of Effingham.
59   *Vice-Chamberlain* Sir Christopher Hatton.
      letter Presumably a temporary 'inhibition' against playing resulted from this letter. The Theatre and Curtain were not 'pulled down'.
60   *Queen's players* a company, under the patronage of the Queen, established in 1583, now probably playing at the Theatre.
60-1 *Lord of Arundel his players* Henry Howard, thirteenth earl. His players were presumably performing at the Curtain.
62   *chiefest......players* either Robert Wilson or Richard Tarlton.
63   *owner of the Theatre* i.e. James Burbage, father of the famous actor Richard Burbage, who created many of the leading roles in Shakespeare's plays. His claim (ll. 64–5) to be 'my Lord of Hunsdon's man' (i.e. Henry Carey, first Lord Hunsdon, who became Lord Chamberlain in 1585 and was the patron of the Lord Chamberlain's Men, later Shakespeare's company) poses an unsolved problem at this date.
65   *come at me* i.e. come at my order.
67   *stouted me out* defied me.

68   *hasty* angrily.
     hand As a member of the Council Lord Hunsdon had signed the letter
     suppressing playing.
69   *to die for it* i.e. he would rather die than be bound over to appear in court
     to answer charges.

iii

A Puritan looks at the drama

From Philip Stubbes, *The Anatomie of Abuses* (1583, 2nd edn), pp. 144–5,
in F. J. Furnivall's edn (1877–9).

Do they not maintain bawdry, insinuate foolery, and renew the
remembrance of heathen idolatry? Do they not induce whoredom
and uncleanness? Nay, are they not rather plain devourers of
maidenly virginity and chastity? For proof whereof but mark the
flocking and running to Theatres and Curtains, daily and hourly,   5
night and day, time and tide, to see plays and interludes, where
such wanton gestures, such bawdy speeches, such laughing and
fleering, such kissing and bussing, such clipping and culling, such
winking and glancing of wanton eyes, and the like is used, as is
wonderful to behold. Then these goodly pageants being done, every   10
mate sorts to his mate, every one brings another homeward of their
way very friendly, and in their secret conclaves (covertly) they play
the sodomites, or worse. And these be the fruits of plays and
interludes, for the most part. And whereas, you say, there are good
examples to be learned in them: truly so there are; if you will learn   15
falsehood; if you will learn cozenage; if you will learn to deceive; if
you will learn to play the hypocrite, to cog, to lie and falsify; if you
will learn to jest, laugh and fleer, to grin, to nod and mow; if you
will learn to play the Vice, to swear, tear and blaspheme both
heaven and earth; if you will learn to become a bawd, unclean, and   20
to devirginate maids, to deflower honest wives; if you will learn to
murder, flay, kill, pick, steal, rob and rove; if you will learn to rebel
against princes, to commit treasons, to consume treasures, to
practise idleness, to sing and talk of bawdy love and venery; if you
will learn to deride, scoff, mock and flout, to flatter and smooth; if   25
you will learn to play the whoremaster, the glutton, drunkard, or

incestuous person; if you will learn to become proud, haughty and
arrogant; and finally, if you will learn to contemn God and all His
laws, to care neither for Heaven nor Hell, and to commit all kind
of sin and mischief, you need to go to no other school, for all these   30
good examples may you see painted before your eyes in interludes
and plays.

NOTES

5   *Theatres and Curtains* See selection (i), ll. 26–9 n.

6   *interludes* a loosely used term describing a variety of plays: 'moral
interlude' (i.e. the anonymous *Marriage of Wit and Science* (*c*.1568));
comedy (i.e. Nicholas Udall's *Ralph Roister Doister* (1545–52); classical
'moral' (i.e. R. B.'s *Appius and Virginia* (1559–67).

8   *fleering* sneering, ridiculing, laughing coarsely (the following pairs, as
here, are essentially tautological – a favourite device of Stubbes's style of
invective).
bussing kissing.
culling embracing.

11 *mate . . . . . . mate* fellow (used contemptuously) consorts with fellow. In
view of what Stubbes has been saying above, the following charge of
homosexual behaviour ('sodomites', l. 13) seems dragged in largely to
paint as black a picture as possible.

12 *conclaves* private rooms.

17 *cog* cheat, deceive (particularly at cards or dice).

18 *mow* make faces.

19 *Vice* figure in moral interludes, who combined in one character all the
seven deadly sins.

20 *bawd* procurer (male or female).

22 *flay* pillage, plunder.
rove wander aimlessly, like a vagabond beggar.

24 *venery* sexual licence.

25 *flout* jeer, insult.
smooth flatter.

28 *contemn* despise.

iv

Thomas Nashe answers the detractors of the theatre

From Thomas Nashe, *Pierce Penilesse* (1592), ed. R. B. McKerrow, *Works*, I, (1904), 211–15.

That state or kingdom that is in league with all the world and hath no foreign sword to vex it, is not half so strong or confirmed to endure, as that which lives every hour in fear of invasion. There is a certain waste of the people for whom there is no use but war: and these men must have some employment still to cut them off. *Nam*   5 *si foras hostem non habent, domi invenient.* If they have no service abroad, they will make mutinies at home. Or if the affairs of the state be such, as cannot exhale all these corrupt excrements, it is very expedient they have some light toys to busy their heads withal, cast before them as bones to gnaw upon, which may keep   10 them from having leisure to intermeddle with higher matters.

To this effect, the policy of plays is very necessary, howsoever some shallow-brained censurers (not the deepest searchers into the secrets of government) mightily oppugn them. For whereas the afternoon, being the idlest time of the day, wherein men that are   15 their own masters (as gentlemen of the Court, the Inns of the Court, and the number of captains and soldiers about London) do wholly bestow themselves upon pleasure, and that pleasure they divide (how virtuously it skills not) either into gaming, following of harlots, drinking, or seeing a play: is it not then better (since of   20 four extremes all the world cannot keep them but they will choose one) that they should betake them to the least, which is plays? Nay, what if I prove plays to be no extreme, but a rare exercise of virtue? First, for the subject of them (for the most part) it is borrowed out of our English chronicles, wherein our forefathers'   25 valiant acts (that have lien long buried in rusty brass and worm-eaten books) are revived, and they themselves raised from the grave of oblivion, and brought to plead their aged honours in open presence: than which, what can be a sharper reproof to these degenerate effeminate days of ours?   30

How would it have joyed brave Talbot (the terror of the French) to think that after he had lien two hundred years in his tomb, he should triumph again on the stage, and have his bones new embalmed with the tears of ten thousand spectators at least (at several times), who in the tragedian that represents his person   35 imagine they behold him fresh bleeding.

I will defend it against any cullion or club-fisted usurer of them all, there is no immortality can be given a man on earth like unto plays. What talk I to them of immortality, that are the only underminers of honour, and do envy any man that is not sprung up   40

by base brokery like themselves? They care not if all the ancient houses were rooted out, so that, like the burgomasters of the Low-countries, they might share the government amongst them as states, and be quarter-masters of our monarchy. All arts to them are vanity; and, if you tell them what a glorious thing it is to have   45
Henry the Fifth represented on the stage, leading the French king prisoner, and forcing both him and the Dolphin to swear fealty, 'Aye but' (will they say) 'what do we get by it?' Respecting neither the right of fame that is due to true nobility deceased, nor what hopes of eternity are to be proposed to advent'rous minds, to   50
encourage them forward, but only their execrable lucre and filthy unquenchable avarice.

They know when they are dead they shall not be brought upon the stage for any goodness, but in a merriment of the Usurer and the Devil, or buying arms of the herald, who gives them the lion,   55
without tongue, tail, or talents, because his master whom he must serve is a townsman and a man of peace, and must not keep any quarrelling beasts to annoy his honest neighbours.

In plays, all cozenages, all cunning drifts over-gilded with outward holiness, all stratagems of war, all the cankerworms that   60
breed on the rust of peace are most lively anatomized: they show the ill-success of treason, the fall of hasty climbers, the wretched end of usurpers, the misery of civil dissension, and how just God is evermore in punishing of murder. And to prove every one of these allegations, could I propound the circumstances of this play and   65
that play, if I meant to handle this theme otherwise than *obiter*. What should I say more? They are sour pills of reprehension, wrapped up in sweet words. Whereas some petitioners of the Council against them object they corrupt the youth of the City and withdraw prentices from their work, they heartily wish they might   70
be troubled with none of their youth nor their prentices; for some of them (I mean the ruder handicrafts' servants) never come abroad but they are in danger of undoing. And as for corrupting them when they come, that's false; for no play they have encourageth any man to tumults or rebellion, but lays before such   75
the halter and the gallows; or praiseth or approveth pride, lust, whoredom, prodigality, or drunkenness, but beats them down utterly. As for the hindrance of trades and traders of the City by them, that is an article foisted in by the vintners, alewives, and victuallers, who surmise, if there were no plays, they should have   80
all the company that resort to them lie boozing and beer-bathing in their houses every afternoon. Nor so, nor so, good Brother Bottle-ale, for there are other places besides where money can bestow itself: the sign of the smock will wipe your mouth clean; and yet I have heard ye have made her a tenant to your tap-houses.   85
But what shall he do that hath spent himself? Where shall he haunt? Faith, when dice, lust, and drunkenness and all have dealt

upon him, if there be never a play for him to go to for his penny, he sits melancholy in his chamber, devising upon felony or treason, and how he may best exalt himself by mischief.   90

In Augustus' time (who was the patron of all witty sports) there happened a great fray in Rome about a player, insomuch as all the city was in an uproar: whereupon the emperor (after the broil was somewhat overblown) called the player before him, and asked what was the reason that a man of his quality durst presume to   95 make such a brawl about nothing. He smilingly replied, 'It is good for thee, O Cæsar, that the people's heads are troubled with brawls and quarrels about us and our light matters; for otherwise they would look into thee and thy matters'.

NOTES

5   *still* . . . . . . *off* continually to limit the number of them.
5–6 *Nam* . . . . . . *invenient* freely translated in ll. 6–7.
8   *exhale* drive or draw off (in vapour).
9   *light toys* slight trifles.
13   *shallow-brained censurers* referring, among others, to writers like Northbrooke, Gosson, and Stubbes, who, generally from a Puritan perspective, had written works attacking the stage. See selections pp. 11, 20.
19   *skills* matters.
20–2 *since* . . . . . . *one* since nothing in the world will prevent them from choosing one of these extremes.
24–5 *subject* . . . . . . *chronicles* Nashe, writing in 1592, is referring to such English public-theatre history plays as the anonymous *Famous Victories of Henry the Fifth* (1583–8) (see below ll. 46–8), the anonymous *Troublesome Reign of King John* (1587–91), Shakespeare's *I–III Henry VI* (1589–91) and perhaps *Richard III* (1592–3), Peele's *Edward I* (1590–3), and Marlowe's *Edward II* (1592).
26   *lien* lain.
     rusty brass i.e. funeral monuments of brass, usually laid into the pavements of churches. 'rusty'=antiquated, unpolished.
30   *effeminate* unmanly.
31   *brave Talbot* John Talbot, first Earl of Shrewsbury (1388?–1453). Nashe is most probably referring to the so-called Talbot scenes in *I Henry VI*.
32   *two hundred years* somewhat of an exaggeration (see preceding note).
35   *tragedian* perhaps Richard Burbage, principal actor of Shakespeare's company, then affiliated with Strange's Men.
37   *cullion* base, despicable fellow.
     club-fisted tight-fisted, avaricious.
41   *brokery* buying and selling, trade (used pejoratively).
42   *burgomasters* chief magistrates of Dutch or Flemish towns.
44   *quarter-masters* naval petty officers, but here used as 'assistant rulers' (McKerrow), i.e. quartering the country up between them.
46   *Henry the Fifth* a reference to *Famous Victories*, not to Shakespeare's play (1599).

47   *Dolphin* Dauphin (usual Elizabethan form).

48   *'what......it?'* i.e. how will it pay off?

51   *lucre* money.

54   *for* because of.

54–5 *merriment......Devil* perhaps a reference to a lost moral interlude
      related to the story of Dives and Lazarus. In Marston's *Histriomastix*
      (*c*.1599), the company poet, Posthaste, includes *The Devil and Dives*
      among the company's repertory, describing it (?ironically) as a 'comedy'
      (see selection on p. 44, l. 31).

56   *talents* talons, claws.

59   *drifts* schemes, plots.

60   *cankerworms* caterpillars.

65   *circumstances* details.

66   *obiter* in passing.

67–8 *sour......words* The sugared-pill defence was common. Compare
      Sidney (*Defence of Poesy*, 1595 [written *c*.1579–80], in *Elizabethan Critical
      Essays*, ed. G. G. Smith, 1904, I, 172): 'the child is often brought to take
      most wholesome things by hiding them in such other as have a pleasant
      taste'.

69   *Council* i.e. the Queen's Privy Council.

73   *but* but that.
      undoing getting into trouble.

74–5 *no play......tumults* The prentices' 'insurrection scene' in Munday and
      Chettle's *Sir Thomas More* (1594–5; preserved only in MS) was forbidden
      by the Master of the Revels, Sir Edmund Tilney, because it was felt to be
      politically dangerous. As a result, Shakespeare (and others) was called in
      to help repair the damage and contributed a scene (II.iii) and at least one
      other speech (III.i.1–21). II.iii (147 lines) is believed by most scholars to be
      in Shakespeare's handwriting.

84   *sign......smock* i.e. brothels.
      wipe......clean i.e. be your undoing.

85   *tenant......tap-houses* i.e. taverns, alehouses, etc., have become
      brothels.

86   *spent himself* depleted himself (physically and financially).

95   *quality* profession or social status.

V

Playbooks banished the Bodleian Library – almost

From a letter of Sir Thomas Bodley to Thomas James, first Keeper of the Bodleian Library, 15 January 1612 (in *Letters of Sir Thomas Bodley to Thomas James*, ed. G. W. Wheeler (1926), pp. 221–2).

...... I can see no good reason to alter my opinion, for excluding such books as almanacs, plays, and an infinite number that are daily printed of very unworthy matters and handling, such as, methinks, both the Keeper and Underkeeper should disdain to seek out to deliver unto any man. Haply some plays may be worthy the keeping, but hardly one in forty. For it is not alike in English plays and others of other nations: because they are most esteemed for learning the languages, and many of them compiled by men of great fame for wisdom and learning, which is seldom or never seen among us. Were it so, again, that some little profit might be reaped (which God knows is very little) out of some of our playbooks, the benefit thereof will nothing near countervail the harm that the scandal will bring unto the Library, when it shall be given out that we stuff it full of baggage books. And though they should be but a few, as they would be very many if your course should take place, yet the having of those few (such is the nature of malicious reporters) would be mightily multiplied by such as purpose to speak in disgrace of the Library. This is my opinion, wherein, if I err, I think I shall err with infinite others; and the more I think upon it, the more it doth distaste me that such kind of books should be vouchsafed a room in so noble a Library ......

5

10

15

20

NOTES

1   *I can......opinion* Apparently Thomas James had been urging that plays, etc. should be given a home in the library (see ll. 15–16). Bodley is writing two years after the Stationers' Company (1610) had made a grant to the Bodleian Library by which a copy of all books printed under their auspices would be presented to the library free of charge. Playbooks had presumably begun to arrive, along with other 'trivia'. Fortunately for us, Bodley's policy did not prevail for long, if at all.

6–7 *not......nations* i.e. English plays are not like those of other nations.

8–9 *many......learning* Bodley is referring to Italian and French plays, which, for the most part, were written in imitation of Seneca (tragedy) and Plautus and Terence (comedy). They were also to be valued 'for learning the languages'.

14   *baggage books* trashy, rubbishy books.

2 The audience

The audience in the days of Elizabeth and James was drawn from all levels of society. Anyone with the necessary money could, and often did, attend the theatres in London, including the so-called 'private' theatres. Until quite recently, however, it has been usual to make a comparatively sharp distinction between the clientele of the public playhouses, the majority of which was believed to be made up of 'commoners' (tradesmen, artificers, yeomen, apprentices, journeymen, 'masterless men', visitors from the country, etc., together with a generous assortment of thieves and prostitutes), and the more educated and socially select patrons (nobility, gentlemen, students at the Inns of Court, etc.) who attended the 'private' theatres (see Alfred Harbage, *Shakespeare's Audience*, 1941, and his later *Shakespeare and the Rival Traditions*, 1952). Though the distinction is not without some truth perhaps, a new study by Ann J. Cook (*The Privileged Playgoers of Shakespeare's London*, 1981) argues that the audiences at both public and 'private' theatres were much more homogeneous and consisted for the most part of a comparatively small core of what she terms 'privileged playgoers' (i.e. those who could afford even the proverbial penny entrance fee to stand in the theatre yard). Drawing on various demographic studies, she suggests (p. 94) that this core represented approximately 15 per cent of London's population between 1576 and 1642, even though that population had increased from roughly 180,000 in 1576 to about 350,000 by 1642. The 'privileged' constituted a great diversity of social levels, from the old nobility and gentry to the upwardly mobile world of business and trade and the landed yeomanry – the key to 'privilege' being, of course, money. Mrs Cook argues further that, given the bare subsistence level on which about 85 per cent of London's population were forced to live and the long and stringently enforced working hours, few apprentices, day labourers, or servants had either time or money to spend on the theatres, except perhaps occasionally on holidays. She does not, of course, deny that such 'lower orders' (including various criminal elements) did from time to time visit the playhouses, but she suggests that their numbers (particularly so far as the public theatres were concerned) were seriously exaggerated for religious (Puritan) and political (law and order) reasons by contemporary critics.

The Puritan view of the audience is adequately represented by selection (i) from Stephen Gosson's *The Schoole of Abuse* (1579). Before a change of heart (about 1579), Gosson, educated at Oxford, had written several plays, none of them extant (one, *Cataline's Conspiracies*, he describes as 'a pig of mine own sow', sig. C7 r) and had, perhaps, been himself an actor. His attack on the stage is rather more tempered than that of others (e.g. Philip Stubbes's in *The Anatomie of Abuses*, 1583) and he even admits that 'Some plays [are] tolerable at sometime [i.e. on occasion]' and that 'Some players [are] modest if I be not deceived' (sig. C6 v). He claims that it is the 'abuses' of poetry, music and plays that he is attacking, though the line is often not very carefully drawn. *The Schoole* was dedicated to Sir Philip Sidney and may, perhaps, have led Sidney to write a kind of answer in his celebrated *Defence of Poesy* (written about 1579–80, published 1595). The official view of the City (as well as a selection from Stubbes's *Anatomie*) will be found above, pages 5–12.

The following three selections ((ii) Thomas Dekker's *The Guls Horne-booke* (1609); (iii) Francis Beaumont's *The Knight of the Burning Pestle* (1607–8); (iv) Edmund Gayton's *Pleasant Notes upon Don Quixot* (1654)) also present the typical audience from a basically satirical point of view (though more tolerantly than Gosson or Stubbes) as boisterous and unruly, tending to disrupt the play and dictate terms to the actors. That performances could be disturbed by brawls and spectator dissatisfaction is amply borne out from other sources, but one must allow for the satirist's natural tendency to exaggerate for his own purposes the less decorous sides of human nature at the expense of its more normal (and less sensational) aspects. Hell is better 'copy' than Heaven. Thus we may suspect that most performances, even at the Fortune, the Curtain and the Red Bull, theatres which gained a reputation for rowdiness, went off smoothly enough, even if noisily by modern standards.

The excerpt from Dekker's *Guls Horne-booke* (ii) is part of Dekker's campaign, carried further in his *Bell-Man of London* (1608), *Lanthorne and Candle-Light* (1608), *The Seven Deadly Sinnes of London* (1606), *Newes from Hell* (1606), etc., to expose the underside of London life (see pp. 230, 238, 240 for similar exposés). Other chapters give satirical advice to the fledgling gallant (or 'gull') on how to dress *à la mode* and how to behave himself in Paul's Walk (see the selection from Dekker's *Dead Tearme* (1608), p. 222), in an ordinary (see the selection, pp. 218–20), and how to escape the Watch in the small hours of the morning.

Aside from their general bearing on the behaviour of the audience, the selections from Beaumont (iii) and Gayton (iv) are of special interest for their comments on the kinds of plays suitable to a 'popular' or citizen audience, whose taste is, of course, held up to ridicule.

i

Elizabethans at the theatre

From Stephen Gosson, *The Schoole of Abuse* (1579), sigs. C1 r–C2 r.

Compare London to Rome, and England to Italy, you shall find
the theatres of the one, the abuses of the other, to be rife among
us. *Experto crede*, I have seen somewhat, and therefore I think
may say the more. In Rome, when plays or pageants are shown,
Ovid chargeth his pilgrims to creep close to the saints whom they   5
serve and show their double diligence to lift the gentlewomen's
robes from the ground for soiling in the dust; to sweep motes from
their kirtles; to keep their fingers in ure; to lay their hands at their
backs for an easy stay; to look upon those whom they behold; to
praise that which they commend; to like every thing that pleaseth   10
them; to present them pomegranates to pick as they sit; and when
all is done to wait on them mannerly to their houses.
    In our assemblies at plays in London, you shall see such
heaving, and shoving, such itching and shouldering to sit by
women: such care for their garments, that they be not trod on: 15
such eyes to their laps, that no chips light in them: such pillows to
their backs, that they take no hurt: such masking in their ears, I
know not what: such giving them pippins to pass the time: such
playing at foot-saunt without cards: such ticking, such toying,
such smiling, such winking, and such manning them home, when   20
the sports are ended, that it is a right comedy to mark their
behaviour, to watch their conceits, as the cat for the mouse, and as
good as a course at the game itself, to dog them a little, or follow
aloof by the print of their feet, and so discover by slot where the
deer taketh soil. If this were as well noted as ill seen, or as openly   25
punished as secretly practised, I have no doubt but the cause would
be seared to dry up the effect, and these pretty rabbits very
cunningly ferreted from their burrows. For they that lack
customers all the week, either because their haunt is unknown, or
the constables and officers of their parish watch them so narrowly   30
that they dare not quetch, to celebrate the Sabbath flock to
theatres, and there keep a general market of bawdry. Not that any
filthiness in deed is committed within the compass of that ground,
as was done in Rome, but that every wanton and his paramour,
every man and his mistress, every John and his Joan, every knave   35
and his quean, are there first acquainted and cheapen the
merchandise in that place, which they pay for elsewhere as they
can agree.

NOTES

3   *Experto crede* Believe one who knows from experience. See introductory note.

5   *Ovid* in *The Art of Love* (*Ars Amatoria*), I, 135–62. Ovid also influences Gosson's account of English behaviour at the theatre.
    pilgrims......saints lovers......ladies. Shakespeare uses this pilgrim / saint metaphor in *Romeo and Juliet*, I.v.93–110.

7   *for* against
    motes specks.

8   *kirtles* skirts or outer petticoats.
    in ure in use, i.e. busy.

9   *easy stay* support offering ease.

14 *itching* hankering, craving.

16 *chips* literally 'wood shavings'; here used, analogous to 'motes' (l. 7), for any 'specks' of foreign matter (not in *OED*).

17 *masking* pretence (of affection); *OED* does not appear to recognize this sense.

18 *pippins* apples. Paul Hentzner (*Itinerarium*, 1612, edn of 1757, p. 43) reports: 'In these theatres fruits, such as apples, pears, and nuts, according to the season, are carried about to be sold, as well as ale and wine.'

19 *foot-saunt* 'Cent' or 'saunt' was a card game, the winner scoring a hundred (cent); 'foot-saunt' is unique to Gosson, but the bawdy implications of 'foot-saunt without cards' is obvious enough.
    ticking......toying dallying......amorous play.

21 *right* true.

22 *conceits* devices, tricks.

23 *course at the game* pursuit of the deer (=game) by hounds; note 'to dog' in l. 23.

24 *slot* mark left by the deer's foot.

25 *taketh soil* takes refuge in a river or lake (here meaning the prostitute's lodging).
    ill seen i.e. the sight of it being evil.

27 *seared* burned (as with a hot iron). The 'cause' presumably refers to the theatres.
    pretty rabbits prostitutes (which haunt the theatre).

28 *ferreted* Rabbits were driven out of their burrows by the use of ferrets.

31 *quetch* stir out, go abroad.

36 *quean* prostitute.
    cheapen bargain for.

ii

From Thomas Dekker, *The Guls Horne-booke* (1609), chap. VI, pp. 27–30.

How a gallant should behave himself in a play-house.
The theatre is your poets' Royal Exchange, upon which their muses (that are now turned to merchants) meeting, barter away that light commodity of words for a lighter ware than words: plaudities and the breath of the great beast, which, like the threatenings of two cowards, vanish all into air. [To] players and their factors, who put away the stuff, and make the best of it they possibly can (as indeed 'tis their parts so to do) your gallant, your courtier, and your captain had wont to be the soundest paymasters, and, I think, are still the surest chapmen: and these, by means that their heads are well stocked, deal upon this comical freight by the gross; when your groundling and gallery-commoner buys his sport by the penny, and, like a haggler, is glad to utter it again by retailing.

Sithence then the place is so free in entertainment, allowing a stool as well to the farmer's son as to your Templar; that your stinkard has the selfsame liberty to be there in his tobacco-fumes, which your sweet courtier hath; and that your carman and tinker claim as strong a voice in their suffrage, and sit to give judgment on the play's life and death, as well as the proudest Momus among the tribe of critic: it is fit that he, whom the most tailors' bills do make room for, when he comes should not be basely (like a viol) cased up in a corner.

Whither therefore the gatherers of the public or private play-house stand to receive the afternoon's rent, let our gallant (having paid it) presently advance himself up to the throne of the stage. I mean not into the lord's room, which is now but the stage's suburbs. No, those boxes, by the iniquity of custom, conspiracy of waiting-women and gentlemen-ushers that there sweat together, and the covetousness of sharers, are contemptibly thrust into the rear; and much new satin is there damned, by being smothered to death in darkness. But on the very rushes where the comedy is to dance, yea, and under the state of Cambyses himself, must our feathered estrich, like a piece of ordnance, be planted valiantly (because impudently), beating down the mews and hisses of the opposed rascality.

For do but cast up a reckoning; what large comings-in are pursed up by sitting on the stage? First a conspicuous eminence is gotten, by which means the best and most essential parts of a gallant (good clothes, a proportionable leg, white hand, the Persian lock, and a tolerable beard) are perfectly revealed.

By sitting on the stage you have a signed patent to engross the

whole commodity of censure, may lawfully presume to be a girder, and stand at the helm to steer the passage of scenes; yet no man shall once offer to hinder you from obtaining the title of an   45
insolent overweening coxcomb.

By sitting on the stage you may (without travelling for it) at the very next door ask whose play it is; and, by that quest of inquiry, the law warrants you to avoid much mistaking. If you know not the author, you may rail against him, and peradventure so behave   50
yourself, that you may enforce the author to know you.

By sitting on the stage, if you be a knight, you may happily get you a mistress; if a mere Fleet-street gentleman, a wife: but assure yourself, by continual residence, you are the first and principal man in election to begin the number of 'We three'.   55

By spreading your body on the stage, and by being a justice in examining of plays, you shall put yourself into such true scenical authority, that some poet shall not dare to present his muse rudely upon your eyes, without having first unmasked her, rifled her, and discovered all her bare and most mystical parts before you at a   60
tavern; when you most knightly shall, for his pains, pay for both their suppers.

By sitting on the stage you may (with small cost) purchase the dear acquaintance of the boys; have a good stool for sixpence; at any time know what particular part any of the infants present; get your   65
match lighted; examine the play-suits' lace, and perhaps win wagers upon laying 'tis copper, &c. And to conclude, whether you be a fool or a justice of peace, a cuckold or a captain, a lord-mayor's son or a dawcock, a knave or an undersheriff, of what stamp soever you be, current or counterfeit, the stage, like time,   70
will bring you to most perfect light, and lay you open. Neither are you to be hunted from thence, though the scarecrows in the yard hoot at you, hiss at you, spit at you, yea throw dirt even in your teeth: 'tis most gentlemanlike patience to endure all this and to laugh at the silly animals. But if the rabble with a full throat cry: 75
'Away with the fool!' you were worse than a madman to tarry by it; for the gentleman and the fool should never sit on the stage together.

Marry, let this observation go hand in hand with the rest; or rather like a country serving-man some five yards before them.   80
Present not yourself on the stage (especially at a new play) until the quaking Prologue hath by rubbing got colour into his cheeks, and is ready to give the trumpets their cue that he is upon point to enter; for then it is time, as though you were one of the properties, or that you dropped out of the hangings, to creep from behind the   85
arras, with your tripos or three-footed stool in one hand and a teston mounted between a fore-finger and a thumb in the other; for, if you should bestow your person upon the vulgar, when the belly of the house is but half full, your apparel is quite eaten up, the

fashion lost, and the proportion of your body in more danger to be   90
devoured than if it were served up in the Counter amongst the
poultry: avoid that as you would the bastone. It shall crown you
with rich commendation to laugh aloud in the midst of the most
serious and saddest scene of the terriblest tragedy; and to let that
clapper (your tongue) be tossed so high, that all the house may   95
ring of it. Your lords use it; your knights are apes to the lords, and
do so too; your Inn-a-court man is zany to the knights, and
(marry, very scurvily) comes likewise limping after it. Be thou a
beagle to them all, and never lin snuffing till you have scented
them: for by talking and laughing (like a ploughman in a morris)   100
you heap Pelion upon Ossa, glory upon glory. As first, all the eyes
in the galleries will leave walking after the players, and only follow
you; the simplest dolt in the house snatches up your name, and,
when he meets you in the streets, or that you fall into his hands in
the middle of a watch, his word shall be taken for you; he'll cry   105
'He's such a gallant,' and you pass. Secondly, you publish your
temperance to the world, in that you seem not to resort thither to
taste vain pleasures with a hungry appetite, but only as a
gentleman to spend a foolish hour or two, because you can do
nothing else. Thirdly, you mightily disrelish the audience, and   110
disgrace the author: marry, you take up (though it be at the worst
hand) a strong opinion of your own judgment, and enforce the
poet to take pity of your weakness, and by some dedicated sonnet
to bring you into a better paradise, only to stop your mouth.

If you can (either for love or money) provide yourself a lodging   115
by the water-side; for, above the convenience it brings to shun
shoulder-clapping, and to ship away your cockatrice betimes in the
morning, it adds a kind of state unto you to be carried from thence
to the stairs of your playhouse. Hate a sculler (remember that)
worse than to be acquainted with one o' th' scullery. No, your oars   120
are your only sea-crabs, board them, and take heed you never go
twice together with one pair; often shifting is a great credit to
gentlemen, and that dividing of your fare will make the poor
water-snakes be ready to pull you in pieces to enjoy your custom.
No matter whether, upon landing, you have money, or no; you   125
may swim in twenty of their boats over the river upon ticket:
marry, when silver comes in, remember to pay treble their fare,
and it will make your flounder-catchers to send more thanks after
you when you do not draw, than when you do: for they know it
will be their own another day.   130

Before the play begins, fall to cards; you may win or lose (as
fencers do in a prize) and beat one another by confederacy, yet
share the money when you meet at supper. Notwithstanding, to
gull the ragamuffins that stand aloof gaping at you, throw the
cards (having first torn four or five of them) round about the stage,   135
just upon the third sound, as though you had lost. It skills not if

the four knaves lie on their backs, and outface the audience;
there's none such fools as dare take exceptions at them, because,
ere the play go off, better knaves than they will fall into the
company.   140

Now, sir, if the writer be a fellow that hath either epigramed
you, or hath had a flirt at your mistress, or hath brought either
your feather, or your red beard, or your little legs, &c. on the stage,
you shall disgrace him worse than by tossing him in a blanket, or
giving him the bastinado in a tavern, if, in the middle of his play   145
(be it pastoral or comedy, moral or tragedy), you rise with a
screwed and discontented face from your stool to be gone. No
matter whether the scenes be good, or no; the better they are, the
worse do you distaste them; and, being on your feet, sneak not
away like a coward, but salute all your gentle acquaintance, that   150
are spread either on the rushes, or on stools about you, and draw
what troop you can from the stage after you. The mimics are
beholden to you for allowing them elbow-room; their poet cries
perhaps, 'A pox go with you', but care not for that; there's no
music without frets.   155

Marry, if either the company or indisposition of the weather
bind you to sit it out, my counsel is then that you turn plain ape:
take up a rush, and tickle the earnest ears of your fellow gallants,
to make other fools fall a laughing; mew at passionate speeches,
blare at merry, find fault with the music, whew at the children's   160
action, whistle at the songs, and, above all, curse the sharers, that
whereas the same day you had bestowed forty shillings on an
embroidered felt and feather (Scotch fashion) for your mistress in
the Court, or your punk in the City, within two hours after you
encounter with the very same block on the stage, when the   165
haberdasher swore to you the impression was extant but that
morning.

To conclude: hoard up the finest play-scraps you can get, upon
which your lean wit may most savourly feed, for want of other
stuff, when the Arcadian and Euphuized gentlewomen have their   170
tongues sharpened to set upon you: that quality (next to your
shuttlecock) is the only furniture to a courtier that's but a new
beginner, and is but in his A B C of compliment.

The next places that are filled, after the play-houses be emptied,
are (or ought to be) taverns; into a tavern then let us next march,   175
where the brains of one hogshead must be beaten out to make up
another.

NOTES

2 *Royal Exchange* the New (or Royal) Exchange, a fashionable resort for shopping, where gallants could encounter ladies, and a haunt for thieves.

5 *plaudities* applause.
   great beast the crowd.

7 *factors* agents (for selling).

10 *chapmen* customers.

11–12 *comical......gross* theatrical wares in great quantities (wholesale).

12–13 *groundling......penny* spectators ('groundlings') who stood to watch the play in the 'yard' or pit for a penny, or those who paid another penny to sit in the galleries.

13–14 *utter......retailing* repeat (with play on 'sell') it again to others by describing it (with pun on 'selling goods in small quantities').

15 *Sithence* since.

16 *stool* i.e. to sit on the stage.
   Templar barrister, with chambers in the Temple.

17 *stinkard* ill-smelling, low fellow.

18 *carman* carter, carrier.

20 *Momus* the Greek god of ridicule, hence a carping critic.

21 *he......tailors' bills* i.e. he who is most expensively dressed and most in debt to his tailor.

22–3 *basely......corner* meanly stood in a corner like a bass-viol in its case.

24 *Whither* where. 1609 edn and earlier editors read 'Whether'.
   gatherers money-takers.

27 *lord's room* a special box, perhaps originally for the company's patron, which had by this time become the resort of disreputable elements in the audience.

30 *sharers* see below, l. 161.

32 *rushes* the stage was 'carpeted' with green rushes, as were the floors in many private houses.

33 *state of Cambyses* throne of Cambyses, a Persian monarch known for his magnificence. 'Cambyses' vein' (*I Henry IV*, II.iv.387) was synonymous with ranting from Thomas Preston's presentation of the figure in *Cambyses* (*c.*1561).

34 *estrich* ostrich (variant form).

41 *Persian lock* love-lock.

43 *girder* sneerer, scoffer.

48 *next door* nearest stage door entrance.
   quest of inquiry search for information.

49 *law warrants you* you are secured by law.

53 *Fleet-street gentleman* probably member of the Inns of Court, not equal to a man of title.

55 *begin......three* stand first, as the viewer, in a picture showing two fools or ass-heads. See *Twelfth Night*, II.iii.17.

58 *muse* i.e. the work of his muse (a play).

59 *rifled* despoiled, stripped bare.

60 *mystical* obscure, hidden.

64 *boys* i.e. the child actors.

67 *copper* i.e. not gold lace as claimed.

68 *fool......peace* The implication is that each of these individuals (here and below) are essentially the same as each other.

69   *dawcock* simpleton.

70   *stamp* character, kind (with a play on stamp' =coin; cf. 'current or counterfeit').

83   *trumpets their cue* i.e. for the third sounding, indicating that the play was about to begin. See the contemporary drawing of the Swan Theatre (*c*.1596).

84   *properties* stage properties.

86   *arras* wall hangings at the rear of the stage, which could be drawn to reveal the discovery space or inner stage; most often referred to as 'curtains'.

      teston sixpence, the price of a stool, which allowed him to sit on the stage.

91   *Counter* the Poultry Counter (hence the following pun), one of London's prisons for debtors.

92   *bastone* cudgel, truncheon.

97   *zany* a clown's assistant, one who mimics his master.

99   *lin* leave off.

100 *morris* i.e. morris dance (see p. 102).

101 *Pelion upon Ossa* i.e. mountain on mountain.

104–5 *you......watch* if you are caught by the night watch, of which he is a member.

111–12 *at the worst hand* though your assumption may be indefensible.

116–17 *convenience......shoulder-clapping* the advantage it affords in being able to escape arrest.

117 *cockatrice* prostitute (so called because of her 'deadly' quality); the cockatrice (or basilisk) was a serpent fabulously supposed to kill by a glance of its eye.

119 *Hate a sculler* Familiarity with a waterman, considered among the social dregs, must be considered more demeaning than social converse with a scullery boy.

120 *oars* rowing-boats (synecdoche).

124 *water-snakes* i.e. watermen. Compare 'flounder-catchers', l. 128.

126 *upon ticket* on credit.

129 *draw* i.e. open your purse-strings to pay.

132 *confederacy* prearrangement (to cheat).

136 *third sound* third trumpet flourish that announced the beginning of the play, usually with the appearance of the Prologue.

137 *knaves* i.e. in the deck of cards.

      outface confront impudently.

139 *go off* be finished.

141 *epigramed* held (you) up to ridicule in an epigram.

142 *flirt* gibe, stroke of wit.

      brought i.e. burlesqued.

145 *bastinado* cudgelling.

146 *pastoral* play set in the countryside, with shepherds and shepherdesses as characters; e.g. John Fletcher's *The Faithful Shepherdess* (1608–9).

      moral moral interlude, or a more developed form of the interlude; e.g. Robert Wilson's *Three Lords and Three Ladies of London* (1588–90).

149 *distaste* show aversion for.

150 *gentle* of the rank of gentleman or above.

152 *mimics* actors.

154 *'A pox......you'* common expression of irritation. 'Pox' = smallpox or venereal disease.

155   *frets* wordplay on (1) vexations, irritations; (2) bars of wood on the fingerboard of a musical instrument.

158   *earnest ears* i.e. of those who are paying attention to the play.

160   *blare* roar, bellow.

160–1   *children's action* action of (1) the boys who played the women's roles, or (2) the all-boy companies such as Paul's Boys.

161   *sharers* senior members in a company of actors who had a financial 'share' in the earnings. Shakespeare was a 'sharer' in the Chamberlain's (later the King's) Men.

163   *felt* hat.
       Scotch fashion unexplained. One would expect 'Spanish', 'French', or 'Flemish'.

165   *block* shape, fashion. Literally 'block', a mould for a hat.

170   *Arcadian and Euphuized gentlewomen* ladies who spoke in the preciously artificial style of Sir Philip Sidney's *Arcadia* (1590), a sophisticated pastoral romance, and John Lyly's *Euphues: The Anatomy of Wit* (1578), a short novel of manners.

172   *only furniture* absolutely necessary equipment.

173   *A B C* primer or 'horn-book'.

176–7   *brains . . . . . . another* Contents of a cask of liquor must be drained out to fill up a human 'hogshead'.

iii

From Francis Beaumont, *The Knight of the Burning Pestle* (1607–8), Induction.

[GENTLEMEN *seated upon the stage. The* CITIZEN, *his* WIFE, *and* RAFE *below among the audience.*]

Enter PROLOGUE

From all that's near the court, from all that's great
Within the compass of the City-walls,
We now have brought our scene.

Enter CITIZEN [*from audience below*]

CITIZEN. Hold your peace, goodman boy.

PROLOGUE. What do you mean, sir?   5

CITIZEN. That you have no good meaning. This seven years there
hath been plays at this house, I have observed it, you have still
girds at citizens; and now you call your play *The London
Merchant*. Down with your title, boy, down with your title!

PROLOGUE. Are you a member of the noble City?   10

CITIZEN. I am.

PROLOGUE. And a freeman?

CITIZEN. Yea, and a grocer.

PROLOGUE. So, grocer, then by your sweet favour, we intend no
abuse to the City.   15

CITIZEN. No, sir! Yes, sir! If you were not resolv'd to play the jacks,
what need you study for new subjects, purposely to abuse your
betters? Why could not you be contented, as well as others,
with *The Legend of Whittington*, or *The Life and Death of Sir
Thomas Gresham, with the Building of the Royal Exchange*, or   20
*The Story of Queen Elenor, with the Rearing of London Bridge
upon Wool-sacks*?

PROLOGUE. You seem to be an understanding man. What would
you have us do, sir?

CITIZEN. Why, present something notably in honour of the   25
commons of the City.

PROLOGUE. Why, what do you say to *The Life and Death of Fat
Drake, or the Repairing of Fleet-privies*?

CITIZEN. I do not like that, but I will have a citizen, and he shall be
of my own trade.   30

PROLOGUE. O, you should have told us your mind a month since,
our play is ready to begin now.

CITIZEN. 'Tis all one for that; I will have a grocer, and he shall do admirable things.

PROLOGUE. What will you have him do? 35

CITIZEN. Marry, I will have him –

WIFE *below*

WIFE. Husband, husband.

RAFE *below*

RAFE. Peace, mistress.

WIFE. Hold thy peace, Rafe; I know what I do, I warrant 'tee. Husband, husband. 40

CITIZEN. What say'st thou, cony?

WIFE. Let him kill a lion with a pestle, husband; let him kill a lion with a pestle.

CITIZEN. So he shall. – I'll have him kill a lion with a pestle.

WIFE. Husband, shall I come up, husband? 45

CITIZEN. Ay, cony. – Rafe, help your mistress this way. – Pray, gentlemen, make her a little room. – I pray you, sir, lend me your hand to help up my wife; I thank you sir. – So.

[WIFE *comes up on the stage*]

WIFE. By your leave, gentlemen all, I'm something troublesome; I'm a stranger here; I was ne'er at one of these plays, as they 50 say, before; but I should have seen *Jane Shore* once, and my husband hath promised me any time this twelvemonth to carry me to *The Bold Beauchamps*, but in truth he did not. I pray you bear with me.

CITIZEN. Boy, let my wife and I have a couple of stools, and then 55 begin, and let the grocer do rare things.

PROLOGUE. But sir, we have never a boy to play him; every one hath a part already.

WIFE. Husband, husband, for God's sake let Rafe play him; beshrew me if I do not think he will go beyond them all. 60

CITIZEN. Well remembered, wife. – Come up, Rafe. – I'll tell you, gentlemen, let them but lend him a suit of reparel, and necessaries, and, by gad, if any of them all blow wind in the tail on him, I'll be hanged.

[RAFE *comes up on the stage*]

WIFE. I pray you, youth, let him have a suit of reparel. – I'll be 65 sworn, gentlemen, my husband tells you true: he will act you sometimes at our house, that all the neighbours cry out on him;

he will fetch you up a couraging part so in the garret, that we
are all as feared, I warrant you, that we quake again. We'll fear
our children with him; if they be never so unruly, do but cry,   70
'Rafe comes, Rafe comes', to them, and they'll be as quiet as
lambs. – Hold up thy head, Rafe, show the gentlemen what
thou canst do; speak a huffing part, I warrant you the
gentlemen will accept of it.

CITIZEN. Do. Rafe, do.   75

RAFE. By heaven, methinks it were an easy leap
　To pluck bright honour from the pale-fac'd moon,
　Or dive into the bottom of the sea,
　Where never fathom line touch'd any ground,
　And pluck up drowned honour from the lake of hell.   80

CITIZEN. How say you, gentlemen, is it not as I told you?

WIFE. Nay, gentlemen, he hath played before, my husband says,
　Mucedorus before the wardens of our company.

CITIZEN. Ay, and he should have played Jeronimo with a
　shoemaker for a wager.   85

PROLOGUE. He shall have a suit of apparel if he will go in.

CITIZEN. In, Rafe, in, Rafe, and set out the grocery in their kind, if
　thou lov'st me.   [*Exit* RAFE]

WIFE. I warrant our Rafe will look finely when he's dressed.

PROLOGUE. But what will you have it called?   90

CITIZEN. *The Grocers' Honour.*

PROLOGUE. Methinks *The Knight of the Burning Pestle* were better.

WIFE. I'll be sworn, husband, that's as good a name as can be.

CITIZEN. Let it be so. Begin, begin; my wife and I will sit down.

PROLOGUE. I pray you, do.   95

CITIZEN. What stately music have you? You have shawms?

PROLOGUE. Shawms? No.

CITIZEN. No? I'm a thief if my mind did not give me so. Rafe plays
　a stately part, and he must needs have shawms; I'll be at the
　charge of them myself, rather than we'll be without them.   100

PROLOGUE. So you are like to be.

CITIZEN. Why, and so I will be. There's two shillings; let's have the
　waits of Southwark. They are as rare fellows as any are in
　England; and that will fetch them all o'er the water with a
　vengeance, as if they were mad.   105

PROLOGUE. You shall have them. Will you sit down then?

CITIZEN. Ay. – Come, wife.

WIFE. Sit you merry all, gentlemen. I'm bold to sit amongst you for
my ease.

PROLOGUE. From all that's near the Court, from all that's great   110
Within the compass of the City-walls,
We now have brought our scene. Fly far from hence
All private taxes, immodest phrases,
Whate'er may but show like vicious:
For wicked mirth never true pleasure brings,   115
But honest minds are pleas'd with honest things.
– Thus much for that we do; but for Rafe's part you must
answer for yourself.   [*Exit*]

CITIZEN. Take you no care for Rafe, he'll discharge himself, I
warrant you.   120

WIFE. I' faith, gentlemen, I'll give my word for Rafe.

NOTES

1–3 A warning to the audience that they are about to witness a bourgeois play
about ordinary citizens.

6 *This seven years* probably dates the play, since the Children of the Queen's
Revels, who performed the play, acted at the Blackfriars Theatre from
about 1600–8.

7 *still* continually.

8–9 *The London Merchant* probably the name of the play as originally
planned, dealing with Venturewell and his family, before the Citizen and
his Wife take over.

9 *title* i.e. the placard bearing the title of the play to be acted, displayed
perhaps at one side of the stage.

13 *grocer* He is a member of one of the twelve powerful livery companies or
trade guilds of London.

16 *jacks* knaves.

17 *study for new subjects* hit at the satiric attitude of plays staged at the
private theatres, particularly by the boys' companies, at the expense of the
'cits'. Beaumont is, of course, satirizing the taste of the public-theatre
audience in the list of plays the Citizen suggests (ll. 19–22), plays like
Thomas Heywood's *The Four Prentices of London* (1592–1600) and his
two-part *Edward IV* (1592–9), both of which celebrated the heroism of
the 'commons'.

23 *understanding man* another hit, aimed at those who stood in the 'yard'
(i.e. stood below the raised stage), the 'groundlings' as Shakespeare calls
them (*Hamlet*, III.ii.11).

28 *Fleet-privies* presumably a reference to Fleet Ditch which by this time had
become a common sewer. Who, if anybody, 'Fat Drake' was is unknown;
'Fat' may mean 'rich'.

39   *'tee* thee.
41   *cony* a young rabbit, a vulgar term of endearment.
42   *kill a lion* The Wife introduces the satire on popular romances such as
       Bevis of Hampton, Guy of Warwick, Palmerin of England, Richard
       Johnson's *The Seven Champions of Christendom* (1596), in which the hero
       was always encountering savage beasts and giants. Beaumont's attitude
       toward romance is influenced by Cervantes' *Don Quixote.*
45   *shall I come up* For a woman to sit on the stage was a serious indecorum,
       an offence against modesty, hence part of Beaumont's satire on the 'cits'.
51   *Jane Shore* probably a reference to Heywood's *Edward IV* plays, in which
       Jane Shore, a goldsmith's wife, figures prominently. Another play of
       Heywood's, *The Bold Beauchamps,* now lost, is mentioned in l. 53.
55   *stools* A stool cost at least an extra sixpence. The practice of sitting on the
       stage began about 1596, both in public and private theatres, and continued
       for many years. The Blackfriars seems especially to have encouraged the
       practice (E. K. Chambers, *Elizabethan Stage,* II, 535–7).
60   *beshrew me* let me be cursed (a common oath).
62   *reparel* apparel.
63   *by gad* softened form of 'by God'.
63–4   *blow . . . . . . him* come near him (from horseracing).
68   *couraging part* a role to raise the spirits (with perhaps a sexual suggestion).
69   *quake again* tremble in response.
73   *huffing part* a role in which one could let out all the stops and rant. The
       speech chosen (ll. 76–80) is from Shakespeare's *I Henry IV* (I.iii.201–5),
       with some slight 'improvements'.
83   *Mucedorus* The play *Mucedorus* (published 1598) was an extremely
       popular public-theatre romantic comedy based on an incident from
       Sidney's *Arcadia* (1590). See below, p. 38.
84   *Jeronimo* hero of Kyd's *The Spanish Tragedy* (*c.*1586), a good 'huffing
       part'.
87   *set . . . . . . kind* properly clothed in the full livery of the Grocers'
       Company.
92   *The Knight . . . . . . Pestle* The title burlesques romance heroes. Compare
       'The Knight of the Burning Sword' in the romance of *Amadis de Gaul.*
       Just why a pestle (a symbol associated with the Apothecaries) is the
       chosen weapon of a grocer's apprentice (Rafe) is not entirely clear
       (perhaps because grocers dealt in spices), though it probably has some
       phallic significance and may be a play on 'pizzle' (bull's penis, often used
       as a flogging instrument).
99   *shawms* wind instruments, like oboes.
103   *waits of Southwark* a small body of wind instrumentalists maintained by a
       town at public charge. Southwark was on the south bank, where most of
       the public theatres (and many bawdy houses) were located. Since the
       Blackfriars Theatre was located on the City side they had be 'fetch[ed]
       o'er the water'.
113   *private taxes* i.e. personal satire on individuals.

iv

The public makes its wishes known

From Edmund Gayton, *Pleasant Notes upon Don Quixot* (1654), pp. 271–2.

......yet men come not to study at a playhouse, but love such expressions and passages which with ease insinuate themselves into their capacities. *Lingua,* that learned comedy of the contention betwixt the five senses for the superiority, is not to be prostituted to the common stage, but is only proper for an academy; to them bring *Jack Drum's Entertainment, Greene's Tu Quoque, The Devil of Edmonton,* and the like; or if it be on holidays, when sailors, watermen, shoemakers, butchers, and apprentices are at leisure, then it is good policy to amaze those violent spirits with some tearing tragedy full of fights and skirmishes: as *The Guelphs and Ghibellines, Greeks and Trojans,* or *The Three London Apprentices,* which commonly ends in six acts, the spectators frequently mounting the stage and making a more bloody Catastrophe amongst themselves than the players did. I have known upon one of these festivals, but especially at Shrovetide, where the players have been appointed, notwithstanding their bills to the contrary, to act what the major part of the company had a mind to; sometimes *Tamburlaine,* sometimes *Jugurth,* sometimes *The Jew of Malta,* and sometimes parts of all these, and, at last, none of the three taking, they were forced to undress and put off their tragic habits, and conclude the day with *The Merry Milkmaids.* And unless this were done, and the popular humour satisfied (as sometimes it so fortuned that the players were refractory), the benches, the tiles, the laths, the stones, oranges, apples, nuts flew about most liberally; and, as there were mechanics of all professions, who fell every one to his own trade and dissolved a house in an instant and made a ruin of a stately fabric, it was not then the most mimical nor fighting man, Fowler nor Andrew Cane, could pacify: Prologues nor Epilogues would prevail; the Devil and the fool were quite out of favour. Nothing but noise and tumult fills the house until a cog take 'um, and then to the bawdy-houses, and reform them; and instantly to the Bank's-side, where the poor bears must conclude the riot and fight twenty dogs at a time beside the butchers, which sometimes fell into the service. This performed, and the horse and Jack-an-Apes for a jig, they had sport enough that day for nothing.

NOTES

3   *Lingua* academic (Cambridge) play (1602–7) by Thomas Tomkis.

6   *them* i.e. the generally non-academic audience of the public and 'private' theatres.

6–7   *Jack Drum's* . . . . . . *Edmonton* three popular plays by John Marston (1600, performed by Paul's Boys at their singing school near St Paul's), John Cooke (1611, performed by Queen Anne's Men at the Red Bull), and (?) Thomas Dekker (1599–1604, performed by the Chamberlain's Men at the Globe) – two public and one 'private' theatre plays.

11–12   *The Guelphs* . . . . . . *Apprentices The Guelphs* is otherwise unknown; *Greeks* is probably a reference to Thomas Heywood's *I* and *II Iron Age* (1612–13, performed by Queen Anne's Men at the Red Bull); *The Three London Apprentices* is almost certainly Heywood's *The Four Prentices of London* (1592–1600, originally performed by the Admiral's Men, later performed by Queen Anne's Men at the Red Bull). Judged by the last named, all three were 'drum and trumpet' plays, with lots of 'fights and skirmishes'.

12   *six acts* i.e. the sixth act being a free-for-all in the theatre.

14   *Catastrophe* technical term for the fifth act in both tragedy and comedy.

15–16   *Shrove-tide* Tuesday before Ash Wednesday, the last opportunity for 'indulgence' before Lent began.

17   *bills* . . . . . . *contrary* i.e. the play advertised for performance.

18–19   *Tamburlaine* . . . . . . *Malta* the first and third, plays by Marlowe (1587–8; 1589); *Jugurth*, a lost play by William Boyle (1600); all three plays, either originally or eventually, associated with the Admiral's Men.

21–2   *The Merry Milkmaids* probably a reference to *The Two Merry Milkmaids* (1619–20), a comedy by I.C., but the reference may not be to a particular title, since Gayton gives it as 'the merry milk-maides', i.e. from tragedy to the comic mode.

26   *mechanics* low persons of manual occupations.

28   *mimical* one giving the impression through acting (of a 'fighting man').

28–9   *Fowler nor Andrew Cane* Richard Fowler and Cane were well-known actors during the 1620s and 30s.

30   *Devil* . . . . . . *fool* i.e. as dramatic characters (usually favourites of the 'mechanics' in the audience).

31   *cog take 'um* device (or sudden whim) strike them; *OED* does not offer a satisfactory definition for the context.

32   *reform them* i.e. to wreck the bawdy-houses as they had been wrecking the theatre, a sport associated with Shrove-Tuesday.
     to the Bank's-side i.e. to Paris Garden located on the Bankside. See 'Bear-baiting', p. 168.

34   *beside* . . . . . . *service* in addition to the butchers, who joined in on the baiting of the bear.

36   *for a jig* A jig was a dance (with dialogues) frequently performed as an afterpiece to a play; here used to mean a final piece of sport to conclude their day's 'performance'. See pp. 363–73.

3 London companies and strolling players

Unlike the powerful City guilds or companies (e.g. Grocers', Haberdashers', Stationers'), acting companies had no established 'union', no single central organization. They existed as separate entities, often rather precariously, depending on the protection of a patron, usually either royal (Elizabeth, James, Queen Anne, Prince Henry, Lady Elizabeth, daughter of James) or noble (Earl of Sussex, Earl of Worcester, Lord Howard, Earl of Derby, Lord Hunsdon (Lord Chamberlain), etc.). Such protection was necessary against the frequently hostile attitude of the City authorities (the Lord Mayor and Aldermen) and the several penal statutes (from 1572 on) which declared unattached actors to be vagabonds and rogues (see pp. 46 n. 1, 97 n. 2).

The history of the various adult and boy companies performing in London between 1558 and 1625 is indeed a bewildering chronicle and often, except in a comparatively few cases, infuriatingly fragmented and confusing. Companies dissolved and disappeared or were reformed under new patronage; actors moved back and forth between old and new companies. E. K. Chambers (*Elizabethan Stage*, II, 77–260) discusses more than twenty adult and some ten boy companies that were either centred in London or had London connections (through Court performances) during these years. Certain companies, of course, gradually emerged and stood out as the principal 'comedians' (a general term for actors) in the 1590s and later, notable among them the Admiral's Men (under the patronage of Lord Howard; becoming in 1604 Prince Henry's Men); the Chamberlain's Men (under the patronage of Lord Hunsdon until 1603 when they became the King's Men; Shakespeare's company); Queen Anne's Men (formerly the Earl of Worcester's Men until 1604); and two of the boy companies, Children of the Chapel Royal and Paul's Boys. A large proportion of the Elizabethan–Jacobean drama that we now read and consider most significant may be associated with these companies or their progenitors.

Chambers describes the economic basis on which a company was formed:

> The basis of this organization was the banding together of players into associations or partnerships, the members of which acted together, held a common stock of garments [properties] and play-books, incurred joint expenditure, and daily or at other convenient periods divided up [as sharers] the profits of their enterprise (*Elizabethan Stage*, I, 352).

The public-theatre companies leased their playhouses from businessmen like James Burbage (Theatre, Globe and second Blackfriars), Philip Henslowe (Rose, Fortune and Hope), Francis Langley (Swan), and

Aaron Holland (Red Bull), paying a part of their proceeds as rent (see 'The playhouses', p. 51). As 'sharers' in a company some of the actors (e.g. Edward Alleyn, Richard Burbage, William Shakespeare) achieved financial independence and some social position (see 'The actors', p. 92), but the lot of the 'hired men', actors who served in a company for wages, was much less rewarding and many actors lived on the edges of poverty.

Unlike many of the acting companies, Shakespeare's company, the Chamberlain's–King's Men, showed an unusual continuity in its personnel from 1594–1642. Already a leading company as the Chamberlain's Men, as the King's Men, under the royal patronage of James, it became the leading London company, a reputation enhanced by Richard Burbage as the most famous actor of his day and by the plays of such dramatists as Shakespeare, Jonson, Beaumont and Fletcher, Chapman, and Webster. It performed, moreover, at two theatres, the first and second Globe, and the second Blackfriars (after 1608), one of the enclosed so-called 'private' theatres. The first selection (i) reproduces the royal licence conferred on the company when it became the King's Men, 19 May 1603. With the list of actors here given, we may compare the later and longer list of 'The Names of the Principall Actors in all these Playes' prefixed to the Shakespeare First Folio (1623).

Although London was, then as now, the centre of dramatic activity, companies of strolling players, 'that (without socks) trot from town to town upon the hard hoof' (Thomas Dekker, *Lanthorne and Candle-Light* (1608), chap. VII), visited with some regularity all the principal cities and towns (even villages) throughout England. Itinerant players also visited Scotland and Ireland, and groups known as *Englische Komödianten* toured on the Continent, particularly in Germany, the Netherlands, and Denmark.

Four kinds of strolling groups may be distinguished: (1) independent provincial companies, under the patronage of members of the nobility, which toured throughout England, rarely or never coming to London; (2) groups from the main London companies, licensed to travel, particularly during outbreaks of the plague in London when the theatres were closed (a two-year 'inhibition' of this kind occurred in 1592–4 which caused great hardship to the then existing London companies); (3) unauthorized groups, who banded together and performed plays in the countryside without a licence (or with a forged one) wherever they could get a precarious foothold; (4) townsmen or villagers who, having decided to put on a play or other entertainment, took their 'production' to neighbouring towns for a few performances. Selections (ii) and (iii) may be taken as illustrating (1) and (3) above; selection (iv) offers a graphic illustration of (4).

The second selection (ii) recalls the vivid childhood recollection of a performance at Gloucester of a moral interlude, *The Cradle of Security*, no longer extant. The author, R. Willis, was born in the same year as Shakespeare in Gloucester, not far from Stratford, and it is possible that the young Shakespeare may have witnessed a performance of the play by the same touring company in Stratford. The play, described in some detail, is typical of the kind of 'moral' popular in the 1560s and 70s, and Willis is careful to 'point the moral' at the conclusion of his account.

In selection (iii), from John Marston's *Histriomastix*, probably an Inns of Court play produced about 1599 (see P. J. Finkelpearl, *John Marston of the Middle Temple* (1969), pp. 119–24), we are given a lively, if obviously burlesque, picture of the kinds and level of dramatic entertainment sometimes offered to unsuspecting country folk by an obviously disreputable band of strolling players. Elsewhere in the play we witness the 'actors' signing articles as a 'company' (they are 'rude mechanicals' as Shakespeare describes Bottom and Co. in *Midsummer Night's Dream*, III.ii.9, a play to which Marston is certainly indebted), dickering for costumes, rehearsing, posting playbills, 'crying the play' at the village cross, squabbling among themselves, running into debt at the tavern and pawning a cloak to pay the shot, being threatened with impressment into the army (compare Thomas Dekker's *The Shoemaker's Holiday*, I.i), and finally falling foul of the law and being deported as rogues and vagabonds. The 'company poet', Posthaste, is generally taken as a satire on Anthony Munday, a prolific, minor playwright and ballader, who is rather extravagantly described by Francis Meres (*Palladis Tamia* (1598), p. 283b) as 'our best plotter'. For other dramatic treatments of strolling or local players, see *Hamlet* (II.ii; III.ii), Munday and Chettle, *Sir Thomas More* (c.1594–5; III.iii), Thomas Middleton, *The Mayor of Queenborough* (c.1615–20; V.i) and *A Mad World My Masters* (c.1604–7; V.i–ii), and Richard Brome, *The Antipodes* (1640).

Selection (iv), from John Rowe's *Tragi-Comœdia* (1653), recounts in unusual detail a 'rustic' performance of an old anonymous (and very popular) romantic comedy called *Mucedorus, The King's Son of Valencia and Amadine, the King's Daughter of Arragon* (c.1588–98) at Witney in Oxfordshire in 1652, a performance that ended in disaster, when the floor of a large upper room in the White Hart Inn collapsed and a number of the audience were killed or injured, a particular judgement of God on the sinful state of the people of Witney according to the preacher John Rowe. Aside from showing the starved appetite for theatre even during the Commonwealth period, Rowe's moral stance illustrates the typical Puritan (and official) reaction to earlier accidents involving death and injury (e.g. at Paris Garden in 1583 or the so-called 'Fatal Vespers' incident connected with the Blackfriars in 1623).

The final selection (v) offers a firsthand account by Fynes Moryson of English Comedians in Germany at Frankfurt am Main in 1592. Moryson takes a dim view of what he witnessed and it is certainly true that almost none of the best actors felt compelled to travel on the Continent, but the members of these touring companies were most often experienced actors, not necessarily the outcasts he suggests. The language barrier which he comments on was obviated by the beginning of the seventeenth century, the actors performing in German versions of English plays.

Most major Elizabethan–Jacobean dramatists (except Middleton) suffered this 'sea change' in adaptations, which, if we may judge by the comparatively few extant specimens, were considerably debased, particularly by the addition of low comic characters and comic business. Such versions of *Hamlet, Titus Andronicus,* and *Romeo and Juliet* may be studied (with English translations) in Albert Cohen's *Shakespeare in Germany* (1865).

i

Royal licence for the King's Men (formerly the Lord Chamberlain's Men), 19 May 1603 (from Malone Society *Collections*, I, iii (1909), pp. 264–5).

Commissio specialis pro Laurencio Fletcher & Willelmo Shackespeare et aliis:

James by the Grace of God, etc. To all justices, mayors, sheriffs, constables, headboroughs, and other our officers and loving subjects, greeting. Know ye that We of our special grace, certain   5 knowledge, and mere motion have licensed and authorized, and by these presents do license and authorize, these our servants, Lawrence Fletcher, William Shakespeare, Richard Burbage, Augustine Phillipps, John Heninges, Henry Condell, William Sly, Robert Armin, Richard Cowley, and the rest of their associates   10 freely to use and exercise the art and faculty of playing comedies, tragedies, histories, interludes, morals, pastorals, stage-plays, and such others like as they have already studied or hereafter shall use or study, as well for the recreation of our loving subjects as for our solace and pleasure when we shall think good to see them during   15 our pleasure. And the said comedies, tragedies, histories, interludes, morals, pastorals, stage-plays, and such like to shew and exercise publicly to their best commodity, when the infection of the plague shall decrease, as well within their now usual house, called the Globe, within our county of Surrey, as also within any   20 town-halls or moot-halls or other convenient places within the liberties and freedom of any other city, university town, or borough whatsoever within our said realms and dominions. Willing and commanding you and every of you as you tender our pleasure not only to permit and suffer them herein without any   25 your lets, hindrances, or molestations during our said pleasure, but also to be aiding and assisting to them if any wrong be to them offered. And to allow them such former courtesies as hath been given to men of their place and quality, and also what further favour you shall show to these our servants, for our sake, We shall   30 take kindly at your hands. In witness whereof, etc. witness ourself at Westminster the nineteenth day of May.

NOTES

1–2 *Superscription: Commissio......aliis* special commission (or licence) for the benefit of Lawrence Fletcher, William Shakespeare and others.
4   *headboroughs* parish officers, with functions of a petty constable.
6   *mere motion* sole instigation.

8–10 *Lawrence Fletcher......Cowley* except for Fletcher, the principal
    actors (and 'sharers') in the King's Men, formerly actors in the
    Chamberlain's Men.

9   *Heninges* either a variant of, or error for, 'Heminges'. Hemingses (or
    Heminge) and Henry Condell (also included in this list) signed two
    dedications honouring their 'fellow' Shakespeare in the so-called 'First
    Folio' of 1623.

15   *when......them* i.e. when the King would order performances at Court.

16–17 *comedies......stage-plays* This list is a regular feature of such licences.
    It is difficult to see how a 'stage-play' differed from the other genres
    listed.

18   *commodity* profit, gain.

20   *Globe......Surrey* Globe Theatre (built 1599) on the Bankside in Surrey.

21   *moot-halls* council-halls, where the town council met.

22   *liberties* districts, like Blackfriars and Whitefriars in London, not strictly
    under the control of the City authorities, which claimed special privileges
    stemming from their religious foundation.

26   *lets* impediments, hindrances.
    molestations hostile interferences.

29   *quality* profession (as actors).

ii

From R. Willis, *Mount Tabor, Or Private Exercises of a Penitent Sinner*
(1639), pp. 110–12.

In the city of Gloucester the manner is (as I think it is in other like
corporations) that when players of interludes come to town they
first attend the Mayor to inform him what nobleman's servants
they are and so to get license for their public playing; and if the
Mayor like the actors, or would show respect to their lord and   5
master, he appoints them to play their first play before himself and
the aldermen and common council of the city; and that is called
the Mayor's Play, where every one that will comes in without
money, the Mayor giving the players a reward as he thinks fit to
show respect unto them. At such a play my father took me with   10
him and made me stand between his legs as he sat upon one of the
benches where we saw and heard very well. The play was called
The Cradle of Security, wherein was personated a King or some
great Prince, with his courtiers of several kinds, amongst which
three ladies were in special grace with him; and they, keeping him   15
in delights and pleasures, drew him from his graver counsellors,
hearing of sermons, and listening to good counsel and admoni-

tions, that in the end they got him to lie down in a cradle upon the
stage, where these three ladies joining in a sweet song rocked him
asleep that he snorted again; and in the mean time closely   20
conveyed under the clothes wherewithal he was covered, a vizard
like a swine's snout upon his face, with three wire chains fastened
thereunto, the other end whereof being holden severally by those
three ladies, who fall to singing again, and then discovered his face
that the spectators might see how they had transformed him,   25
going on with their singing; whilst all this was acting, there came
forth of another door at the farthest end of the stage two old men,
the one in blue like a Sergeant at Arms, his mace on his shoulder,
the other in red with a drawn sword in his hand, and leaning with
the other hand upon the other's shoulder, and so they two went   30
along in a soft pace around about by the skirt of the stage, till at
last they came to the cradle, when all the court was in greatest
jollity, and then the foremost old man with his mace struck a
fearful blow upon the cradle, whereat all the courtiers, with the
three ladies and the vizard, all vanished, and the desolate Prince   35
starting up barefaced, and, finding himself thus sent for to
judgment, made a lamentable complaint of his miserable case, and
so was carried away by wicked spirits. This Prince did personate in
the moral the wicked of the world; the three ladies, Pride,
Covetousness, and Luxury; the two old men, the end of the world   40
and the Last Judgment. This sight took such impression in me
that when I came towards man's estate it was as fresh in my
memory as if I had seen it newly acted.

NOTES

8   *Mayor's Play* This seems to have been a wide-spread custom not only in
Gloucester but in many other provincial towns.

9   *reward* The 'rewards' given varied from a few shillings (in the early years
of Elizabeth) up to £3 by 1616 (E. K. Chambers, *Elizabethan Stage*, I,
335).

13   *The Cradle of Security* The play is lost, but is referred to in Munday and
Chettle's *Sir Thomas More* (*c.* 1594–5; III.iii), where the visiting players
list it among their repertory. 'Security' here means 'thoughtless
indolence, culpable lack of moral awareness'.

20   *snorted again* fell asleep as a result.

28   *like* substituted for 1639 edn 'with'.
      mace heavy metal-headed club borne by a sergeant at arms as an insignia
of office.

35   *vanished* It is not clear how this was accomplished. Probably all it means
is that the actors exited hastily. The use of a trap in this provincial
performance seems unlikely.

38   *wicked spirits* This is reminiscent of the Vice figure in moral interludes,
who was often carried off the stage by the Devil.

39   *moral* morality play or moral interlude.

iii

From John Marston, *Histriomastix* (*c*.1599), Act II.

Enter PLAYERS, *with them* POSTHASTE *the Poet*

USHER. Sir Oliver Owlet's men welcome, by God's will,
It is my Lord's pleasure it should be so.

POSTHASTE. Sir, we have carous'd like kings,
For here is plenty in all things.

USHER. Look about you, masters; be uncover'd. 5

Enter SEWER *with service, in side livery coats*

The Players' Song

Brave lads come forth and chant it, chant it,
for now 'tis supper time.
See how the dishes flaunt it, and flaunt it,
with meat to make up rhyme.
Pray for his Honour truly, and truly, 10
in all he undertakes;
He serves the poor most duly, and duly,
as all the country speaks.

POSTHASTE. God bless my Lord Mavortius and his merry men
all,
To make his Honour merry, we sing in the hall. 15

USHER. My masters, for that we are not only (for causes)
Come new to the house; but also (for causes)
I marvel where you will lodge.

POSTHASTE. We hope (for causes) in the house, though drink be
in our heads,
Because to *Plenty* we carouse, for beef and beer, and beds. 20

USHER. Said like honest men: what plays have you?

BELCH. Here's a gentleman scholler writes for us: I pray, Master
Posthaste, declare for our credits.

POSTHASTE. For mine own part, though this summer season, I am
desperate of a horse. 25

USHER. 'Tis well; but what plays have you?

POSTHASTE. A gentleman's a gentleman that hath a clean shirt on,
with some learning, and so have I.

USHER. One of you answer the names of your plays.

POSTHASTE. *Mother Gurton's Needle* (a tragedy);   30
    The Devil and Dives (a comedy);
    A Russet Coat and a Knave's Cap (an infernal);
    A Proud Heart and a Beggar's Purse (a pastoral);
    The Widow's Apron-Strings (a nocturnal).

USHER. I promise ye, pretty names.   35
    I pray what ye want in anything,
    To take it out in drink.
    And so go make ye ready masters.   *Exeunt* PLAYERS

Enter MAVORTIUS, PHILARCHUS, *with* LANDULPHO (an *Italian*
    Lord) *and other Nobles and Gentles to see the play*

    *   *   *   *   *   *   *   *

USHER. Room, my masters, take your places.   58
    Hold up your torches for dropping there.

MAVORTIUS. Usher, are the players ready? bid them begin.   60

Enter PLAYERS *and sing*

    Some up and some down, there's players in the town,
      You wot well who they be:
    The sum doth arise, to three companies,
      One, two, three, four make we.
    Besides we that travel, with pumps full of gravel,   65
      Made all of such running leather,
    That once in a week, new masters we seek,
      And never can hold together.

Enter PROLOGUE

[PROLOGUE.] *Phillida was a fair maid; I know one fairer than she:*
    Troylus was a true lover; I know one truer than he: 70
    And Cressida that dainty dame, whose beauty fair and sweet,
    Was clear as is the crystal stream, that runs along the street.
    How Troyl he that noble knight, was drunk in love and bade
      good-night:
    So bending leg likewise; do you not us despise.

LANDULPHO. Most ugly lines and base brown-paper-stuff   75
    Thus to abuse our heavenly poesy,
    That sacred off-spring from the brain of Jove,
    Thus to be mangled with profane absurds,
    Strangled and chok'd with lawless bastard's words.

MAVORTIUS. I see, my Lord, this homespun country stuff   80
    Brings little liking to your curious ear;
    Be patient for perhaps the play will mend.

Enter TROYLUS *and* CRESSIDA

TROYLUS. *Come Cressida, my cresset-light,*
   Thy face doth shine both day and night.
   Behold, behold, thy garter blue!   85
   Thy knight his valiant elbow wears,
   That when he shakes his furious spear,
   The foe in shivering fearful sort,
   May lay him down in death to snort.

CRESSIDA. *O knight, with valour in thy face,*   90
   Here take my screen, wear it for grace,
   Within thy helmet put the same,
   Therewith to make thine enemies lame.

LANDULPHO. Lame stuff indeed, the like was never heard.

     Enter a roaring DEVIL *with the* VICE *on his back,*
       INIQUITY *in one hand, and* JUVENTUS *in the other*

VICE. *Passion of me, sir, puff, puff, how I sweat, sir;*   95
   The dust out of your coat, sir, I intend for to beat, sir.

JUVENTUS. *I am the prodigal child, ay, that I am;*
   Who says I am not, I say he is to blame.

INIQUITY. *And I likewise am Iniquity,*
   Beloved of many, alas for pity.   100

DEVIL. *Ho, ho, ho, these babes mine are all,*
   The Vice, Iniquity, and child prodigal.

LANDULPHO. Fie, what unworthy foolish foppery
   Presents such buzzardly simplicity?

MARVORTIUS. No more, no more, unless 'twere better,   105
   And for the rest ye shall be our debtor.

POSTHASTE. My Lords, of your accords,
   Some better pleasure for to bring,
   If you a theme affords,
   You shall know it,   110
   That I, Posthaste the Poet,
   Extempore can sing.

LANDULPHO. I pray, my Lord, let's ha't: the play is so good
   That this must needs be excellent.

MAVORTIUS. Content, my Lord, pray give a theme.   115

Theme

LANDULPHO. *Your poets and your pots*
   Are knit in true-love knots.

The song extempore

[POSTHASTE]

> Give your scholar degrees, and your lawyer his fees,
>   And some dice for Sir Petronel Flash:
> Give your courtier grace, and your knight a new case,   120
>   And empty their purses of cash.
> Give your play-gull a stool, and my Lady her fool,
>   And her usher potatoes and marrow,
> But your poet were he dead, set a pot to his head,
>   And he rises as pert as a sparrow.   125
> O delicate wine, with thy power so divine,
>   Full of ravishing sweet inspiration;
> Yet a verse may run clear that is tapp'd out of beer,
>   Especially in the vacation.
> But when the term comes, that with trumpets and drums,   130
>   Our playhouses ring in confusion,
> Then Bacchus me murder, but rhyme we no further,
>   Some sack now, upon the conclusion.

MAVORTIUS. Give them forty pence, let them go.
How likes Landulpho this extempore song?   135

[Exeunt Players]

[Landulpho calls it 'trash' and expatiates on the superiority of Italian theatre and wit, and Marvortius, agreeing with him, says he will henceforth study Italian fashions. The scene ends with a speech from Philarchus, defending the English tradition.]

PHILARCHUS. By'r Lady, sir, I like not of this pride.   155
Give me the ancient hospitality;
They say, 'tis merry in hall when beards wag all.
The Italian Lord is an ass; the song is a good song. *[Exeunt.]*

NOTES

1   *Owlet's men* In an earlier scene (Act I) Posthaste and three others (Belch, a beard maker; Gut, a fiddle-string maker; Incle, a pedlar) had incorporated themselves as a company, claiming the patronage of Sir Oliver Owlet in an attempt to circumvent the 1598 *Act for punishment of rogues, vagabonds and sturdy beggars* (a renewal of the similar 1572 act), among which 'common players of interludes and minstrels' were included unless vouched for by 'any Baron of this realm'. By the end of the play, they are caught and, as the act orders in aggravated cases, deported.

5   *be uncovered* remove your hats.
   SD SEWER attendant who supervised the table arrangements and the serving of food.

16   *SD service* other servants bearing dishes.
    SD side livery coats long coats, distinguished by the badge of Lord Mavortius.

16   *for causes* ?for good reasons.

25   *desperate of* desperately in need of.

30–4   The only one of these plays, if indeed they are meant to be taken as actual plays, now extant is *Mother Gurton's Needle*, which is presumably *Gammer Gurton's Needle* by W.S. (*c*.1553), though here absurdly described as a tragedy. The other genre identifications are also probably intentionally inaccurate: 'an infernal' seems merely invented, but 'a nocturnal', which should mean a 'night-piece' of some kind, may have been a formal term (see Thomas Dekker, *The Seven Deadly Sinnes of London* (1606; ed. Grosart, II, 41): 'and all the City looked like a private playhouse, when the windows are clapped down, as if some *Nocturnal*, or dismal *Tragedy*, were presently to be acted......'.

65   *pumps......gravel* Jonson seems to echo this in *Poetaster* (1601), III.iv.167–70: 'If he pen for thee once, thou shalt not need to travel with thy pumps full of gravel any more, after a blind jade and a hamper, and stalk upon boards and barrel-heads to an old cracked trumpet'. Note Jonson's description of a typical provincial stage.

74   *bending leg* i.e. making his bow to the audience.

75   *brown-paper-stuff* coarse, low matter.

78   *absurds* unreasonable statements (a Marston neologism).

83   *cresset-light* beacon-light, with play on Cressida as a 'light' woman.

85   *garter blue* a love token from Cressida, which Troylus wears on his 'valiant elbow'.

87   *shakes......spear* a possible, but doubtful, reference to Shakespeare.

89   *snort* sleep.

91   *screen* ?a veil, used to shield the face from the sun.

94   *SD Devil......back* By tradition the Vice (a useful composite of the seven deadly sins) was supposed to be carried off by the Devil (crying 'ho, ho, ho'; see l. 101) at the end of a morality play or moral interlude.
    Juventus i.e. youth (as in the moral interlude *Lusty Juventus* (*c*.1550)), here presented in the role of the Prodigal Son, whose story was a favourite of Protestant dramatists because it illustrated salvation through faith alone.

113   *ha't* have it.

115   *theme* a subject for extempore improvisation, a popular device in the period, particularly paradoxical themes.

119   *Sir Petronel Flash* A blustering gallant with this name ('petronel' = carbine or horse-pistol) appears in *Eastward Ho!* (by Jonson, Chapman, and Marston) produced in 1604.

120   *case* suit of clothes.

122   *play-gull a stool* See the excerpt from Dekker's *Guls Horne-booke*, p. 22.

123   *potatoes and marrow* considered to be aphrodisiacs.

129   *vacation* i.e. when the Inns of Court were not in session, out of term.

iv

From John Rowe, *Tragi-Comœdia. Being a Brief Relation of the Strange and Wonderfull hand of God discovered at Witny, in the Comedy Acted there February the third* (1653), sigs. ¶4 v–*2 v.

The actors of the play [*Mucedorus*] were countrymen, most of them, and for any thing I can hear, all of Stanton-Harcourt parish. The punctual time of their first learning the play cannot be certainly set down, but this we have been told, they had been learning it ever since Michaelmas [29 September] and had been   5 acting privately every week. This we are informed upon more certain grounds, that they began to act it in a more public manner about Christmas, and acted it three or four times in their own parish; they acted it likewise in several neighbouring parishes, as Moore, Standlake, South-Leigh, Cumnor. The last place that they   10 came at was Witney, where it pleased the Lord to discover his displeasure against such wicked and ungodly plays by an eminent hand. Some few days before the play was to be acted, one of Stanton came to the Bailiff of Witney, telling him *that there were some countrymen that had learned to make a play, and desired his*   15 *leave to show it,* his aim being (as the Bailiff conceived) that they might have the liberty of the Town-hall. Leave also was desired of the other Bailiff, but they being denied by both the Bailiffs, they pitched on the White Hart, a chief inn of the town, to act their play there. The day when it was acted was the third of February,   20 the same day when many godly people, townsmen and scholars of Oxford, kept a solemn day of fast at Carfax. About seven a'clock at night they caused a drum to beat and a trumpet to be sounded to gather the people together. The people flocked in great multitudes, men, women, and children, to the number (as is   25 guessed) of three hundred, some say four hundred, and the chamber where the play was acted being full, others in the yard pressed sorely to get in. The people which were in the room were exceeding jovial and merry before the play began, young men and maids dancing together, and so merry and frolic were many of the   30 spectators that the players could hardly get liberty that they themselves might act, but, at last, a little liberty being obtained, the play itself began. . . . . .

[Rowe quotes substantial passages from the Induction to *Mucedorus*, in which Envy, much to Rowe's satisfaction, promises to 'mix' Comedy's 'music with a tragic end. . . . . . And drench thy methods in a sea of blood', noting also a passage that required the actor of Bremo to say 'To dare the greatest Gods to fight with thee' (III.iii.42), 'but the words were so ghastly, and had such a face of impiety in them, that he durst not say *Gods,* but (as one that excused him would have us believe) he said *Gobs.*']

Thus had they continued their sport for an hour and half, as some of the spectators say, but as is more probable about two 35 hours, for they were ordinarily three hours in acting it (as the players say) and there were above two parts in three of the play that were passed over in this action. At which time it pleased God to put a stop to their mirth, and by an immediate hand of his own, in causing the chamber to sink and fall under them, to put an end 40 to this ungodly play before it was thought or intended by them.

[Rowe concludes his 'Narrative' with a long and very graphic account (sigs. *3 v–¶¶2 r) of the hysteria and confusion which followed the collapse of the floor, in which five children were killed and about 'threescore' injured.]

NOTES

2   *Stanton-Harcourt* like Witney and the other towns mentioned below (except Cumnor), a town in Oxfordshire; Cumnor is in Berkshire.

3   *punctual time* exact time.

12   *eminent* conspicuously displayed.

14   *Bailiff* chief administrative officer of the town (Witney seems to have had two bailiffs).

22   *Carfax* name of a major intersection in Oxford.

27   *chamber* The 'chamber', on the second floor, was large and had formerly been used as a 'malting room, having a part of it covered with earth to that purpose' (sig. *3 r).

35–6   *two hours* . . . . . . *three hours* The conventional time is usually given as 'two hours' (compare *Romeo and Juliet*, Prologue, 12, 'the two hours' traffic of our stage'), but 'three hours' is occasionally mentioned.

V

From Fynes Moryson's *Itinerary* (in Charles Hughes, *Shakespeare's Europe: Unpublished Chapters of Fynes Moryson's 'Itinerary'* (1903), p. 304; the passage does not appear in the published *Itinerary* (1617)). Moryson visited Frankfurt in 1592.

Germany hath some few wand'ring comedians, more deserving pity than praise, for the serious parts are dully penned and worse acted, and the mirth they make is ridiculous and nothing less than witty (as I formerly have showed). So as I remember that when some of our cast despised stageplayers came out of England into   5
Germany, and played at Frankfort in the time of the Mart, having neither a complete number of actors nor any good apparel, nor any ornament of the stage, yet the Germans, not understanding a word they said, both men and women, flocked wonderfully to see their gesture and action, rather than hear them speaking English which   10
they understood not, and pronouncing pieces and patches of English plays, which myself and some Englishmen there present could not hear without great wearisomeness. Yea, myself, coming from Frankfort in the company of some chief merchants, Dutch and Flemish, heard them often brag of the good market they had   15
made, only condoling that they had not the leisure to hear the English players.

NOTES

3–4 *nothing......witty* i.e. the antithesis of witty.
4 *as......showed* In a later comment (see Hughes, p. 373) Moryson says of Dutch actors: 'But for the comedians, they little practise that art and are the poorest actors that can be imagined.'
5 *cast* dismissed from service or otherwise unemployed. Moryson is probably over-harsh in his characterization of these actors. The troupe he saw was that headed by Robert Browne, travelling under special passport from the Lord Admiral; all but one of the actors there named, Robert Jones, are best known as English actors on the Continent. They are reported to have performed W.S.'s *Gammer Gurton's Needle* (*c.* 1553) and some of Marlowe's plays.
6 *Mart* i.e. the autumn fair (one of two famous annual fairs held in Frankfurt).
7 *neither......actors* Only four are named in the Lord Admiral's licence, but they probably had 'hirelings' as well.
11–12 *pieces......plays* This suggests that they performed detached scenes from several plays. This was done at fairs in England during the Commonwealth period, the detached scenes being known as 'drolls'.

4 The playhouses

Elizabethan–Jacobean London was well supplied with theatres, more so than any of the other European capitals. Among them, the most important were: the Theatre (the earliest regular public theatre, built in 1576 and torn down to furnish materials for the first Globe in 1598–9); the Curtain (built 1577); the Rose (built 1587); the Swan (built 1595–6); the Globe (built 1599, burned down 1613, rebuilt 1614 as the so-called second Globe); the Fortune (built 1600, burned down 1621, rebuilt in circular form by 1623); the Red Bull (built 1605); the Hope (built 1614; also used for bear-baiting); and four so-called 'private' enclosed theatres: the first (1576–7–84) and second (1597) Blackfriars; the Whitefriars (built 1606); the Cockpit or Phoenix (originally built (1609) for cock-fighting but converted to a 'private' theatre in 1616–17); and the 'song school' near St Paul's where the Paul's Boys performed up to 1606. All, except the first Fortune (square) and the 'private' theatres (rectangular), were either circular or polygonal, and all, except the Rose, the Globe, the Swan, and the Hope, which were located on the Bankside, were in the City or in its immediate environs.

Our knowledge of the physical characteristics, both inside and out, of the London playhouses is drawn from a variety of sources: panoramic maps (by Ralph Agas, c.1570, showing only two bull- and bear-baiting arenas on the Bankside; John Norden, 1600; J. C. Visscher, 1616; Wenzel Hollar, 1647, etc.); a sketch of the interior of the Swan (c.1596), originally by Johannes de Witt; two builders' contracts, one (see selection (i)) for the Fortune (1600) and one for the Hope (1613); stage directions and dialogue in contemporary plays; and scattered allusions in legal and other official documents and in the literature of the period (see illustrations 3 and 4).

Even so our knowledge remains infuriatingly incomplete (and hypothetically controversial) on a number of important details, particularly in relation to the actual stage itself. In neither the Fortune nor Hope contracts, for example, is any mention made of stage entrance doors, stage traps, the inner or rear stage (or 'discovery space' as it has more recently been called), or the upper stage, the front part of which was often referred to as the 'tarras'; while the De Witt drawing of the Swan, though it shows two stage entrances with heavy wooden closed doors, pictures spectators sitting in 'rooms' above the rear back wall of the stage, where the upper stage would be expected, and includes no sign of any inner stage or discovery space. It is possible that De Witt depicted conditions at the Swan accurately, but the drawing is probably misleading so far as most of the other playhouses were concerned. There is ample evidence from many stage directions, drawn from plays performed in different theatres, both public and 'private', that an upper and inner stage were regular features in most theatres. Again and again characters are described as entering 'above', 'aloft', 'at a window', or 'upon the walls' (*Enter* [Barabas] *with a hammer above, very busy*', Marlowe, *Jew of Malta*, V.v; '[*Trumpet*] *sounds. Enter* General [*and others*] *aloft*', Shakespeare, *I Henry VI*, IV.ii.2; '*Enter Romeo and Juliet at the window*', Shakespeare, *Romeo and Juliet* (Q1), III.v; '*The drums sounds a parle.* Perseda *comes upon the walls in man's apparel.* Basilisco *and* Piston, *upon the walls*' and l. 55, '*Then* Perseda *comes down to* Soliman, *and* Basilisco *and* Piston' (entering on the main stage from the inner stage, which would here represent the gates of a castle or city), Kyd, *Soliman and Perseda*, V.iv.15).

'Discoveries', calling for the use of an inner stage, are also common ('*Enter* Faustus *in his study*', Marlowe, *Dr Faustus*, I.i; '*A room in Frippery's house.* Frippery *discovered summing up his pawns, one fellow standing by him*', Middleton, *Your Five Gallants*, I.i; '*Here Prospero discovers* Ferdinand *and* Miranda *playing at chess*', Shakespeare, *The Tempest*, V.i.171). Such 'discoveries' were made by opening the curtains (of painted cloth or arras) covering the recessed space at the rear centre of the main stage; once the curtains were opened the inner stage could be absorbed into the action on the main stage (as in the tomb scene (V.iii) of *Romeo and Juliet*).

In the public theatres, a third level, above the upper stage, seems to have been occasionally used. In Kyd's *Soliman and Perseda* a stage direction (V.iii. 121) reads: '*Then the Marshal bears them to the tower top*', and eight lines later: '*Then they are both tumbled down*'; and in Shakespeare's *I Henry VI* (III.ii.25) we find: '*Enter* Pucelle *on the top, thrusting out a burning torch*' (the 'top' being later described as 'yonder turret').

Some critics have argued that in some theatres, the Swan perhaps, when needed, a removable 'pavilion' or tent-like structure was used in place of a permanent inner stage, or that instead of a recessed inner and upper stage, a more permanent structure projected from the rear stage wall (this last seems to be the orthodoxy of the moment). I have chosen to follow the more old-fashioned view, since the evidence for any of the views remains highly controversial, where it exists at all. In any case, the necessity for some kinds of inner- and upper-stage areas is incontrovertible, whether recessed or projecting.

What do we really know about the most famous of Elizabethan–Jacobean theatres, Shakespeare's Globe (both first and second)? There is an exterior view of the second Globe in Hollar's panoramic *Long View of London from Bankside* (1647), in which the Globe is mislabelled 'Beere bayting h.' and what is probably the Hope noted as 'The Globe'. This, plus a slightly more detailed pencil sketch (*c*.1640) also by Hollar, is all we have, since the building labelled 'The Globe' in Visscher's view (1616) is in all likelihood the Rose. Hollar shows a more or less cylindrical structure with a twin-dormered superstructure, topped by a small domed turret, rising above the third-gallery roof level from the tiring-house area, perhaps projecting also over the 'heavens'. Being built on the burned-out foundations of the first Globe, the size of the second Globe was of necessity identical so far as the ground dimensions were concerned. Recent studies (by Richard Hosley and John Orrell in *The Third Globe*, ed. by C. W. Hodges, S. Schoenbaum, and Leonard Leone, 1981), based on mathematical computations extrapolated from Hollar's *Long View* and *East Part of Southwarke* (the second a sketch), suggest that the second Globe was a twenty-four- (or sixteen-) sided polygonal structure, about 100 feet wide and 33 or 34 feet high (the height being based on analogy with the Fortune). Of the interior and the stage, except for what may be assumed by analogy from the information in the Fortune and Hope contracts and the De Witt drawing, we have almost no concrete information.

The seating–standing capacity of the public theatres was surprisingly large. Ann J. Cook (*The Privileged Playgoers of Shakespeare's London* (1981), pp. 175–9) offers a recent summary of the evidence. The larger houses (Swan, Globe, Fortune and Rose) could attract audiences estimated at something over three thousand, and the older theatres (Theatre and Curtain) could probably accommodate around two thousand. The capacity of the 'private' houses was, however, much less and has been variously estimated as between five and six hundred.

Selection (ii) recounts the visit of the Swiss traveller Thomas Platter to several London theatres (among them the Globe and probably the Curtain) in the later part of 1599. His account is of special interest because he witnessed a performance of what was almost certainly Shakespeare's *Julius Caesar* at the Globe ('the house with the thatched roof').

For detailed studies of the London theatres (not always agreeing with each other), see the following works: E. K. Chambers, *The Elizabethan Stage* (4 vols., 1923); G. E. Bentley, *The Jacobean and Caroline Stage* (7 vols. 1941–68); C. W. Hodges, *The Globe Restored* (2nd edn., 1968); Glynne Wickham, *Early English Stages* (vol. II, parts I and II, 1963–72); Irwin Smith, *Shakespeare's Blackfriars Playhouse* (1964); *The Third Globe* (1981) (referred to above).

i

From the contract for the building of the Fortune Theatre (drawn between Philip Henslowe, Edward Alleyn, and Peter Street), 8 January 1600 (MS in the Alleyn Papers at Dulwich College, Muniment No. 22).

...... The frame of the said house to be set square and to contain four score foot of lawful assize every way square without, and fifty-five foot of like assize square every way within, with a good, sure, and strong foundation of piles, brick, lime and sand both without and within to be wrought one foot of assize at the least above the ground. And the said frame to contain three storeys in height, the first or lower storey to contain twelve foot of lawful assize in height, the second storey eleven foot of lawful assize in height, and the third or upper storey to contain nine foot of lawful assize in height. All which storeys shall contain twelve foot and a half of lawful assize in breadth throughout, besides a jutty forwards in either of the said two upper storeys of ten inches of lawful assize, with four convenient divisions for gentlemen's rooms and other sufficient and convenient divisions for two-penny rooms, with necessary seats to be placed and set as well in those rooms as throughout all the rest of the galleries of the said house and with such-like stairs, conveyances, and divisions without and within as are made and contrived in and to the late erected playhouse on the Bank, in the said parish of St Saviour's, called the Globe; with a stage and tiring-house to be made, erected, and set up within the said frame with a shadow or cover over the said stage...... And which stage shall contain in length forty and three foot of lawful assize and in breadth to extend to the middle of the yard of the said house. The same stage to be paled in below with good, strong, and sufficient new oaken boards, and likewise the lower storey of the said frame withinside; and the same lower storey to be also laid over and fenced with strong iron pikes. And the said stage to be in all other proportions contrived and fashioned like unto the stage of the said playhouse called the Globe, with convenient windows and lights glazed to the said tiring-house, and the said frame, stage, and staircases to be covered with tile and to have a sufficient gutter of lead to carry and convey the water from the covering of the said stage to fall backwards. And also all the said frame and the staircases thereof to be sufficiently enclosed without with lath, lime and hair, and the gentlemen's rooms and two-penny rooms to be sealed with lath, lime and hair, and all the floors of the said galleries, storeys, and stage to be boarded with good and sufficient new deal boards of whole thickness where need shall be. And the said house, and other things before-mentioned, to be made and done, to be in all other contrivitions, conveyances, fashions, thing and things effected, finished, and done, according to the manner

5

10

15

20

25

30

35

40

and fashion of the said house called the Globe, saving only that all
the principal and main posts of the said frame and stage forward
shall be square and wrought pilaster-wise with carved proportions
called satyrs to be placed and set on the top of every of the same   45
posts......

NOTES

1   *set square* Unlike most other theatres of the time, which were polygonal
    or round, the Fortune was square.

2   *lawful assize* prescribed (by law) standard.

11 *jutty* projection (presumably to afford some protection from rain).

13 *gentlemen's rooms* probably private rooms, in which a seat cost six or (later)
    twelve and eight pence.

14 *two-penny rooms* rooms in which one could sit by paying an extra penny
    above the initial entrance penny.

19 *St Saviour's* parish in Southwark on the Bankside, west of London Bridge.
    Globe theatre of the King's Men (Shakespeare), built in 1599 (rebuilt after
    a fire in 1614). This and the following references to the Globe (ll. 29, 42)
    are tantalizing, since we don't really know a great deal about the details of
    structure in the Globe.

20 *tiring-house* i.e. attiring house, where the actors costumed themselves, and
    from which they entered, and into which they exited, through two or
    more doorways placed on either side at the rear of the stage in most public
    theatres.

21 *shadow or cover* i.e. a roof-like projection from well above the upper stage
    extending over probably three-quarters of the main stage (the Hope
    contract of 1613 seems to suggest over the whole stage) and supported by
    two pillars (see ll. 42–6) at the front of the stage; it was known as 'the
    heavens' (so called in the Hope contract, where, however, there were no
    supporting pillars, since the stage, raised on trestles, was removable to
    accommodate bear- and bull-baiting); in the Globe 'the heavens' was, we
    believe, painted sky-blue, with golden stars.

22–3 *stage......yard* The stage thus would have been 43 feet across (back and
    front) and about $27\frac{1}{2}$ feet deep, projecting out 'to the middle of the yard'.
    The 'yard', unroofed, occupied a 55-by-$27\frac{1}{2}$-foot area at the front of the
    stage, with two narrow 6-foot areas running down either side of the stage;
    thus it surrounded the stage on three sides. It was in the yard, unprotected
    from the elements, that the 'groundlings', 'who for the most part are
    capable of nothing but inexplicable dumb shows and noise' (*Hamlet*,
    III.ii.11–12), stood to enjoy their pennyworths. The standing areas on each
    side of the stage would have been rather more roomy in a polygonal
    structure such as the Globe.

27 *iron pikes* The position and purpose of these 'pikes' (=spikes) is not clear.
    They appear to be associated with the 'lower storey'; perhaps, however,
    they were meant to be placed across the front and on either side of the
    stage as a protection for the actors from obstreperous 'groundlings'. The
    Globe is believed to have had a low, openwork fence surrounding the
    exposed edges of the stage as Thomas Middleton suggests: [Lucifer

speaking] 'And now that I have vaulted up so high / Above the stage-rails of this earthen globe, / I must turn actor and join companies' (*The Blacke Book*, (1604), in *Works*, ed. A. H. Bullen, VIII, 8).

31   *covered with tile* i.e. roofed with tile. The first Globe (1599) was thatched (see selection (ii)) and burned to the ground (1613) when, in the masquing scene of *Henry VIII* (I.iv.49 SD), 'chambers' (= small pieces of ordnance, used for firing salutes) discharged burning materials which alighted on the thatch.

32–3   *water......backwards* i.e. so that the rain-water would not fall on the 'groundlings' in the yard.

40   *contrivitions* ? contrivances (not in *OED*).

44   *wrought pilaster-wise* i.e. finished decoratively in the fashion of pilasters (= square or rectangular columns).

44–5   *proportions called satyrs* figures carved to resemble satyrs.

ii

From the diary of Thomas Platter (1599) (as translated by Clare Williams in *Thomas Platter's Travels in England, 1599* (1937), pp. 166–7).

On September 21st after lunch, about two o'clock, I and my party crossed the water, and there in the house with the thatched roof witnessed an excellent performance of the tragedy of the First Emperor Julius Caesar with a cast of some fifteen people; when the play was over, they danced very marvellously and gracefully   5
together as is their wont, two dressed as men and two as women.

On another occasion not far from our inn, in the suburb at Bishopsgate, if I remember, also after lunch, I beheld a play in which they presented diverse nations and an Englishman struggling together for a maiden; he overcame them all except the   10
German who won the girl in a tussle, and then sat down by her side, when he and his servant drank themselves tipsy, so that they were both fuddled and the servant proceeded to hurl his shoe at his master's head, whereupon they both fell asleep; meanwhile the Englishman stole into the tent and absconded with the German's   15
prize, thus in his turn outwitting the German; in conclusion they danced very charmingly in English and Irish fashion. Thus daily at two in the afternoon, London has two, sometimes three plays running in different places, competing with each other, and those which play best obtain most spectators. The playhouses are so   20
constructed that they play on a raised platform, so that everyone

has a good view. There are different galleries and places, however, where the seating is better and more comfortable and therefore more expensive. For whoever cares to stand below only pays one English penny, but if he wishes to sit he enters by another door, 25 and pays another penny, while if he desires to sit in the most comfortable seats which are cushioned, where he not only sees everything well, but can also be seen, then he pays yet another English penny at another door. And during the performance food and drink are carried round the audience, so that for what one 30 cares to pay one may also have refreshment. The actors are most expensively and elaborately costumed; for it is the English usage for eminent lords or knights at their decease to bequeath and leave almost the best of their clothes to their serving men, which it is unseemly for the latter to wear, so that they offer them then for 35 sale for a small sum to the actors.

How much time then they may merrily spend daily at the play everyone knows who has ever seen them play or act.

NOTES

2   *house . . . . . . roof* i.e. the Globe, only completed earlier in 1599.
5   *they danced* i.e. they performed a stage jig (see p. 363).
8   *Bishopsgate* one of the old gates in the north-eastern part of the City, between Aldgate and Aldersgate. Platter probably means 'near Bishops-gate'.
   beheld a play probably at the Curtain; the play has not survived.

5 Play genres and repertories

Any discussion of play genres and the Elizabethan–Jacobean repertory must begin with Polonius' hyperbolic comment on the range and capabilities of the company of strolling players which is revisiting Elsinore (*Hamlet*, II.ii.396–402): 'The best actors in the world, either for tragedy, comedy, history, pastoral, pastoral-comical, historical-pastoral, tragical-historical, tragical-comical-historical-pastoral, scene individable, or poem unlimited; Seneca cannot be too heavy, nor Plautus too light, for the law of the writ and the liberty: these are the only men.' Even though Shakespeare is writing tongue in cheek, poking fun at the pomposity of Polonius, most of the 'kinds' he makes Polonius reel off may be illustrated from the extant drama of the period. Polonius also touches, though somewhat ambiguously, on certain aspects of critical theory which were being debated in some quarters at this time. It was a debate between the Ancients and the Moderns, between those who insisted that a play must observe the so-called 'classical' laws of the drama (the unities of time, place, and action, i.e. 'scene individable' and 'the law of the writ') and those, the great majority of Elizabethan–Jacobean playwrights, including, of course, Shakespeare, who generally ignored the 'classical' prescripts and produced 'poem[s] unlimited' with complete 'liberty', i.e. plays like *Hamlet*. (On the three unities, see selection (i) from Sidney's *Defence*, notes on ll. 9–10, 52, below).

Both Sir Philip Sidney and Ben Jonson (see selections (i) and (ii)) argued from the classically oriented point of view so far as the unities were concerned, though Jonson, when it suited him (as in *Every Man out of His Humour* (1599)), modelled on '*vetus comoedia*', i.e. 'old comedy', based on Aristophanes, or, even in a 'Senecan' tragedy like *Sejanus* (1603)), was ready to overlook one or more of them, and the Aristotelian unity of action (a single plot, with or without 'discovery') held little appeal either for him or for the other popular dramatists who wrote for the public stage. Indeed, it may be noted that, in his strictures on contemporary drama (selection (ii)), Jonson makes no mention of the unity of action. On the other hand, although little heed was accorded to the unities by the professional dramatists, classical Latin drama, particularly the tragedies associated with Seneca and the comedies of Terence and Plautus were widely influential: Seneca for the rhetorical tone (the 'high style' proper to tragedy), psychological probing of character, sensational and 'bloody' subject matter, etc.; Terence and Plautus, especially the former, for the so-called five-act structure (see selection (iii), note to ll. 8–12) in both comedy and tragedy and for the kinds of language ('middle' or 'low style') and the social level of the characters proper to the comic mode according to the doctrine of decorum (see selection (ii), note to l. 14). Thus Thomas Heywood (selection (iii)), a 'popular' dramatist, who claimed to have had a hand in over two hundred plays, which, if his extant plays are any guide, violated the unities at every turn, is obviously much concerned to establish, the unities aside, the continuing debt of contemporary drama, structurally and in terms of general subject matter and purpose, to its classical antecedents.

An example of the structural influence of the five-act formula may be clearly seen in Sir William Davenant's 'play recipe' offered in his *Preface to Gondibert* (1650):

> The first *Act* is the general preparative, by rend'ring the chiefest characters of persons, and ending with something that looks like an obscure promise of design. The second begins with an introduction of new persons, so finishes all the characters, and ends with some little performance of that design which was promised at the parting of the first *Act*. The third makes a visible correspondence in the underwalks (or lesser intrigues) of persons; and ends with an ample turn of the main design, and expectation of a new [i.e. turn]. The fourth (ever having occasion to be the longest) gives a notorious turn to all the underwalks, and a counterturn to that main design which changed in the third. The fifth begins with an entire diversion of the main and dependent plots; then makes the general correspondence of the persons more discernible, and ends with any easy untying of those particular knots which made a contexture of the whole, leaving such satisfaction of probabilities with the spectator, as may persuade him that neither Fortune in the fate of the persons, nor the writer in the representment, have been unnatural or exorbitant.

Plays were written for and became the property of particular companies, each of which jealously guarded its rights. The majority of the plays written during the Elizabethan–Jacobean period can be assigned to specific companies (see Harbage and Schoenbaum, *Annals of English Drama, 975–1700*, rev. edn, 1964), but for only one (the Admiral's Men) do we possess any extended and detailed, day-by-day record. This we owe to Philip Henslowe, who, as a keen businessman and owner (among other theatrical properties) of the Rose playhouse (built 1587), kept a daily record of his rental receipts (half the gallery takings; after 1598 all the gallery takings) from performances by the Admiral's Men, who occupied the Rose from 1594–1600. A short sample from Henslowe's so-called *Diary* (ed. R. A. Foakes and R. T. Richert, 1961) from October of 1954, in Henslowe's idiosyncratic spelling, will give some idea of the kind of information he furnishes.

```
17 of octobr 1594    Rd at tamberlen ........................ xxxx s
18 of octobr 1594    Rd at the frenshe docter .............. xxij s
20 of octobr 1594—Rd at the Jew of malta 1594   ......... xiij s
21 of octobr 1594    Rd at docter ffostus 1594 ............ xxxiij s
22 of octbr 1594 ne—Rd at a Knacke to Know
                       a noneste  ....................... xxxx s
```

Here we have a record of the performance of three of Marlowe's plays (*Tamburlaine* (probably Part I), *The Jew of Malta*, and *Dr Faustus*), an anonymous lost play, *The French Doctor* (perhaps the same as the lost *The Venetian Comedy* performed as 'ne' (i.e. new) on 25 August 1594), and a new play, *Knack to Know an Honest Man*, possibly by Thomas Heywood or Anthony Munday: two tragedies, a 'history' (*Tamburlaine*), a comedy (?), and a tragi-comedy (*Knack*). It will be noticed that the 'bill' changed each night, though a play might be repeated (especially if new) within a few days. Consecutive 'runs' were essentially unknown, the exception being a nine-day (Sunday excepted) run of Middleton's *A Game at Chess*, a contemporary anti-Spanish political satire, at the Globe in 1624 to an audience of never less than three thousand.

A quick analysis of Henslowe's records for September and October of 1595, a year for which he records a total of 214 performances for the Admiral's Men and the production of 15 new plays, shows 27 performances for September of 16 different plays, two of them new; for October, 27 performances of 14 different plays, three of them new. One play (*Crack Me This Nut*, anonymous and lost) was played as new on 5 September and repeated six more times during September and October; another anonymous, lost play, *The Seven Days of the Week*, produced as new on 10 June 1595, received seven performances during the same period. Two-part plays were often given consecutively (*I* and *II Hercules*, 1,2; 22,23 September) but not always (*I Hercules* only 25 October).

Something of the relative popularity of different plays may be gauged by the amount of Henslowe's gallery takings. New plays tended to bring in more money than old plays (e.g. *Dr Faustus* (an old play) netted Henslowe 13 shillings on 26 September; *Crack Me This Nut* (new on 5 September, when it netted Henslowe 61 shillings) brought him 66 shillings on 28 September). Generally, though there seem to be exceptions, performances were prohibited (since about 1583) on Sundays and during the period of Lent.

How applicable to other companies is the picture here sketched from Henslowe's accounts for the Admiral's Men? Judged by some earlier comparatively limited records for Lord Strange's Men, the Earl of Sussex's Men, and the Chamberlain's Men included by Henslowe in the *Diary*, the answer would seem to be that on the whole the picture is typical for the 1590s and may be taken as representative of the repertory performance patterns during the first three decades of the seventeenth century.

For comment on academic drama (grammar school, university, and Inns of Court), see the introductory note to 'Education', pp. 143–4.

i

The state of English drama in 1579–80

From Sir Philip Sidney, *The Defence of Poesy* (written about 1579–80, published 1595), in G. G. Smith, ed., *Elizabethan Critical Essays* (1904), I, 196–201 (under the alternative title 'An Apology for Poetry').

Our tragedies and comedies (not without cause cried out against), observing rules neither of honest civility nor of skilful poetry, excepting *Gorboduc* (again, I say, of those that I have seen), which, notwithstanding as it is full of stately speeches and well-sounding phrases, climbing to the height of Seneca his style, and as full of   5
notable morality, which it doth most delightfully teach, and so obtain the very end of poesy, yet in troth it is very defectious in the circumstances, which grieveth me, because it might not remain as an exact model of all tragedies. For it is faulty both in place and time, the two necessary companions of all corporal actions. For   10
where the stage should always represent but one place, and the uttermost time presupposed in it should be, both by Aristotle's precept and common reason, but one day, there is both many days and many places, inartificially imagined.

But if it be so in *Gorboduc*, how much more in all the rest?   15
where you shall have Asia of the one side, and Afric of the other, and so many other under-kingdoms, that the player, when he cometh in, must ever begin with telling where he is, or else the tale will not be conceived. Now ye shall have three ladies walk to gather flowers, and then we must believe the stage to be a garden.   20
By and by, we hear news of shipwrack in the same place, and then we are to blame if we accept it not for a rock. Upon the back of that, comes out a hideous monster with fire and smoke, and then the miserable beholders are bound to take it for a cave. While in the meantime two armies fly in, represented with four swords and   25
bucklers, and then what hard heart will not receive it for a pitched field?

Now of time they are much more liberal, for ordinary it is that two young princes fall in love. After many traverses, she is got with child, delivered of a fair boy, he is lost, groweth a man, falls in   30
love, and is ready to get another child; and all this in two hours' space: which how absurd it is in sense, even sense may imagine, and art hath taught, and all ancient examples justified, and at this day the ordinary players in Italy will not err in. Yet will some bring in an example of *Eunuchus* in Terence, that containeth matter of   35
two days, yet far short of twenty years. True it is, and so was it to be played in two days, and so fitted to the time it set forth. And though Plautus hath in one place done amiss, let us hit with him, and not miss with him. But they will say, how then shall we set

forth a story which containeth both many places and many times?   40
And do they not know, that a tragedy is tied to the laws of poesy,
and not of history? not bound to follow the story, but having
liberty either to feign a quite new matter, or to frame the history to
the most tragical conveniency. Again, many things may be told
which cannot be showed, if they know the difference betwixt   45
reporting and representing. As for example, I may speak (though I
am here) of Peru, and in speech digress from that to the
description of Calicut; but in action, I cannot represent it without
Pacolet's horse; and so was the manner the ancients took, by some
Nuntius to recount things done in former time or other place.   50

   Lastly, if they will represent an history, they must not (as
Horace saith) begin *ab ovo*, but they must come to the principal
point of that one action which they will represent. By example this
will be best expressed. I have a story of young Polydorus, delivered
for safety's sake, with great riches, by his father Priamus to   55
Polymnestor, king of Thrace, in the Trojan war time; he after
some years, hearing the overthrow of Priamus, for to make the
treasure his own murdereth the child; the body of the child is
taken up by Hecuba; she the same day findeth a sleight to be
revenged most cruelly of the tyrant. Where now would one of our   60
tragedy writers begin, but with the delivery of the child? Then
should he sail over into Thrace, and so spend I know not how
many years, and travel numbers of places. But where doth
Euripides? Even with the finding of the body, leaving the rest to be
told by the spirit of Polydorus. This need no further to be   65
enlarged; the dullest wit may conceive it.

   But besides these gross absurdities, how all their plays be
neither right tragedies nor right comedies, mingling kings and
clowns, not because the matter so carrieth it, but thrust in clowns
by head and shoulders, to play a part in majestical matters, with   70
neither decency nor discretion, so as neither the admiration and
commiseration, nor the right sportfulness, is by their mongrel
tragi-comedy obtained. I know Apuleius did somewhat so, but
that is a thing recounted with space of time, not represented in
one moment: and I know the ancients have one or two examples of   75
tragi-comedies, as Plautus hath *Amphitrio*; but if we mark them
well, we shall find, that they never, or very daintily, match horn-
pipes and funerals. So falleth it out, that having indeed no right
comedy, in that comical part of our tragedy we have nothing but
scurrility, unworthy of any chaste ears, or some extreme show of   80
doltishness, indeed fit to lift up a loud laughter, and nothing else:
where the whole tract of a comedy should be full of delight, as the
tragedy should be still maintained in a well-raised admiration.

   But our comedians think there is no delight without laughter;
which is very wrong, for though laughter may come with delight,   85
yet cometh it not of delight, as though delight should be the cause

of laughter; but well may one thing breed both together; nay, rather in themselves they have, as it were, a kind of contrariety; for delight we scarcely do but in things that have a conveniency to ourselves or to the general nature. Laughter almost ever cometh of things most disproportioned to ourselves and nature. Delight hath a joy in it, either permanent or present. Laughter hath only a scornful tickling......

But I have lavished out too many words of this play matter. I do it because, as they are excelling parts of poesy, so is there none so much used in England, and none can be more pitifully abused: which, like an unmannerly daughter, shewing a bad education, causeth her mother Poesy's honesty to be called in question.

NOTES

3   *Gorboduc* the first so-called 'regular' English tragedy, written by Thomas Sackville and Thomas Norton in 1562 and acted at the Inner Temple. In form it is an imitation of Seneca (five-act structure, choruses, reported action, comparatively small cast).

5   *height......style* Considering the usual Renaissance view of Seneca, no higher praise could have been given.
Seneca his Seneca's.

7   *end of poesy* Although Sidney here would seem to say that the sole aim of poetry was to teach or profit mankind, he also believed, following Horace (*Ars Poetica*, ll. 333–4: 'Aut prodesse volunt aut delectare poetae......omne tulit punctum qui miscuit utile dulci, lectorem delectando pariterque monendo.', i.e. Poets aim either to profit [teach] or to amuse......He has won every vote who has blended profit and pleasure, at once delighting and instructing the reader.), that successfully to move the reader it must combine both profit *and* pleasure ('that delightful teaching, which must be the right describing note to know a poet by', ed. G. G. Smith, I, 160).
defectious defective.

8   *circumstances* particulars, details.

9–10 *faulty......time* Sidney is here referring, for the first time in England, to the doctrine of the 'three unities' (time, place, and action), for which Continental critics claimed authority in Aristotle's *Poetics* and classical drama. Aristotle does discuss unity of action (in terms of a single or complex plot) and mentions unity of time in a single passing reference to 'a single revolution of the sun' (i.e. twenty-four hours), but says nothing of unity of place, which limited the action to a single locale and was formulated into a 'law of the drama', on the basis of general classical practice, by Lodovico Castelvetro in 1571. Much of what Sidney criticizes in contemporary English drama arises out of its failure to observe these 'laws'. Fortunately, popular English drama, unlike much French drama for example, paid little or no attention to the 'laws' of neo-classical criticism.

16 *one side* i.e. of the stage.

18   *begin......he is* Compare, for example, *Twelfth Night*, I.ii.1–2: '*Viola*. What country, friends, is this? / *Captain*. This is Illyria, lady.'

19   *conceived* understood.

29–32   *After......space* Sidney is thinking of plays like *Common Conditions* (anon., 1576), *Clyomon and Clamydes* (anon., 1570–83), but the description might also fit much later plays like Shakespeare's *Pericles* (1607–8) or *The Winter's Tale* (1610–11). Sidney may have been thinking of George Whetstone's comment in his Dedication to *Promos and Cassandra* (1578): 'then in three hours runs he through the world, marries, gets children, makes children men, men to conquer kingdoms, murder monsters, and bringeth gods from heaven, and fetcheth devils from hell' (ed. G. G. Smith, *Elizabethan Critical Essays*, I, 59).

31–2   *two hours' space* See p. 49, ll. 35–6n.

35–6   *Eunuchus......days* Sidney is confused; he is probably thinking of Plautus' *Captivi*, to which he appears to refer in ll. 37–8. His explanation of the 'two days' is pure nonsense.

43–4   *frame......conveniency* i.e. adjust history in order to achieve the most tragic effect.

44–5   *many......showed* i.e. often through the use of reported action, most usually through the Nuntius or messenger (see l. 50).

48   *Calicut* Calcutta (in India).

49   *Pacolet's horse* The dwarf Pacolet (in the French romance of *Valentine and Orson*, trans. *c*.1550) had a magic horse that could convey him immediately to any place he wished to be.

52   *ab ovo* from the egg; a reference to Horace, *Ars Poetica*, l. 147. Sidney is beginning his discussion of what may be called classical 'crisis' construction (i.e. the choice of 'the day' on which events unfold, antecedent events being reported by the Chorus or other characters) versus what has been described as the 'and then, and then, and then' type of construction (events being dramatized over a series of years), the kind of construction then and later usually employed by English dramatists.

53   *example* Sidney chooses Euripides' *Hecuba* to illustrate classical 'crisis' construction.

68–9   *mingling......clowns* Classical precept (except in the satyr play) frowned on the mingling of tragic and comic matter in the same play, though Renaissance critics admitted that Plautus' *Amphitrio* (see l. 76), which he himself described as 'tragicomoedia' (Prologue, l. 59), successfully combined 'tragic' and 'comic' elements. Sidney is objecting to plays like Thomas Preston's *Cambyses* (1559–69) and R. B.'s *Appius and Virginia* (1559–67), which interspersed the tragic story with low comedy scenes usually associated with the Vice. Sidney again seems to be recalling Whetstone.

73   *Apuleius* Sidney is referring to Apuleius' 'novel' called *The Golden Asse* (trans. W. Adlington, 1566) as an example of mixed genres. As a narrative it did not need to observe the unities of time and place.

73   *tragi-comedy* The term here is loosely used to describe plays like *Cambyses* and *Appius and Virginia*. The full theory of the genre which we call tragi-comedy, and which became so popular in England around 1608, was only formulated by Guarini in 1590 in defence of his tragi-comedy, *Il Pastor Fido*.

77   *daintily* elegantly, deftly.

82   *tract* duration of the action.

83   *admiration* wonder.
88   *contrariety* natural opposition.
88–9 *for. . . . . . do* i.e. we scarcely do delight.
95–6 *there. . . . . .used* i.e. more plays are written than any other kind of
     'poesy'.
98   *honesty* with play on the frequent Elizabethan sense of 'chastity'.

ii

The state of English drama about 1610

From Ben Jonson, *Every Man in His Humour* (revised text *c.*1610), The
Prologue.

> Though need make many poets, and some such
> As art and nature have not better'd much;
> Yet ours for want hath not so lov'd the stage,
> As he dare serve th'ill customs of the age,
> Or purchase your delight at such a rate   5
> As for it he himself must justly hate:
> To make a child, now swaddled, to proceed
> Man, and then shoot up, in one beard and weed,
> Past threescore years; or, with three rusty swords,
> And help of some few foot-and-half-foot words,   10
> Fight over *York* and *Lancaster's* long jars,
> And in the tiring-house bring wounds to scars.
> He rather prays you will be pleas'd to see
> One such, today, as other plays should be.
> Where neither *Chorus* wafts you o'er the seas,   15
> Nor creaking throne comes down the boys to please,
> Nor nimble squib is seen to make afeard
> The gentlewomen, nor roll'd bullet heard
> To say it thunders, nor tempestuous drum
> Rumbles to tell you when the storm doth come;   20
> But deeds and language such as men do use,
> And persons such as *Comedy* would choose,
> When she would show an image of the times,
> And sport with human follies, not with crimes –
> Except we make 'hem such by loving still   25

Our popular errors, when we know th'are ill.
I mean such errors as you'll all confess,
By laughing at them, they deserve no less:
Which when you heartily do, there's hope left then,
You, that have so grac'd monsters, may like men.   30

NOTES

3   *ours* i.e. the author, Ben Jonson.
     for want out of poverty.
5–6 *purchase......hate* i.e. Jonson refuses to prostitute his talents, making
     him despise himself, by pandering to the popular taste and serving 'th'ill
     customs of the age'.
7–9 *To make......swords* Jonson obviously is recalling Sidney's strictures
     (see selection (i), ll. 24–34).
10   *foot-and-half-foot words* polysyllabic words. Jonson is translating part of
     Horace's caveat against 'sesquipedalia verba' (*Ars Poetica*, l. 97).
11   *York......jars* a reference to Shakespeare's three parts of *Henry VI* and
     Richard III, and possibly to his *Richard II* to *Henry V* tetralogy.
12   *bring......scars* i.e. heal immediately the supposed wounds (with their
     fake blood) inflicted during fights on the stage.
14   *as other......be* This is the sort of statement that earned Jonson (rightly
     or wrongly) the reputation of arrogance. He means, of course, that *Every
     Man in His Humour* observes the 'rules of art' so far as time (one day) and
     place (London) are concerned and that the level of characters (middle and
     lower class), the language they employ, and the subject matter ('human
     follies' not 'crimes') are, according to the classical doctrine of decorum,
     proper to true comedy (see ll. 21–4). Note, however, that in his strictures
     on other contemporary plays for their failure to observe the unities of time
     and place (ll. 7–15), he says nothing about the genuinely Aristotelian unity
     of action. Like his contemporaries, Jonson liked multiple and complicated
     plots; not even the 'double plots' sanctioned by some of Terence's plays
     satisfied his truly Elizabethan taste for 'infinite variety'.
15   *Chorus......seas* possibly a reference to Shakespeare's use of the Chorus
     in *Henry V*.
16–20 For illustrations, see pp. 70–1.
19   *tempestuous drum* Perhaps a reference to *The Tempest*; if so, it has been
     suggested that 'monsters' (l. 30) is meant to recall Caliban.
23   *image......times* Although Jonson is probably thinking of a definition
     of comedy attributed to Cicero ('imitatio vitae'), compare *Hamlet*,
     III.ii.20–4.
25   *'hem* them.
30   *grac'd* approved of.

iii

Plays: their genres and uses

From Thomas Heywood, *An Apology for Actors*, 1612, sigs. F1 v–F4 r.

Tragedies and comedies, saith Donatus, had their beginning *a rebus divinis*, from divine sacrifices. They differ thus: in comedies, *turbulenta prima, tranquilla ultima*; in tragedies, *tranquilla prima, turbulenta ultima*: comedies begin in trouble and end in peace; tragedies begin in calms and end in tempest.   5

Of comedies there be three kinds: moving comedies, called *motoriae*; standing comedies, called *statariae*; or mixed betwixt both, called *mistae*. They are distributed into four parts: the *Prologue*, that is, the preface; the *Protasis*, that is, the proposition, which includes the first act and presents the actors; the *Epitasis*,   10
which is the business and body of the comedy; the last, the *Catastrophe* and conclusion. The definition of the comedy, according to the Latins: a discourse consisting of divers institutions, comprehending civil and domestic things, in which is taught what in our lives and manners is to be followed, what to be   15
avoided. The Greeks defined it thus: Κωμῳδία ἐστὶν ἰδιωτικῶν καὶ πολιτικῶν πραγμάτων ἀκίνδυνος περιοχή. Cicero saith, a comedy is the imitation of life, the glass of custom, and the image of truth. In Athens they had their first original......

If we present a tragedy, we include the fatal and abortive ends   20
of such as commit notorious murders, which is aggravated and acted with all the art that may be, to terrify men from the like abhorred practices. If we present a foreign history, the subject is so intended that in the lives of Romans, Grecians, or others either the virtues of our countrymen are extolled, or their vices repro-   25
ved......If a moral, it is to persuade men to humanity and good life, to instruct them in civility and good manners, showing them the fruits of honesty and the end of villainy......

If a comedy, it is pleasantly contrived with merry accidents and intermixed with apt and witty jests, to present before the prince at   30
certain times of solemnity, or else merrily fitted to the stage. And what is then the subject of this harmless mirth? Either, in the shape of a clown, to show others their slovenly and unhandsome behaviour, that they may reform that simplicity in themselves, which others make their sport, lest they happen to become the like   35
subject of general scorn to an auditory; else it entreats of love, deriding foolish inamorates, who spend their ages, their spirits, nay themselves, in the servile and ridiculous employments of their mistresses. And these are mingled with sportful accidents to recreate such as of themselves are wholly devoted to melancholy,   40
which corrupts the blood; or to refresh such weary spirits as are

tired with labour or study, to moderate the cares and heaviness of the mind that they may return to their trades and faculties with more zeal and earnestness after some soft and pleasant retirement. Sometimes they discourse of pantaloons, usurers that have unthrifty sons, which both the fathers and sons may behold to their instructions; sometimes of courtezans, to divulge their subtleties and snares, in which young men may be entangled, showing them the means to avoid them.   45

If we present a pastoral, we show the harmless love of shepherds diversely moralized, distinguishing betwixt the craft of the city and the innocency of the sheepcote. Briefly, there is neither tragedy, history, comedy, moral, or pastoral from which an infinite use cannot be gathered. I speak not in the defence of any lascivious shows, scurrilous jests, or scandalous invectives. If there be any such, I banish them quite from my patronage.   50   55

NOTES

1   *Donatus* Aelius Donatus, fourth-century-AD grammarian, who wrote a very influential commentary on the plays of Terence. Heywood is drawing, directly or indirectly, on early treatises on comedy by Diomedes, Evanthius, and Donatus (see Georgius Kaibel, ed., *Comicorum Graecorum Fragmenta*, 1899, I, 53–71).

1–2   *a rebus divinis* from sacred events (i.e. sacrifices).

3–5   *turbulenta......tempest* These definitions of comedy and tragedy, like everything that Heywood says, were commonplaces of sixteenth-century critical theory, though the distinction here drawn was well known in medieval times.

6–8   *three kinds......mistae* In his treatise 'On Comedy', Franciscus Robortellus explains: '*Stataria* is such as the *Andrian* [Terence], for it is acted in the quieter manner; *motoria* is more boisterous, such as the *Eunuch* [Terence]; *mixta* is in both manners, such as the *Brothers* [Terence, *Adelphi*]' (see M. T. Herrick, *Comic Theory in the Sixteenth Century*, 1950, p. 231).

8–12   *four parts......conclusion* Donatus discussed the structure of Terentian comedy in this four-fold division, but the usual division was three-fold, since the Prologue was not an integrated part of the action. Horace, however, had said (*Ars Poetica*, ll. 189–90) that a play must have five acts. Landinus, in his commentary on Horace (1482), sketched the action of a Terentian comedy in these terms: 'the first part [act] unfolds the argument. The second seeks to bring to an end the things which already have been begun. The third brings on the perturbation and the impediments and despair of the desired thing. The fourth brings a remedy for the impending evil. The fifth brings the whole to the desired outcome' (see T. W. Baldwin, *Shakspere's Five-Act Structure*, 1947, p. 112). Sixteenth-century continental critics combined the Donation three-fold structure and the Horatian five-act structure: *protasis*, first two acts; *epitasis*, acts three and four; *catastrophe*, act five; and Robortellus completed the picture to everyone's satisfaction by fitting Aristotle (*Poetics*) into the five-act structure: prologue, three episodes, and an exode for Greek tragedy (Baldwin, p. 273). Everybody was very happy!

10   *the first act* Most authorities say acts I and II.

16–17 Κωμῳδία......περιοχῇ Comedy is a collection of private and public actions involving no danger (of disaster in the outcome). Heywood's quotation has been corrected from Diomedes.

17   *Cicero saith* The definition is attributed to Cicero by Donatus: 'Comoediam esse Cicero ait imitationem vitae, speculum consuetudinis, imaginem veritatis'. Compare *Hamlet*, III.ii.20–4.

26   *moral* moral interlude or morality play.

29   *accidents* incidents.

33   *clown* ill-bred rustic or country fellow.

34   *simplicity* natural rusticity, lack of sophistication.

35–6 *lest......auditory* i.e. lest they themselves are held up to scorn (on the stage) before an audience.

37   *inamorates* lovers.

44   *soft* refined, delicate.

45   *pantaloons* doddering old men (from 'pantalone' a character in the Italian *commedia dell'arte*).

50   *pastoral* kind of play, like John Fletcher's *The Faithful Shepherdess* (1608) or Guarini's *Il Pastor Fido* (1590), laid in the country and having shepherds and shepherdesses as characters. The pastoral element was strongly influential in the development of tragi-comedy as a genre.

6 Costumes, properties and scenery

The open platform stage of the Elizabethan public theatres (as of the so-called 'private' theatres) did not (indeed could not, lacking a proscenium arch) employ scenery in the usually accepted modern sense. Sometimes a painted backdrop or arras might be used (see selection (ii), ll. 7, 16), but generally the actors depended on comparatively lavish costuming, most of it bought second- or third-hand (see selection (i)), and a probably fairly sparing use of common properties (bed, throne of state, chairs, stools, trestle tables, tree, rock, chariot, etc.; see selection (ii)). Special effects might be attempted for a particular play (see selection (ii)): 'one Hell mouth' (l. 1), 'one tomb of Dido' (l. 2; like the other tombs mentioned and 'Belin Dun's stable' (l. 19) these were presumably wooden constructs that could be moved on and off stage for certain scenes), 'two steeples and one chime of bells' (l. 4), 'one lion skin' (l. 11), 'Argus' head' (l. 12), 'one frame for the heading in *Black Joan*' (l. 33), etc. The Induction to the fifth act of George Peele's *The Battle of Alcazar* (1588–9) suggests how some of the special properties were used:

> *Lightning and thunder*
> Now through the heavens forth their lightning flames,
> And thunder over Afric's fatal fields;
> Blood will have blood, foul murder scape no scourge.
> *Enter Fame like an angel, and hangs the crowns*
>
> *upon a tree*
> At last descendeth Fame as Iris,
> To finish fainting Dido's dying life;
> Fame from her stately bower doth descend,
> And on the tree, as fruit new ripe to fall,
> Placeth the crowns of these unhappy kings,
> That erst she kept in eye of all the world.
> *Here the blazing star*
> Now fiery stars and streaming comets blaze,
> That threat the earth and princes of the same.
> *Fireworks*
> Fire, fire about the axletree of heaven
> Whirls round, and from the foot of Casiopa
> In fatal hour consumes these fatal crowns.
> *One falls*
> Down falls the diadem of Portugal.
> *The other falls*
> The crowns of Barbary and kingdoms fall.

Here we have both visual and sound effects (thunder being made by rolling a cannon-ball down a wooden or metal trough, or by drum-rolls). Stage blood was plentiful (*'Friar stoops and looks on the blood and weapons'*, *Romeo and Juliet* (Q1), V.iii) and the extent to which a kind of crude realism could go is suggested by two property-notes, for a performance in 1598–9, in 'The Plot of the Battle of Alcazar' (a skeletal plot outline used in the theatre to aid the prompter in getting the actors on and off stage at the right times and in seeing that necessary stage properties were ready). In a scene (lacking in the extant text), where three men are put to the torture, the prompt-note calls for 'Three vials of blood and a sheep's gather [i.e. liver, lungs, and heart]', for an organ is to be torn out of each of the victims, and a later prompt-note specifies 'Dead men's heads [in dishes] and bones. Banquet. Blood.'

Another example of crude realism appears in Robert Yarington's *Two Tragedies in One* (1594–*c*.1598), II.i: 'When the boy goeth into the shop, Merry striketh six blows on his head and, with the seventh, leaves the hammer sticking in his head; the boy groaning must be heard by a maid, who must cry to her master.' In II.iv, someone 'Brings him forth in a chair with a hammer sticking in his head.' When asked why the hammer has not been removed, a neighbour explains:

> That must not be before the youth be dead,
> Because the crowner and his quest may see
> The manner how he did receive his death.

Night scenes were signalled by the use of torches (performances beginning about two or three o'clock in the public theatres, which were without artificial lighting); rain and hail storms were simulated by 'raining' down dried peas from the 'heavens' (from which also a *deus ex machina*, such as Fame in the passage quoted above, could be lowered; compare *Cymbeline*, V.iv and Greene's *Alphonsus King of Arragon* (1587–8), Prologue); mists and fogs could be produced from stage-traps (the section under the stage being commonly known as 'Hell' [Thomas Dekker, *Works*, ed. Grosart, II, 92]), and various noises (battles, the tread of horses, a noise of hunters, bird songs, thunder, etc.) were reproduced off-stage. John Melton (*Astrologaster* (1620), p. 31) describes a performance of Marlowe's *Dr Faustus* (*c*.1592) at 'the *Fortune* in Golding Lane': 'There indeed a man may behold shag-hair'd devils run roaring over the stage with squibs in their mouths, while drummers make thunder in the tiring-house, and the twelve-penny hirelings make artificial lightning in their heavens.'

The stock list (i) records the sale of an assortment of used costumes and other stage accessories sold by John Alleyn, the brother of the celebrated actor, Edward Alleyn, to some kind of touring company (note the 'waggon' and the two playbooks) and is the earliest such stock list associated with the public theatre, dating probably from about 1589–90. The inventory of properties (ii) was prepared by Philip Henslowe, owner of the Rose playhouse, in 1598, listing all properties then belonging to the Admiral's Men (there are other lists, several of costumes, compiled at about the same time; see *Diary*, ed. Foakes and Rickert, pp. 291–4,

317–23). The costume and property stocks (including the manuscript playbooks belonging to the company, of which Henslowe includes a list for 1598) constituted a company's most valuable asset and represented a comparatively large financial outlay, an amount sometimes larger than the value of the theatre in which they acted. Lacking scenic spectacle, the public theatres made lavish use of costuming and pageantry, though, so far as we know, little or no attempt was made to costume a play with local or historical accuracy. As the inventory lists show, most of the costumes used were those worn in contemporary England. Perhaps some effort was made to approximate Roman costume. The sketch of *Titus Andronicus* (*c.*1594–5), sometimes attributed to Henry Peacham (illustration 5), shows some of the characters, including Titus and Aaron, dressed in vaguely Roman 'habits', but the effect is somewhat dissipated by two attendant soldiers in contemporary Elizabethan military costumes, each bearing a most un-Roman halbert. See M. C. Linthicum, *Costume in the Drama of Shakespeare and his Contemporaries* (1936) (contains good illustrations).

So far as scenery is concerned the story was very different for the entertainments, especially masques, put on at the Court. Influenced by Italian and French models, the Court masque employed a wide variety of intricately sophisticated scenery and theatrical effects. The best known practitioner of 'scenes', as they were called, was Inigo Jones (1573–1652), who after study in Italy returned to England in 1604 and became, for many years, the principal designer of scenic spectacles for the extravagantly mounted Court masques. The average cost of a masque has been estimated at around £2000, a very large sum of money for the period and one that utterly dwarfs the possible outlay for a single play in the public theatres. A large collection of Jones's scenic and costume designs has been preserved in the collection of the Duke of Devonshire at Chatsworth House (see *Designs by Inigo Jones for Masques and Plays at Court*, ed. Percy Simpson and C. F. Bell (1924)).

These 'toys', as Francis Bacon dubbed them in his rather grudging essay 'Of Masques and Triumphs' (in *Essayes* (1625), no. 37), somewhat patronizingly since he himself had had a hand in designing masques, required the closest sort of collaboration between author, scenic artist, and composer (songs and incidental music being a regular feature of the masque). Such a successful collaboration, albeit a stormy one (see selection (iii), ll. 65–8 and note), was achieved between Inigo Jones and Ben Jonson in masque after masque during the first thirty years of the seventeenth century. Jonson's descriptive directions in his *Masque of Queens* (1609), selection (iii), are generally representative of the kinds of scenic display and sumptuous costuming characteristic of the typical Court masque, and Jones's pen sketch for the 'House of Fame' has survived (see Simpson and Bell, plate IV). The elaborate scenic effects were made possible by the use of a 'stage frame', or proscenium, with a curtain, which effectively separated the stage from the audience as in most modern theatres, and behind which scene shifts and other stage business could, more or less quietly, be 'secretly' engineered. The *Masque of Queens* was performed in the newly erected (1608) Banqueting house near Whitehall, the inside structure of which, along with the stage area and seating arrangements, is described in some detail by Orazio Busino, chaplain to the Venetian ambassador, who attended a performance there of Jonson's *Pleasure Reconciled to Virtue* in 1618. Jammed in the Venetian 'box' for two hours before the masque began, he had plenty of time to observe everything, including the rest of the audience, which he estimates at six hundred (see a translation of his letter in *Calendar of Venetian State Papers*, XV (1909), 110–14). In 1623 another banqueting hall, designed by Inigo Jones, was built and may still be seen in Whitehall today (see Jones's sketch-plan of the interior (stage and seating) reproduced in L. B. Campbell, *Scenes and Machines on the English Stage During the Renaissance* (1923), plate IV, p. 178).

i

An Elizabethan theatrical stock list

From a manuscript (Thr. 276) in the Harvard College Library (see G. B. Evans, 'An Elizabethan Theatrical Stock List', *Harvard Library Bulletin*, XXI (1973), 254–70).

Item, one scarlet cloak faced with green velvet and silver lace...£3
Item, one scarlet cloak caped with blue velvet and with gold
    lace...£4 10s
Item, *Charlemagne's* cloak with fur...£1 6s 8d
Item, a Spanish cape cloak...£1 6s 8d
Item, a short cloak with bugle...10s   5
Item, one orange tawney velvet pee with [g]old lace...20s
Item, one black velvet pee with gold lace and blue satin
    sleeves...£3 10s
Item, one green satin doublet...15s
Item, one white satin doublet...40s
Item, one white satin suit, hose and doublet...40s   10
Item, one antic coat...10s
Item, a red scaffler...
Item, a pair of old purple velvet hose, laced...15s
Item, a pair of embroidered paned hose scaled with red velvet...15s
Item, a pair of embroidered paned hose scaled with murrey satin...30s   15
Item, a pair of embroidered paned hose scaled with black
    taffeta...13s 4d
Item, a pair of silver paned hose scaled with yellow damask...20s
Item, a pair of gold paned hose scaled with peach-coloured
    velvet...35s
Item, a woman's gown of cloth of gold...50s
Item, a hermit's gray gown   20
Item, a parasite's suit for a boy
Item, a clown's suit
Item, six beards *Item*, a white hair and cap, two yellow hairs...13s 4d
Item, two head-tires (*Item*, two rebatos. *Item*, two hairs)...6s 8d
Item, waggon, and waggon cloth...£4   25
Item, two rebatos...23s 4d
Item, two periwigs...6s
Item, a trunk...6s
Item, *Saul and David. Charlemagne*...£4
Item, a hair and beard for *Charlemagne* and *Saul and David*...10s   30

NOTES

1 *faced* trimmed.

2 *caped* having a cape.

3 *Charlemagne's cloak* See l. 29.

4 *cape coat* cloak with a hood.

5 *bugle* tube-shaped glass bead, used to ornament wearing apparel.

7 *velvet pee* originally a coat of coarse cloth for men, but by the end of the sixteenth century made of fine fabrics. Compare modern 'pea-jacket'.

10 *suit, hose and doublet* i.e. matching set ('suit') of breeches ('hose') and doublet (close-fitting garment, with or without sleeves).

11 *antic coat* coat for an antic or clown.

12 *scaffler* meaning unknown.

14 *paned hose* breeches made of strips of different coloured cloth joined together.
    scaled ornamented with strips of inset or overlaid cloth, giving something like the appearance of scales (not in *OED*).

15 *murrey* purple-red or blood-coloured.

21 *parasite's suit* The parasite was a character from Roman comedy (e.g. Peniculus in Plautus' *Menaechmi*).
    boy i.e. a child actor.

23 *white hair* white wig.

24 *head-tires* head-dresses.
    (Item . . . . . . hairs) Crossed through; the price, therefore, applies only to the 'head-tires'. The two items may turn up in ll. 26, 27. 'rebatos' are stiff collars (or wire frames to support such a collar) worn by both sexes from about 1590 to 1630.

25 *waggon . . . . . . cloth* The 'waggon' and the 'trunk' (l. 28) strongly suggest a touring company of strolling players. The 'cloth' would be some kind of covering (canvas perhaps) to serve as protection from the weather.

27 *periwigs* curled wigs, at this time worn by women.

29 *Saul and David. Charlemagne* two lost plays, otherwise unrecorded. *Saul and David* may well have been a first part of George Peele's *David and Bethsabe* (c.1581–94), and it is possible that *Charlemagne* was also by Peele, since he refers to 'King Charlemaine' as a dramatic character in his 'Farewell to Norris and Drake' written in 1589. Neither was a new play as the price of £2 each strongly suggests.

Henslowe's list of properties for the Lord Admiral's Men, 10 March 1598

'*The Enventary tacken of all the properties for my* Lord Admeralles men, *the* 10 *of Marche* 1598', first printed from a manuscript (now lost) among the Alleyn Papers at Dulwich College by Edmond Malone in *Plays and Poems of William Shakespeare* (1790), vol. I, part ii, pp. 302–3 (see *Henslowe's Diary*, ed. R. A. Foakes and R. T. Rickert (1961), pp. 319–21).

Item, one rock, one cage, one tomb, one Hell mouth.
Item, one tomb of Guido, one tomb of Dido, one bedstead.
Item, eight lances, one pair of stairs for *Phaëton.*
Item, two steeples and one chime of bells and one beacon.
Item, one heckfer [i.e. heifer] for the play of *Phaëton*, the limbs dead.   5
Item, one globe and one golden sceptre; three clubs.
Item, two marchpanes and the city of Rome.
Item, one golden fleece; two rackets; one bay tree.
Item, one wooden hatchet; one leather hatchet.
Item, one wooden canopy; old Mahomet's head.   10
Item, one lion skin; one bear's skin; and Phaëton's limbs, and
     Phaëton['s] charet [i.e. chariot]; and Argus' head.
Item, Neptune['s] fork and garland.
Item, one croser's staff [i.e. cross-staff or bishop's crosier]; Kent's
     wooden leg.
Item, Iras's head and rainbow; one little altar.
Item, eight vizards; Tamburlaine['s] bridal; one wooden mattock.   15
Item, Cupid's bow and quiver; the cloth of the Sun and Moon.
Item, one boar's head and Cerberus' three heads.
Item, one caduceus; two moss banks and one snake.
Item, two fans of feathers; Belin Dun's stable; one tree of golden
     apples; Tantalus' tree; nine iron targets [i.e. light round shields].
Item, one copper target and seventeen foils.   20
Item, four wooden targets; one greave armour [i.e. armour for the legs].
Item, one sign for Mother Redcap; one buckler [i.e. small round shield].
Item, Mercury's wings; Tasso['s] picture; one helmet with a dragon; one
     shield with three lions; one elm bowl.
Item, a chayne [i.e. chain?] of dragons [i.e. snakes?]; one gilt spear.
Item, two coffins; one bull's head; and one vylter [i.e. philtre? or vulture?].   25
Item, three timbrels; one dragon in *Faustus.*
Item, one lion; two lion heads; one great horse with his legs; one sackbut.
Item, one wheel and frame in the *Siege of London.*
Item, one pair of rough gloves.
Item, one Pope's mitre.   30
Item, three imperial crowns; one plain crown.
Item, one ghost's crown; one crown with a sun.

Item, one frame for the heading in *Black Joan*.
Item, one black dog.
Item, one cauldron for *The Jew*.   35

NOTES

1   *one cage* perhaps for Marlowe's *Tamburlaine, Part I* (1587–8). See l. 15 below.
   one Hell mouth perhaps for Marlowe's *Dr Faustus* (1592–3), v.ii. See l. 7 below.

2   *tomb of Dido* probably for an anonymous lost play, *Dido and Aeneas* (1598), presumably to be distinguished from Marlowe's *Tragedy of Dido* (1587–91).

3   *Phaëton* lost play by Thomas Dekker (1598).

5   *heckfer......dead* It is not clear what a heifer has to do with the story of Phaëton. Perhaps one of the animals killed by his disastrous attempt to drive the 'charet' (l. 11) of Phoebus. 'the limbs dead', one may suppose, suggests that it was not made to stand upright.

6   *globe* i.e. the golden orb borne with the sceptre as an emblem of sovereignty.

7   *marchpanes* moulded, ornamental cakes for a banquet (here not really made of marzipan but made to look as if they were).
   city of Rome for Marlowe's *Dr Faustus*, probably a painted-cloth.

10   *old Mahomet's head* perhaps for an anonymous lost play, *Mahomet* (c.1594).

11   *Phaëton['s]* The original 'Faeton charete' may be an example of an uninflected genitive, occasionally found in Elizabethan usage (cf. 'for God sake'). I have used the regular possessive form here and in some other examples below.
   Argus' head mythological person fabled to have had a hundred eyes.

12   *fork* trident.

15   *vizards* masks (perhaps of a grotesque kind).

16   *cloth......Moon* a painted-cloth (or arras) displaying the Sun and Moon. This and 'the city of Rome' (l. 7) are the nearest approach to what we would call 'scenery' that the list contains.

18   *caduceus* wand, represented with two serpents twined round it, associated with the god Mercury.

19   *Belin Dun's stable* property for an anonymous lost play called *Belin Dun* (1594); Henslowe's form is 'Belendon'.
   Tantalus' tree Tantalus, king of Phrygia, was doomed in Tartarus (Hell) to stand up to the chin in water, which receded when he tried to drink, and with a fruit tree above him, the branches of which always evaded his grasp.

22   *sign......Redcap* presumably a tavern sign for a lost play called *Mother Redcap* (1597–8) by Michael Drayton and Anthony Munday.

23   *Tasso['s] picture* property for a lost anonymous play called *Tasso's Melancholy* (1594; altered by Thomas Dekker in 1602).

24   *chayne of dragons* i.e. ?a chain of snakes. Unexplained, but perhaps with
     reference to the play of *Troy* (see note l. 27) and the death of the Trojan
     Laocoon, who, for trying to destroy the Trojan Horse, was stung to death
     by large snakes. Heywood dramatizes the incident in *II Iron Age*, II.i.

26   *dragon in Faustus* See Marlowe's *Dr Faustus*, I.iii.

27   *great......legs* i.e. the Trojan horse, property for Thomas Heywood's
     (?)*Troy* (1596); later perhaps reworked as *I* and *II Iron Age* (1612–13).

28   *Siege of London* lost anonymous play, not new in 1594, perhaps reworked
     by Thomas Heywood as *I Edward IV* (1598–9).

33   *frame......Joan* stage machine to simulate a beheading in an
     anonymous lost play called *Black Joan* (?date).

35   *cauldron......Jew* See Marlowe's *The Jew of Malta* (1589–90), v.v.

iii

Scenic directions from Ben Jonson's *The Masque of Queens*, presented at
Whitehall 2 February 1609

[The masque begins with an anti-masque of eleven Witches,
played by women, perhaps minor Court functionaries.]

First, then, his Majesty [King James] being set, and the whole
company in full expectation, that which presented itself was an
ugly *Hell*, which, flaming beneath, smok'd unto the top of the
roof...... These Witches, with a kind of hollow and infernal
music, came forth from thence. First one, then two, and three, and   5
more, till their number increas'd to eleven; all differently attir'd:
some with rats on their heads; some, on their shoulders; others
with ointment pots at their girdles; all with spindles, timbrels,
rattles, or other *venefical* instruments, making a confused noise,
with strange gestures. The device of their attire was Master Jones   10
his, with the invention and *architecture* of the whole *scene* and
machine. Only I prescrib'd them their properties, of vipers,
snakes, bones, herbs, roots, and other ensigns of their magic, out
of the authority of ancient and late writers......

[After their dance the Witches call upon their 'Dame' (in the
character of Ate), who hails them as 'faithful opposites / To *Fame*
and *Glory*', 'fraught with spite / To overthrow the glory of this
night'. They 'wind up' an evil 'charm'.]

At which, with a strange and sudden music, they fell into a   15
magical dance, full of preposterous change and gesticulation, but
most applying to their property; who, at their meetings, do all
things contrary to the custom of men, dancing back to back, hip
to hip, their hands join'd, and making their circles backward to
the left hand, with strange phantastic motions of their heads and   20
bodies......

In the heat of their dance, on the sudden, was heard a sound of
loud music, as if many instruments had given one blast. With
which, not only the *Hags* themselves, but their *Hell*, into which
they ran, quite vanish'd; and the whole face of the *scene* alter'd,   25
scarce suff'ring the memory of any such thing: but in the place of
it appear'd a glorious and magnificent building, figuring the *House
of Fame*, in the upper part of which were discover'd the twelve
Masquers sitting upon a throne triumphal, erected in form of a
pyramid and circled with all store of light; from whom a person, by   30
this time descended, in the furniture of Perseus, and, expressing
heroical and *masculine Virtue* began to speak......

[Perseus, as presenter, explains who the twelve Masquers are
('each of them a Queen'), the last being Bel-anna, played by Queen
Anne herself, the consort of King James, to whom the speech is
directed.]

Here the throne wherein they sat, being *machina versatilis*,
suddenly chang'd; and in the place of it appear'd *Fama
bona*,......attir'd in white, with white wings, having a collar of   35
gold about her neck and a heart hanging from it;......In her
right hand she bore a trumpet, in her left an olive branch, and for
her state, it was as Virgil describes her, at the full, her feet on the
ground and her head in the clouds......At which [after *Fame*
had ended her speech], the loud music sounded as before, to give   40
the Masquers time of descending......

[Jonson here interpolates a long account of the suitability of each
of the twelve Queens for celebration by *Fama bona*, ending with
Bel-anna, 'royal Queen of the Ocean'.]

There rests, now, that we give the description (we promis'd) of
the *scene*, which was the *House of Fame*. The structure and
ornament of which (as is profess'd before) was entirely Master
Jones his invention and design. First, for the lower columns, he   45
chose the statues of the most excellent poets, as Homer, Virgil,
Lucan, etc., as being the substantial supporters of *Fame*. For the
upper, Achilles, Aeneas, Caesar, and those great *Heroës*, which
those poets had celebrated. All which stood as in massy gold.
Between the pillars, underneath, were figur'd land battles, sea   50
fights, triumphs, loves, sacrifices, and all magnificent subjects of
honour, in brass and heighten'd with silver. In which he profess'd

to follow that noble description made by Chaucer of the like place.
Above, were plac'd the Masquers, over whose heads he devis'd two
eminent figures of *Honour* and *Virtue* for the arch. The friezes,   55
both below and above, were fill'd with several-colour'd lights, like
emeralds, rubies, sapphires, carbuncles, etc. The reflex of which,
with other lights plac'd in the concave, upon the Masquers' habits
was full of glory. These habits had in them the excellency of all
device and riches; and were worthily varied, by his invention, to   60
the nations whereof they were Queens. Nor are these alone his
due, but divers other accessions to the strangeness and beauty of
the spectacle, as the *Hell*, the going about of the chariots, the
binding of the Witches, the turning machine with the presentation
of *Fame*: all which I willingly acknowledge for him, since it is a   65
virtue, planted in good natures, that what respects they wish to
obtain fruitfully from others, they will give ingenuously themselves.

By this time imagine the Masquers descended; and again
mounted into three triumphant chariots ready to come forth. The   70
first four were drawn with eagles . . . . . ., their four torch-bearers
attending on the chariot sides, and four of the *Hags* [i.e.
Witches] bound before them. Then follow'd the second, drawn by
griffins, with their torch-bearers and four other *Hags*. Then the
last, which was drawn by lions, and more eminent (wherein her   75
Majesty was), and had six torch-bearers more (peculiar to her),
with the like number of *Hags*. After which, a full triumphant
music, singing this song, while they rode in state about the
stage . . . . . . Here [after the song] they alighted from their
chariots and danc'd forth their first dance; then a second,   80
immediately following it: both right curious and full of subtile and
excellent changes, and seem'd perform'd with no less spirits than
those they personated. The first was to the cornets, the second to
the violins. After which they took out the men and danc'd the
measures, entertaining the time almost to the space of an hour   85
with singular variety . . . . . . After which [i.e. another song], they
danc'd their third dance; . . . . . . After this, they danc'd galliards
and corantos. And then their last dance, no less elegant (in the
place) than the rest; with which they took their chariots again and,
triumphing about the stage, had their return to the *House of*   90
Fame . . . . . . [The masque concludes with another song.]

NOTES

3   *ugly Hell* a very sophisticated version of 'one Hell mouth' in Henslowe's
    list (ii).
8   *spindles* slender rounded rods, which being revolved in the hands, twisted
    into thread the fibres drawn out of a bunch of wool.

	timbrels percussion instruments, like tambourines.
9	*venefical* relating to magic.
10–11	*Jones his* i.e. Jones's.
	scene Here, and later, means the total stage picture as represented by the 'scenery'.
12	*machine* i.e. 'ugly *Hell*'.
16	*preposterous change* inverted, unnatural alteration.
17	*property* peculiar attribute (as witches).
27–8	*House of Fame* See ll. 42–61.
28–9	*twelve Masquers* i.e. the twelve Queens, played by Queen Anne and eleven other ladies of the Court: Countess of Arundel, Countess of Derby, Countess of Bedford, Countess of Essex, etc. (all listed by Jonson at the end of the masque).
31	*furniture* apparel.
	Perseus in mythology, the slayer of the Gorgon and the rescuer of Andromeda, considered, along with Hercules and Bellerophon, one of the three classical types of '*masculine Virtue*' (Jonson).
33	*machina versatilis* revolving machine or mechanism.
38	*state* bodily form.
	Virgil describes in *Aeneid*, IV, 176–7.
48	*Heroës* (trisyllabic) heroes.
53	*description . . . . . . Chaucer* in *The House of Fame*, ll. 1181ff.
55	*friezes* entablatures which come between the architrave and cornice.
57	*reflex* reflection.
58	*habits* costumes.
60–1	*varied . . . . . . nations* adapted to the different countries.
63	*going . . . . . . chariots* See ll. 69–91.
65–8	*all which . . . . . . themselves* This comment reveals Jonson's defensiveness as the librettist *vs.* Inigo Jones's position as contriver of the scenic spectacle, on which, Jonson felt, too much attention and honour were lavished compared with that accorded his 'book'. This attitude later led to an open break between the two men.
70	*triumphant chariots* chariots suitable to a military or civic triumph, specially ornamented.
72	*chariot sides* uninflected genitive.
77	*like number* i.e. four.
78	*state* great pomp.
81	*subtile* fine, delicate.
82	*changes* variety of footwork.
84	*took out the men* i.e. led out members of the audience to dance. This dance, in which the masquers danced with members of the audience, was more or less the climax of the masque form from very early times.
85	*measures* dances (usually stately).
87	*galliards* quick lively dances in triple time.
88	*corantos* 'running' dances also in triple time. These and the 'galliards' were danced with members of the audience.

7 Acting

Our knowledge of the acting styles in Elizabethan–Jacobean times is limited and there is some disagreement as to the extent to which the formal, rhetorical style predominated. There are enough references to make it clear that the actor and orator were thought of as close cousins (see selection (i) and 'The actors', selection (iii), p. 99), and Bertram L. Joseph (*Elizabethan Acting*, (1951)), drawing heavily on John Bulwer's *Chirologia: Or the Naturall Language of the Hand* (1644; ed. J. W. Cleary, 1974), declares for a formal acting style based in good part on the dictates of the oratorical mode. Two examples from *Chirologia* (Cleary, pp. 32, 36) will suggest the implied connection:

> Gestus [Gesture] III: *Ploro* [I lament]. *To wring the hands* is a natural expression of *excessive grief*, used by those who *condole, bewail*, and *lament*......Indeed, the *folding* and *wringing of the hands* in the natural equipage of *sorrow* hath ever passed for a note of *lamentation*......

> Gestus VII: *Explodo* [I reject (in anger)]. *To clasp the right fist often on the left palm* is a natural expression used by those who *mock, chide, brawl*, and *insult, reproach, rebuke*, and *explode* (or *drive out with noise*), commonly used by the vulgar in their *bickerings*, as being the scold's *taunting* dialect, and the loud natural rhetoric of those who declaim at Billingsgate [former London fish-market, the name synonymous with 'foul language']......

While is is certainly true that Elizabethan acting would, one may be sure, strike a modern viewer as unbearably stylized and over stagey (as would the acting styles of the eighteenth and nineteenth centuries), more recent criticism suggests that Joseph lays too much stress on the merely formal conventions (such as tearing the hair or lying on the ground, as Romeo does (III.iii.68–70), to express despair), and Michael Hattaway (*Elizabethan Popular Theatre: Plays in Performance* (1982), pp. 76–7) points out that many of Bulwer's gestures would not be considered 'formal' even by a modern audience. On the other hand, he notes (pp. 77–8) that the Elizabethans, following classical precedent, viewed characters as types or emblems, with which, in terms of the classically derived 'doctrine of decorum', certain characteristics were regularly associated (see selection (ii)), and that the modern ideal of naturalistic acting, presenting the uniqueness of an individual psyche, would have been foreign to an age that tended to see man (and his seven ages) in terms of universal types in the manner of Milton's *Il Penseroso* and *L'Allegro*. Thus Hamlet, as Hattaway observes, describes a good actor as one who 'hold[s] as 'twere the mirror up to nature: to show virtue her feature, scorn her own image, and the very age and body of the time his form and pressure' (III.ii.22–4). These lines, of course, are part of Hamlet's famous advice to the players (III.ii.1–45) on what constitutes 'good' and 'bad' acting, advice which Richard Brome builds on for a lively scene in *The Antipodes* (1640, II.ii), in which Lord Le Toy lectures his personal troupe of players on the special pitfalls of bad acting, echoing Hamlet ('Suit the action to the word, the word to the action, with this special observance, that you o'erstep not the modesty of nature: for any thing so o'erdone is from the purpose of playing.'):

> I'll none of these absurdities in my house,
> But words and action married so together
> That shall strike harmony in the ears and eyes
> Of the severest, if judicious, critics.

Some years earlier, Thomas Nashe (*Summer's Last Will and Testament* (1592), ll. 96–103) had already offered his advice on acting:

> Actors, you rogues, come away; clear your throats, blow your noses, and wipe your mouths ere you enter, that you may take no occasion to spit or to cough when you are *non plus* [i.e. have forgotten your lines]. And this I bar, over and besides, that none of you stroke your beards to make action, play with your cod-piece points, or stand fumbling on your buttons when you know not how to bestow your fingers.

Selection (i), from Thomas Heywood's *An Apology for Actors* (1612), illustrates the frequently stated relationship between the precepts of oratory and the practice of acting. Bulwer also makes the connection explicit in a second work called *Chironomia* (1644; ed. J. W. Cleary (1974), p. 161), comparing 'the famous orator Cicero and Roscius, the great master in the art of action', the second of whom 'wrote a book wherein he compared eloquence with the art or science of stage-players.'

Selection (ii), the highly self-conscious, extra-dramatic 'Induction' from John Marston's *Antonio and Mellida* (*c.*1599), presents a device in which Marston may have been an innovator (Jonson's 'Induction' to *Every Man out of His Humour* (1599) being a possible earlier rival). Such a *Vorspiel* allows a dramatist (sometimes through a character representing the author, e.g. Asper in *Every Man out*) to direct the audience's attention to aspects of the play he wishes to emphasize (or defend in an attempt to forestall criticism) and to comment (as Marston here does) on the various characters being presented. This extra-dramatic form of Induction, as distinct from the earlier supernatural-prologue type inherited from Senecan tragedy in such English plays as Kyd's *Spanish Tragedy* (*c.*1586–8) or *Locrine* (*c.*1591–5), attributed to W.S. (not William Shakespeare), became popular, particularly with Jonson, and John Webster, curiously enough, composed such an Induction for a revival of Marston's own *Malcontent* (*c.*1604).

Marston was a 'word-smith' and was fond of sometimes outrageous neologisms, a tendency for which Jonson took him to task in his

Poetaster (1601), Jonson's final stroke in the so-called 'War of the Theatres' conducted between Jonson and his rivals, Marston and Thomas Dekker (and, perhaps, Shakespeare). Even in the present short selection there is an unusual number of neologisms; they are distinguished in the notes by an asterisk.

Reference to two other 'acting scenes' may be found in the introductory note to 'The actors', p. 92.

85

i

From Thomas Heywood, *An Apology for Actors* (1612), sigs. c3 v–C4 r.

To come to Rhetoric, it not only emboldens a scholar to speak,
but instructs him to speak well,......to keep a decorum in his
countenance, neither to frown when he should smile, nor to make
unseemly and disguised faces in the delivery of his words, not to
stare with his eyes, draw awry his mouth, confound his voice in the   5
hollow of his throat, or tear his words hastily betwixt his
teeth......It instructs him to fit his phrases to his action, and
his action to his phrase, and his pronunciation to them both.
......be his invention never so fluent and exquisite, his
disposition and order never so composed and formal, his eloquence   10
and elaborate phrases never so material and pithy, his memory
never so firm and retentive, his pronunciation never so musical and
plausive, yet without a comely and elegant gesture, a gracious and
a bewitching kind of action, a natural and a familiar motion of the
head, the hand, the body, and a moderate and fit countenance   15
suitable to all the rest, I hold all the rest as nothing......And
this is the action behooveful in any that profess this quality, not to
use any impudent or forced motion in any part of the body, no
rough or other violent gesture, nor, on the contrary, to stand like a
stiff starched man, but to qualify everything according to the   20
nature of the person personated: for in overacting tricks, and
toiling too much in the antic habit of humours, men of the ripest
desert, greatest opinions, and best reputations may break into the
most violent absurdities.

NOTES

7–8 *fit......both* Compare *Hamlet*, III. ii.17–18: 'Suit the action to the word,
    the word to the action.'
9 *invention* the first of the five special qualities required of an orator in the
    anonymous *Ad Herennium* (generally assigned to Cicero at this time).
    After listing the five qualities, Heywood adds a sixth, Action.
13 *plausive* pleasing, calling for applause.
17 *quality* here, the profession of acting.

ii

The actors discuss their parts

From John Marston, *Antonio and Mellida* (*c*.1599), Induction.

Enter GALEATZO, PIERO, ALBERTO, ANTONIO, FOROBOSCO, BALURDO, MATZAGENTE, *and* FELICHE, *with parts in their hands, having cloaks cast over their apparel*

GALEATZO. Come, sirs, come; the music will sound straight for
    entrance. Are ye ready? are ye perfect?

PIERO. Faith, we can say our parts, but we are ignorant in what
    mould we must cast our actors.

ALBERTO. Whom do you personate? 5

PIERO. Piero, Duke of Venice.

ALBERTO. O ho! then thus frame your exterior shape
    To haughty form of elate majesty,
    As if you held the palsy-shaking head
    Of reeling chance under your fortune's belt 10
    In strictest vassalage; grow big in thought,
    As swol'n with glory of successful arms.

PIERO. If that be all, fear not, I'll suit it right.
    Who cannot be proud, stroke up the hair, and strut!

ALBERTO. Truth! such rank custom is grown popular; 15
    And now the vulgar fashion strides as wide
    And stalks as proud upon the weakest stilts
    Of the slight'st fortunes, as if Hercules,
    Or burly Atlas, should'red up their state.

PIERO. Good; but whom act you? 20

ALBERTO. The necessity of the play forceth me to act two parts:
    Andrugio, the distressed Duke of Genoa, and Alberto, a
    Venetian gentleman, enamoured on the Lady Rossaline; whose
    fortunes being too weak to sustain the port of her, he proved
    always disastrous in love; his worth being much underpoised by 25
    the uneven scale that currents all things by the outward stamp
    of opinion.

GALEATZO. Well; and what dost thou play?   [*To* BALURDO]

BALURDO. The part of all the world.

ALBERTO. 'The part of all the world'? What's that? 30

BALURDO. The fool. Ay, in good deed law now, I play Balurdo, a
    wealthy mountbanking burgomasco's heir of Venice.

ALBERTO. Ha, ha! one whose foppish nature might seem great only
for wise men's recreation; and, like a juiceless bark, to preserve
the sap of more strenuous spirits; a servile hound that loves the   35
scent of forerunning fashion; like an empty hollow vault still
giving an echo to wit, greedily champing what any other well-
valued judgement had beforehand chewed.

FOROBOSCO. Ha, ha, ha! tolerably good, good faith, sweet wag.

ALBERTO. Umh, why tolerably good, good faith, sweet wag? Go,   40
go, you flatter me.

FOROBOSCO. Right; I but dispose my speech to the habit of my
part.

ALBERTO. Why, what plays he?   *To* FELICHE

FELICHE. The wolf, that eats into the breast of princes,   45
That breeds the lethargy and falling sickness
In honour, makes justice look asquint,
And blinks the eye of merited reward
From viewing desertful vertue.

ALBERTO. What's all this periphrasis? ha?   50

FELICHE. The substance of a supple-chapped flatterer.

ALBERTO. O, doth he play Forobosco, the parasite? Good, i'faith!
Sirrah, you must seem now as glib and straight in outward
semblance as a lady's busk, though inwardly as cross as a pair of
tailor's legs; having a tongue as nimble as his needle, with   55
servile patches of glavering flattery to stitch up the bracks of
unworthily honoured –

FOROBOSCO. I warrant you, I warrant you. You shall see me prove
the very periwig to cover the bald pate of brainless gentility.
Ho, I will so tickle the sense of *bella gratiosa madonna* with the   60
titillation of hyperbolical praise that I'll strike it in the nick, in
the very nick, chuck.

FELICHE. Thou promisest more than I hope any spectator gives
faith of performance. But why look you so dusky? ha?
                                                 To ANTONIO   65

ANTONIO. I was never worse fitted since the nativity of my
actorship. I shall be hissed at, on my life now.

FELICHE. Why, what must you play?

ANTONIO. Faith, I know not what: an hermaphrodite, two parts in
one; my true person being Antonio, son to the Duke of Genoa;   70
though for the love of Mellida, Piero's daughter, I take this
feigned presence of an Amazon, calling myself Florizell, and I
know not what. I, a voice to play a lady! I shall ne'er do it.

ALBERTO. O, an Amazon have such a voice, virago-like. Not play
two parts in one? away, away! 'Tis common fashion. Nay, if you   75
cannot bear two subtle fronts under one hood, idiot, go by, go
by – off this world's stage. O times' impurity!

ANTONIO. Ay, but when use hath taught me action to hit the right
point of a lady's part, I shall grow ignorant, when I must turn
young prince again, how but to truss my hose.   80

FELICHE. Tush, never put them off, for women wear the breeches
still.

MATZAGENTE. By the bright honour of a Milanoise,
And the resplendent fulgor of this steel,
I will defend the feminine to death;   85
And ding his spirit to the verge of hell
That dares divulge a lady's prejudice.
                Exeunt [MATZAGENTE, FOROBOSCO *and* BALURDO]

FELICHE. Rampum scrampum, mount tufty Tamburlaine!
What rattling thunderclap breaks from his lips?   90

ALBERTO. O, 'tis native to his part; for, acting a modern
braggadoch under the person of Matzagente, the Duke of
Milan's son, it may seem to suit with good fashion of
coherence.

PIERO. But methinks he speaks with a spruce Attic accent of   95
adulterate Spanish.

ALBERTO. So 'tis resolved. For Milan being half Spanish, half high
Dutch, and half Italians, the blood of chiefest houses is corrupt
and mongreled; so that you shall see a fellow vain-glorious for a
Spaniard, gluttonous for a Dutchman, proud for an Italian, and   100
a fantastic idiot for all. Such a one conceit this Matzagente.

FELICHE. But I have a part allotted me, which I have neither able
apprehension to conceit, nor what I conceit gracious ability to
utter.

GALEATZO. Whoop, in the old cut? Good, show us a draught of thy   105
spirit.

FELICHE. 'Tis steady, and must seem so impregnably fortressed
with his own content that no envious thought could ever invade
his spirit: never surveying any man so unmeasuredly happy,
whom I thought not justly hateful for some true impoverish-   110
ment; never beholding any favour of Madam Felicity gracing
another, which his well-bounded content persuaded not to

hang in the front of his own fortune; and therefore as far from envying any man, as he valued all men infinitely distant from accomplished beatitude. These native adjuncts appropriate to me the name of Feliche. [*To* GALEATZO] But last, good, thy humour? 115

Exeunt ALBERTO [*and* PIERO]

ANTONIO. 'Tis to be described by signs and tokens; for unless I were possessed with a legion of spirits, 'tis impossible to be 120 made perspicuous by any utterance: for sometimes he must take austere state, as for the person of Galeatzo, the son of the Duke of Florence, and possess his exterior presence with a formal majesty; keep popularity in distance, and on the sudden fling his honour so prodigally into a common arm, that he may seem 125 to give up his indiscretion to the mercy of vulgar censure. Now as solemn as a traveller and as grave as a Puritan's ruff; with the same breath as slight and scattered in his fashion as – as – as a – a – anything. Now as sweet and neat as a barber's casting-bottle; straight as slovenly as the yeasty breast of an ale-knight; 130 now lamenting, then chafing; straight laughing, then –

FELICHE. What then?

ANTONIO. Faith, I know not what; 't had been a right part for Proteus or Gew. Ho, blind Gew would ha' done't rarely, rarely.

FELICHE. I fear it is not possible to limn so many persons in so 135 small a tablet as the compass of our plays afford.

ANTONIO. Right; therefore I have heard that those persons, as he and you, Feliche, that are but slightly drawn in this comedy, should receive more exact accomplishment in a second part, which, if this obtain gracious acceptance, means to try his 140 fortune.

FELICHE. Peace, here comes the Prologue; clear the stage.

Exeunt

NOTES

1   *music* Since the play was acted in a private theatre, 'music' here probably refers to instrumental performance, not to the third sounding of the trumpet, which announced the entry of the Prologue in the public theatres.

5   **personate* act the part of.

8   *elate* exalted, lofty.

13   *suit it right* fit the role exactly.

18–19 *Hercules......Atlas* In Greek mythology, Atlas was supposed to bear
       up the heavens on his shoulders and was relieved of his burden for a while
       by Hercules.

21   *necessity of the play* i.e. the play called for more characters than the
       company could furnish; hence some roles had to be doubled. Doubling of
       this kind (sometimes of several roles) was common, usually a 'necessity'.

24   *the port of her* her style of living, social position.

25   **underpoised* undervalued, outweighed.

26   **currents* gives currency to, makes acceptable.

31   *law* i.e. la (exclamation).

32   **mountbanking* (form of 'mountebanking') making an impudent pretence
       to skills he doesn't possess.
       burgomasco Italianate form of 'burgomask', chief magistrate of a Dutch
       town, though here applied to Venice.

34   *to preserve* i.e. seem to preserve.

35–6   *loves......fashion* loves to follow the scent of the latest fashion and, like
       a hunted animal, is always running ahead of the pack.

37   *champing* munching.

39   *wag* droll fellow.

48   *blinks* closes.

50   *periphrasis* many words to express one, circumlocution.

51   *supple-chapped* having a (too) pliant lower-jaw (i.e. being a facile talker).

52   *parasite* a stock figure of Latin comedy. Jonson's Mosca (in *Volpone*, III.i)
       hails himself as a master parasite.

54   *busk* strip (wooden, whalebone, metal) used to stiffen and support a corset.
       cross crooked.

56   *glavering* deceitful, blandishing.
       bracks flaws (in cloth, etc.).

59   *periwig* curled wig (originally worn by women).

60   *bella gratiosa madonna* beautiful and gracious lady.

61   *nick* precisely right moment.

62   *chuck* familiar term of endearment.

63–4   *Thou......performance* i.e. I hope no spectator expects as much in
       performance as you are promising.

64   **dusky* gloomy, melancholy.

72   *Amazon* female warrior (from the race of warlike women supposed to have
       existed in Scythia).

74   *virago-like* like that of a bold, impudent woman, a scold.

76–7   *idiot, go by, go by* a parody of Thomas Kyd's *The Spanish Tragedy* (c.1587),
       III.xii.31 ('Hieronimo, beware: go by, go by'), a frequently quoted tag; 'go
       by' =stand aside.

80   *truss my hose* tie the points of my breeches.

84   **fulgor* dazzling brightness.

85   *the feminine* women.

86   *ding* beat with heavy blows.

87   *divulge* publish abroad.
       a lady's prejudice something damaging to a lady's honour.

89   *Rampum......Tamburlaine* satiric reference to Marlowe's *I* and *II*
       Tamburlaine (1587–8) and his 'mighty line', which by this time was
       associated with the huffy-puffy style, particularly as it was practised by his

many imitators. Ironically, 'rampum scrampum' (onomatopoeic to describe 'ranting and roaring') describes all too accurately Marston's own early verse style (as in the two parts of *Antonio and Mellida*, especially part II).

tufty Hunter (Regents edn, 1965) suggests this may mean 'proud' (i.e. dressed luxuriously in 'tuftaffeta', a kind of taffeta with a nap arranged in tufts).

91–2 *modern braggadoch* trifling braggart.

95 *spruce *Attic* neatly elegant (ironic).

97 *resolved* i.e. decided (as the proper accent for his part).

99 **mongreled* mixed.

101 *conceit* conceive.

105 *old cut* old fashion (i.e. with modesty).
show......draught give us a sketch or sample.

109–11 *never......impoverishment* i.e. ?never considering any man whom I believed justly to have some real fault to be completely happy.

111 *Madam Felicity* i.e. Dame Fortune.

112–13 *his well-bounded......fortune* i.e. ?his sense of properly controlled contentment persuaded him to consider it one of the foremost aspects of his own lot in life.

115 *accomplished beatitude* complete happiness.

116 *Feliche* Means 'the happy man'.
SD *To Galeatzo* Antonio answers Feliche's question to Galeatzo; perhaps a line or more, in which Galeatzo briefly identifies his role, has dropped out of the text.

121–2 *take austere state* assume an appearance of haughty dignity.

124 *keep......distance* abstain from over-familiarity of deportment or vulgarity in conversation.

125 *into......arm* ?into consorting with low characters.

126 *vulgar censure* plebeian judgement.

127 *Puritan's ruff* i.e. small, unostentatious ruff.

129–30 *casting-bottle* small bottle for sprinkling perfumed waters.

130 *yeasty breast* breath smelling of ale.

133 *'t had* it had.

134 *Proteus* sea-god, who could change into various shapes.
blind Gew not an actor, but (as other references suggest) a blind performing ape.

135 *limn* paint, portray.

136 *tablet* little panel (of wood, etc.) on which to paint (the comparatively short length of a play).
our plays afford i.e. plays generally, not this particular play.

137 *he* Galeatzo.

139 *second part* i.e. *Antonio's Revenge* (*c*.1600). Actually, Feliche appears only as a hanged corpse in the second part and Galeatzo there receives no 'more exact accomplishment'.

8 The actors

The actors' 'quality' or profession was not generally highly regarded by many segments (particularly the Puritan groups) of the Elizabethan–Jacobean public. As John Earle put it (*Micro-cosmographie* (1628), no. 21, 'A player'): 'His profession has in it a kind of contradiction, for none is more disliked, and yet none more applauded.' Unattached actors, those not under royal patronage or that of other noblemen as members of an officially allowed company, e.g. the King's Men (under Elizabeth, the Lord Chamberlain's Men), the Admiral's Men, Queen Anne's Men, etc., were always in danger of the Statute of 1572 (and its successors), which declared them to be rogues and vagabonds punishable by law. On the other hand, a few actors, like Richard Burbage, Edward Alleyn, and Shakespeare, achieved some financial and limited social status, while others, like Richard Tarlton, William Kemp, and Robert Armin, became widely honoured as comedians, particularly for their 'clown' roles. Burbage (1571?–1619), who was the leading actor of Shakespeare's company (the Chamberlain's, later the King's, Men), shared his honours with his principal rival, Edward ('Ned') Alleyn (1566–1626), widely acclaimed tragedian of the Admiral's Men. It has been suggested that Hamlet in his advice to the players (III.ii.28–35) was comparing the strutting and bellowing of Alleyn with the more natural style of Burbage. Alleyn, it may be noted, had created the title-role of Marlowe's *Tamburlaine* (1587–88) and the mad Orlando in Robert Greene's *Orlando Furioso* (1588–92). Some of Burbage's best-known roles are referred to in 'A funeral elegy on the death of the famous actor Richard Burbage' (see C. M. Ingleby, *Shakespeare, the Man and the Book* (1881), II, 180–2, lines 12–16):

He's gone, and with him what a world are dead,
Which he reviv'd; to be revived so
No more: young Hamlet, old Hieronimo [in *The Spanish Tragedy*],
Kind Lear, the grieved Moor, and more beside,
That liv'd in him, have now forever died.

Burbage and Kemp appear as characters in the anonymous Cambridge play, *The Return from Parnassus, Part II* (1602), IV.iii–iv, where they try out two Cambridge students, Philomusus and Studioso, in passages from Thomas Kyd's *Spanish Tragedy* and Shakespeare's *Richard III*. Since this is a university play, they are presented as more or less illiterate. Ben Jonson has a similar try-out scene in *Poetaster* (1601), III.iv.

Thomas Nashe compares English actors, very favourably, with their Continental counterparts:

Our players are not as the players beyond sea, a sort of squirting, bawdy comedians, that have whores and common courtezans to play women's parts [boys played women's roles in England], and forbear no immodest speech or unchaste action that may procure laughter; but our scene is more stately furnished than ever it was in the time of Roscius, our representations honourable and full of gallant resolution, not consisting, like theirs, of a pantaloon, a whore, and a zany [stock characters in Italian *commedia dell'arte*], but of emperors, kings, and princes, whose true tragedies (*Sophocleo cothurno* [in Sophocles' tragic style]) they do vaunt.

Not Roscius nor Aesop, those admired tragedians that have lived ever since before Christ was born, could ever perform more in action than famous Ned Alleyn [see above]. I must accuse our poets of sloth and partiality that they will not boast in large impressions [printed books] what worthy men (above all nations) England affords. . . . . .

. . . . . . if I ever write anything in Latin (as I hope one day I shall [he never did]), not a man of any desert here amongst us but I will have up. Tarlton [principal comedian of the Queen's Men], Ned Alleyn, [?William] Knell, [John] Bentley shall be made known to France, Spain, and Italy; and not a part that they surmounted in, more than other, but I will there note and set down, with the manner of their habits and attire (*Pierce Penilesse* (1592), ed. McKerrow, I, 215).

The first selection (i), from Anthony Munday's *Second and Third Blast of Retrait from Plaies and Theaters* (1580), is a typical Munday attempt to 'cash in' on Gosson's recent *Schoole of Abuse* (1579). Aside from his somewhat novel charge that actors choose their roles in order to express their real characters, Munday's attack is interesting because he had probably been an unsuccessful actor himself and was, very shortly, to become a mediocre dramatist, prolific ballad writer, and purveyor of civic pageants (see the satiric portrait of Munday as the poet Posthaste in Marston's *Histriomastix*, p. 43). He unintentionally describes himself, when, in a side note, he says: 'Players cannot better be compared than to the *Chameleon*.' He seems, indeed, to have been ready to espouse any side that promised possible financial gain.

Selection (ii), from John Stephens' *Satyricall Essayes, Characters and Others* (1615, 2nd edn) catches up in the somewhat scattered manner of the prose 'character' most of the charges usually levelled at 'A common Player', some of them not without some justification. John Webster, the dramatist, leapt to the defence in a pendant character, 'An excellent Actor' (selection (iii) from *New Characters (drawne to the life)* in the second edition, 1615, of Sir Thomas Overbury's *A Wife*), inducing Stephens to soften somewhat his sweeping criticisms in a revised and extended version (here reprinted) of his original character (see notes to ll. 66, 70-5).

i

From Anthony Munday, *A Second and Third Blast of Retrait from Plaies and Theaters* (1580), pp. 110–116.

As I have had a saying to these versifying play-makers, so must I likewise deal with shameless enactors. When I see by them young boys, inclining of themselves unto wickedness, trained up in filthy speeches, unnatural and unseemly gestures, to be brought up by these schoolmasters in bawdry and in idleness, I cannot choose but with tears and grief of heart lament......

    And as for those stagers themselves are they not commonly such kind of men in their conversation as they are in profession? Are they not as variable in heart as they are in their parts? Are they not as good practisers of bawdry as enactors? Live they not in such sort themselves as they give precepts unto others? Doth not their talk on the stage declare the nature of their disposition? Doth not every one take that part which is proper to his kind? Doth not the ploughman's tongue walk of his plough; the seafaring man of his mast, cable, and sail; the soldier of his harness, spear, and shield; and bawdy mates of bawdy matters? Ask them, if in their laying out of their parts, they choose not those parts which is most agreeing to their inclination and that they can best discharge? And look what every of them doth most delight in, that he can best handle to the contentment of others. If it be a roisting, bawdy, and lascivious part, wherein are unseemly speeches, and that they make choice of them as best answering and proper to their manner of play, may we not say, by how much he exceeds in his gesture, he delights himself in his part? And by so much it is pleasing to his disposition and nature?......

    Are they not notoriously known to be those men in their life abroad as they are on the stage: roisters, brawlers, ill-dealers, boasters, lovers, loiterers, ruffins? So that, they are always exercised in playing their parts and practising wickedness, making that an art to the end they might the better gesture in their parts. For who can better play the ruffin than a very ruffin? Who better the lover than they who make it a common exercise? To conclude, the principal end of all their interludes is to feed the world with sights and fond pastimes; to juggle in good earnest the money out of other men's purses into their own hands.

5

10

15

20

25

30

35

NOTES

1   *had a saying* i.e. spoken my mind.
2   *enactors* actors (Munday's form is 'inactors').
    by them in their company.

7   *stagers* actors.
8   *conversation* behaviour, manner of life.
13   *kind* nature.
14   *walk* move briskly (i.e. talk continually).
16   *mates* fellows (used pejoratively).
16–17 *laying out of* apportioning of.
17   *is* A singular verb with a plural subject is not uncommon in Elizabethan
     English (see Abbott 332).
19   *that* is that which.
20   *roisting* roistering, blustering, noisy. Compare 'roisters' in l. 27.
21   *that* so that, if.
28   *ruffins* ruffians (variant form).
30   *art* technical skill.
34   *fond* foolish, trivial.

                                    ii

From John Stephens, *Satyricall Essayes, Characters and Others* (1615;
second edn), pp. 295–301.

A common Player
Is a slow payer, seldom a purchaser, never a Puritan. The statute
hath done wisely to acknowledge him a rogue errant; for his chief
essence is *A daily counterfeit.* He hath been familiar so long with
outsides that he professes himself (being unknown) to be an
apparent gentleman. But his thin felt and his silk stockings, or his   5
foul linen and fair doublet, do (in him) bodily reveal the broker. So
being not suitable, he proves a *motley*: his mind observing the same
fashion of his body; both consists of parcels and remnants. But his
mind hath commonly the newer fashion and the newer stuff; he
would not else harken so passionately after new tunes, new tricks,   10
new devices. These together apparel his brain and understanding,
whilst he takes the materials upon trust, and is himself the tailor to
take measure of his soul's liking. He doth conjecture somewhat
strongly, but dares not commend a play's goodness till he hath
either spoken, or heard, the *Epilogue*; neither dares he entitle good   15
things *good*, unless he be heart'ned on by the multitude. Till then,
he saith faintly what he thinks, with a willing purpose to recant or
persist. But howsoever he pretends to have a royal master, or
mistress, his wages and dependence prove him to be the servant of

the people. When he doth hold conference upon the stage and   20
should look directly in his fellow's face, he turns about his voice
into the assembly for applause-sake, like a trumpeter in the fields
that shifts places to get an echo. The cautions of his judging
humour (if he dares undertake it) be a certain number of saucy
rude jests against the common lawyer, handsome conceits against   25
the fine courtiers, delicate quirks against the rich cuckold a
citizen, shadowed glance[s] for good innocent ladies and
gentlewomen, with a nipping scoff for some honest justice, who
hath imprisoned him, or some thrifty tradesman, who hath
allowed him no credit: always rememb'red, his object is *A new*   30
play or *A play newly revived.* Other poems he admits, as good
fellows take tobacco or ignorant burgesses give a voice for
company sake, as things that neither maintain nor be against him.
To be a player is to have a *mithridate* against the pestilence; for
players cannot tarry where the plague reigns; and therefore they be   35
seldom infected. He can seem no less than one in honour, or at
least one mounted; for unto miseries which persecute such, he is
most incident. Hence it proceeds that in the prosperous fortune of
a play frequented he proves immoderate and falls into a drunkard's
paradise, till it be *last* no longer. Otherwise, when adversities   40
come, they come together; for Lent and Shrove Tuesday be not far
asunder; then he is dejected daily and weekly; his blessings be
neither lame nor monstrous; they go upon four legs, but move
slowly, and make as great a distance between their steps as
between the four terms. Reproof is ill bestowed upon him; it   45
cannot alter his conditions; he hath been so accustomed to the
scorn and laughter of his audience that he cannot be ashamed of
himself; for he dares laugh in the middest of a serious conference
without blushing. If he marries, he mistakes the woman for the
boy in woman's attire by not respecting a difference in the   50
mischief. But so long as he lives unmarried, he mistakes the boy,
or a whore, for the woman, by courting the first on the stage, or
visiting the second at her devotions. When he is most commendable, you must confess there is no truth in him; for his best action is
but an imitation of truth, and *nullum simile est idem.* It may be   55
imagined I abuse his carriage, and he perhaps may suddenly be
thought fair-conditioned: for he *plays above board.* Take him at
the best, he is but a shifting companion; for he lives effectually by
putting on and putting off. If his profession were single, he would
think himself a simple fellow, as he doth all professions besides his   60
own. His own, therefore, is compounded of all natures, all
humours, all professions. He is politic also to perceive the
commonwealth doubts of his licence, and therefore in spite of
parliaments or statutes he incorporates himself by the title of a
brotherhood. Painting and fine clothes may not by the same   65
reason be called abusive, that players may not be called rogues *for*

they be chief ornaments of his Majesty's Revels. I need not multiply his character; for boys, and everyone, will no sooner see men of this faculty walk along but they will (unasked) inform you what he is by the vulgar title. Yet in the general number of them, many may 70 deserve a wise man's commendation; and therefore did I prefix an epithet of *common* to distinguish the base and artless appendants of our City companies, which often times start away into rustical wanderers and then (like Proteus) start back again into the City number. 75

NOTES

1   *Puritan* Puritans, of course, considered actors as 'limbs of Satan', but the principal suggestion here is that actors were loose livers.
      statute i.e. the Act of 1572 (and later versions of the same Act), in which 'common players of interludes' (i.e. those without the patronage of a nobleman or other authority), in company with jugglers, bearwards, tinkers, petty chapmen, etc., were 'deemed rogues, vagabonds, and sturdy beggars'.

2   *errant* vagrant, wandering.

5   *apparent gentleman* gentleman in appearance (judged from his clothes). Earle ('A player') makes the same point.
      thin felt poor-quality hat (of felt).

6   *reveal the broker* betray the second-hand clothes dealer.

7   *suitable* properly suited or clothed.
      motley one dressed, like the professional fool, in bits and pieces (particoloured) which clash with each other.

8   *parcels* fragments, pieces.

12   *upon trust* without any investigation.

15   *Epilogue* i.e. the outcome or conclusion (of a play).

18   *royal master* perhaps a reference to the King's Men (Shakespeare's company), who were under the patronage of King James.

20   *hold conference* take part in the stage dialogue.

23-4 *cautions......humour* warning hints of his critical temperament.

25   *conceits* fancies, notions, expressions.

26   *quirks* quips, witty turns.

26-7 *cuckold a citizen* The cuckolding of citizen tradesmen was a favourite plot device of City comedy.

27   *shadowed glance[s]* covert hits. The first edn (1615) reads 'glaunces'.

28   *nipping scoff* biting mockery or jest.

31   *Other poems* i.e. poems other than plays, which were often so termed (e.g. by Ben Jonson).

34   *mithridate* medicine regarded as a universal antidote against poisons and infectious diseases.

35   *cannot......reigns* The theatres were closed in London during attacks of the plague and the actors were forced to leave the city and tour in the provinces.

36   *one in honour* i.e. a gentleman (from outward appearance).

37   *one mounted* i.e. a person on his way up the social ladder.

38–9 *prosperous......frequented* a play which has been successful and drawn a full house, particularly a new play for which the entrance fees were sometimes doubled.

40   *be last* meaning unclear. Perhaps 'be' should be deleted; in which case '*last*' would refer to a play that had outlived its popularity.

41–2 *Lent......asunder* Shrove Tuesday (a day of feasting, called 'pancake day') preceded Ash Wednesday, the first day of Lent (a long stretch of forty weekdays, a period of fasting).

43   *neither......monstrous* i.e. of a middling nature, not extreme.
      go......legs i.e. crawl.

45   *four terms* term-days, or quarter-days, when wages were paid.

48   *middest* midst.
      conference See above, l. 20.

49–51 *If he......mischief* meaning not clear, though there is obviously, as in ll. 51–2, some suggestion of homosexuality: 'mistake' = choose in error; 'mischief' = source of harm or evil.

53   *devotions* ironic.

55   *nullum......idem* nothing merely like is the thing itself.

56   *carriage* social behaviour toward others.

57   *fair-conditioned* well-natured; of good social standing.
      plays above board (1) deals honestly; (2) acts on the boards of the stage.

58   *shifting companion* fellow who lives by questionable means or shifts; here, with play on 'shift' = to change costumes.
      effectually explicitly, in fact.

59   *single* i.e. devoted to one pursuit or profession. As an actor he is compounded of all professions, playing many different roles (see ll. 61–2).

64–5 *incorporates......brotherhood* sets himself up as part of a licensed company of actors.

65–6 *by......reason* according to the same argument.

66   *abusive* improper, deceitful, corrupt. This is part of one of the insertions in the second edition and refers to ll. 12–14 and 30–2 of 'An excellent Actor' (selection (iii)).

70   *vulgar title* familiar name, i.e. common player.

70–5 *Yet......number* an addition to the second edition, intended, like the addition of 'errant' in l. 2, to answer some of the criticisms in 'An excellent Actor'.

72   *appendants* adjuncts, i.e. minor members (of a company).

73–4 *rustical wanderers* i.e. strolling players. See selection, p. 43.

74   *Proteus* mythical sea-god, famous for his ability to change shapes at will.

iii

From John Webster, *New Characters* (*drawne to the life*) in Sir Thomas
Overbury's *A Wife* (1615; 2nd edn).

An excellent Actor
Whatsoever is commendable to the grave orator is most exquisitely
perfect in him; for by a full and significant action of body he
charms our attention. Sit in a full theatre and you will think you
see so many lines drawn from the circumference of so many ears,
whiles the *actor* is the *centre*. He doth not strive to make nature   5
monstrous: she is often seen in the same scene with him, but
neither on stilts nor crutches; and for his voice, 'tis not lower than
the prompter, nor lowder than the foil and target. By his action he
fortifies moral precepts with examples; for what we see him
personate we think truly done before us: a man of a deep thought   10
might apprehend the ghosts of our ancient *heroes* walked again,
and take him (at several times) for many of them. He is much
affected to painting, and 'tis a question whether that make him an
excellent player, or his playing an exquisite painter. He adds grace
to the poet's labours: for what in the poet is but ditty, in him is   15
both ditty and music. He entertains us in the best leisure of our
life, that is between meals, the most unfit time either for study or
bodily exercise. The flight of hawks and chase of wild beasts,
either of them are delights noble; but some think this sport of men
the worthier despite all *calumny*. All men have been of his   20
occupation, and, indeed, what he doth feignedly that do others
essentially: this day one plays a monarch, the next a private person;
here one acts a tyrant, on the morrow an exile; a parasite this man
tonight, tomorrow a precisian; and so of divers others. I observe,
of all men living, a worthy actor in one kind is the strongest   25
motive of affection that can be; for when he dies, we cannot be
persuaded any man can do his parts like him. Therefore the
imitating characterist was extreme idle in calling them rogues. His
muse it seems, with all his loud invocation, could not be waked to
light him a snuff to read the statute; for I would let his malicious   30
ignorance understand that rogues are not to be employed as main
ornaments to his Majesty's revels . . . . . . But to conclude, I value a
worthy actor by the corruption of some few of the quality, as I
would do gold in the ore; I should not mind the dross but the
purity of the metal.   35

NOTES

2   *him* i.e. the excellent actor.

4–5   *lines......centre* Note the implication of the generally circular structure of the 'full theatre'. Compare *Troilus and Cressida* (I.iii.65–8), where Shakespeare suggests that Nestor's speech 'Should with a bond of air....../......knit all the Greekish ears / To his experienc'd tongue'.

6   *monstrous* unnatural.

8   *prompter* A prompter would naturally speak 'low' so that only the actor might hear him.
    lowder i.e. he would not rant and roar, making more noise than the clashing of 'foil' (=kind of small-sword with a blunt edge and a button at the point) and 'target' (=light round shield).

11   *ancient heroes* English military leaders, particularly earlier kings, who figured in the history plays. The passage is borrowed from Thomas Nashe (*Pierce Penilesse*, ed. McKerrow, I, 212–13), who specifically mentions Talbot (*I Henry VI*) and Henry V.

12   *several* different.

13   *affected to painting* given to using make-up. We know almost nothing of the extent to which make-up was used on the stage at this time. Webster may, indeed, be using 'painting' as a metaphor for drawing pictures through language.

15   *ditty* any composition in verse, not merely a song lyric.

17   *between meals* i.e. after dinner, which was usually eaten around noon.

19   *sport* i.e. acting.

20   *calumny* a reference to Stephens' 'A common Player' and to the numerous Puritan attacks on the immorality of stage plays and actors. See pp. 11, 94.

22   *essentially* according to their essential nature.
    one i.e. mankind generally.

23   *parasite* one who sponges off the rich, a yes-man. A type-character in Latin comedy, imitated by English dramatists of the period.

24   *precisian* one punctilious in the observance of rules and forms (with a hit at the Puritans).

25   *kind* manner.

26   *motive of* emotion producing.

28   *imitating characterist* i.e. John Stephens, whose character of 'A common Player' Webster is answering.

30   *snuff* candle-end.
    statute See note to l. 1, 'A common Player'.

33   *corruption......few* an unwilling admission that Stephens' charges are not unjustified in a 'few' cases.
    quality acting fraternity.

9 Country festivals and entertainments

Village and town life was for most people a long round of hard work, but when holidays came they were gratefully celebrated with gusto and some abandon. Elizabethans and Jacobeans were physically high-spirited and exerted themselves energetically in working off various kinds of pent-up steam whenever occasion offered. In several of the following selections, we get, I think, a strong sense of close community spirit and echoes of long-forgotten folk rituals expressing the passing of the seasons in what were originally fertility rites. As C. J. Sisson (*Lost Plays of Shakespeare's Age* (1936), p. 157) explains: 'The May Game [see selection (ii)] is held to be a form of rite arising out of the Fertility Cult. Its personages are vegetation deities or priests. The Maypole is a sacred tree, and the Game a kind of sacrifice. This kind of explanation takes also within its ambit the Morris Dance, Sword Dance, St George and the Dragon, and Robin Hood and his merry men.' It is thus impossible always to distinguish the various strands of influence in such festival entertainments and assuredly the Elizabethans were unworried by the kinds of gallimaufries that resulted. Sisson describes a May Game festival at Wells in 1607 (p. 168) in which the Lord of May was followed by Morris Dancers, the Pinner of Wakefield and his troupe, Robin Hood and his merry men, St George and his knights (with the Dragon), Old Mother Bunch (making black puddings as she was trundled in a wheelbarrow), a pageant of Diana and Acteon, Noah (from the Mystery Plays), a Giant and Giantess, and an oriental pageant of the Soldan of Egypt and his Queen (more properly connected with the legend of St George, who had rescued their daughter). What more could heart desire!

It may seem strange that we should turn to Philip Stubbes's *The Anatomie of Abuses* (1583) (selections (i)–(iii)) for an account of such fun-filled occasions, but, despite his vociferously moralistic, Puritan approach and threats of Hell fire, which for the most part we may discount, he is so unconsciously attracted to the very 'enormities' he describes that he gives us the best and most colourful accounts anywhere to be found. In fairness to Stubbes, it was the 'abuses' rather than the things themselves that he intended to attack (see his 'Preface to the Reader' in the first edition of 1583; dropped in later editions: 'That whereas . . . . . . I have entreated of certain exercises usually practised among us, as namely plays and interludes, of dancing, gaming, and such like, I would not have thee so to take me as though my speeches tended to the overthrow and utter disliking of all kind of exercises in general: . . . . . . but the particular abuses which are crept into every one of these several exercises is the only thing which I think worthy of reprehension.'). Unfortunately, a narrow moral zeal usually obliterates this nice distinction. He admits, for example, the propriety of some kinds of dancing (for which he gives biblical precedent), but when he comments on the kind of dancing practised at popular festivals he loses control: 'For what clipping, what

culling [embracing], what kissing and bussing [kissing], what smouch-
ing [kissing] and slabbering [beslobbering] one of another, what filthy
groping and unclean handling is not practised everywhere in these
dancings' (p. 155 in Furnivall's edn).

Stubbes's treatment of the Lord of Misrule (selection (i)) is somewhat
misleading. He appears to associate this custom only with country life
and seems to suggest that it was a summer festival. In fact, however, the
selection of a Lord or Prince of Misrule was most generally associated
with the Christmas season at Court, the universities, and the Inns of
Court. A detailed account of the revels held at Gray's Inn in 1594–5 is
preserved in the *Gesta Grayorum* published in 1688.

The morris dance is well illustrated by a lively scene in Fletcher and
Shakespeare's *The Two Noble Kinsmen* (III.v; written 1613), in which a
morris dance is performed under the direction of Master Gerrold, the
schoolmaster, as a May Game in honour of Duke Theseus. Although the
play is based on Chaucer's 'Knight's Tale', Fletcher, who is responsible
for this scene, turned for the *dramatis personae* of the dance to Francis
Beaumont's very recent (20 February 1613) *Inner Temple and Gray's Inn
Masque*, in which, as an anti-masque, a morris was danced by essentially
the same cast of characters. Casts varied considerably from morris to
morris, sometimes incorporating characters from the tales of Robin
Hood and Maid Marian (in the roles played by the Lord and Lady of
May in *Noble Kinsmen*); one of the most popular performers in earlier
morrises, the hobby-horse, however, 'is forgot' (see selection (i), l. 21).
And William Kemp, the celebrated comedian, danced a solo morris from
London to Norwich (about a hundred miles), which he describes in his
Kemps Nine Daies Wonder (1600), accompanied only by a taborer with
drum and pipe (see illustrations 7 and 8).

The final selection (iv), from Robert Laneham's *Letter* (1575), gives us
an eyewitness account of an 'old storial show' put on by 'certain good-
hearted men of Coventry' at Kenilworth Castle, the seat of the Earl of
Leicester, to honour Queen Elizabeth in 1575. The 'show', which
describes the massacre of the Danes by order of King Ethelred 'the
redeless [resourceless]' in 1002, may be considered a kind of forerunner
of the many plays on all periods of British and English history that
became so popular in the late 1580s and 90s. Presentation of dramatic
entertainments by local 'actors' on festival occasions was a long
established practice (several other 'shows' were presented to the Queen
during her nineteen-day visit at Kenilworth), a practice kindly satirized
by Shakespeare in *A Midsummer Night's Dream*, where Bottom and his
fellow 'rude mechanicals' celebrate the marriage of Duke Theseus with
the play of 'Pyramus and Thisbe', or in *Love's Labour's Lost* with the
'Masque of the Worthies'. Local plays on St George and the Dragon and
the Robin Hood legend were widespread (see J. M. Manley, *Specimens of
the Pre-Shakesperean Drama*, I (1897), pp. 279–95, for such texts as have
survived) and a 'literary' entertainment may be sampled in Sir Philip
Sidney's *The Lady of May* (1578–82).

For a detailed account of folk entertainment and drama, see E. K. Chambers, *The Mediaeval Stage* (1903), I, 89–419.

i

Lords of Misrule in Ailgna [i.e. Anglia or England]

From Philip Stubbes, *The Anatomie of Abuses* (1583, 2nd edn), pp. 146–8 in F. J. Furnivall's edn (1877–9).

The name, indeed, is odious both to God and good men, and such as the very heathen people would have blushed at, once to have named amongst them. And if the name importeth some evil, then what may the thing itself be, judge you? But because you desire to know the manner of them, I will show you as I have seen them 5 practised myself. First, all the wildheads of the parish, conventing together, choose them a Grand-Captain (of all mischief) whom they ennoble with the title of 'my Lord of Misrule', and him they crown with great solemnity, and adopt for their king. This king anointed, chooseth forth twenty, forty, threescore or a hundred 10 lusty guts, like to himself, to wait upon his lordly majesty, and to guard his noble person. Then, every one of these his men, he investeth with his liveries of green, yellow, or some other light wanton colour; and as though that were not (bawdy) gaudy enough I should say, they bedeck themselves with scarfs, ribbons, and laces 15 hanged all over with gold rings, precious stones, and other jewels: this done, they tie about either leg twenty or forty bells, with rich handkerchiefs in their hands, and sometimes laid across over their shoulders and necks, borrowed for the most part of their pretty Mopsies and loving Besses, for bussing them in the dark. Thus all 20 things set in order, then have they their hobby-horses, dragons and other antics, together with their bawdy pipers and thundering drummers to strike up the devil's dance withal. Then march these heathen company towards the church and church-yard, their pipers piping, their drummers thund'ring, their stumps dancing, 25 their bells jingling, their handkerchiefs swinging about their heads like madmen, their hobby-horses and other monsters skirmishing amongst the throng: and in this sort they go to the church (though the minister be at prayer or preaching), dancing and swinging their handkerchiefs, over their heads in the church, like devils 30 incarnate, with such a confused noise, that no man can hear his own voice. Then, the foolish people they look, they stare, they laugh, they fleer, and mount upon forms and pews to see these goodly pageants solemnized in this sort. Then, after this, about the church they go again and again, and so forth into the church- 35 yard, where they have commonly their summer-halls, their bowers, arbours, and banquetting houses set up, wherein they feast, banquet and dance all that day and (peradventure) all the night too. And thus these terrestrial furies spend the Sabbath day.

Then for the further ennobling of this honourable lurden (lord, 40

I should say) they have also certain papers, wherein is painted some babblery or other of imagery work, and these they call 'my Lord of Misrule's badges': these they give to every one that will give money for them to maintain them in this their heathenry, devilry, whoredom, drunkenness, pride, and what not. And who   45
will not show himself buxom to them, and give them money for these the devil's cognizances, they shall be mocked and flouted at shamefully. And so assotted are some, that they not only give them money to maintain their abomination withal, but also wear their badges and cognizances in their hats or caps openly. But let them   50
take heed; for these are the badges, seals, brands, and cognizances of the devil, whereby he knoweth his servants and clients from the children of God; and so long as they wear them, *Sub vexillo diaboli militant contra Dominum et legem suam*: they fight under the banner and standard of the devil against Christ Jesus, and all his   55
laws. Another sort of fantastical fools bring to these hell-hounds (the Lord of Misrule and his complices) some bread, some good ale, some new cheese, some old cheese, some custards, and cakes, some flawns, some tarts, some cream, some meat, some one thing, some another; but if they knew that as often as they bring any to   60
the maintainance of these execrable pastimes, they offer sacrifice to the devil and Sathanas, they would repent and withdraw their hands; *which God grant they may!*

NOTES

6   *conventing* assembling.
11   *lusty guts* merry (or strong) fellows (literally 'gluttons').
13   *investeth* clotheth.
     liveries distinctive uniforms worn by a person's servants.
20   *for bussing* as a reward for kissing.
21   *hobby-horses* The 'hobby-horse' was frequently a character in a morris dance.
     dragons A 'dragon' figured in the folk-play of St George and the Dragon.
22   *antics* grotesquely dressed performers, such as the Bavian (or baboon) in a morris dance.
33   *fleer* make wry faces or laugh coarsely.
36   *summer-halls* summer-houses, light structures for protection from the sun.
     bowers shady recesses (= 'arbours').
40   *lurden* vagabond, rascal.
42   *babblery* here confused with 'babery' or 'baublery' = grotesque ornamentation.
     imagery work i.e. pictures.
43   *badges* cognizances, indicating that they were followers or servants of the Lord of Misrule. See ll. 45ff.

46   *buxom* indulgent, submissive.
53–4 *Sub. . . . . . suam* translated immediately following.
59   *flawns* cheese-cakes or pancakes.
62   *Sathanas* Satan.

ii

May games

From Philip Stubbes, *The Anatomie of Abuses* (1583, 2nd edn), p. 149 in
F. J. Furnivall's edn (1877–9).

Against May, Whitsunday, or some other time of the year, every
parish, town and village assemble themselves together, both men,
women, and children, old and young, even all indifferently; and
either going all together or dividing themselves into companies,
they go some to the woods and groves, some to the hills and   5
mountains, some to one place and some to another, where they
spend all the night in pleasant pastimes; and in the morning they
return, bringing with them birch boughs and branches of trees, to
deck their assemblies withal. And no marvel, for there is a great
lord present amongst them, as superintendent and lord over their   10
pastimes and sports, namely Sathan, prince of hell. But their
chiefest jewel they bring from thence is their May-pole, which
they bring home with great veneration, as thus. They have twenty
or forty yoke of oxen, every ox having a sweet nose-gay of flowers
placed on the tip of his horns; and these oxen draw home this   15
May-pole (this stinking idol, rather) which is covered all over with
flowers and herbs, bound round about with strings from the top to
the bottom, and sometime painted with variable colours, with two
or three hundred men, women, and children following it with
great devotion. And thus being reared up with handkerchiefs and   20
flags streaming on the top, they straw the ground about, bind
green boughs about it, set up summer-halls, bowers, and arbours
hard by it; and then fall they to banquet and feast, to leap and
dance about it, as the heathen people did at the dedication of their
idols, whereof this is a perfect pattern, or rather the thing itself.   25

NOTES

1   *Whitsunday* the seventh Sunday and fiftieth day after Easter, Pentecost.
3   *indifferently* without distinction.
17 *strings* ribbons, tapes.
23–4 *leap and dance* Dances associated with the May-pole were the morris dance and the sword dance.

iii

The manner of church-ales in Ailgna [i.e. Anglia or England]

From Philip Stubbes, *The Anatomie of Abuses* (1583, 2nd edn), pp. 150–1 in F. J. Furnivall's edn (1877–9).

In certain towns, where drunken Bacchus bears the sway, against Christmas and Easter, Whitsunday, or some other time the churchwardens (for so they call them) of every parish, with the consent of the whole parish, provide half a score or twenty quarters of malt, whereof some they buy of the church-stock, and some is   5
given them of the parishioners themselves, everyone conferring somewhat, according to his ability; which malt, being made into very strong ale or beer, is set to sale, either in the church or some other place assigned to that purpose.
 Then, when this nippitatum, this huff cap (as they call it) and   10
this nectar of life is set abroach, well is he that can get the soonest to it and spend the most at it; for he that sitteth the closest to it, and spends the most at it, he is counted the godliest man of all the rest and most in God's favour because it is spent upon his church, forsooth . . . . . . [The money so collected was spent to repair the   15
church, buy service books, surplices, etc., but the disapproving Stubbes objects to the means: 'do they think that the Lord will have his house built with drunkenness, gluttony, and suchlike abominations?'.]

NOTES

5   *church-stock* church funds.
10 *nippitatum* ale of prime quality.
 huff-cap strong, heady ale.
15 *forsooth* in truth (ironic).

iv

The locals put on a play for Queen Elizabeth

From Robert Laneham's *Letter* (1575; ed. F. J. Furnivall (1887), pp. 26–32).

Hock Tuesday by the Coventry men. And hereto followed as good a sport (me thought), presented in an historical cue, by certain good-hearted men of Coventry, my Lord's neighbours there: who......made petition that they mought renew now their old storial show. Of argument: how the Danes whilom here in a 5 troublous season were for quietness borne withal and suffer'd in peace; that anon, by outrage and importable insolency, abusing both Ethelred, the King then, and all estates everywhere beside; at the grievous complaint and counsel of Huna, the King's chieftain in wars, on Saint Brice's night, Ann. Dom. 1012,......that 10 falleth yearly on the thirteenth of November, were all dispatch'd and the reame rid. And for because the matter mentioneth how valiantly our English women for love of their country behaved themselves, expressed in actions and rhymes after their manner, they thought it mought move some mirth to her Majesty the 15 rather.

The thing, said they, is grounded on story, and for pastime wont to be played in our city yearly, without ill example of manners, papistry, or any superstition; and else did so occupy the heads of a number that likely enough would have had worse 20 meditations; had an ancient beginning and a long continuance; till now of late laid down, they knew no cause why, unless it were by the zeal of certain their preachers, men very commendable for their behaviour and learning, and sweet in their sermons, but somewhat too sour in preaching away their pastime: wish'd, 25 therefore, that as they should continue their good doctrine in pulpit, so, for matters of policy and governance of the city, they would permit them to the Mayor and magistrates, and said......they would make their humble petition unto her Highness that they might have their plays up again. 30

But aware, keep back, make room now, here they come ......Captain Cox came marching on valiantly before, clean truss'd and gartered above the knee, all fresh in a velvet cap (Master Goldingham lent it him), flourishing with his tonsword, and another fence-master with him: thus in the forward making 35 room for the rest. After them proudly prick'd on foremost the Danish lance-knights on horseback and then the English, each with their alder pole martially in their hand. Even at the first entry the meeting wax'd somewhat warm; that by and by kindled with courage a'both sides grew from a hot skirmish unto a blazing 40

battle: first by spear and shield, outrageous in their races as rams at
their rut, with furious encounters, that together they tumble to the
dust, sometime horse and man; and after fall to it with sword and
target, good bangs a'both sides. The fight so ceasing, but the
battle not so ended, followed the footmen, both the hosts, ton   45
after tother; first marching in ranks, then warlike turning; then
from ranks into squadrons, then into triangles; from that into
rings, and so winding out again. A valiant captain of great
prowess, as fierce as a fox assaulting a goose, was so hardy to give
the first stroke; then get they grisly together, that great was the   50
activity that day to be seen there a'both sides; ton very eager for
purchase of prey, tother utterly stout for redemption of liberty:
thus quarrel inflamed fury a'both sides. Twice the Danes had the
better, but at the last conflict, beaten down, overcome, and many
led captive for triumph by our English women.   55

NOTES

1   *Hock Tuesday* i.e. the Hock Tuesday (second Tuesday after Easter
     Sunday) play.
2   *in......cue ?*i.e. in a manner conformable to history.
3   *my Lord's* the Earl of Leicester's.
4   *mought* might.
5   *storial* historical.
     whilom erewhile.
6   *suffer'd* allowed (to live).
7   *importable* unbearable.
10   *Ann. Dom.* 1012 more correctly 1002, though Holinshed gives the date as
     1012 (*Chronicles*, edn of 1807, I, 708).
12   *reame* realm. Ethelred, with great barbarity, secretly ordered the murder
     of all Danes throughout the kingdom. The kind of pitched battle here
     suggested romanticizes a nasty incident.
14   *rhymes* verses.
15   *move some mirth* give some pleasure. The Queen is reported to have
     'laugh'd well' and given the performers 'two bucks and five mark in
     money'.
17   *story* i.e. history.
22   *laid down* forbidden.
22-5 Note the diplomacy of the actors' comments on the more extreme
     Protestant clergy, whose reactions to drama and festival entertainment
     may be sampled in the section on 'Attitudes toward the drama' and in
     selections (i) and (ii) above.
28   *permit them to* leave them in the control of.
31   *aware* Beware.
32   *Captain Cox* Laneham describes Cox as 'an odd man, I promise you; by
     profession a mason, and that right skilful, very cunning in fence and
     hardy as Gawain' with 'great oversight [learning]......in matters of
     story [fabulous and popular history]'. Laneham then lists some 59 titles,
     plus almanacs, that Cox claimed to have in his 'library'.

32–3 *clean truss'd* i.e. his doublet and hose were neatly fastened with points or laces.

34   *tonsword* ?large two-handed sword (the term is unique to Laneham).

37   *lance-knights* literally, mercenary foot-soldiers, armed with lance or pike (but here mounted like knights for combat).

38   *alder pole* poles or lances made of alder wood.

40   *a'* on or of.

41–2 *at their rut* in heat.

44   *target* light round shield.

45–6 *ton after tother* the one after the other.

47   *triangles* wedge-shaped formations.

49   *fierce......goose* ironic.

50   *grisly* grimly, terrifyingly.

52   *stout* furious, menacing.

55   *led......women* probably a reference to a Hock-Monday custom according to which women caught and bound any men they met and exacted a forfeit.

1 An Elizabethan courtier à la mode. A miniature, on fine parchment, by
Nicholas Hilliard (1547–1619), one of the most admired artists and miniaturists of
the time and the author of the first treatise in English on painting, *The Arte of
Lymning* (*c.* 1600). Note the large starched ruff, intricately cut and embroidered
doublet with its row of big buttons, long hose, and silk or velvet cloak (see pages
128–33). The garden setting and the young man's rather affected pose, hand over
heart, suggest perhaps the plight of a lover caught in the rose-bush thorns of
unrequited passion, a favourite Petrarchan theme.

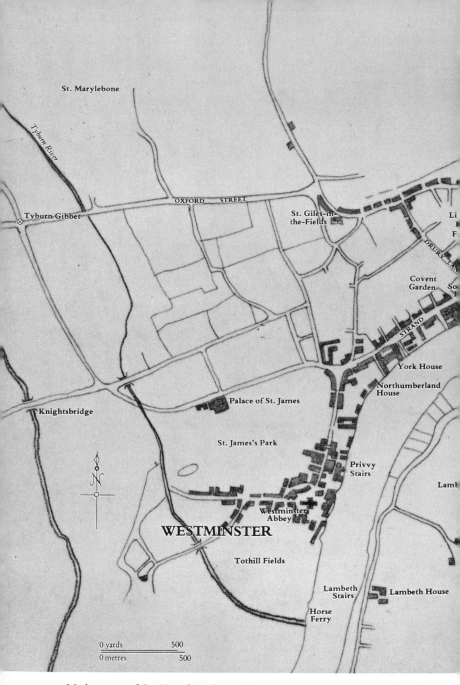

2 Modern map of the City of London and its environs as they were in the time of Elizabeth I and James I. Note the location of several of the playhouses: the Theatre and Curtain in the upper right corner, below Finsbury Fields; the Swan,

Rose and Globe on the south bank of the River Thames, west of London Bridge.
Compare Visscher's contemporary view (*c.* 1616) in illustration 3 overleaf.

3a

3 J. C. Visscher's striking panoramic view of London, published in four sections, dating from 1616. It is probably the best known of early seventeenth-century views of the City and its environs (see page 51). Although Visscher is believed to have known little of London at first hand, depending largely on earlier maps, and those not always the best, the overall effect is generally accurate enough, and manages to convey an unusually vivid sense of time and place. Note the prominence of old St Paul's (minus its steeple–see page 222) in the centre of **3a** and London Bridge (displaying the heads of traitors on its South Gate–see page 209) in **3b**. Opposite St Paul's, on the south bank of the Thames, are the Bear Garden (i.e. Paris Garden–see page 168) and a theatre labelled 'The Globe' to the right. They can be seen in greater detail in **3c**. Probably, in view of its location shown here, the theatre designated as the Globe (see pages 52–3) is actually the Rose theatre. The theatre in **3d** is the Swan (see page 51) from the left-hand section of the panorama, not otherwise reproduced here.

ON

FLUVIUS

South Warke

ꞈLawrence Pountney
the Stak Bridge
St. Michaels
St. Peters
Michaell hall
St. Helens
St. Andrew
St. Dunston in the 296

Old Swan
T... hell
The Bishops
Longe

Win hyde boats
St. Mary Oues

3b

The Bear Gardine   The Globe

3c

The Swan

Wenceslas Hollar fecit

3d

4 Sketch of the interior of the Swan theatre (*c.* 1596) by Johannes de Witt (preserved in a copy by his friend Arend van Buchell). De Witt's drawing, sketched on the spot or from memory, is the only contemporary representation we possess of the interior of an Elizabethan public playhouse. In its larger details it generally confirms much of what we know from other kinds of sources about the structure of the Elizabethan–Jacobean public theatres: a more or less circular structure (except for the Fortune: see pages 54–5), open to the sky apart from three galleries (the top gallery roofed) and the covering (known as the 'heavens'), supported on two pillars, over the rear half of the stage; a raised platform stage (*'proscænium'*), somewhat wider than deep, extending into the middle of the 'yard' (*'planities siue arena'*), where the 'groundlings', entering from either side (*'ingressus'*), and surrounding the stage on three sides, stood to watch a performance; the tiring-house (*'mimorum ædes'*); and the third-level 'hut', from which a flag (here bearing the 'sign' of the Swan) was flown during performances and a trumpeter (as shown) announced, on the third call, the beginning of the play. De Witt's depiction of the rear stage wall (or 'scene'), however, raises a number of problems (see pages 51–2) so far as other public theatres are concerned.

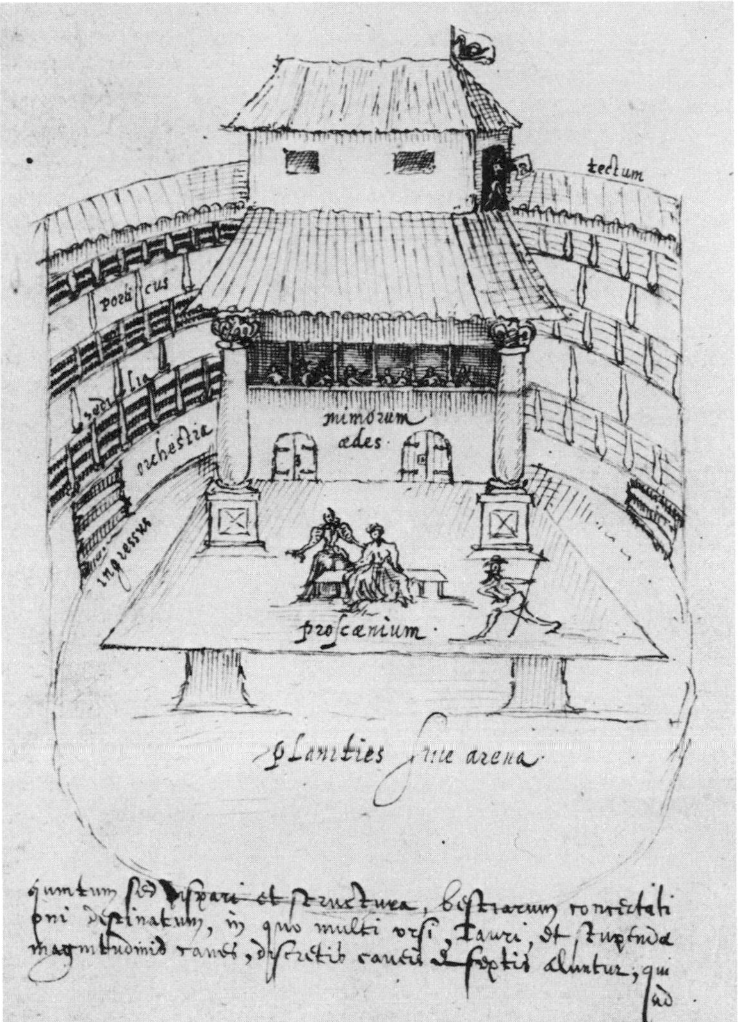

tectum

porticus

sedilia

orchestra

mimorum
aedes

ingressus

proscaenium

planities siue arena

quintum est Diuersi et permixtura, bestiarum conflicta-
oni destinatum, in quo multi ursi, Tauri, et stupenda
magnitudinis canes, distinctis cautis et septis aluntur, qui
ad

5 This pen-and-ink sketch, possibly by Henry Peacham, dates perhaps as early as 1594–95, and represents the earliest-known attempt to illustrate a scene from one of Shakespeare's plays–a point in Act I of *Titus Andronicus* which, however, the artist has apparently somewhat confused. Tamora is shown kneeling (crowned as stage kings and queens usually were), interceding for two of her sons, not merely for Alarbus as in the text of the play, while Aaron the Moor, with drawn sword and dramatic gesture, appears to be taking a more active role in the scene than his mute presence in Act I would seem to allow for. If, as seems likely, the artist is recalling a performance he has seen, the costumes are of special interest as indicating that some attempt was made to give an effect of Roman costuming to the principal characters. Note, however, the two guards, standing to the left, who are dressed in contemporary Elizabethan costume and are holding very sixteenth-century halberds.

6 Richard Burbage (*c.* 1567–1619). Painting at Dulwich College, London. Burbage, for more than twenty-five years the principal actor of Shakespeare's company (the Chamberlain's Men, later the King's Men), was famous as a tragic actor. He is credited with creating such Shakespearean roles as Richard III, Romeo, Hamlet, Othello, and Lear (see page 92), as well as Ferdinand in Webster's *The Duchess of Malfi* and Malvole in Marston's *The Malcontent*. He is also believed to have created a number of major roles in plays by Beaumont and Fletcher (e.g. Philaster in *Philaster*, Amintor in *The Maid's Tragedy*, and Arbaces in *A King and No King*).

7 William Kemp, comedian. From Kemp's *Nine Daies Wonder* (1600). Kemp, famous for his roles in comedy, particularly clowns, and as a dancer of stage jigs (see pages 363–4), was a member of Shakespeare's company (the Chamberlain's, later the King's, Men). Amongst others, he is believed to have created the roles of Costard (*Love's Labour's Lost*), Bottom (*Midsummer Night's Dream*), Dogberry (*Much Ado about Nothing*), and probably Falstaff. He danced his famous solo morris (note the bells on his legs), accompanied only by a taborer (note the drum and pipe), from London to Norwich, about a hundred miles, in the early months of 1600 and immediately after published his lively account of his Terpsichorean progress through the English countryside.

8 (right) The morris dance. An engraving of a mid fifteenth-century window at Betley in Staffordshire from Edmund Malone's edition of Shakespeare's *Works* (1790, vol. V). The intermingling of the morris dance (an early medieval folk dance, possibly English in origin), the Sword Dance, the May Game (note the maypole in no. 8), and the Robin Hood stories is clearly exhibited in the characters represented (see pages 101–2): Maid Marian (no. 2), Robin Hood as the Hobby-Horse (no. 5), both crowned as the Lord and Lady of May (Robin Hood bearing the sword of authority as well as the ladle for collecting from the spectators), and Friar Tuck (no. 3). Note also the Fool (no. 12), the Taborer (no. 9) and the dancers (nos. 1, 4, 6, etc.) who, like the Fool, wear bells on their legs.

9 From the frontispiece to Francis Kirkman's *The Wits, or, Sport upon Sport* (1672), a collection of 'drolls' (single or combined scenes from earlier plays, performed at fairs, etc. during the Commonwealth period when the theatres were officially closed, a tradition that lasted until at least the end of the eighteenth century). Note (1) the indoor platform stage, surrounded on three sides by spectators (?standing) and lighted by 'footlights' and candelabra; (2) the spectators' gallery above the 'scene'; (3) the curtained area at the rear of the stage, perhaps some kind of inner stage, or perhaps only a stage entrance, and the curtained area above, which may represent an upper-stage playing place. The engraving contains the earliest-published depiction of Shakespearean characters (Falstaff and Mistress Quickly), as well as of characters from Fletcher and Massinger's *Beggars' Bush* (Clause), Middleton and William Rowley's *The Changeling* (Antonio), Cavendish's *The Variety* (French Dancing Master), and Cooke's *Greene's Tu Quoque* (Bubble, in fool's costume, peeking out from the curtains). Simpleton figures in a droll ascribed to Robert Cox.

10 A wedding masque. This scene (see page 72), part of a larger birth-to-death memorial painting featuring the career of Sir Henry Unton (1557–96), a soldier and diplomat, is our only extant representation of an Elizabethan masque in performance. Unton, his bride, and guests are shown seated round a banqueting table. In a sunken area below them a broken consort of six musicians plays, while the costumed masquers, led in by a taborer and 'truchman' (or presenter), the latter with a paper (presumably a sort of programme note) in his hand for presentation to Lady Unton, approach the bridal party. As the mythological figures so common in masques, the masquers appear as Mercury, Diana, and six Nymphs, all wearing red masks, with ten Cupids (five white paired with five black), who act as torchbearers for the principals.

11 Pen-and-ink costume sketch by Inigo Jones for one of the twelve Queens in Ben Jonson's *The Masque of Queens* (1609). See pages 78–80. This one shows Elizabeth de Vere, Countess of Derby, as Zenobia, Queen of Palmyra, the colours of her costume noted (upper right corner) as 'watchet [light blue] the middle/carnation the petticoat/white the upperbodice'.

12 Pen-and-ink sketch by Inigo Jones of 'The House of Fame' in Ben Jonson's *The Masque of Queens* (1609). Following the anti-masque of twelve witches, set in 'an ugly *Hell*', the principal masquers were presented in 'a glorious and magnificent building, figuring the *House of Fame*', a *machina versatilis* (or revolving mechanism), which turned to reveal the figure of *Fama bona* (see Jonson's full description, pages 79–80). The twelve Queens are here shown seated in a triangular formation, with Bel-anna, Queen of the Ocean (played by Queen Anne herself) at its apex. The large doors below were used for the triumphal entry of the Queens in their chariots (see page 80).

13 A country gentleman's 'great house' or 'palace'. Photograph of the front façade of Montacute House, in Somerset, built for Sir Edward Phelips and completed about 1600. Constructed on the frequently employed H-plan of local gold-brown stone, its style represents the recently imported Italianate-classical school of architecture (see page 124). Note the forecourt, the central area probably originally arranged as a formal garden (see pages 122–3), with handsome balustrades on either side.

14 Thomas Arden's house, Faversham, Kent. Photograph of a fairly typical example of an English timbered and plastered house (see pages 123–4). Note how the second and third stories each project about a foot and that the third storey appears to be fronted by plastered wattle-work. In 1551 Thomas Arden was murdered at the instigation of his wife and her lover in the bow-windowed ground-floor room, and the whole story, as reported in detail by Holinshed (*Chronicles*, 2nd edition, 1587), became the source for a powerful domestic tragedy (anonymous) called *Arden of Faversham* (1585–92).

15 Hunting the deer. From George Turbervile's *The Noble Arte of Venerie or Hunting* (1575). Queen Elizabeth, here pictured at 'the kill' (see page 156), is being offered a knife by the Master of the Hunt to 'make assay' (i.e. to test how fat, hence flavoursome, the slain deer is). For a description of a hunt, see pages 160–3. Note the two grooms, bearing the royal cognizance on their doublets, who attend the Queen's elaborately appointed horse.

The Booke of Faulconrie or Hau-KING, FOR THE ONELY DE-

light and pleasure of all Noblemen and Gentlemen:

Collected out of the best authors, aswell Italians as Frenchmen,
and some English practises withall concernyng Faulconrie, the contentes
whereof are to be seene in the next page folowyng.
By *George Turberuile* Gentleman.

NOCET EMPTA DOLORE VOLVPTAS.

Imprinted at London for Christopher Barker, at the signe of
the Grashopper in Paules Churchyarde.   *Anno.* 1575.

16 Falconry. From the title page of George Turbervile's *The Booke of Faulconrie or Hauking* (1575). The woodcut shows three gentlemen (note their quite elaborate costumes–see pages 128–33), one bearing a falcon, hooded, belled, and leashed, on a perch held in his left hand (see pages 165–7). The dogs are spaniels, trained to retrieve birds 'hawk'd at, and kill'd' by the falcon or hawk, 'tow'ring in her pride of place' (*Macbeth*, II. iv. 12–13).

17 The game of tennis. From *Illustrissimi Wirtembergici Ducalis Novi Collegii Quod Tubingae* (n.d., c. 1589). Tennis in the sixteenth and seventeenth centuries, a favourite sport among courtiers and gallants, was an indoor game. It was played in a walled, roofed court, in which the end and side walls were used to ricochet the ball into the opponent's court. Points could also be scored by hitting the ball into one of several specially placed apertures of different sizes (dedans, grille, lunes) in each of the end walls. The projecting penthouse roof shown on the left end wall of the court (called the 'service side', the right being called the 'hazard side') also figured in the game.

Rapier and dagger

Sword and buckler

The two-handed broadsword

A 'case of rapiers'

Rapier and cloak

18 The art of defence. From Di Grassi's *His True Arte of Defence* (translated by I. G. Gentleman, 1594). See pages 158–9.

19 An Elizabethan garden. Two woodcuts from Didymus Mountain's (i.e. Thomas Hill's) *The Gardeners Labyrinth* (1577). The first pictures a fairly typical walled garden (with a single entrance at top centre), the fenced flower beds and

20 A schoolroom. Woodcut from Alexander Nowell, *Catechismus parvus pueris primum qui ediscatur, proponendus in Scholis* (1574 edition). Note the schoolboy standing before the master's desk to recite his lesson and several pleasantly humanizing touches: a boy pinching his neighbour's ear; another sneaking in late at the door; two boys, books abandoned, sharing (or fighting over) what looks like a loaf of bread; and the dog, happy with his bone, stretched out in the middle of the floor. The inevitable bundle of birch rods, badge of the master's authority (clearly visible in the cut in the first edition (1573), from which, incidentally, the nice little touches noted above are missing), is presumably hidden to the left of the desk. See pages 140–1, 145–7.

(19 continued)
grass plots laid out in a geometrical formal style, intersected and surrounded by gravel paths (see pages 122–3). Fruit trees were trained to grow flat against the inner walls, and beehives, complete with bees, may be seen in the upper right corner. To the left a gardener operates a comparatively sophisticated watering device. The second shows an intricately constructed arbour, complete with table and benches, where the master of the house, protected from the sun (shining brightly, upper right), might entertain guests with food and drink.

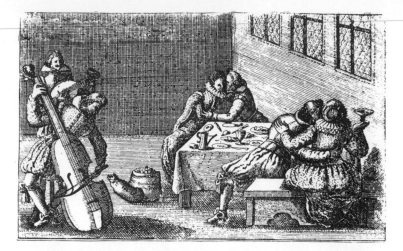

21 A tavern scene. From *Le Centre de l'Amour* (1630?). As pointed out (page 207), tavern scenes abound in the drama of the period, especially in City comedy. A tavern or ordinary was not only a place in which young gallants, *et al.*, could procure their dinner (around noon) or supper (see pages 218–20) but, as Shakespeare shows in a scene between Falstaff and Doll Common in *II Henry IV* at the Boar's Head Tavern in Eastcheap (II, iv), often a favourite locale for amorous dalliance. Like Falstaff, the two gallants here pictured have imported 'a music' to set the desired tone for their obvious intentions.

22 An Upright Man and Counterfeit Crank. From Thomas Harman, *A Caveat or Warening for Common Cursetors* (1573 edition). This rough woodcut depicts one man in two roles. As Nicholas Blunt, he was known as an Upright Man, a person of consequence and power among the fraternity of rogues and vagabonds (see page 226); as Nicholas Genings, he assumed the disguise of a counterfeit crank (a rogue who feigned various forms of debilitating sickness in order to arouse pity and collect money by begging). See Harman's lively story of his capture and unmasking (pages 230–3).

23 Fleeing the plague. Woodcut from a broadside printed in London in 1632. The focus here is on the flight of London's rich, borne off in their coaches, to the country during a plague epidemic (see pages 333–9). As the lengthy exhortation to repentance, printed below the cut, says: 'How little do they regard the poor, which they leave behind them.' But as the selection from Thomas Dekker's *The Wonderfull Yeare* (1603) emphasizes (see page 337), such escape to the countryside was often of no avail, a sad fact underscored by the artist who depicts Death, brandishing his arrow and holding an hourglass upright (time running out), astride the coach horses, and then shows him, with his hourglass reversed (time run out), standing over one of the coach passengers as she lies dead on the ground, her rich friends mourning beside her. In the background other less well-to-do Londoners are shown fleeing on horseback and on foot.

aue thriues
neuer so fast:
imblest baste.

24 Dr Faustus conjuring in his study. From the title page of Christopher
Marlowe's *Dr Faustus* (1624 edition). Faustus, dressed in full academic garb and
holding a magic staff in his right hand and a conjuring book in his left, is shown
standing warily within the cabbalistic circle he has inscribed on the pavement to
protect himself from the Devil (Mephostophilis), who may be seen starting up
through the tiles, complete with horns and tail. We may contrast Faustus' tragic
end with that of Shakespeare's Prospero, a 'white magician', who, after
promising to 'abjure rough magic', says: 'I'll break my staff,/Bury it certain
fadoms in the earth,/And deeper than did ever plummet sound/I'll drown my
book' (*The Tempest*, v.i.54–7). Note the clasped volumes arranged on a shelf with
their spines facing in, the usual way of shelving books at this period. See pages
262–4.

25 Witches and 'witch finders'. From Matthew Hopkins' *Discovery of Witches*
(1647). Hopkins, a notorious so-called 'witch finder', was responsible in one year
alone (1645–6) for sending some sixty-eight 'witches' to the gallows. He is here
pictured observing two such 'witches', who are shown accompanied by their
'familiars' (imps of Satan or demons), which were believed to assume the forms of
various domestic animals and through which they were supposed to work their
maleficia (see pages 262–71).

26 Stocking of religious dissenters. From John Foxe, *Actes and Monuments* (1583 edition). Stocks set up in an open public place were often used to punish rogues and vagabonds (see page 288), a place where the individuals stocked might conveniently be pelted with refuse by righteous citizens. Here, however, they are being employed as a form of torture inflicted during Queen Mary's reign on Protestant dissidents who have been incarcerated in the Lollards' Tower, near St Paul's, a prison where the notorious Bonner, Bishop of London, sent such 'heretics' awaiting trial. All four persons here pictured escaped being burned at the stake by dying as a result of the 'strait handling' they had received in prison. (William Andrew was actually a prisoner in Newgate Prison, not in the Lollards' Tower.) Their bodies were thrown into the open fields and only buried through the humane ministry of the 'faithful brethren' (i.e. fellow Protestants). Note the Keeper at the door, with his hand on the lever which operated the stocks. Some difference in degree of torture seems to be indicated by whether both hands and feet were stocked (cf. Leyes and Wade).

27 Pressing to death. From the title page of the anonymous *The Life and Death of Griffin Flood, Informer* (1623). Practised as late as 1716, this particularly barbarous form of torture was resorted to for those accused of felony who refused to plead (see page 288). By so refusing, the accused, if he were convicted, was able to prevent the law from confiscating his estate, thus protecting his family and heirs. The Press-yard in Newgate Prison (see page 205) was the original scene of this form of torture.

28 The Four Humours. From Thomas Walkington's *The Optick Glasse of Humors* (1639). This schema diagrams the interrelations between the four humours or body fluids (sanguine, choleric, phlegmatic, and melancholic), different combinations of which served to determine a man's or woman's temperament or personality (known as 'complexion'–see pages 324–8). Each of these humours in the microcosm (or 'little world' of man–see page 313) is interconnected with and influenced by constituents of the macrocosm (or 'great world'). Thus the sanguine humour, for example, is here shown as associated with the age of youth, the season of spring, the south wind, the element of air, the planet Jupiter, and three (Gemini, Libra, Aquarius) of the twelve signs of the zodiac.

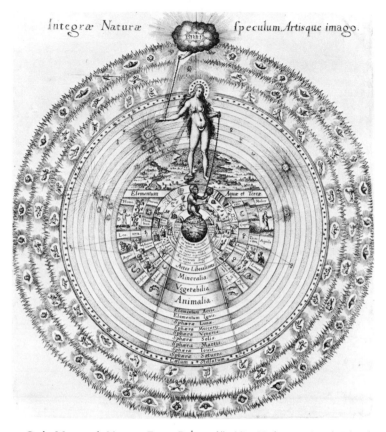

29 God, Man and Nature. From Robert Fludd's *Utriusque Cosmi Historia* (1617–19). Based on the Ptolemaic geocentric (earth-centred) concept of the universe, this imaginatively constructed schema illustrates the integration of the cosmos (macrocosm) and man (microcosm) (see pages 313, 316–17). At the top God's creating hand is shown as linked by a chain to Nature's right hand, while Nature's left hand is similarly connected to the left hand of a monkey (i.e. Man, the 'ape of Nature'), which is perched on the 'centre' (i.e. the Earth). Nature stands on the animal, vegetable, and mineral kingdoms (man and woman being shown as part of the animal kingdom), while Man, as the 'ape of Nature', measures a globe (again the Earth) with a pair of compasses, applying, symbolically, Man's reason and art to the interpretation and use of Nature. Above the Earth, which embraces the so-called elements of earth and water, range, in ascending order, the elements of air and fire, the seven planets (Moon, Mercury, Venus, Sun, Mars, Jupiter, and Saturn), the circle of the fixed stars, and the Empyrean Heaven.

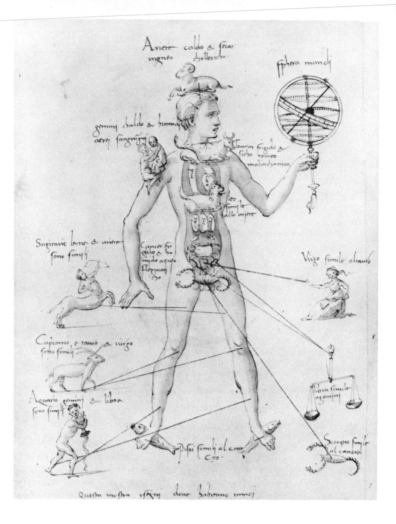

30 Man and the zodiac. From *Grilandus Inventum Libri IV* (MS, 1506–8). Each of the twelve signs of the zodiac was believed to govern a particular part of man's body. Thus, for example, the head is here shown as under the influence of Aries (the Ram) and associated with choleric humour, hot and dry; the arms as under Gemini (the Twins) and associated with the sanguine humour, hot and moist; the intestines, as under Cancer (the Crab) and associated with the phlegmatic humour, cold and moist; and the knees, as under Capricorn (the Goat). The young man bears a globe ('*sphæra mundi*') in his left hand to indicate the relation between him (microcosm) and the great world (macrocosm).

Part II

The World and the Theatre

This royal throne of kings, this sceptred isle,
This earth of majesty, this seat of Mars,
This other Eden, demi-paradise,
This fortress built by Nature for herself
Against infection and the hand of war,
This happy breed of men, this little world,
This precious stone set in the silver sea,
Which serves it in the office of a wall,
Or as a moat defensive to a house,
Against the envy of less happier lands;
This blessed plot, this earth, this realm, this England,
This nurse, this teeming womb of royal kings,
Fear'd by their breed, and famous by their birth,
Renowned for their deeds as far from home,
For Christian service and true chivalry,
As is the sepulchre in stubborn Jewry
Of the world's ransom, blessed Mary's Son; . . . . . .

Shakespeare, *Richard II*, II.i.40–56.

1 Domestic life

Food and drink

William Harrison's *The Description of England*, prefixed to Raphael Holinshed's *Chronicles of England, Scotlande, and Irelande* (1578; 2nd edn, 1587) and described by himself as 'this foul frizzled treatise', is our most immediate and detailed account of life in the England of Elizabeth. Drawing on a variety of sources, written and oral, some of them not always entirely accurate, it is also packed with his personal observations on men and manners, some of them coloured by a perhaps too fervent patriotism and his middle-class upbringing. Almost nothing is too trivial to be noticed and commented upon, often with a strongly moralistic flavouring, for, as he says in his dedicatory letter to Lord Cobham, 'I have had an especial eye unto the truth of things', a 'truth' that for him was rooted in the Elizabethan religious and political compromise; and it is characteristic that one of his favourite ways of introducing a sentence is with 'certes' (i.e. of a truth, certainly). Despite his modest disclaimer, Harrison's *Description* is, in its special way, a remarkable achievement and opens a window on the contemporary, everyday life of sixteenth-century England that students of the period still find unrivalled. There are modern editions of *The Description of England* edited by F. J. Furnivall (1877) and Georges Edelen (1968).

Selection (i), from 'Of the food and diet of the English', aside from detailing the kinds and variety of food and drink generally available, lays special stress on the comparative temperance exercised by the English, as compared with Europeans generally, in their eating and drinking. But one becomes a little sceptical about the actual restraint exercised by the English gentry when one encounters the domestic accounts of William Darrell of Littlecote. Darrell, in the role of bachelor-courtier, resided in London between 16 April and 14 July 1589, during which time he spent a grand total of £42 6s 10d for food (more, indeed, than Harrison's yearly income, which he tells us was £40). Here is a typical entry for his dinner (midday) and supper. *Dinner*: 'A piece of beef, 19 pence; a leg of mutton, 20 pence; two chickens and bacon, 20 pence (cost of roasting, 18 pence); for dressing all, 7 pence; for parsley, cloves, and sauce for the mutton, 6 pence; bread and beer, 16 pence.' *Supper*: 'A shoulder of mutton, 20 pence; three pigeons, 8 pence; for roasting the mutton, pigeons, two chickens and two rabbits, 11 pence; for sauce, sops [pieces of bread, etc., dipped in water or wine before eating or cooking], and parsley, 5 pence; bread and beer, 14 pence' (see Hubert Hall, *Society in the Elizabethan Age* (1886), p. 212). Temperance must, I think, be considered a relative term. Falstaff's famous tavern reckoning comes inevitably to mind: '*Item*, a capon, 2 shillings, 2 pence; *Item*, sauce, 4 pence; *Item*, sack, two gallons, 5 shillings, 8 pence; *Item*, anchovies and sack after supper, 2 shillings, 6 pence; *Item*, bread, a halfpenny' (*1 Henry IV*, II.iv.535–9). A good account of the domestic arrangements for food and drink in a middle-rank country household (Ingatestone Hall in Essex, the seat of Sir William Petre) may be found in F. G. Emmison's *Tudor Food and Pastimes* (1964), pp. 36–59 and Appendix A (menus).

Selection (ii), Ben Jonson's urbane verses 'Inviting a friend to supper', though suggested in many details by three of Martial's *Epigrams*, is thoroughly English and breathes an air of tolerance, good manners, and genuine conviviality – a good example of how Englishmen then and later naturalized their classical heritage.

i

From William Harrison, *The Description of England*, bk. II, chap. 6 (in Holinshed's *Chronicles*, 2nd edn, 1587).

Of the food and diet of the English
The situation of our region, lying near unto the north, doth cause the heat of our stomachs to be of somewhat greater force: therefore our bodies do crave a little more ample nourishment than the inhabitants of the hotter regions are accustomed withal,...... 5

It is no marvel therefore that our tables are oftentimes more plentifully garnished than those of other nations,......

In number of dishes and change of meat the nobility of England (whose cooks are for the most part musical-headed 10 Frenchmen and strangers) do most exceed, sith there is no day in manner that passeth over their heads wherein they have not only beef, mutton, veal, lamb, kid, pork, cony, capon, pig, or so many of these as the season yieldeth, but also some portion of the red or fallow-deer, beside great variety of fish and wild-fowl,......so 15 that for a man to dine with one of them, and to taste of every dish that standeth before him (which few use to do, but each one feedeth upon that meat him best liketh for the time, the beginning of every dish notwithstanding being reserved unto the greatest personage that sitteth at the table, to whom it is drawn up still by 20 the waiters as order requireth, and from whom it descendeth again even to the lower end, whereby each one may taste thereof), is rather to yield unto a conspiracy with a great deal of meat for the speedy suppression of natural health, than the use of a necessary mean to satisfy himself with a competent repast to sustain his body 25 withal......

The chief part likewise of their daily provision is brought in before them (commonly in silver vessel, if they be of the degree of barons, bishops, and upwards) and placed on their tables, whereof, when they have taken what it pleaseth them, the rest is reserved 30 and afterward sent down to their serving-men and waiters, who feed thereon in like sort with convenient moderation, their reversion also being bestowed upon the poor which lie ready at their gates in great numbers to receive the same......As for drink, it is usually filled in pots, goblets, jugs, bowls of silver, in 35 noblemen's houses; also in fine Venice glasses of all forms, and, for want of these elsewhere, in pots of earth of sundry colours and moulds, whereof many are garnished with silver, or at the leastwise in pewter, all which notwithstanding are seldom set on the table, but each one, as necessity urgeth, calleth for a cup of such drink as 40 him listeth to have,......

It is a world to see in these our days, wherein gold and silver most aboundeth, how that our gentility, as loathing those metals (because of the plenty) do now generally choose rather the Venice glasses, both for our wine and beer, than any of those metals or stone wherein before time we have been accustomed to drink; but such is the nature of man generally that it most coveteth things difficult to be attained;...... And as this is seen in the gentility, so in the wealthy communalty the like desire of glass is not neglected,...... 45

50

The poorest also will have glass if they may; but, sith the Venetian is somewhat too dear for them, they content themselves with such as are made at home of fern and burned stone; but in fine all go one way – that is, to shards at the last, so that our great expenses in glasses (beside that they breed much strife toward such as have the charge of them) are worst of all bestowed in mine opinion, because their pieces do turn unto no profit...... 55

To be short, at such time as the merchants do make their ordinary or voluntary feasts, it is a world to see what great provision is made of all manner of delicate meats, from every quarter of the country, wherein, beside that they are often comparable herein to the nobility of the land, they will seldom regard anything that the butcher usually killeth, but reject the same as not worthy to come in place. In such cases also gellifs of all colours, mixed with a variety in the representation of sundry flowers, herbs, trees, forms of beasts, fish, fowls and fruits, and thereunto marchpane wrought with no small curiosity, tarts of divers hues and sundry denominations, conserves of old fruits, foreign and home-bred, suckets, codinacs, marmalets, marchpane, sugar-bread, gingerbread, florentines, wild-fowl, venison of all sorts, and sundry outlandish confections, altogether seasoned with sugar,......do generally bear the sway, besides infinite devices of our own not possible for me to remember. Of the potato, and such venerous roots as are brought out of Spain, Portingal, and the Indies to furnish up our banquets, I speak not...... 60

65

70

75

[Harrison describes the various kinds of wines, homegrown and imported, light (of which there were fifty-six kinds) and strong.]

The beer that is used at noblemen's tables in their fixed and standing houses is commonly of a year old, or peradventure of two years' tunning or more, but this is not general. It is also brewed in March, and therefore called March beer. But for the household, it is usually not under a month's age,...... 80

The artificer and husbandman make greatest account of such meat as they may soonest come by, and have it quickliest ready,......Their food also consisteth principally in beef and such meat as the butcher selleth, that is to say, mutton, veal, lamb, 85

pork, etc., whereof he [the artificer] findeth great store in the markets adjoining, beside souse, brawn, bacon, fruit, pies of fruit, fowls of sundry sorts, cheese, butter, eggs, etc.; as the other wanteth it not at home, by his own provision, which is at the best hand and commonly least charge. In feasting also this latter sort (I   90
mean the husbandman) do exceed after their manner, especially at bride-ales, purifications of women, and such odd meetings, where it is incredible to tell what meat is consumed and spent, each one bringing such a dish, or so many with him as his wife and he do consult upon,......   95

I might here talk somewhat of the great silence that is used at the tables of the honourable and wiser sort generally over all the realm,...... likewise of the moderate eating and drinking that is daily seen, and finally of the regard that each one hath to keep himself from the note of surfeiting and drunkenness......but, as   100
in rehearsal thereof I should commend the nobleman, merchant, and frugal artificer, so I could not clear the meaner sort of husbandmen and country inhabitants of very much babbling (except it be here and there some odd yeoman), with whom he is thought to be the merriest that talketh of most ribaldry or the   105
wisest man that speaketh fastest among them, and now and then surfeiting and drunkenness, which they rather fall into for want of heed-taking than wilfully following or delighting in those errors of set mind and purpose. It may be that divers of them living at home, with hard and pinching diet, small drink, and some of them   110
having scarce enough of that, are soonest overtaken when they come unto such banquets; howbeit they take it generally as no small disgrace if they happen to be cupshotten,...... If the friends also of the wealthier sort come to their houses from far, they are commonly so welcome till they depart as upon the first   115
day of their coming; whereas in good towns and cities, as London, etc., men oftentimes complain of little room, and, in reward of a fat capon or plenty of beef and mutton largely bestowed upon them in the country, a cup of wine or beer with a napkin to wipe their lips and an 'You are heartily welcome!' is thought to be great   120
entertainment......

The bread throughout the land is made of such grain as the soil yieldeth; nevertheless the gentility commonly provide themselves sufficiently of wheat for their own tables, whilest their household and poor neighbours in some shires are enforced to content   125
themselves with rye or barley, yea, in time of dearth, many with bread made either of beans, peasen, or oats, or of all together and some acorns among, of which scourge the poorest do soonest taste, sith they are least able to provide themselves of better......   130

With us the nobility, gentry, and students do ordinarily go to dinner at eleven before noon, and to supper at five or between five

and six at afternoon. The merchants dine and sup seldom before twelve at noon, and six at night, especially in London. The husbandmen dine also at high noon as they call it, and sup at seven   135
or eight; but out of the term in our universities the scholars dine at ten. As for the poorest sort they generally dine and sup when they may, so that to talk of their order of repast it were but a needless matter......But whereas we commonly begin with the most gross food, and end with the most delicate, the Scot, thinking   140
much to leave the best for his menial servants, maketh his entrance at the best, so that he is sure thereby to leave the worst. We use also our wines by degrees, so that the hottest cometh last to the table: but to stand upon such toys would spend much time and turn to small profit.   145

NOTES

10   *musical-headed* ?light-headed.
11–12 *in manner* of any kind.
13   *cony* rabbit.
15   *fallow-deer* species of deer, smaller than the red deer.
33   *reversion* leavings.
36   *Venice glasses* Then, as now, Venice was famous for the manufacture of glass-ware of all kinds.
37   *pots of earth* earthenware pots, stoneware.
42   *It......world* It is a marvel.
46   *stone* i.e. stoneware.
49   *communalty* citizens below the rank of gentlemen.
53   *fern......stone* earthenware fired in fern faggots.
53–4 *in fine* in the end.
54   *shards* fragments
59   *ordinary* regularly instituted (by a particular guild).
      voluntary unscheduled, special.
64   *gellifs* ?jellies (not in *OED*).
67   *marchpane* marzipan, confection made of the paste of ground almonds, sugar, etc.
      curiosity artistic workmanship.
69   *suckets* sweetmeats of candied fruit or vegetable products.
      codinacs codiniacs, quince marmalades.
      marmalets marmalades.
70   *sugar-bread* bread sprinkled with sugar.
      florentines meat baked in a dish with a pastry cover.
71   *outlandish* foreign.
72   *sugar* See below, p. 178, ll. 13–15.
74   *potato......roots* Sweet potatoes were generally thought to act as an aphrodisiac; common white potatoes were not known in England until about 1596 (Edelen).
77–8 *fixed......houses* permanent residences.

79 *tunning* storage in cask or tun.
80 *household* i.e. the servants.
80–1 *it.......age* i.e. it is usually aged over a month, but presumably not much
      more.
82 *artificer* craftsman.
    husbandman farmer.
87 *souse* pickled meat, mostly pork (feet and ears).
    brawn pickled or potted boar's flesh.
89–90 *at......hand* most handily located.
92 *bride-ales* wedding feasts.
    purifications of women celebrations of thanksgiving for recovery from
    childbirth. The Prayer Book (1549/52) contains an 'Order of the
    Purification [*or* Churching] of Women'.
    odd special (not occurring at set times).
104 *odd yeoman* occasional small landholder, under the rank of gentleman.
113 *cupshotten* intoxicated.
116 *good* i.e. good-sized.
117 *in reward of* in comparison with.
127 *peasen* peas (plural form).
140–1 *thinking much* i.e. thinking it too much.
143 *hottest* ?strongest; ?wine that has been heated, e.g. burnt sack.

ii

From Ben Jonson, *Epigrammes*, no. 101, in *The Workes* (1616).

Inviting a friend to supper

Tonight, grave sir, both my poor house and I
    Do equally desire your company:
Not that we think us worthy such a guest,
    But that your worth will dignify our feast
With those that come; whose grace may make that seem   5
    Something, which, else, could hope for no esteem.
It is the fair acceptance, sir, creates
    The entertainment perfect, not the cates.
Yet shall you have, to rectify your palate,
    An olive, capers, or some better sallad   10
Ush'ring the mutton; with a short-legg'd hen,
    If we can get her, full of eggs, and then
Limons, and wine for sauce; to these, a cony
    It is not to be despair'd of for our money;
And though fowl, now, be scarce, yet there are clerks,   15
    The sky not falling, think we may have larks.
I'll tell you of more, and lie, so you will come:
    Of partrich, pheasant, wood-cock, of which some
May yet be there; and godwit, if we can:
    Gnat, rail, and ruff too. Howsoe'er, my man   20
Shall read a piece of Virgil, Tacitus,
    Livy, or of some better book to us,
Of which we'll speak our minds, amidst our meat;
    And I'll profess no verses to repeat:
To this, if ought appear, which I do not know of,   25
    That will the pastry, not my paper, show of.
Digestive cheese and fruit there sure will be;
    But that which most doth take my *Muse*, and me,
Is a pure cup of rich canary wine,
    Which is the Mermaid's now, but shall be mine;   30
Of which had Horace or Anacreon tasted,
    Their lives, as do their lines, till now had lasted.
Tobacco, nectar, or the Thespian spring
    Are all but Luther's beer to this I sing.
Of this we will sup free, but moderately,   35
    And we will have no Pooly or Parrot by;
Nor shall our cups make any guilty men,
    But, at our parting, we will be as when
We innocently met. No simple word
    That shall be utter'd at our mirthful board   40
Shall make us sad next morning, or affright
    The liberty that we'll enjoy tonight.

NOTES

1ff.   Jonson's poem is indebted to three of Martial's *Epigrams* (bk. V, lxxviii; X, xlviii; XI, lii).

3–6   This beautifully turned compliment is Jonson's own.

7–8   *It . . . . . . cates* i.e. the generous reception of the entertainment as a whole is what makes the occasion perfect, not the delicacies ('cates') served.

13   *Limons* lemons (variant form).

15   *clerks* learned men.

16   *sky not falling* Even though the sky doesn't fall. The proverb is 'When the sky falls, we shall have larks' (Tilley S517), said about something most unlikely to happen.

18   *partrich* partridge (variant form).

19   *godwit* marsh-bird resembling a curlew.

20   *Gnat* kind of sandpiper.
     rail corn-crake.
     ruff small freshwater fish of the perch family.
     my man my servant (?Richard Brome).

24   *profess . . . . . . repeat* i.e. promise not to recite any of my poems.

25   *To this* in addition to all this.

26   *paper* i.e. the present 'paper' of verses.

29   *canary wine* light sweet wine from the Canary Islands.

30   *Which . . . . . . mine* i.e. wine, at present at the Mermaid Tavern, which I will procure for the feast. The Mermaid was a favourite haunt of Jonson's.

33   *Thespian spring* Thespis was traditionally the father of Greek tragedy; hence the 'Thespian spring' was the source from which dramatists drew their inspiration.

34   *Luther's beer* ?German beer of poor quality.

36   *Pooly or Parrot* two known government informers, who might report one for supposedly treasonous remarks made *in vino*.

Houses and furniture

The following selection from William Harrison's *The Description of England* (in Holinshed's *Chronicles*, 2nd edn, 1587) is taken from bk. II, chap. 12: 'Of the manner of building and furniture of our houses'. The second half of the sixteenth century was a period of heavy inflation and economic growth, and Harrison is keenly conscious that he is living in rapidly changing times. His attitude, as one who must have felt the financial pressure, is a mixture of admiration for the growing signs of England's prosperity, measured by a new comparatively lavish standard of living, tinged with a strong sense of outrage at the greed and (to him) extreme luxury which characterized the behaviour of too many in positions of authority or in mercantile pursuits: the 'good old days' versus the new age of 'progress'. Harrison would have shared Ben Jonson's admiration for the old-fashioned virtues, architectural, agricultural and social, which still distinguished the Sidney family's 'great house' and estate at Penshurst in Kent (see his well-known topographical poem 'To Penshurst').

When Harrison talks of 'furniture' he is referring to household furnishings generally; the only pieces of 'furniture' in our present sense that he lists are a bed and a cupboard (or sideboard). Descriptions and illustrations of Elizabethan–Jacobean tables, chairs, stools, beds, cupboards, settles, etc. may be found in *Shakespeare's England*, ed. Sidney Lee (1916), II, 119–33, and Percy MacQuoid, *A History of English Furniture*, 4 vols. (1904–8). For stage 'furniture', see the section on 'Costumes, properties and scenery', p. 70.

Formal gardens (as well as herb, fruit and vegetable gardens) were, of course, a regular part of the exterior 'furniture' of both the so-called 'great houses' and the houses of the well-to-do gentry. As Harrison ('Of gardens and orchards', bk. II, chap. 20) exclaims:

> If you look into our gardens annexed to our houses, how wonderfully is their beauty increased, not only with flowers, ... and variety of curious and costly workmanship, but also with rare and medicinable herbs sought up [searched for] in the land within these forty years; so that, in comparison of this present, the ancient gardens were but dunghills and laystows [refuse heaps] to such as did possess them. How art also helpeth nature in the daily colouring, doubling, and enlarging the proportion of our flowers, it is incredible to report: for so curious and cunning [learned] are our gardeners now in these days that they presume to do in manner what they list with nature, and moderate her course in things as if they were her superiors.

The English love of gardens is proverbial and even the cool-tempered Francis Bacon waxes enthusiastic when, in 'Of Gardens' (*Essayes* (1625), no. 46)), he turns to describe the ideal garden proper for a noble house, the kind of 'palace' he had sketched in the complementary essay, 'Of Building' (no. 45). On a less rarefied level, Didymus Mountain (i.e. Thomas Hill), in *The Gardeners Labyrinth* (1577), affords detailed practical advice on the planning, planting and loving care of gardens generally. See Roy Strong, *The Renaissance Garden* (1982) and illustration 19.

i

Of the manner of building and furniture of our houses

From William Harrison, *The Description of England*, bk. II, chap. 12 (in Holinshed's *Chronicles*, 2nd edn, 1587).

The greatest part of our building in the cities and good towns of England consisteth only of timber, for as yet few of the houses of the communalty (except here and there in the west-country towns) are made of stone, although they may (in my opinion) in divers other places be builded so good cheap of the one as of the other.   5
In old time the houses of the Britons were slightly set up with a few posts and many raddles, with stable and all offices under one roof, the like whereof almost is to be seen in the fenny countries and northern parts unto this day, where for lack of wood they are enforced to continue this ancient manner of building......In   10
like sort as every country house in thus apparelled on the outside, so is it inwardly divided into sundry rooms above and beneath; and, where plenty of wood is, they cover them with tiles, otherwise with straw, sedge, or reed, except some quarry of slate be near-hand, from whence they have for their money so much as may suffice them.   15
The clay wherewith our houses are impanelled is either white, red, or blue; and of these the first doth participate very much with the nature of our chalk, the second is called loam, but the third eftsoons changeth colour so soon as it is wrought, notwithstanding that it look blue when it is thrown out of the pit......   20
The walls of our houses on the inner sides......be either hanged with tapestry, arras work, or painted cloths, wherein either divers histories, or herbs, beasts, knots and such like are stained, or else they are ceiled with oak of our own, or wainscot brought hither out of the east countries, whereby the rooms are not a little   25
commended, made warm and much more close than otherwise they would be. As for stoves, we have not hitherto used them

greatly, yet do they now begin to be made in divers houses of the
gentry and wealthy citizens, who build them not to work and feed
in, as in Germany and elsewhere, but now and then to sweat in, as   30
occasion and need shall require it.

This also hath been common in England, contrary to the
customs of all other nations, and yet be seen (for example, in most
streets of London), that many of our greatest houses have
outwardly been very simple and plain to sight, which inwardly   35
have been able to receive a duke with his whole train, and lodge
them at their ease. Hereby, moreover, it is come to pass that the
fronts of our streets have not been so uniform and orderly builded
as those of foreign cities, where (to say truth) the utterside of their
mansions and dwellings have oft more cost bestowed upon them   40
than all the rest of the house, which are often very simple and
uneasy within, as experience doth confirm. Of old time, our
country houses, instead of glass, did use much lattice, and that
made either of wicker or fine rifts of oak in chequerwise. I read
also that some of the better sort, in and before the times of the   45
Saxons......did make panels of horn instead of glass, and fix
them in wooden calms. But as horn in windows is now quite laid
down in every place, so our lattices are also grown into less use,
because glass is come to be so plentiful and within a very little so
good cheap, if not better than the other......   50

The ancient manors and houses of our gentlemen are yet, and
for the most part, of strong timber, in framing whereof our
carpenters have been and are worthily preferred before those of
like science among all other nations. Howbeit, such as be lately
builded are commonly either of brick or hard stone, or both, their   55
rooms large and comely, and houses of office further distant from
their lodgings. Those of the nobility are likewise wrought with
brick and hard stone, as provision may best be made, but so
magnificent and stately as the basest house of a baron doth often
match in our days with some honours of princes in old time. So   60
that if ever curious building did flourish in England, it is in these
our years,......

The furniture of our houses also exceedeth, and is grown in
manner even to passing delicacy: and herein I do not speak of the
nobility and gentry only, but likewise of the lowest sort in most   65
places of our south country that have anything at all to take to.
Certes, in noblemen's houses it is not rare to see abundance of
arras, rich hangings of tapestry, silver vessel, and so much other
plate as may furnish sundry cupboards to the sum oftentimes of a
thousand or two thousand pounds at the least,......Likewise in   70
the houses of knights, gentlemen, merchantmen, and some other
wealthy citizens, it is not geason to behold generally their great
provision of tapestry, Turkey work, pewter, brass, fine linen, and
thereto costly cupboards of plate, worth five or six hundred or a

thousand pounds to be deemed by estimation. But, as herein all   75
these sorts do far exceed their elders and predecessors, and in
neatness and curiosity the merchant all other, so in time past the
costly furniture stayed there, whereas now it is descended yet lower
even unto the inferior artificers and many farmers, who, by virtue
of their old and not of their new leases, have for the most part   80
learned also to garnish their cupboards with plate, their joined
beds with tapestry and silk hangings, and their tables with carpets
and fine napery, whereby the wealth of our country (God be
praised therefore, and give us grace to employ it well) doth
infinitely appear......   85

There are old men yet dwelling in the village where I remain
which have noted three things to be marvellously altered in
England within their sound remembrance, and other three things
too too much increased.

One is the multitude of chimneys lately erected, whereas in   90
their young days there were not above two or three, if so many, in
most uplandish towns of the realm (the religious houses and manor
places of their lords always excepted, and peradventure some great
personages), but each one made his fire against a reredos in the
hall, where he dined and dressed his meat.   95

The second is the great (although not general) amendment of
lodging; for, said they, our fathers, yea and we ourselves also, have
lien full oft upon straw pallets, on rough mats covered only with a
sheet, under coverlets made of dagswain or hop-harlots (I use their
own terms), and a good round log under their heads instead of a   100
bolster or pillow. If it were so that our fathers or the goodman of
the house had within seven years after his marriage purchased a
mattress or flock-bed, and thereto a sack of chaff to rest his head
upon, he thought himself to be as well lodged as the lord of the
town,.....which also is not very much amended as yet in some   105
parts of Bedfordshire, and elsewhere, further off from our southern
parts. Pillows (said they) were thought meet only for women in
childbed. As for servants, if they had any sheet above them, it was
well, for seldom had they any under their bodies to keep them
from the pricking straws that ran oft through the canvas of the   110
pallet and rased their hardened hides.

The third thing they tell of is the exchange of vessel, as of treen
platters into pewter, and wooden spoons into silver or tin. For so
common were all sorts of treen stuff in old time that a man should
hardly find four pieces of pewter (of which one was peradventure a   115
salt) in a good farmer's house, and yet for all this frugality (if it
may so be justly called) they were scarce able to live and pay their
rents at their days without selling of a cow or a horse or more,
although they paid but four pounds at the uttermost by the
year......Whereas in my time, although peradventure four   120
pounds of old rent be improved to forty, fifty, or a hundred

pounds, yet will the farmer, as another palm or date tree, think his gains very small toward the end of his term if he have not six or seven years' rent lying by him, therewith to purchase a new lease, beside a fair garnish of pewter on his cupboard, with so much   125 more in odd vessel going about the house, three or four feather beds, so many coverlets and carpets of tapestry, a silver salt, a bowl for wine (if not a whole nest), and a dozen of spoons to furnish up the suit......

NOTES

1   *good* i.e. good-sized.

3   *communalty* citizens below the rank of gentlemen.

5   *so good cheap* as cheaply.

7   *raddles* slender rods, wattles or lath, fastened to or twisted between upright stakes or posts to form a fence, partition, or wall (in the latter case usually plastered over with clay).

       offices i.e. the kitchen, pantry, scullery, laundry, etc.

13–14 *with straw......reed* i.e. with thatching.

16   *impanelled* plastered, as panelling, between the cross-beams of the walls (both inner and outer).

18   *loam* composition of moistened clay and sand, mixed with horse-dung, chopped straw, etc.

19   *eftsoons* at once.

22   *arras work* tapestry fabric, sometimes hung, on screens, around apartments far enough from the wall that an individual could be concealed behind it. Polonius hides behind the arras (*Hamlet*, IV.i.8–10).

       painted cloths the poor man's tapestry, suitable to a tavern. See *I Henry IV*, IV.ii.25–6, referring to the story ('history') of Dives and Lazarus.

23   *knots* figures of intertwined flowers, etc.

24   *ceiled* panelled.

       wainscot oak panelling, imported from eastern Europe ('east countries').

26   *commended* set off to advantage.

       close tight, less draughty.

27   *stoves* hot air baths, sweating-rooms.

39   *utterside* outerside.

42   *uneasy* uncomfortable.

43   *lattice* openwork screen used in windows in place of glass.

44   *fine rifts* narrow strips of oak, split not sawed.

47   *calms* frames.

47–8 *laid down* abandoned.

54   *science* craft, trade.

59   *baron* member of the lowest order of the nobility.

60   *honours* manors.

61   *curious* skilful, expert.

63   *furniture* furnishings generally.

64   *passing delicacy* extreme luxuriousness.

66   *have......take to* i.e. have any means to undertake (such purchases).

68   *vessel* vessels, utensils (collective singular).

69   *plate* silver and silver-gilt serving-dishes.
      cupboards sideboards.
72   *geason* rare, uncommon.
73   *Turkey work* Turkish tapestry work.
77   *neatness and curiosity* elegance and elaborateness (with a suggestion of excess).
80   *leases* Rent leases for tenant farmers were sharply increased during the second half of the sixteenth century. See ll. 120–2.
81–2 *joined beds* beds made by a joiner, as distinguished from those of more clumsy workmanship (carpenter's work).
82   *carpets* i.e. used as table coverings.
88   *other three things* Harrison lists these, later, as (1) the sharp increase in rents; (2) the extortionate rise in rates to tenants who held their lands by copyhold from the lord of the manor; (3) the steadily growing practice of usury (see p. 284).
92   *uplandish* inland, remote, hence rustic and rude.
94   *reredos* brick or stone back of a fire place or open hearth.
97   *lodging* bedding (earliest use 1683 *OED*).
98   *lien* lain.
99   *dagswain or hop-harlots* rough shaggy material or patches of coarse material.
101   *bolster* long, rounded stuffed pillow, now used only as an under-pillow.
103   *flock-bed* mattress filled with tufts and refuse of wool or cotton.
111   *rased* scratched or cut.
114   *treen* wooden.
116   *salt* salt-cellar.
122   *as . . . . . . tree* as though he were a palm or date tree. Palm trees were reputed to thrive under heavy weights. See Tilley P37.
129   *suit* set.

Clothes

The excessive fondness of Elizabethans and Jacobeans for expensive, overdecorated, unfunctional clothing and foreign fashions drew fire from many sources, particularly from Puritan writers or from those who could not afford such clothing. The complaints were not new. William Harrison (*The Description of England*, bk. II, chap. 7, edn of 1587) begins his account of 'Their apparel and attire' by recalling how Andrew Borde in his *Introduction of Knowledge* (1547) had thrown up his hands when it came to describing an Englishman's clothes and satisfied himself by showing a woodcut of a naked man with a pair of shears in one hand and a remnant of cloth over his other arm 'to the end he should shape his apparel after such fashion as himself liked, sith he could find no kind of garment that could please him any while together; and this he called an Englishman.' As Harrison notes a little later:

> And as these fashions are divers, so likewise it is a world [i.e. marvel] to see the costliness and the curiosity [excessive ingenuity], the excess and the vanity, the pomp and the bravery [ostentation], the change and the variety, and finally the fickleness and the folly that is in all degrees [social levels], insomuch that nothing is more constant in England than inconstancy of attire.

And Ulpian Fulwell in the interlude *Like Will to Like, Quoth the Devil to the Collier* (1562–8) introduces a Vice figure named Nichol Newfangle, who in his service to the Devil boasts:

> I learn'd to make gowns with long sleeves and wings;
> I learn'd to make ruffs like calves' chitterlings [mesenteries],
> Caps, hats, coats, with all kinds of apparels,
> And especially breeches as big as good barrels;
> Shoes, boots, buskins, with many pretty toys:
> All kinds of garments for men, women, and boys.

See, also, the historical description of English clothing in the section on 'Apparel' in William Camden's *Remaines of a Greater Worke Concerning Britaine* (1605).

As we might expect, Thomas Nashe (*Christes Teares over Jerusalem* (1593), ed. McKerrow, II, 142) takes his fling at the 'immorality' of the extreme fashions:

> England, the players' stage of gorgeous attire, the ape of all nations' superfluities, the continual masquer in outlandish [foreign] habiliments, great plenty-scanting calamities art thou to await for wanton disguising thyself against kind [nature] and digressing from the plainness of thine ancestors.

And Thomas Dekker (*The Seven Deadly Sinnes of London* (1606), ed. A. B. Grosart, *Prose Works*, II, 59–60) echoes the common complaint:

For an Englishman's suit is like a traitor's body that hath been hanged, drawn, and quartered and is set up in several places: his codpiece is in Denmark, the collar of his doublet and the belly in France, the wing and narrow sleeve in Italy; the short waist hangs over a Dutch botcher's [tailor who does repairs] stall in Utrecht, his huge slops [wide, baggy breeches] speaks Spanish, Polonia gives him the boots, the block [hat-mould] for his head alters faster than the feltmaker [hatter) can fit him, and thereupon we are called in scorn *blockheads*.

Or, as Fynes Moryson (*Itinerary* (1617), bk. III, part iii, chap. 2) puts it: 'they have in this one age worn out all the fashions of France and all the nations of Europe and tired their own inventions, which are no less busy in finding out new and ridiculous fashions than in scraping up money for such idle expences'. Finally, Henry Peacham at the end of our period, looking back, thus describes an Elizabethan gallant:

In Queen Elizabeth's time were the great-bellied doublets, wide saucy sleeves that would be in every dish before their master, and buttons as big as tablemen [pieces used in a board game] or the lesser sort of Sandwich turnips, with huge ruffs that stood like cartwheels about their necks, and round breeches not much unlike St Omer's onions, whereunto the long stocking without garters was joined ('Of Following the Fashion' in *The Truth of Our Times* (1638)).

In selections (i) and (ii), from *The Anatomie of Abuses* (1583, 2nd edn), Philip Stubbes, despite his usual fulminating style, casts a surprisingly microscopic eye (one might almost say a grudgingly fascinated eye) on the 'wicked' excesses of Elizabethan costume, men's (i) and women's (ii). He has really studied his subject and affords us lovingly detailed descriptions of the 'enormities' he holds up for moral and social condemnation. Stubbes again attacks tailors, shoemakers, and expensive fashions in *The Second Part of the Anatomie of Abuses* (1583), sigs. E8 v–F4 v.

It will be noticed that Stubbes (along with Harrison and others) is disturbed not only by the fantastic elaboration and wasteful expense involved, an expense that many could ill afford, but by the way in which commoners (tradesmen, apprentices, artisans, yeomen, even labourers, their wives and children) insisted upon aping the fashions of their presumed betters (the nobility and gentry). Such ostentation among the lower orders tended to blur the lines of what a proper-thinking Elizabethan believed to be natural class distinctions, and the government, in 1565, re-enacted several of the sumptuary laws from the earlier times of Henry VIII. These laws, for example, made it illegal for any but the nobility to wear imported woollen fabrics; only those with an income in excess of £200 a year might wear 'velvet or embroidery, or pricking with gold, silver, or silk'; and only those with £100 a year might wear satin, damask, silk, camlet, or taffeta (see H. D. Traill, *Social England* (1898), III, 389). But England's was an upwardly mobile economy, in which the new wealth of middle-class tradesmen and other business entrepreneurs was beginning to exercise its growing power, and such sumptuary laws had little significant effect in stemming the tide of social change. 'Many good laws have been made against this Babylonian confusion, but either the merchants buying out the penalty, or the magistrates not inflicting punishments, have made the multitude of laws hitherto unprofitable' (Moryson, *Itinerary* (1617), bk. III, part iii, chap. 2).

Peter Erondell, in *The French Garden* (1605), one of the popular language manuals, despite its obviously didactic burden and rather stiff dialogue, offers a usefully detailed contemporary picture (with passing reference to all the common appurtenances of an Elizabethan lady's bedchamber and to a wide variety of specific articles of clothing) that would be hard to improve upon for sheer concentration. Erondell gets everything in and manages a little mild dramatic byplay at the same time, particularly in the character of the Lady, whose demanding petulance nicely illustrates part of the proverb reported by Fynes Moryson (*Itinerary*, bk. III, part iii, chap. 3): 'England is the Hell of horses, the purgatory of servants, and the paradise of women; because they ride horses without measure, and use their servants imperiously and their women obsequiously.'

It is important to recognize, however, that the strictures of Stubbes and his fellow critics were aimed at a comparatively small proportion of the population, the privileged or those who had enough money to pay for anything more than the bare necessities of life, a group that, between say 1576 and 1642, represented only roughly about four to seven per cent (see Ann J. Cook, *The Privileged Playgoers of Shakespeare's London* (1981), p. 94). The great majority, including many well-to-do members of the middle class (as Moryson is careful to point out) and, of course, the poor, were generally unaffected by the everchanging tides of fashion, particularly in the countryside.

Elizabethan–Jacobean drama is packed with references, frequently mysterious to the modern reader, to the clothing of the period. Most plays were acted in contemporary costumes, with little or no attention to time or locale. See 'Costumes, properties and scenery', particularly selection (i); Philip Henslowe's lists of costumes in the possession of the Admiral's Men in 1598 (*Henslowe's Diary*, ed. R. A. Foakes and R. T. Richert (1961), pp. 317–23); M. C. Linthicum, *Costume in the Drama of Shakespeare and his Contemporaries* (1936).

i

A particular description of [men's] apparel in Ailgna [i.e. Anglia or England] by degrees

From Philip Stubbes, *The Anatomie of Abuses* (1583, 2nd edn), pp. 49–61 in F. J. Furnivall's edn (1877–9).

......Wherefore to begin first with their hats. Sometimes they use them sharp on the crown, perking up like the sphere, or shaft of a steeple, standing a quarter of a yard above the crown of their heads, some more, some less, as please the fantasies of their inconstant minds. Othersome be flat, and broad on the crown, like 5 the battlements of a house. Another sort have round crowns, sometimes with one kind of [coloured] band, sometime with another......And as the fashions be rare and strange, so is the stuff whereof their hats be made divers also: for some are of silk, some of velvet, some of taffety, some of sarcenet, some of wool, 10 and, which is more curious, some of a certain kind of fine hair......These they call beaver hats, of twenty, thirty, or forty shillings price, fetched from beyond the seas, from whence a great sort of other [vanities] do come besides......

They have great and monstrous ruffs, made either of cambric, 15 holland, lawn, or else of some other the finest cloth that can be got for money, whereof some be a quarter of a yard deep, yea, some more, very few less. So that they stand a full quarter of a yard (and more) from their necks, hanging over their shoulder points instead of a veil. But if Aeolus with his blasts, or Neptune with his storms, 20 chance to hit upon the crazy bark of their bruised ruffs, then they go flip-flap in the wind like rags that flew abroad, lying upon their shoulders like the dishclout of a slut. But wot you what? The Devil ...hath..... now found out also two great pillars to bear up and maintain this his kingdom of great ruffs,......the 25 one arch or pillar whereby his kingdom of great ruffs is underpropped is a certain kind of liquid matter which they call starch, wherein the Devil hath willed them to wash and dive their ruffs well,......The other pillar is a certain device made of wires crested for the purpose, whipped over either with gold thread, 30 silver, or silk, and this he calleth a supportasse or underpropper. This is to be applied round about their necks under the ruff,......

Their shirts, which all in a manner do wear (for if the nobility or gentry only did wear them, it were somedeal more tolerable) are 35 either of cameric, holland, lawn, or else of the finest cloth that may be got......And these shirts (sometimes it happeneth) are wrought throughout with needlework of silk,......

Their doublets are no less monstrous than the rest; for now the fashion is to have them hang down to the middle of their thighs, 40 or at least to their privy members, being so hard-quilted, stuffed, bombasted, and sewed, as they can neither work, nor yet well play in them, through the excessive heat thereof, and therefore are forced to wear them loose about them, otherwise they could very hardly either stoop or decline themselves to the ground, so stiff and sturdy they stand about them......

Then they have hosen, which as they be of divers fashions so are they of sundry names. Some be called French hose, some gally-hose, and some Venetians. The French hose are of two divers makings, for the common French hose (as they list to call them) containeth length, breadth, and sideness sufficient, and is made very round. The other containeth neither length, breadth, nor sideness (being not past a quarter of a yard side),...... The gally-hosen are made very large and wide, reaching down to their knees only, with three or four guards apiece laid down along either hose. And the Venetian hosen, they reach beneath the knee to the gartering place of the leg, where they are tied finely with silk points, or some such like,...... They be made of silk, velvet, satin, damask, and other such precious things beside. Yea, everyone, servingman and other inferior to them in every condition, will not stick to flaunt it out in these kind of hosen, with all other their apparel suitable thereunto......

Then have they netherstocks to these gay hosen, not of cloth (though never so fine), for that is thought too base, but of Jarnsey worsted, crewel, silk, thread, and such like, or else at the least of the finest yarn that can be, and so curiously knit with open seam down the legs, with quirks and clocks about the ankles, and sometime (haply) interlaced with gold or silver threads, as is wonderful to behold......

To these their netherstocks, they have corked shoes, pinsnets, and fine pantofles, which bear them up a finger or two from the ground, whereof some be of white leather,......black, and......red; some of black velvet,......white,...... red,......green; raced, carved, cut, and stitched all over with silk and laid on with gold, silver, and such like. Yet, notwithstanding, to what good uses serve these pantofles, except it be to wear in a private house, or in a man's chamber, to keep him warm?......

Their coats and jerkins, as they be divers in colours, so be they divers in fashions; for some be made with colours, some without, some close to the body, some loose, covering the whole body down to the thigh, like bags or sacks that were drawn over them, hiding the dimensions and lineaments of the body;......

They have cloaks there also in nothing discrepant from the rest, of divers and sundry colours, white, red, tawny, black, green, yellow, russet, purple, violet, and infinite other colours; some of cloth, silk, velvet, taffety, and such like, whereof some be of the Spanish, French, and Dutch fashion; some short, scarcely reaching

to the girdlestead or waist, some to the knee, and othersome
trailing upon the ground (almost), liker gowns than cloaks . . . . . .

They have also boot-hose, which are to be wondered at, for   90
they be of the finest cloth that may be got, yea, fine enough to
make any band, ruff, or shirt needful to be worn; yet this is bad
enough to wear next their greasy boots. And would God this were
all; but (O fie, for shame!) they must be wrought all over, from the
gartering place upward, with needlework, clogged with silk of all   95
colours, with birds, fowls, beasts, and antics portrayed all over in
sumptuous sort.

NOTES

2	*sharp* i.e. rising sharply. Stubbes is describing a 'copatain', a high, conical or sugar-loaf hat.
10	*taffety* (variant of 'taffeta') thin, fine silk fabric of various colours, often 'tufted' and called 'tuftaffety'.
	sarcenet fine, soft silk material of various colours.
11–12	*kind of fine hair* Stubbes is referring to felt hats made of wool and fur or hair, closely compacted under pressure to give a stiff texture.
15	*ruffs* neckwear of starched linen or muslin, arranged in horizontal flutings and standing out all round the neck, making the head appear to be standing on a platter; worn by both men and women.
	cambric fine white linen. Stubbes later uses the variant form 'cameric'.
16	*holland* linen cloth, originally made in Holland.
	lawn very fine linen cloth, perhaps taking its name from Laon in France.
20	*Aeolus . . . . . . Neptune* In classical mythology, the God of the Winds and the God of the Sea.
21	*crazy* frail, unsound, damaged.
23	*dishclout* cloth for drying dishes.
	wot know.
28	*dive* submerge, soak.
30	*crested* ribbed.
	whipped over bound round.
31	*supportasse* a word peculiar to Stubbes (explained in the context).
35	*somedeal* somewhat.
41	*hard-quilted* stiffly sewn in layers, usually with some soft thick substance between.
42	*bombasted* padded (with four to six pounds of cotton-wool, etc.).
47	*hosen* here used both for a pair of breeches (i.e. upper or trunk hose) and for what was worn below the breeches (canons, long hose, or even netherstocks; see Linthicum, p. 204). Stubbes's description of French hose (ll. 49–53) is very confusing.
49	*gally-hose . . . . . . Venetians* See below, ll. 53–9.
50	*common French hose* i.e. trunk hose, 'usually mid-thigh length, shaped like pumpkins, and stuffed with hair, flocks, or bombast' (Linthicum, p. 205).
51	*sideness* length (*OED*), but since this repeats 'length', Stubbes appears to

be using the word in the earlier obsolete sense of 'side' meaning 'large or ample', hence 'roominess'.

52 *The other* 'refers to the short hose, cut in panes, with tubular extensions below the knee-cap' (Linthicum, p. 206).

53 *side* long.

54 *gally-hosen* same as 'galligascons', shipmen's hose, reaching only to the knee, loose 'slops'.

55 *guards* ornamental borders or trimmings.

56 *Venetian hosen* breeches that fitted the hips, but were full at the knee (Linthicum, p. 208).

58 *points* tagged laces.

59 *damask* rich silk, with floral or geometric designs (named from Damascus).

63 *netherstocks* stockings.

64–5 *Jarnsey worsted* wool fabric, originally produced in Jersey.

65 *crewel* thin worsted yarn.

67 *quirks and clocks* ornamental patterns in silk worked on the side of stockings. 'quirks' = clocks.

70 *corked shoes* i.e. shoes with cork soles.
   pinsnets (variant of 'pinson') thin shoes of some kind, slippers or pumps.

71 *pantofles* either (a) high-heeled cork-soled shoes, or (b) indoor slippers. Stubbes rather confusingly seems to refer to both.

74 *raced* slashed (same as 'carved' and 'cut').

78 *jerkins* short coats, sleeved or without sleeves.

84 *tawny* brown, which is red-yellow in hue.

85 *russet* reddish-brown (from the reddish-brown or neutral colour of the coarse woollen cloth called 'russet').

86 *cloth* i.e. woollen cloth.

88 *girdlestead* waist.

90 *boot-hose* footless leggings, worn under the boot to protect stockings and long hose from staining (Linthicum, p. 262).

95 *clogged* ?loaded, burdened; possibly a form of 'clocked' = embroidered with a pattern or figure; cf. selection (ii), l. 35.

96 *antics* grotesque figures.

ii

A particular description of the abuses of women's apparel in Ailgna [i.e. Anglia or England]

From Philip Stubbes, *The Anatomie of Abuses* (1583, 2nd edn), pp. 63–80 in F. J. Furnivall's edn (1877–9).

The women of Ailgna use to colour their faces with certain oils, liquors, unguents, and waters made to that end, whereby they think their beauty is greatly decored; but who seeth not that their souls are thereby deformed and they brought deeper into the displeasure and indignation of the Almighty,......   5

Then followeth the trimming and tricking of their heads in laying out their hair to the show, which of force must be curled, frizzled, and crisped, laid out (a world to see!) on wreaths and borders from one ear to another. And lest it should fall down, it is underpropped with forks, wires, and I cannot tell what, rather like   10
grim stern monsters than chaste Christian matrons. Then on the edges of their bolstered hair......there is laid great wreaths of gold and silver, curiously wrought and cunningly applied to the temples of their heads......

If curling and laying out their own natural hair were   15
all......it were the less matter, but they are not simply content with their own hair, but buy other hair, dying it of what colour they list themselves;.....

Then on tops of these stately turrets......stand their other capital ornaments, as French hood, hat, cap, kercher, and such   20
like, whereof some be of velvet, some of taffety, some (but few) of wool,......

Another sort of dissolute minions......are so far bewitched as they are not ashamed to make holes in their ears, whereat they hang rings and other jewels of gold and precious stones......But   25
because this is not so much frequented amongst women as men, I will say no more thereof......

The women there use great ruffs and neckerchers of holland, lawn, cameric, and such cloth,......then lest they should fall down, they are smeared and starched in the Devil's liquour, I mean   30
Starch; after that dried with great diligence, streaked, patted, and rubbed very nicely, and so applied to their goodly necks, and, withal, underpropped with supportasses......The skirts then of these great ruffs are long and side every way, pleated and crested full curiously, God wot. Then last of all, they are either clogged   35
with gold, silver, or silk lace of stately price, wrought all over with needlework, speckled and sparkled here and there with the sun, the moon, the stars, and many other antics strange to behold......

The women also there have doublets and jerkins as men have   40
here, buttoned up the breast, and made with wings, welts, and
pinions on the shoulder points, as man's apparel is, for all the
world; and though this be a kind of attire appropriate only to man,
yet they blush not to wear it,......

Their gowns be no less famous than the rest, for some are of   45
silk, ... velvet, ... grogram, ... taffety, ... scarlet,
and......fine cloth, of ten, twenty, or forty shillings a yard. But
if the whole gown be not silk or velvet, then the same shall be laid
with lace, two or three fingers broad, all over the gown or else the
most part......Some with sleeves hanging down to their skirts,   50
trailing on the ground and cast over their shoulders like cow-tails.
Some have sleeves much shorter, cut up the arm and pointed with
silk ribbons very gallantly, tied with true-loves' knots (for so they
call them)......Then have they petticoats of the best cloth
......And sometimes they are not of cloth neither, for that is   55
thought too base, but of scarlet, grogram, taffety, silk, and such
like, fringed about the skirts with silk fringe of changeable colour.
But which is more vain, of whatsoever their petticoats be, yet must
they have kirtles (for so they call them) either of silk, velvet,
grogram, taffety, satin, or scarlet, bordered with guards, lace,   60
fringe, and I cannot tell what besides......

Their netherstocks, in like manner, are either of silk, Jarnsey
worsted, crewel, or at least of as fine yarn, thread, or cloth as is
possible to be had......whereto they have corked shoes,
pinsnets, pantofles, and slippers, some of black velvet,......   65
white,......green, and......yellow; some of Spanish
leather and some of English, stitched with silk and embroidered
with gold and silver all over the foot, with other gewgaws
innumerable......

Is not this a certain sweet pride to have civet, musk, sweet   70
powders, fragrant pomanders, odorous perfumes, and such like,
whereof the smell may be felt and perceived not only all over the
house or place where they be present, but also a stone's cast off
almost?......

After all this, when they have attired themselves thus in the   75
midst of their pride, it is a world to consider their coyness in
gestures, their mincedness in words and speeches, their ginger[li]-
ness in tripping on toes like young goats, their demure nicety and
babishness, and withal their haughty stomachs and more than
Cyclopical countenances. Their fingers must be decked with gold,   80
silver, and precious stones, their wrists with bracelets and armlets
of gold and other costly jewels, their hands covered with their
sweet washed gloves embroidered with gold, silver, and what not;
and to such abomination is it grown as they must have their
looking glasses carried with them wheresoever they   85
go......Then must they have their silk scarves cast about their

faces and fluttering in the wind, with great tassels at every end
either of gold, silver, or silk . . . . . . When they use to ride abroad,
they have visors made of velvet (or in my judgement they may
rather be called invisories), wherewith they cover all their faces,   90
having holes made in them against their eyes, whereout they look.

NOTES

[Note: see the notes to the preceding selection on men's clothes for many of the
terms here repeated by Stubbes.]

1   *use . . . . . . faces* Although he fulminates at length on 'painting', Stubbes is
surprisingly 'un-particular' on the details of the various 'oils, liquors,
unguents, and waters' widely employed by the upper classes (including the
Queen). He would have agreed with Claudius: 'The harlot's cheek,
beautied with plast'ring art, / Is not more ugly to the thing that helps it /
Than is my deed to my most painted word' (*Hamlet*, III.1.50–2).

3   *decored* adorned, embellished.

6   *tricking* decking out, ornamentation.

8   *crisped* stiffly curled (same as 'frizzled').
    a world a marvel.

12   *bolstered* propped up, supported.

14   *temples* (a) the flattened region on each side of the forehead; (b) sacred
edifices (ironic).

19   *on tops* i.e. on the tops.

20   *capital* pertaining to the head.
    French hood softly pleated hood with a round front.
    kercher (variant of 'kerchief') cloth used to cover the head.

23   *minions* darlings, lady-loves.

26   *frequented* resorted to.

28   *neckerchers* kerchief worn about the neck.

31   *streaked* smoothed, ironed.

34   *side* hanging far down.

37   *sparkled* sprinkled.

41   *wings* lateral projecting shoulder pieces.
    welts borders or fringes.

42   *pinions* shoulder (or sleeve) embellishments.

46   *grogram* or 'grograin', coarse fabric of silk, mohair or wool, or these
mixed with silk, often stiffened with gum.
    scarlet rich cloth, usually of a bright red colour, though sometimes green,
blue or brown.

52   *pointed* tied, laced.

53   *true-loves' knots* complicated knots, with double-looped bow or two loops
intertwined, symbols of true love.

59   *kirtles* second or outer petticoats.

68   *gewgaws* gaudy trifles, baubles.

70   *civet* yellowish or brownish unctuous substance, having a strong musky
scent and obtained from animals of the civet genus or civet-cat.
    musk odoriferous, reddish-brown substance, obtained from the male
musk-deer.

77   *mincedness* affected manner.
77–8 *ginger[li]ness* walking daintily or mincingly.
78   *nicety* shyness, coyness.
79   *babishness* babyishness.
      stomachs dispositions, temperaments.
80   *Cyclopical* monstrous (like the Cyclops).
90   *invisories* visors or masques (found only in Stubbes).
91   *against* opposite to.

2 Education

The education of youth was taken very seriously in England during the sixteenth and seventeenth centuries, that is to say, education for those who could afford it. As William Harrison (*The Description of England*, bk. II, chap. 3, 1587 edn of Holinshed's *Chronicles*) tells us: 'there are not many corporate towns, now under the Queen's dominion, that han [have] not one grammar school at the least, with a sufficient living for a master and usher appointed to the same.' Though called 'free schools', in as much as the actual teaching cost the students nothing, there were entrance fees, 'voluntary' gifts to the master, books, writing materials, etc., to be paid for, extras which effectively excluded the children of the really poor (see Joan Simon, *Education and Society in Tudor England* (1966), pp. 369–70). Money was the key, as Philip Stubbes (*The Second Part of the Anatomie of Abuses*, 1583, sig. D3 v) complains: 'So that the places in the universities and free schools seem rather to be sold for money and friendship than given *gratis* to them that have need as they ought to be.' Stubbes may, as usual, exaggerate, but the problem was very real, especially so far as the universities were concerned.

Girls, of course, did not attend a grammar school, but in noble or well-to-do families were educated at home by private tutors, as for the most part were the sons of the aristocracy. In addition a continental tour (France, Italy, the Netherlands, Spain) was often a recognized part of a young gentleman's education (see J. W. Stoye, *English Travellers Abroad, 1604-1667* (1952)). Sir Walter Raleigh, for example, sent his son to France under the tutelage of Ben Jonson:

> . . . . . .this youth, being knavishly inclined, among other pastimes (as the setting of the favour [love token] of damosels on a codpiece) caused him [Jonson] to be drunken and dead drunk, so that he knew not where he was; thereafter laid him on a car [cart], which he made to be drawn by pioners [labourers] through the streets, at every corner showing his governor stretched out and telling them that was a more lively image of the crucifix than any they had. At which sport young Raleigh's mother delighted much (saying his father young was so inclined), though the father abhorred it. (*Conversations with Drummond* in *Works*, ed. C. H. Herford and P. Simpson, I (1925), 140–1.)

Careful advice on how the youthful traveller should behave, and what, and whom, he should see, is offered by Francis Bacon in 'Of Travel' (in *Essayes* (1625; no. 18) and by James Howell (*Instructions for Forreine Travell* (1642)); and, aside from the many accounts left by English voyagers (see 'At sea', p. 341), the pleasures of travel may best be sampled in the work of that prototypical busybody traveller Thomas Coryate (*Coryats Crudities*, 1611), in Fynes Moryson's *Itinerary* (1617), and in

William Lithgow's *A Most Delectable, and True, Discourse of a Peregrination in Europe, Asia, etc.* (1614).

'Then the whining schoolboy, with his satchel / And shining morning face, creeping like snail / Unwillingly to school' (*As You Like It*, II.vii.145–7): Shakespeare's famous lines should be read in the context of selection (i) from John Brinsley's *Ludus Literarius, or The Grammar Schoole* (1612). For Brinsley, as for Roger Ascham (*The Scholemaster* (1570)) and Richard Mulcaster (*Positions* (1581), and *The Elementarie* (1582)) – all of them humane and dedicated teachers – school was a deadly serious, no-nonsense, no-frill institution, and students were expected, 'painfully' if necessary, to master their work to the greater glory of God and the commonweal. Aside from some study of the Scriptures and perhaps arithmetic, the curriculum was almost wholly devoted to a day-in and day-out study of classical Latin authors in order to gain, through 'imitation', some facility in translating and writing Latin prose and verse, with, as Mulcaster complains (see selection (ii)) comparatively little attention to their native language. All this may sound rather grim (and in some schools it was apparently worse than grim) but, narrowly focused as it may seem to us today, it gave the grounding for many years after Ascham and Brinsley to generations of our greatest poets, philosophers, and scientists.

A school day (see selection (i)) of between eight and nine hours, even with two hours off for midday dinner and two fifteen-minute 'intermissions', may strike us (soft moderns!) as excessive, but the Elizabethan authorities (and the parents) did not think so. For many parents it meant 'out of sight and out of mischief' in a milieu where a troublesome 'twig' might be 'bent' so as to become in process of time a moderately learned and useful citizen.

The fear of corporal punishment was accepted as an incentive to learning, at home, at school, and even at the university. Henry Peacham (*The Compleat Gentleman* (1622), chap. III) describes how pupils were 'pulled by the hair, lashed over the face, beaten about the head with the great end of the rod, smitten upon the lips for every slight offence with the *ferula*'. If this emphasis on corporal punishment in the schools seems barbarous, even in the comparative moderation prescribed by Brinsley (see his chapter 'Of the execution of justice in schools by punishment'), it took its cue from biblical authority (Proverbs 13:24) and, sadly, widespread parental practice. Ascham (*The Scholemaster*, ed. W. A. Wright (1904), in *English Works*, pp. 201–2) recounts a revealing conversation with Lady Jane Grey:

One of the greatest benefits that ever God gave me is that He sent me so sharp and severe parents and so gentle a schoolmaster. For when I was in presence either of father or mother, whether I speak, keep silence, sit, stand, or go [walk], eat, drink, be merry or sad, be sewing, playing, dancing, or doing anything else, I must do it, as it were, in such weight, measure, and number, even so perfitly [perfectly] as God made the world, or else I am so sharply taunted, so cruelly threatened, yea, presently sometimes with pinches, nips, and bobs [blows], and other ways, which I will not name for the honour I bear them, so without measure misordered, that I think myself in hell till time come that I must go to Master Aylmer, who teacheth me so gently,......

Unfortunately, as Ascham notes (p. 176), many thought that the 'best schoolmaster' was the 'greatest beater'; hence his (and Brinsley's) insistence that 'love' rather than 'fear' was the best teacher. As Brinsley (p. 50) put it (echoing Ascham), it was his wish

......to make the schoolhouse to be *ludus literarius*, indeed a school of play and pleasure...and not of fear and bondage: although there must be always a meet and loving fear, furthered by wise severity, to maintain authority, and to make it also *ludus a non ludendo*, a place void of all fruitless play and loitering,......

Selection (ii), from Richard Mulcaster's *The First Part of the Elementarie* (1582), deals with the problem of proper instruction in the reading and writing of English in schools which were dominated by Latin. 'I honour the Latin, but I worship the English' (p. 254), cries Mulcaster. Such enthusiasm may seem natural enough to us, but Mulcaster, even as late as 1582, felt that a substantial book (272 pages) was called for to counter the still widely held belief that English, when compared with Latin, was 'uncouth' ('But you will say it is uncouth. Indeed, being unused', p. 255) and irsular ('......it stretcheth no further than this island of ours, nay not thei. overall', p. 256), a language unfit for serious and learned discourse.

As a result of this attitude, little or no attention was being paid to the writing of 'good' English in the schools, except as an ancillary tool to the study of Latin and (some) Greek (compare Ascham's insistence on the value of 'double translation' – from Latin to English and back into Latin). Without Latin, considered basic to the whole educational system, no one could pretend to be educated. This attitude outraged Mulcaster, himself 'learned' both in Latin and Greek: 'For is it not indeed a marvellous bondage to become servants to one tongue for learning sake the most of our time, with loss of most time, whereas we may have the very same treasure in our own tongue with the gain of most time?' (p. 254). And he argues for early mastery, before the serious study of Latin is begun, of the rules of English grammar and 'correct' orthography. Brinsley later supports the same view (chap. III).

Selection (iii), from Donald Lupton's *London and the Countrey Carbonadoed and Quartred into Severall Characters* (1632), offers a fairly enough balanced and witty 'character' of 'Country schoolmasters'. Prior to the Reformation in England, teaching on the grammar-school level had been largely in the hands of the local clergy, but by Queen

Elizabeth's time school-teaching was gradually becoming recognized as a layman's profession, partly as a result of the increasing number of new grammar schools which were being founded throughout the country (see Penry Williams, *Life in Tudor England* (1964), p. 125). Schoolmasters, apart from those at the great schools, Westminster, St Paul's, Eton, Winchester, and Shrewsbury, were most often badly underpaid. The annual £20 stipend, for example, paid to the schoolmaster at the Stratford grammar school was unusually good, better, in fact, than the stipends granted to Fellows at Oxford and Cambridge (see E. K. Chambers, *William Shakespeare* (1930), I, 9–10). It is scarcely surprising, then, that, as Lupton charges, the profession of teaching did not always, outside the universities (and not always there), attract well prepared and responsible teachers. Shakespeare, who despite his truncated grammar school education may, according to a report by one of his contemporaries, William Beeston, have served 'as a schoolmaster in the country' before going to London, has given us a satiric (but kindly) portrait of a country schoolmaster in Holofernes (*Love's Labour's Lost*), who, with all the insensitivity of the true pedant, showers his little learning on anyone who will listen (IV.ii, V.i). As Moth, page to the braggart, Don Armado, aptly puts it; 'They [Holofernes, Sir Nathaniel (the curate) and Armado] have been at a great feast of languages, and stol'n the scraps' (V.i.36–7). Another sketch of a country schoolmaster may be found in Fletcher and Shakespeare's *The Two Noble Kinsmen* (III.v).

There is a good schoolroom scene in Thomas Heywood's (?) *How to Choose a Good Wife from a Bad* (1602; II.i), in which a lot of Latin is thrown about; and the kind of grilling in Latin grammar, with its heavy emphasis on rote learning, that students 'enjoyed' daily throughout the year, and what could happen when memory faltered, may be seen in John Marston's *What You Will* (1601; II.ii), a scene for which Marston may have taken a hint from Shakespeare's *The Merry Wives of Windsor* (IV.i), when Sir Hugh Evans, the Welsh parson and schoolmaster, puts young William through his Latin grammar paces for the benefit of his mother, Mistress Page, much to the wonderment of Mistress Quickly.

The last selection (iv), 'The three universities', is taken from William Harrison's *The Description of England* (1587). Harrison (1534–93), who had studied first at Cambridge and then taken his BA and MA from Oxford (for which he shows a preference), writes from personal experience. He is, however, obviously less at home in treating the 'third university', the Inns of Court in London, and his opinion of the general run of lawyers is not high, an opinion endorsed by that universal critic Philip Stubbes (see p. 283).

Students at Oxford and Cambridge were called 'freshmen' in their first year and 'sophisters' (at least at Cambridge) in their second and third, 'from whence', as Harrison says, 'when they have learned more sufficiently the rules of logic, rhetoric, and obtained thereto competent skill in philosophy and in the mathematicals, they ascend higher unto the estate of Bachelor of Arts, after four years of their entrance into their sophistry.' The university curriculum still followed, more or less, the medieval division of the seven liberal arts into the 'trivium' (grammar, which included Greek and Hebrew, Latin being taken as already learned, rhetoric, and logic) and the 'quadrivium' (arithmetic, geometry, astronomy and music), all considered as introductory to the study of the 'three philosophies' (natural, moral and metaphysical), plus divinity. Harrison complains that the subjects of the 'quadrivium' 'are now smally regarded' in either university.

A fairly regular adjunct to the educational process was the performance of plays in the grammar schools, universities, and Inns of Court. In addition to the performance of classical plays (Seneca, Plautus, Terence), a substantial number of original plays were produced, both Latin and English, several of which exercised an important influence on later Elizabethan–Jacobean drama. Thus, in comedy, for example, Nicholas Udall's *Ralph Roister Doister* (1545–52), an early form of which may possibly have been performed at Eton College, and W. S.'s *Gammer Gurton's Needle* (1552–63, Christ's College, Cambridge) introduced formal structural elements and type characters from Latin comedy in a recognizably English setting; George Gascoigne's *Supposes* (1566, Gray's Inn), a translation of Ariosto's *I Suppositi*, naturalized Italian *commedia erudita* and was the first English play written in prose. In tragedy, Sackville and Norton's *Gorboduc* (1562, Inner Temple), the first 'regular' tragedy in the Senecan mode in English, introduced blank verse to the drama, popularized the use of a chorus, reported action, and dumb shows (see 'Play genres', selection (i)), and became, along with a Latin play like Thomas Legge's *Richardus Tertius* (1580, St John's College, Cambridge) or the anonymous *True Tragedy of Richard III* (1588–94, Queen's College, Oxford), the forerunner of the many English history plays so popular in the 1590s, and Robert Wilmot's (with others) *Gismond of Salerne* (c.1566, Inner Temple), as the first English love tragedy, prepared the way for Shakespeare's *Romeo and Juliet*.

One academic play, *Club Law* (1599–1600, Clare Hall, Cambridge), written perhaps by George Ruggle, the author of the comparatively well-known satiric Latin comedy on lawyers, *Ignoramus* (1615, also Clare Hall), is particularly interesting for the light it throws on the longstanding hostility between town and gown, generated in good part by the special legal privileges and immunities enjoyed by the universities, privileges which the town authorities of Oxford and Cambridge insisted, and not without reason, infringed on their civic rights and freedoms (see Rowland Parker, *Town and Gown: The 700 Years' War in Cambridge* (1983)). Written of course, with a strong university bias, *Club Law* presents the town faction in a highly ludicrous and morally questionable light, including among the principal characters satiric portraits of the then Mayor and other Cambridge officials. Thomas Fuller (*History of the University of Cambridge* (1655), p. 156) records an amusing, though perhaps apocryphal, account of the performance:

> The young scholars, conceiving themselves somewhat wronged by
> the townsmen,......betook them for revenge to their wits, as
> the weapon wherein lay their best advantage. These, having gotten
> a discovery of some town privacies [secrets] from Miles Goldsbo-
> rough (one of their own Corporation), composed a merry (but
> abusive) comedy (which they called *Club Law*) in English, as
> calculated for the capacities of such whom they intended
> spectators thereof. Clare Hall was the place wherein it was acted,
> and the Mayor, with his brethren, and their wives, were invited to
> behold it, or rather themselves abused therein. A convenient place
> was assigned to the townsfolk (rivetted in with scholars [students]
> on all sides), where they might see and be seen. Here they did
> behold themselves in their own best clothes (which the scholars
> had borrowed) so lively personated, their habits, gestures,
> language, leger-jests [trifling jokes], and expressions, that it was
> hard to decide which was the true townsman, whether he that sat
> by, or he who acted on the stage. Sit still they could not for
> chafing, go out they could not for crowding, but impatiently
> patient were fain to attend till dismissed at the end of the comedy.

Although the corporation complained violently, the university 'only sent
some slight and private check [reprimand] to the principal actors
therein.'

For education, generally, see Joan Simon (cited above) and Kenneth
Charlton, *Education in Renaissance England* (1965); for academic drama,
see T. H. Vail Motter, *The School Drama in England* (1929), F. S. Boas,
University Drama in the Tudor Age (1914), and A. W. Green, *The Inns of
Court and Early English Drama* (1931). John Stow (*Survay of London*
(1603 edn), ed. C. L. Kingsford (1908), I, 76–9 affords a more detailed
contemporary account of the Inns of Court, and Thomas Powell (*Tom of
All Trades, or The Plaine Path-way to Preferment*, 1631) offers advice for
succeeding in grammar school, university, and the Inns of Court.

i

A day in the grammar school

From John Brinsley, *Ludus Literarius, or The Grammar Schoole* (1612),
'Of School-times, Intermissions, and Recreations', pp. 296–301.

Philoponus.   The school-time should begin at six:......

Spoudeus.   But it is hard for the little children to rise so early,
and in some families all lie long: how would you have them come
so soon then? You would not have them beaten every time they
come over-late, as the custom is in some schools.   5

Philoponus.   That I take far too great severity and whereby
many a poor child is driven into wonderful fear, and either to play
the truant, or make some device to leave the school; at least to
come with a marvellous ill will, and oft to be dragged to the
school, to the reproach of the master and the school.   10

The best means that ever I could find to make them to rise
early, to prevent all this fear of whipping, is this: by letting the
little ones to have their places in their forms daily, according to
their coming after six of the clock: so many as are there at six, to
have their places as they had them by election or the day before; all   15
who come after six, every one to sit as he cometh, and so to
continue that day and until he recover his place again by the
election of the form or otherwise. Thus deal with them at all
times, after every intermission, when they are to be in their places
again, and you shall have them ever attending who to be first in his   20
place; so greatly even children are provoked by the credit of their
places.

If any cannot be brought by this, then to be noted in the black
bill by a special mark, and feel the punishment thereof: and
sometimes present correction to be used for terror, though this (as   25
I said) to be more seldom, for making them to fear coming to the
school.

The higher scholars must of necessity rest to do their exercises,
if their exercises be strictly called for. Thus they are to continue
until nine, signified by monitors, subdoctor, or otherwise. Then at   30
nine I find that order which is in Westminster to be far the best: to
let them to have a quarter of an hour at least, or more, for
intermission, either for breakfast, for all who are near unto the
school, that can be there within the time limited, or else for the
necessity of everyone, or their honest recreation, or to prepare   35
their exercises against the master's coming in.

After, each of them to be in his place in an instant upon the
knocking of the door or some other sign given by the subdoctor or
monitors, in pain of loss of his place, or further punishment,......so to continue until eleven of the clock, or somewhat   40

after, to countervail the time of the intermission at nine.

To be again all ready and in their places at one, in an instant; to continue until three or half an hour after: then to have another quarter of an hour or more, as at nine, for drinking and necessities; so to continue till half an hour after five, thereby in that half hour   45
to countervail the time at three; then to end so as was showed, with reading a piece of a chapter and with singing two staves of a psalm; lastly with prayer to be used by the master.

For the psalms, every scholar should begin to give the psalm and the tune in order, and to read every verse before them; or every   50
one to have his book (if it can be) and read it as they do sing it. Where anyone cannot begin the tune, his next fellow beneath is to help him and take his place. By this they will all learn to give the tunes sweetly, which is a thing very commendable; and also it will help both reading, voice, and audacity in the younger.   55

Spoudeus. But these intermissions at nine and three may be offensive. They who know not the manner of them may reproach the school, thinking that they do nothing but play.

Philoponus. We are, so much as may be, in all things to avoid offence; but when by long custom the order is once made known,   60
it will be no more offensive than it is at Westminster, or than it is at noon and night; so that it be done in a decent order.

Spoudeus. ......But what say you for their recreations? Let me also hear your judgment in them; for I see that you would have in like manner a special regard to be kept thereof.   65

Philoponus. I would indeed have their recreations as well looked unto, as their learning; as you may perceive plainly by their intermissions at nine and at three. Besides those, and all other their intermissions, it is very requisite also that they should have weekly one part of an afternoon for recreation, as a reward of their   70
diligence, obedience, and profiting; and that to be appointed at the master's discretion, either the Thursday after the usual custom, or according to the best opportunity of the place......

Before their breaking up also, it shall not be amiss to give them a theme to make some verses of, *ex tempore*, in the highest forms,   75
after they have been for a time exercised therein, or if time permit, sometime to cap verses. In capping verses, the way to provoke them the most, and to have most variety of good verses, is to appoint some one or two of the best to challenge their fellows to come one after another, and ever as anyone but sticketh or misseth   80
in a syllable, the other to tell him, and another to come in his place; or else to try adversaries of forms together. This exercise will much help capacity and audacity, memory, right pronunciation, to furnish with store of authorities for poetry and the like; so as that they may be very cunning in their Poets by it......   85

All recreations and sports of scholars would be meet for gentlemen. Clownish sports, or perilous, or yet playing for money

are no way to be admitted. The recreations of the studious are as
well to be looked unto, as the study of the rest: that none take hurt
by his study, either for mind or body, or any way else.   90

Yet here of the other side, very great care is to be had in the
moderating of their recreation. For schools, generally, do not take
more hindrance by any one thing, than by over-often leave to play.
Experience teacheth that this draweth their minds utterly away
from their books, that they cannot take pains for longing after play   95
and talking of it; as also devising means to procure others to get
leave to play: so that ordinarily when they are but in hope thereof,
they will do things very negligently; and after the most play, they
are evermore far the worst.

NOTES

3   *how......come* how would you arrange matters so that they would come.
8   *make some device* invent some trick.
13   *forms* one or other of the numbered class divisions.
15   *or* perhaps an error for 'on'.
19   *intermission* 'break' in the school day.
21   *provoked......credit* incited (to emulation) by the (relative) honour.
23–4 *black bill* some kind of memorandum book in which the child's 'faults'
     were registered for present or future reference.
25   *present* immediate.
28   *higher scholars* i.e. those in the upper forms.
     exercises i.e. imitations, in Latin and English, of classical authors (Cicero,
     Terence, Ovid, Virgil, etc.).
29   *if......called for* i.e. if they are to be held strictly accountable for their
     exercises
30   *monitors* senior pupils.
     subdoctor student assistant, appointed from the highest forms.
31   *Westminster* Westminster School, one of the best grammar schools in
     London, founded by Queen Elizabeth in 1560.
35   *necessity* i.e. calls of nature.
     honest seemly, befitting.
44   *drinking* i.e. of water!
47   *chapter* of the Bible.
     staves verses.
48   *psalm* i.e. in the Sternhold and Hopkins metrical version (1549), which
     included musical notation for each psalm (the 'tune').
72   *after* according to.
75   *theme* topic.
77   *cap verses* reply to one verse, previously quoted, with another that begins
     with the final or initial letter of the first, or that rhymes or otherwise
     corresponds with it.
80   *sticketh* is unable to proceed.
80–1 *misseth in* gets (a syllable) wrong.

82   *try adversaries of* set up a competition between.
84   *store of authorities* abundance of classical quotations.
85   *cunning* learned.
95   *take pains for* i.e. study well because of.

ii

Latin vs. English in the schools

From Richard Mulcaster, *The First Part of the Elementarie, Which Entreateth of Right Writing in Our English Tung* (1582), pp. 258–9.

But why not all in *English*, a tongue of itself both deep in conceit and frank in delivery? I do not think that any language, be it whatsoever, is better able to utter all arguments, either with more pith or greater plainness than our *English* tongue is, if the English utterer be as skilful in the matter which he is to utter as the foreign   5
utterer is. Which methink I durst prove in any most strange argument even mine own self, though no great clerk, but a great wellwiller to my natural country. And though we use, and must use, many foreign terms when we deal with such arguments, we do not any more than the bravest tongues do and even very those   10
which crake of their cunning . . . . . . But grant it were an heresy, seeing our training up is in the foreign tongues, even to wish all in English. Certainly it is no fault to handle that in *English* which is proper to *England*, though the same argument well handled in *Latin* were like to please *Latinists*. But an *English* profit must not   15
be measured by a *Latinist's* pleasure, which is not for studies to play with but for students to practise, and there the better where every one can judge: the principal benefit of our *English* penning. Besides all this, to confirm a true ground with a trial as true, how many slender things are ofttimes uttered in the *Latin* tongue, and   20
other foreign speeches, which under the bare vail of a strange covert do seem to be somewhat for to countenance study, which if they were *Englished*, and the mask pulled off that every man might see them, would seem very miserable and make a sorry show of simple substance and be soon disclaimed in of the parties   25
themselves with some thought at the least of the old saying, *Had I wist, I would not?* And were it not then better to gain judgement thoroughout in our own *English*, than either to leese it or to lame

[it] in the foreign *Latin* or any tongue else? To be led on a long
time with the opinion of something which in the end will prove 30
plain nothing or but a simple something?

NOTES

1	*conceit* conception, thought.
6	*strange* (1) foreign; (2) uncommon, out of the way.
11	*crake......cunning* boast of their learning.
18	*penning* writing, composition.
19	*confirm......as true* verify (or assert) a right position with a test equally right.
21	*bare* mere, simple
21–2	*strange covert* foreign cover.
22	*countenance study* make studying (them) seem worthwhile.
25	*simple* slight, insignificant.
	disclaimed in of repudiated by.
27	*wist* known.
28	*thoroughout* throughout.
	leese......lame fail to profit by......make (it) defective or maimed.

iii

Country schoolmasters

From Donald Lupton, *London and the Countrey Carbonadoed and Quartred into Severall Characters* (1632), pp. 115–19.

If they be well gowned and bearded, they have two good apologies ready made; but they are beholden to the tailor and barber for both: if they can provide for two pottles of wine against the next lecture-day, the school being void, there are great hopes of preferment: if he gets the place, his care next must be for the demeanour of his countenance: he looks over his scholars with as great and grave a countenance, as the emperor over his army. He will not at first be over busy to examine his usher, for fear he should prove, as many curates, better scholars than the chief master. As he sits in his seat, he must with a grace turn his muchatoes up; his sceptre lies not far from him, the rod: he uses martial law most, and the day of execution ordinarily is the Friday: at six o'clock his army all begin to march; at eleven they keep rendezvous, and at five or six at night, they take up their quarters. There are many set in authority to teach youth which never had much learning themselves; therefore if he cannot teach them, yet his looks and correction shall affright them. But there are some who deserve the place by their worth and wisdom, who stayed with their mother the university, until learning, discretion and judgement had ripened them for the well-managing of a school. These I love, respect, and wish that they may have good means either here, or somewhere else. These come from the sea of learning, well furnished with rich prizes of knowledge and excellent qualities, ballasted they are well with gravity and judgement, well steered by religion and a good conscience. And these abilities make them the only fit men to govern and instruct tender age; he learns the cradle to speak several languages and fits them for places of public note: being thus qualified, 'tis pity he should either want means or employment.

NOTES

1   *apologies* excuses (against being underrated).
3   *pottles* vessels containing about two quarts (to entertain his prospective employer).
    against in time for.
4   *school being void* school having a vacancy.
8   *usher* assistant to the master. Lupton also has a 'character' of 'Country Ushers' (pp. 119–22).

9   *curates* assistants to parish priests.

11   *muchatoes* mustachios.

12   *martial law* under which ordinary law is suspended and offenders are punished without trial.

13   *six o'clock* Compare the hours of the schoolday given in selection (i).

14   *keep rendezvous* i.e. return to school-work after a short break for breakfast.

14-15 *take......quarters* occupy their rooms (if a boarding-school) or go to their homes.

22   *means* pecuniary support.

      here......else either as a schoolmaster or in some other position (where their learning may be useful).

27   *learns* teaches.

iv

The three universities

From William Harrison, *The Description of England*, bk. II, chap. 3 (in Holinshed's *Chronicles*, edn of 1587).

In my time there are three noble universities in England, to wit, one at Oxford, the second at Cambridge and the third in London, of which the first two are the most famous, I mean Cambridge and Oxford, for that in them the use of the tongues, philosophy, and the liberal sciences, besides the profound studies of the civil law,　　5
physic, and theology are daily taught and had: whereas in the latter the laws of the realm are only read and learned by such as give their minds unto the knowledge of the same. In the first there are not only divers goodly houses builded four-square for the most part of hard freestone or brick, with great numbers of lodgings and　　10
chambers in the same for students, after a sumptuous sort, through the exceeding liberality of kings, queens, bishops, noblemen and ladies of the land; but also large livings and great revenues bestowed upon them (the like whereof is not to be seen in any other region, as Peter Martyr did oft affirm) to the maintainance　　15
only of such convenient numbers of poor men's sons as the several stipends bestowed upon the said houses are able to support. . . . . . .

The colleges of Oxford, for curious workmanship and private commodities, are much more stately, magnificent, and commodi-　　20
ous than those of Cambridge, and thereunto the streets of the town for the most part more large and comely. But for uniformity of building, orderly compaction, and politic regiment, the town of Cambridge, as the newer workmanship, exceedeth that of Oxford (which otherwise is and hath been the greater of the two by many　　25
a fold, as I guess, although I know divers that are of the contrary opinion). This also is certain, that whatsoever the difference be in building of the town streets, the townsmen of both are glad when they may match and annoy the students by encroaching upon their liberties, and keep them bare by extreme sale of their wares,　　30
whereby many of them become rich for a time, but afterward fall again into poverty, because that goods evil gotten do seldom long endure. . . . . . .

In each of these universities also is likewise a church dedicated to the Virgin Mary, wherein once in the year, to wit, in July, the　　35
scholars are holden, and in which such as have been called to any degree in the year precedent do there receive the accomplishment of the same in solemn and sumptuous manner. In Oxford this solemnity is called an Act, but in Cambridge they use the French word 'Commencement'; and such resort is made yearly unto the　　40

same from all parts of the land, by the friends of those which do proceed, that all the town is hardly able to receive and lodge those guests........

The manner to live in these universities is not as in some other of foreign countries we see daily to happen, where the students are enforced, for want of such houses, to dwell in common inns and taverns, without all order or discipline. But in these our colleges we live in such exact order, and under so precise rules of government, as that the famous learned man Erasmus of Rotterdam, being here among us fifty years past, did not let to compare the trades in living of students in these two places even with the very rules and orders of the ancient monks, affirming moreover, in flat words, our orders to be such as not only came near unto, but rather far exceeded, all the monastical institutions that ever were devised.

In most of our colleges there are also great numbers of students, of which many are found by the revenues of the houses and other by the purveyances and help of their rich friends; whereby in some one college you shall have two hundred scholars, in others an hundred and fifty, in divers a hundred and forty, and in the rest less numbers, as the capacity of the said houses is able to receive: so that at this present, of one sort and other, there are about three thousand students nourished in them both (as by a late survey it manifestly appeared). They were erected by their founders at the first only for poor men's sons, whose parents were not able to bring them up unto learning; but now they have the least benefit of them, by reason the rich do so encroach upon them. And so far hath this inconvenience spread itself that it is in my time an hard matter for a poor man's child to come by a fellowship (though he be never so good a scholar and worthy of that room). Such packing also is used at elections that not he which best deserveth, but he that hath most friends, though he be the worst scholar, is always surest to speed; which will turn in the end to the overthrow of learning. That some gentlemen also, whose friends have been in times past benefactors to certain of those houses, do intrude into the disposition of their estates without all respect of order or estatutes devised by the founders, only thereby to place whom they think good (and not without some hope of gain), the case is too too evident: and their attempt would soon take place if their superiors did not provide to bridle their endeavours. In some grammar schools likewise, which send scholars to these universities, it is lamentable to see what bribery is used; for, yer the scholar can be preferred, such bribage is made that poor men's children are commonly shut out, and the richer sort received (who in time past thought it dishonour to live as it were upon alms), and yet, being placed, most of them study little other than histories, tables, dice, and trifles, as men that make not

the living by their study the end of their purposes, which is a
lamentable hearing. Beside this, being for the most part either
gentlemen or rich men's sons, they oft bring the universities into   90
much slander. For, standing upon their reputation and liberty,
they ruffle and roist it out, exceeding in apparel and haunting
riotous company (which draweth them from their books unto
another trade); and for excuse, when they are charged with breach
of all good order, think it sufficient to say that they be gentlemen,   95
which grieveth many not a little.

To these two also we may in like sort add the third, which is at
London (serving only for such as study the laws of the realm),
where there are sundry famous houses, of which three are called by
the name of Inns of the Court, the rest of the Chancery, and all   100
builded beforetime for the furtherance and commodity of such as
apply their minds to our common laws. Out of these also come
many scholars of great fame, whereof the most part have
heretofore been brought up in one of the aforesaid universities,..... They have also degrees of learning among themselves   105
and rules of discipline under which they live most civilly in their
houses, albeit that the younger sort of them abroad in the streets
are scarce able to be bridled by any good order at all. Certes, this
error was wont also greatly to reign in Cambridge and Oxford
between the students and the burgesses; but as it is well left in   110
these two places, so in foreign count[r]ies it cannot yet be
suppressed.

NOTES

6   *had* i.e. learned.
7   *read* studied.
9   *four-square* having four equal sides.
10   *freestone* fine-grained sandstone or limestone.
11   *after......sort* in a lavish manner.
15   *Peter Martyr* Italian biblical scholar (1500–62), who, because of his
      sympathies with Protestant theology, fled Italy and became Regius
      professor of divinity at Oxford in 1548.
23   *compaction* being fitted or framed in a compact manner.
      politic regiment judicious governance.
24   *newer workmanship* Harrison, in a side-note, observes that Cambridge
      'burned not long since'.
25–6 *by......fold* in many ways.
29   *match* encounter as adversaries.
30   *liberties* privileges or rights (granted to them as students under university
      rules).
      bare needy, impoverished.
      by......wares by the exorbitant prices of their goods or provisions.
36   *scholars are holden* the students are brought together.

42 *proceed* advance to the degree of BA, MA or higher.
44 *manner to live* manner of living.
46 *houses* i.e. the colleges.
49 *Erasmus* great biblical scholar and educator (1466?–1536).
50–1 *let......living* forbear to compare the ways of life.
57 *found* maintained, supported.
58 *purveyances* provisions.
71 *room* appointment.
       packing corrupt practice.
73 *speed* succeed.
77 *estatutes* statutes, ordinances.
78 *think good* i.e. wish to have appointed.
83 *yer* ere.
86 *alms* charity.
87 *histories* stories, tales, romances (e.g. *Bevis of Hampton, Guy of Warwick, Huon of Bordeaux*).
       tables backgammon.
92 *ruffle......out* arrogantly swagger and bluster (like bullies) in an extreme way.
94 *another trade* i.e. whoring.
99–100 *three......Chancery* Harrison slips here. There were four Inns of Court (Lincoln's Inn, Inner Temple, Middle Temple, and Gray's Inn); to each of these, as subordinate, were attached several Inns of Chancery (e.g. Furnival's Inn and Thavie's Inn to Lincoln's Inn). Students were first admitted to the Inns of Chancery (ten all told) and then, if promising, graduated to one of the Inns of Court.
107 *albeit that* even though.
       younger sort Law students were notorious as disturbers of the peace and riotous livers. Shakespeare (*2 Henry IV*, III.ii.13–34) recounts Justice Shallow's nostalgic memories of his wild youth at Clement's Inn (it is doubtful that he was ever admitted to the Inner Temple); as he says, 'I would have done any thing indeed too, and roundly too.'
       Certes (disyllabic) Certainly.

3 Sports

Hunting, hawking and other pastimes

The royal and noble sports of hunting and hawking were widely honoured and practised in Elizabethan–Jacobean England. As George Gascoigne, in a commendatory poem prefixed to George Turbervile's *The Noble Arte of Venerie or Hunting* (1575), assures us:

> But let these few suffice: it is a *noble sport*,
> To recreate the minds of men, in good and godly sort,
> A sport for noble peers, a sport for gentle bloods;
> The pain I leave for servants such as beat the bushy woods,
> To make their masters sport.

Few Elizabethans would have quarrelled with such a description, whatever some more modern sensibilities may now feel. Even the 'servants' would have accepted their 'pain' with some enthusiasm, since, in the ceremonial 'breaking up' of the deer (its dismemberment at the 'kill' by the hunters), they received the neck and the chine (the upper part of the back between the shoulders) as their rightful reward, the sides and other 'dainty morsels' being reserved for the Master of the Hunt. Turbervile describes the whole gory business in detail (pp. 127–35), including the taking of assay (compare Falstaff's 'three fingers in the ribs', *I Henry IV*, IV.ii.74) and the cutting off of the deer's head, both performed by the 'chief personage' ('they take delight to cut off his head with their woodknives, skenes [daggers], or swords to try their edge and the goodness or strength of their arm'). A royal hunt, with Queen Elizabeth present, is described by Robert Laneham in his famous *Letter* (1575; ed. F. J. Furnivall (1887) pp. 13–14).

Turbervile devotes most of his attention in *The Noble Arte of Venerie* to the hunting of the hart and other kinds of deer (see selection (i)), but he also discusses the techniques of hunting boars, hares, foxes ('the unspeakable in full pursuit of the uneatable' as Oscar Wilde was to put it), badgers, otters, wolves, etc.

Turbervile also compiled a book on the noble science of hawking, *The Booke of Faulconrie or Hauking* (1575) and, in an introductory poem, he exclaims with infectious enthusiasm:

> So as by hawks doth pleasure grow unto the gazing eye,
> And dogs delight the list'ning ears, before the hawks
> do fly.
> What dolt so dull but takes delight, when once the span'el
> springs

The fearful fowl, and when the hawk lies long upon her
wings?
What sense so sad, what mind so maz'd, but sets his sorrows
by,
When once the falcon free begins to scud amid the sky,
To turn and wind a bird by sleight, and eke at last to slay,
With strong encounter, doves and ducks and every other
prey?

But his book does not lend itself to excerpting and selection (ii) has been taken from the lively scene in Thomas Heywood's *A Woman Kill'd with Kindness* first produced in 1603. Although Heywood is a little shaky on technical hawking terms, which he lifts from Gervase Markham's *The Gentlemans Academie* (1595; a reworking of the much earlier *Boke of St Albans* (1486)), and is primarily interested in the moral implications of a quarrel arising out of a foolishly excessive wager, he effectively catches something of the exhilaration and involvement experienced by true *aficionados* of the sport. Real hawks were not employed, however, the scene beginning after the two hawks have been 'cast off'.

Aside from Heywood's scene, there are many other references to hunting and hawking in Elizabethan–Jacobean drama. Shakespeare offers a 'moralized' commentary on a stag hunt as witnessed by the Melancholy Jaques in *As You Like It* (II.i.21–66), followed later (IV.ii) by a mock triumphal presentation of a slain deer to the Duke, and in *Love's Labour's Lost* (IV.i–ii) he performs some verbal gymnastics with hunting terms, when the Princess of France is so stationed during a deer hunt that she may shoot a deer with bow and arrow ('The preyful Princess pierc'd and prick'd a pretty pleasing pricket', as Holofernes immortalizes the event). Thomas Dekker employs a hunting scene in *The Shoemaker's Holiday* (1599; II.i–ii) to introduce his heroine to one of her (unsuccessful) suitors, and the anonymous Cambridge play, *The Return from Parnassus, Pt. II* (1603; II.v) uses a long technical discussion of hunting as a ploy to confuse a university student who applies for some financial aid from a rich young gallant.

Hawk-taming is the central metaphor in Shakespeare's *The Taming of the Shrew*, where Katherine ('Kate the curst') is brought to apparent submission by the falconer (Petruchio), and in *II Henry VI*, according to the 'bad quarto' text, Queen Margaret enters (II.i) '*with her hawk on her fist*', following an off-stage hawking contest.

A great variety of other sports, games, and pastimes were widely practised both in town and country (see Joseph Strutt, *The Sports and Pastimes of the People of England* , 1801). Robert Burton (*The Anatomy of Melancholy* (1621), ed. A. R. Shilleto from 6th edn 1651–2 (1896), II, 83–6), after favourable comments on hunting, hawking, fowling ('with guns, lime, nets, glades [openings in woods, for snaring birds], gins [traps], strings, baits, pitfalls, pipes, calls, stalking-horses, setting-dogs, coy-ducks, &c.'), and fishing ('a kind of hunting by water'), continues:

Many other sports and recreations there be, much in use, as
ringing [?playing at quoits], bowling, shooting [archery],
......keelpins [?ninepins], trunks [blow-guns], quoits, pitching
bars, hurling, wrestling, leaping, running, fencing, mustering
[assembling for the purposes of military exercises], swimming,
wasters [cudgels], foils, football, baloon [inflated ball of leather,
struck to and fro by the arm protected by a wooden brace],
quintain [wooden post or plank set up to be tilted at], &c. and
many such, which are the common recreations of the country
folks; riding of great horses, running at rings, tilts and
tournaments, horse-races, wild-goose chases [horse-races in which
the object was to follow the leader at all costs], which are the
disports of greater men, and good in themselves, though many
Gentlemen, by that means, gallop quite out of their fortunes.

As Burton implies, some sports were more approved of, or more
socially acceptable, than others. Philip Stubbes's opinion of football is
classic (*The Anatomie of Abuses* (1583), 2nd edn; p. 184 in F. J. Furnivall's
edn (1877–9)):

For as concerning football playing, I protest unto you it may rather
be called a friendly kind of fight than a play or recreation; a bloody
and murdering practice than a fellowly sport or pastime. For doth
not everyone lie in wait for his adversary, seeking to overthrow
him and to pick [pitch] him on his nose, though it be upon hard
stones, in ditch or dale, in valley or hill, or what place soever it be,
he careth not, so he may have him down? And he that can serve
the most of this fashion, he is counted the only fellow, and who
but he? So that by this means, sometimes their necks are broken,
sometimes their backs, sometime their legs, sometime their
arms;......But whosoever scapeth away the best goeth not scot-
free, but is either sore wounded and bruised, so as he dieth of it, or
else scapeth very hardly; and no marvel, for they have sleights
[tricks] to meet one betwixt two, to dash him against the heart
with their elbows, to hit him under the short ribs with their griped
[closed] fists, and with their knees to catch him upon the hip, and
to pick him on his neck, with a hundred such murdering devices.

And James I prohibited the playing of football in the confines of the
Court. Roger Ascham (*Toxophilus, The Schole of Shootinge* (1545), ed. W.
A. Wright (1904), in *English Works*, p. 18) considered 'running, leaping,
and quoiting too vile for scholars', but archery or shooting (which he
contrasts with cards and dice, pp. 21–3) was 'a pastime wholesome and
equal for every part of the body, pleasant and full of courage for the
mind.'

Some competence in the art of fencing or sword-play of various kinds
was thought of as a natural part of a gentleman's education, indeed a
necessary part given the military and hot-blooded constitution of an age

in which the concept of 'honour', despite Falstaff, was still more than a 'mere scutcheon'. Fencing schools flourished in London and other towns (see Donald Lupton's 'character' of 'Fencing Schools' in *London and the Countrey Carbonadoed* (1632), pp. 83–6) and practitioners vied with each other over the respective merits of the old mode of short sword and buckler (shield) (for striking and slashing) versus the recently imported (in the 1570s) Italian–French–Spanish school of rapier and dagger (for foining and thrusting), the first school represented by a manual like George Silver's *Paradoxes of Defence* (1599), the second, by *Di Grassi His True Arte of Defence* (trans. I. G., 1594) and Vincentio Saviolo's *His Practise* (1595), which treated not only of the correct use of rapier and dagger, but of the proper observance of honour and honourable quarrels. We may recall Mercutio's disdain for Tybalt's new-fangled duelling terms and techniques (*Romeo and Juliet*, II.iv.10–26) and Hamlet's teasing of the 'fashionable' Osric (v.ii.105–81) for his fencing-school jargon. See Egerton Castle, *Schools and Masters of Fence from the Middle Ages to the Eighteenth Century* (1885).

Battle scenes, armed combat, and sword-play are an indigenous part of Elizabethan–Jacobean drama, particularly so, of course, in the English and Roman history plays or conqueror 'tragedies' like Greene's (?) *Selimus*. In such instances, the old style of sword-and-buckler combat probably predominated, but the new school also leaves its mark, increasingly so in the Jacobean period, in scenes of personal quarrels on points of honour (the duello). See, for example, Shakespeare's *Romeo and Juliet* (III.i, perhaps intended as a mixture of old and new so far as Mercutio and Tybalt are concerned) and *Hamlet* (v.ii, ostensibly a contest of fencing skill); George Chapman's *Bussy D'Ambois* (c.1604), II.i.25–137 (a long report of a six-man duel, two seconds on each side, in which all but Bussy himself are slain); John Webster's *The Devil's Law Case* (c.1610), II.ii; and William Cartwright's *The Lady-Errant* (1633–5), III.ii. The comic potentialities of the duel are exploited in Shakespeare's *Twelfth Night* (III.iv) and Ben Jonson's *Epicoene* (1609), IV.v.

i

Hunting the hart

From George Turbervile, *The Noble Arte of Venerie or Hunting* (1575), chaps. 38–41, pp. 100–27.

Relays must be set according to the seasons and growth of springs. For in winter when the hart's head is hard they keep the strong coverts and thickets. And in spring time when their heads are tender, they keep in young friths and coppices, and in the weakest coverts that they can find, for fear lest they should knock and hurt their heads against the boughs. And therefore it is requisite to set men abroad which are brought up in hunting, and understand well their advantages, and with them a good pricker or huntsman on horseback, mounted upon a good curtal, which should be lightly clad, having good boots and high, with an horn about his neck. Phoebus saith that they ought to be clad in green when they hunt the hart or buck and in russet when they hunt the boar, but that is of no great importance, for I remit the colours to the fantasies of men. These horsemen should go over night to their master's chamber, or if they serve a prince to the Master of the Games or his lieutenants, to know which of them shall follow the kennel, and which shall be for the relays, and in which relays and where they shall bestow themselves, and what hounds they shall lead with them, what helps and varlets shall go with them. And those of the relays shall do well to have every man a little billet to remember the names of their relays . . . . . . Afterwards they must look that their horses be well shod and in good plight, giving them oats sufficient; that done, they shall go to bed that they might rise in the morning two hours before day . . . . . . Their guide being come, they shall break their fasts all together. And instead of pistolets, they shall have each of them a bottle full of good wine at the pommel of their saddles. And when day shall begin to peep, then must they get on horseback, having with them their guide, their relays, and all their equipage . . . . . . When they are come to the place appointed for their relay, they shall place their hounds in some fair place at the foot of some tree, forbidding the varlet that he uncouple them not without their knowledge and commandment, and that he stir not from thence nor make any noise. Then shall they go three or four hundred paces from thence, on that side that the hunting is ordained, and shall harken if they hear anything or can discover the hart, for, seeing him afar off, they shall better judge whether he be spent or not than if they mark him when he is hallowed or cried at. For an hart when he is spent doth bear his head low if he see no man, showing thereby how weary he is. But when he seeth a man, he raiseth up his head and maketh great bounds, as though he

5

10

15

20

25

30

35

40

would have men think that he is strong and stout. As also the
horseman shall withdraw himself aside for another reason. And
that is, because the pages and they which hold the horses do
commonly make such a noise that he cannot hear the cry. And
also when the hart doth hear noise, or hath the dogs in the wind,   45
they will either turn back again or wheel aside from the
relay;......And if he pass by his relay, he shall mark diligently
whether he sink or be spent, and also whether he hear the hounds
in chase coming after him or not. And methinks that in hunting
an hart at force, it were not best to cast off your relays until you see   50
the hounds of the kennel which began the cry. So should you see
who hunteth best, and also the swiftness of your hounds. But
nowadays I see few hunt the hart as he ought to be hunted; for
men give not their hounds leisure to hunt, neither is there passing
two or three that can hunt; for there are so many hunters on   55
horseback which can neither blow, hallow, nor prick perfectly,
which mingle themselves amongst the hounds, crossing them and
breaking their course in such sort, that it is not possible they
should hunt truly: and therefore I say it is the horses which hunt
and not the hounds......   60

   When the Prince or Lord which hunteth shall have heard all
reports, and that the relays are well set and placed,......then he
which seemed to have harboured the greatest and oldest deer, and
him which lieth in the fairest covert,......shall take his
bloodhound and go before to the blemishings with his companions   65
and with all the prickers or hunters on horseback which hunt with
the kennel, who should have every one of them a good cudgel in
his hand, which is called a *Hunting cudgel* or a *Truncheon* to turn
the boughs and bear them from his face as he followeth the
hounds in the woods and thicks;......being come to the   70
blemishes, let them alight to behold the slot and such other marks
as may be taken by the view or foot of a deer, to the end they may
the better know whether their hounds hunt change or not. Then
when the Prince or Master of the Game is come, and the hounds
for the cry, all the horsemen must quickly cast abroad about the   75
covert to discover the hart when he rouseth and goeth out of his
hold that they may the better know him afterwards by the coat and
by his head. And when the huntsman which harboured shall see all
the rest of his companions about him with the hounds for the cry,
he shall then go before them and rouse the deer, for the honour is   80
due to him; and then the rest shall cast off their hounds, he and all
they crying *To him, to him, that's he, that's he* and such other words
of encouragement......Afterwards when he seeth that they are
in full cry, and take it right, he may go out of the thick and give
his hound to his boy or servant and get up on horseback, keeping   85
still under the wind and coasting to cross the hounds which are in
chase to help them at default if need require......

You shall understand herewith that when a hart feels that the hounds hold in after him, he fleeth and seeketh to beguile them, with change in sundry sorts; for he will seek other harts and deer   90
at lair and rouseth them before the hounds to make them hunt change; therewithal he will lie flat down upon his belly in some of their lairs and so let the hounds overshoot him; and because they should have no scent of him, nor vent him, he will truss all his four feet under his belly and will blow and breathe upon the ground in   95
some moist place, in such sort that I have seen the hounds pass by such an hart within a yard of him and never vent him; and this subtlety doth nature endow him with, that he knoweth his breath and his feet to give greater scent unto the hounds than all the rest of his body. . . . . . You shall understand that when a hart is spent   100
and sore run, his last resort is to the water, which hunters call the soil, ... for sometimes the hart will lie under the water all but his very nose; . . . . . . a deer that is spent or sore hunted, and that seeketh to forloin or break from the hounds, will never tarry to cross or double but holdeth head onwards still as long as breath   105
serveth him, unless he have some soil in the wind, then he may chance go aside to take the soil, but else not. . . . . . .

When a hart is at bay, it is dangerous to go in to him and especially in rutting time. For at that time their heads are venemous and most perilous, and thereupon came this proverb: 110

If thou be hurt with hart, it brings thee to thy bier,
But barber's hand will boar's hurt heal, thereof thou needst
    not fear. . . . . . .

You shall understand then that there are bays in the water and bays on the land, and if an hart be in a deep water, where the huntsman cannot come at him, the best thing that he can do shall   115
be to couple up his hounds, ... For a hart which is spent will not willingly leave a great water when he seeth the hounds and the huntsmen come in to him, but will swim up and down in the midst of the stream and never come near the banks . . . . . . And if the huntsmen stand close and upon a clear wind, he may chance to   120
have a blow at him with his sword as he cometh out. . . . . . But if he perceive that the hart will not come out of the water, then let him get a boat, or if he can swim let him put off his clothes and swim to him with a dagger ready drawn to kill him, and yet let him well beware how he assail him unless the water be very   125
deep . . . . . . As touching the bay on the land, ... if it be in a plain and open place where there is no wood nor covert, it is dangerous and hard to come in to him; but if it be by an hedge side, or in a strong thick or queach, then whiles the hart doth stare and look upon the hounds, the huntsman may come covertly   130
amongst the bushes behind him and so may easily kill him; and if the hart turn head upon him, let him run behind some tree or

cover himself in the thick quickly or shake some bough rudely and boisterously before him.

NOTES

1 *Relays* sets of fresh hounds (and horses) posted to take up the chase of a deer in place of those already tired out.
2 *head* antlers.
3 *coverts* thickets.
4 *friths* lands grown sparsely with trees or with underwoods only.
8 *advantages* superiority arising from special knowledge (of hunting).
   pricker mounted attendant.
9 *curtal* horse with its tail docked.
11 *Phoebus* ?Gaston Phoebus, Comte de Foix (died 1391), known for his collection of illustrated hunting manuals.
12 *russet* reddish-brown, also a coarse cloth of that colour.
13 *fantasies* caprices, inclinations.
16 *kennel* pack of hounds, here applied to those hounds beginning the chase as opposed to the 'relays'.
19 *varlets* servants, grooms.
20 *billet* note.
25 *pistolets* small fire-arms, pistols. One may recall Falstaff's 'bottle of sack' carried in his pistol case (*I Henry IV*, v.iii.53–4).
31 *forbidding. . . . . . not* forbidding the groom to uncouple them (a form of the Elizabethan double negative).
37 *hallowed* i.e. hallooed (to incite dogs in the chase).
   cried = 'hallowed'.
44 *cry* yelping of hounds in the chase.
49–50 *hunting. . . . . . force* hunting in the open with the hounds in full cry.
54 *passing* above, more than.
56 *blow* sound the correct calls on the hunting horn. Turbervile lists the various calls (with notation) at the conclusion of his book.
   prick ride fast.
59 *hunt truly* i.e. retain the scent.
63 *harboured* traced a deer to his 'harbour' or lair.
65 *blemishings* 'marks which are left to know where a deer hath gone in or out' (Turbervile).
68 *Truncheon* short thick staff, cudgel.
70 *thicks* thickets.
71 *blemishes* = 'blemishings'.
   slot mark left by the deer's foot.
72 *view* footprint.
73 *hunt change* pick up a fresh scent, not the one they are supposed to be following.
77 *hold* lair or 'harbour'.
80 *rouse* cause to leave his 'hold' (see l. 77).
81 *cast off* uncouple, unleash.
86 *under the wind* on the side away from the wind.
   coasting riding by the side of.

cross intercept (in order to redirect).

87   *at default* i.e. in failing to follow the scent.

90   *change* counter-moves.

94   *vent* snuff up the air in order to pick up the scent.

104   *forloin* leave the hounds far behind.

109   *rutting time* certain period when an animal is in a state of sexual excitement.

113   *bays* those places where the hunted animal stands 'at bay', unable to flee further.

120   *upon......wind* i.e. standing in such a position that the wind does not blow his scent in the direction of the deer.

129   *queach* thicket or dense growth of bushes.

ii

A hawking contest

From Thomas Heywood, *A Woman Kill'd with Kindness* (1607), I.iii.
[Hawking and dog-coursing matches have been arranged (I.i) between
Sir Charles Mountford and Sir Francis Acton, a hundred pounds being
laid on each match by the principals.]

Wind horns. Enter SIR CHARLES [MOUNTFORD], SIR FRANCIS
  [ACTON], MALBY, CRANWELL, WENDOLL, *Falconer[s], and
  Huntsmen*

SIR CHARLES. So; well cast off! Aloft, aloft! Well flown!
  O now she takes her at the souse, and strikes her
  Down to the earth, like a swift thunder-clap.

WENDOLL. She hath struck ten angels out of my way.

SIR FRANCIS. A hundred pound from me.   5

SIR CHARLES. What, falc'ner!

FALCONER. At hand, sir.

SIR CHARLES. Now she hath seiz'd the fowl and 'gins to plume
    her;
  Rebeck her not; rather stand still and cherk her.
  So! seize her gets, her jesses, and her bells.   10
  Away!

SIR FRANCIS. My hawk kill'd, too.

SIR CHARLES.   Ay, but 'twas at the querre,
  Not at the mount like mine.

SIR FRANCIS.   Judgement, my masters!

CRANWELL. Yours miss'd her at the ferre.

WENDOLL. Ay, but our merlin first had plum'd the fowl,   15
  And twice renew'd her from the river too.
  Her bells, Sir Francis, had not both one weight.
  Nor was one semi-tune above the other.
  Methinks these Milan bells do sound too full,
  And spoil the mounting of your hawk.

SIR CHARLES.   'Tis lost.   20

SIR FRANCIS. I grant it not. Mine likewise seiz'd a fowl
  Within her talents; and you saw her paws
  Full of the feathers. Both her petty singles
  And her long singles grip'd her more than other;

The terrials of her legs were stain'd with blood,   25
Not of the fowl only; she did discomfit
Some of her feathers, but she brake away.
Come, come, your hawk is but a rifler.

SIR CHARLES.   How!

SIR FRANCIS. Ay, and your dogs are trindle-tails and curs.

SIR CHARLES. You stir my blood!   30
You keep not one good hound in all your kennel,
Nor one good hawk upon your perch.

SIR FRANCIS.   How, knight!

SIR CHARLES. So, knight! you will not swagger, sir?

SIR FRANCIS.   Why, say I did?

SIR CHARLES. Why, sir, I say you would gaine as much by
   swagg'ring
As you have got by wagers on your dogs.   35
You will come short in all things.

SIR FRANCIS.   Not in this!
Now I'll strike home.   [*Strikes Sir Charles*]

SIR CHARLES.   Thou shalt to thy long home,
Or I will want my will.

SIR FRANCIS. All they that love Sir Francis, follow me!

SIR CHARLES. All that affect Sir Charles, draw on my part!   40

CRANWELL. On this side heaves my hand.

WENDOLL.   Here goes my heart.

SIR CHARLES,CRANWELL, *Falconer, and Huntsmen fight against*
   SIR FRANCIS, WENDOLL, *his Falconer and Huntsman; and* SIR
   CHARLES *hath the better and beats them away, killing both of* SIR
   FRANCIS *his men* [*Exeunt all but* SIR CHARLES]

SIR CHARLES. My God, what have I done! What have I done!
My rage hath plung'd into a sea of blood,
In which my soul lies drown'd. Poor innocents,
For whom we are to answer! Well, 'tis done,   45
And I remain the victor. A great conquest!
When I would give this right hand, nay, this head,
To breathe in them new life whom I have slain.
Forgive me, God! 'twas in the heat of blood,
And anger quite removes me from myself.   50
It was not I, but rage, did this vile murder;

Yet I, and not my rage, must answer it.
Sir Francis Acton, he is fled the field;
With him all those that did partake his quarrel;
And I am left alone, with sorrow dumb,   55
And in my heighth of conquest overcome.

[Later in the scene Sir Charles is arrested and sent to prison, but, by ruining himself financially, buys his freedom.]

NOTES

1   *cast off* turned off the fist to fly up.

2   *at the souse* i.e. swooping down on its prey from above.

8   *'gins......her* begins to tear out her feathers.

9   *Rebeck her not* Don't call her off.
    cherk chirrup (like a bird), one way a falconer 'talked' to his bird (Turbervile, p. 143). 'cherk' is K. L. Bates's emendation of the 1607 reading 'checke'.

10   *gets* ?some part of a hawk's harness.
    jesses short leather or silk straps fastened to the legs of a hawk, with a small ring on their free ends for attachment to the falconer's leash.
    bells Two bells, tuned a semi-tone apart (see l. 18), were fastened one on each leg.

12   *at the querre* i.e. before the prey rose from the ground (an unsporting kill).

13   *at the mount* i.e. after the prey had risen in the air.

14   *at the ferre* i.e. at the further bank of the river.

15   *merlin* species of falcon. 'They fly with greater fierceness and more hotly than any other hawk of prey' (Turbervile, p. 52).

16   *renew'd* drove (by a fresh attack).

17   *one weight* Hawk bells had to be of equal weight to avoid unbalancing the hawk's flight.

18   *semi-tune* semi-tone (see above, l. 10).

19   *Milan bells* silver bells, supposed to be the best.
    sound too full have too much resonance.

22   *talents* talons (variant form).

23–4   *petty singles......long singles* outer and inner claws.

24   *grip'd* past tense of 'gripe'=grip.
    other i.e. the other (Sir Charles's hawk).

25   *terrials* probably a misprint for 'terrets'=each of the two rings by which the leash is attached to the jesses.

28   *rifler* spoiler, plunderer.

29   *trindle-tails* curly-tailed, low-bred dogs.

32   *perch* cross-stick stand for a falcon.

33   *swagger* talk insolently (as to an inferior).

37   *long home* eternity in death.

40   *affect* prefer.

41   SD *Francis his* Francis's.

51   *It was......murder* Compare Hamlet's excuse to Laertes for his killing of Polonius (V.ii.234–9).

Bear-baiting and cock-fighting

Bear-baiting, bull-baiting, and cock-fighting were among the most popular diversions for people of all levels until the middle of the seventeenth century (cock-fighting indeed was not outlawed in England until the middle of the nineteenth century). Even so generally humane a person as Roger Ascham promised a treatise on cock-fighting (which, if he wrote, has not, happily, survived), and bear- and bull-baiting were under royal and noble patronage and control. John Stow (*A Survay of London* (edn 1603), ed. C. L. Kingsford (1908), II, 54) describes two bear-gardens in Southwark on the West Bank: '......there be two bear-gardens, the old and new places, wherein be kept bears, bulls, and other beasts to be baited. As also mastiffs in several kennels, nourished to bait them. These bears and other beasts are there baited in plots of ground, scaffolded about for the beholders to stand safe.' The better known was called Paris Garden, a 'circular', tiered structure similar to the London theatres, where regular performances (most commonly on Wednesdays and Sundays) took place, unless the Court, which had a virtual monopoly on such 'sports' in London, required attendance for the entertainment of visiting dignitaries (e.g. in 1559, 'after dinner to bear and bull baiting, and the Queen's grace and the [French] ambassadors stood in the gallery [at Whitehall] looking of the pastime till six at night' (E. K. Chambers, *Elizabethan Stage*, II, 453)). The tone of these 'pastimes' is nicely caught by an early Jacobean advertisement: 'Tomorrow, being Thursday, shall be seen at the Bear-garden on the Bankside a great match played by the gamesters of Essex, who hath challenged all comers whatsoever to play five dogs at the single bear for five pounds [the bear was chained to a stake] and also to worry a bull dead at the stake, and for your better content shall have pleasant sport with the horse and ape and whipping of the blind bear. *Vivat Rex*' (Chambers, II, 458).

Selection (i), from Robert Laneham's *Letter* (1575), describes one of the numerous entertainments arranged for Queen Elizabeth on her nineteen-day visit to Kenilworth Castle, the seat of the Earl of Leicester, in 1575. Laneham's whole *Letter* is well worth reading. Written in a highly colloquial, undress style, it is packed with detail and gives a vivid picture of the costly (often ruinous) lengths to which members of the nobility were forced to go in entertaining the Queen and her household on one of her famous 'progresses'.

Like most of his contemporaries, Laneham obviously enjoyed and approved of the nasty business of bear-baiting, but selection (ii), from Philip Stubbes's *The Anatomie of Abuses* (1583), presents what was a minority opinion at the time, one that was, however, gradually gaining ground, particularly among the more pronounced Puritan groups. Stubbes's reaction, as usual, is vitriolic, but it is a pleasure, for once, to find his vituperative and fire-eating moralism wholly agreeable. Some years later, Thomas Dekker (*Work for Armourers* (1609), ed. A. B.

Grosart, IV, 98–9) echoes his view. Describing the whipping of 'Monsieur Hunks', the blind bear, by 'a company of creatures that had the shapes of men and faces of Christians (being either colliers, carters, or watermen)', he says it 'moved as much pity in my breast towards him as the leading of poor starved wretches to the whipping posts in London (when they had more need to be relieved with food) ought to move the hearts of citizens, though it be the fashion now to laugh at the punishment.' This particular inhumanity is also singled out for criticism by the German traveller Paul Hentzner (*Itinerarium* (1612, edn of 1757), pp. 42–3), but his Swiss contemporary, Thomas Platter, evinces no disgust when he confides to his diary how 'Lastly they brought in an old blind bear which the boys hit with canes and sticks; but he knew how to untie his leash and he ran back to his stall' (Clare Williams, *Thomas Platter's Travels in England, 1599* (1923), p. 169). Platter also notes that 'The bears' teeth were not sharp so they could not injure the dogs; they have them broken short', and that, after the second bear had been baited, 'a large white powerful bull was brought in, and likewise bound in the centre of the theatre, and one dog only was set on him at a time, which he speared with his horns and tossed in such masterly fashion, that they could not get the better of him.' The general level of the audience is thus described by Donald Lupton in his 'character' of Paris Garden: 'Here come......the swaggering roarer, the cunning cheater, the rotten bawd, the swearing drunkard, and the bloody butcher' (*London and the Countrey Carbonadoed* (1632), pp. 66–9).

Selection (iii), from Gervase Markham's *Country Contentments: or The Husbandmans Recreations* (1631), describes in loving detail the care, preparation and 'matching' of fighting cocks for 'battle' in the cock-pit. Henry VIII had erected a special cock-pit in the palace at Whitehall (Stow, II, 102), which under James I was occasionally used for plays, and many other less elaborate cock-pits existed in London and the provinces. In 1609 John Best built a public cock-pit in St Giles In the Fields, bordering on Drury Lane, which later was converted into a 'private' theatre (1616–17) known as the Phoenix.

The indefatigable Platter (pp. 167–8) witnessed a cock-fight in a 'house' 'built like a theatre. In the centre of the floor stands a circular table covered with straw and with high ledges round it, where the cocks are teased and incited to fly at one another, while those with wagers as to which cock will win sit closest around the circular disk, but the spectators who are merely present on their entrance penny sit around higher up, watching with eager pleasure the fierce and angry fight between the cocks, as these wound each other to death with spurs and beaks.' He adds that the stakes 'often amount to many thousands of crowns' and that the 'game' could last four or five hours.

i

From Robert Laneham's *Letter* (1575; ed. F. J. Furnivall (1887), pp. 16–17).

Thursday, the fourteenth of this July [1575], and the sixth day of her Majesty's coming, a great sort of bandogs were there tied in the utter court and thirteen bears in the inner......

    Well, sir, the bears were brought forth into the court, the dogs set to them,......Very fierce, both ton and tother, and eager in argument......   5

    Therefore thus, with fending and proving, with plucking and tugging, scratting and biting, by plain tooth and nail a'to[n] side and tother, such expense of blood and leather was there between them, as a month's licking (I ween) will not recover......   10

    It was a sport very pleasant of these beasts to see the bear with his pink neyes leering after his enemy's approach, the nimbleness and wait of the dog to take his advantage, and the force and experience of the bear again to avoid the assaults. If he were bitten in one place, how he would pinch in an other to get free; that if he   15
were taken once, then what shift, with biting, with clawing, with roaring, tossing, and tumbling, he would work to wind himself from them; and when he was loose, to shake his ears twice or thrice with the blood and the slaver about his physnomy, was a matter of a goodly relief.   20

NOTES

2   *sort of bandogs* number of mastiffs or bloodhounds (frequently kept chained because of their fierceness).
3   *utter* outer.
5   *ton and tother* the one and the other.
     eager savage, biting (with reference to their teeth).
7   *fending and proving* warding off and making trial.
8   *scratting* scratching, lacerating.
12   *neyes leering after* eyes looking from side to side watching.
13   *wait* watchfulness.
14   *If he* i.e. if the bear.
16   *were taken once* were ever caught (by the dogs).
     shift evasive stratagem. The bear was chained to a stake, which made his defence more difficult.
19   *physnomy* physiognomy.
20   *matter......relief* This may mean that the onlookers were relieved when the bear extricated itself, but, more probably, it means that the 'sport' was a good way to while away the time, a form of 'comic relief'.

ii

From Philip Stubbes, *The Anatomie of Abuses* (1583; 2nd edn), pp. 177–8 in F. J. Furnivall's edn (1877–9).

These heathnical exercises upon the Sabaoth day, which the Lord would have consecrated to holy uses for the glory of his name and our spiritual comfort, are not in any respect tolerable or to be suffered. For the baiting of a bear, besides that it is a filthy, stinking, and loathsome game, is it not a dangerous and a perilous   5
exercise, wherein a man is in danger of his life every minute of an hour? Which thing, though it were not so, yet what exercise is this meet for any Christian? What Christen heart can take pleasure to see one poor beast to rent, tear, and kill another, and all for his foolish pleasure? And although they be bloody beasts to mankind,   10
and seek his destruction, yet we are not to abuse them, for his sake who made them and whose creatures they are......It is a [com]mon saying amongst all men, borrowed from the French, 'Qui aime Jean, aime son chien', love me, love my dog; so, love God, love his creatures......   15
   And some, who take themselves for no small fools, are so far assotted that they will not stick to keep a dozen or a score of great mastiffs, to their no small charges, for the maintenance of this goodly game (forsooth!), and will not make any bones of twenty, forty, yea, an hundred pound at once to hazard at a bait – with,   20
'Fight dog!, Fight bear!, The devil part all!'. And to be plain, I think the Devil is the Master of the Game, bearward and all! A goodly pastime, forsooth, worthy of commendation and well fitting these gentlemen of such reputation!

NOTES

1   *heathnical* heathenish.
     Sabaoth from the Hebrew, meaning 'hosts', 'armies', frequently used for 'Sabbath' (i.e. Sunday) in English usage.
6   *a man* referring, presumably, to the bearward, or keeper of the bears (see l. 22), who superintended their performance, though some reference to the spectators may be included.
14   *'Qui......chien'* Who loves John, loves his dog. See Tilley D496.
16   *some......fools* i.e. some men, who consider themselves in no way even slightly foolish.
17   *assotted* infatuated, acting like fools.
     stick hesitate.
19   *not......bones of* will have no scruples about (in wagering).
21   *'Fight dog......all!'* Tilley (D467) lists as proverbial, Stubbes's use being the earliest. 'devil part all' means '?the devil go shares in everything', as

did the 'Master of the Game' in a deer hunt (see l. 22). 'Master of the Game' was also the official title of Queen Elizabeth's officer responsible for the procurement and care of all the royal bears, bulls and mastiffs.

iii

Cock-fighting

From Gervase Markham, *Country Contentments: or The Husbandmans Recreations* (1631), bk. I, pp. 114–17.

After the end of six weeks' feeding, finding your cock in lust and breath, you may fight him at your pleasure, observing that he have at least three days' rest before he fight, and well emptied of his meat before you bring him into the pit.

Now when you bring him into the pit to fight, you must have   5
an especial care to the matching of him, for in that art consisteth the greatest glory of the cock-master; for what availeth it to feed never so well, if in the matching you give that advantage which overthroweth all your former labour? Therefore, in your matching; there are two things to be considered: that is, the length of cocks,   10
and the strength of cocks. For, if your adversary cock be too long, yours shall hardly catch his head, and then he can neither endanger eye or life; and if he be the stronger, he will overbear your cock, and not suffer him to rise and strike with any advantage. Therefore, for the knowledge of these two rules,   15
though experience be the best tutor, yet the first, which is length, you shall judge by your eye, when you gripe the cock about the waist and make him shoot out his legs, in which posture you shall see the utmost of his height, and so compare them in your judgement. Now for his strength, which is known by the thickness   20
of his body (for that cock is ever held the strongest which is largest in garth), you shall know it by the measure of his hands, griping the cock about from the points of your great fingers to the joints of your thumbs. And either of these advantages by no means give to your adversary; but if you doubt loss in the one, yet be sure to gain   25
in the other; for the weak long cock will rise at more ease, and the short strong cock will give the surer blow, so that, because all cocks are not cast into a mould, there may be a reconciliation of the advantages; yet by all means give as little as you can.

When your cock is equally matched, you shall thus prepare him 30
to the fight. First, with a pair of fine cock-shears you shall cut all
his mane off, close unto his neck, even from his head unto the
setting on of his shoulders. Then you shall clip off all the feathers
from his tail close unto his rump; where, the more scarlet that you
see his rump, in the better estate of body the cock is. Then you 35
shall take his wings, and, spreading them forth by the length of
the first feather of his wing, clip the rest slope-wise with sharp
points, that in his rising he may therewith endanger the eyes of his
adversary. Then, with a sharp knife, you shall scrape smooth and
sharpen his beak; then shall you smooth and sharpen his spurs. 40

Lastly, you shall see that there be no feathers above the crown
of his head for his foe to take hold on, and then, with your spittle
moist'ning his head all over, turn him into the pit to prove his
fortune. When the battle is ended, the first thing you do, you shall
search his wounds, and, as many as you can find, you shall with 45
your mouth suck the blood out of them; then wash them very well
with warm urine to keep them from rankling; and then presently
give him a roll or two of your best scouring, and so stove him up as
hot as you can, both with sweet straw and blanketing, in a close
basket for all that night, ... 50

But if he have received any hurt or blemish in his eye, then
shall you take a leaf or two of right ground ivy, ... and, having
chewed it very well in your mouth and sucked out the juice, spit it
into the eye of the cock, and it will not only cure it of any wound
or any blow in the eye, where the sight is not pierced, but also 55
defend it from the breeding of films, haws, warts, or any such
other infirmities which quite destroy the sight. . . . . . .

NOTES

1   *lust* appetite (for fighting).
7–8 *feed . . . . . . well* i.e. feed (the cock) all the correct foods, which Markham
     has earlier detailed.
14   *rise* spring or mount up (beating its wings).
22   *garth* girth, measurement round about.
      his i.e. your.
23   *great fingers* i.e. the second finger of each hand.
25   *doubt* fear.
28   *cast . . . . . . mould* i.e. are not all alike.
32   *mane* hackles or neck-feathers.
47   *rankling* festering.
48   *roll* pill (shaped like a small roll).
      scouring purgative medicine.
      stove him up i.e. make him sweat.
49   *close* covered.

52 *right* true.
56 *films, haws* morbid eye-growths, infected triangular cartilages in the eyes, considered as 'excrescences'.

4 The Court

Queen Elizabeth

The following four selections give us an intimate contemporary glimpse of Queen Elizabeth I, the 'Star of England', in her long reign (1558–1603) and in her death. In each something of the remarkable force and quality of Elizabeth, the awe and admiration that she generated among her subjects both high and low, may be felt behind the words. It was the 'Age of Elizabeth'.

The first selection (i) is from Paul Hentzner's *Itinerarium* (1612). Hentzner, a native of Brandenburg, toured England in 1598 as tutor to Christoph Rehdiger, a young Silesian nobleman. Horace Walpole, who first published a translation of Hentzner's work, notes (p. iii) that he 'had that laborious and indiscriminate passion for SEEING, which is remarked in his countrymen', a backhanded compliment, perhaps, but, fortunately for us, abundantly true. His eye for detail, generally accurate, is extraordinary, and he not only looked but listened as well. Following the present selection, Hentzner describes the lavish ceremonial that attended the preparations for the Queen's dinner (mid-day), which, after the elaborate public presentation, she ate in the privacy of her own chamber alone. On this occasion there were twenty-four dishes borne in by the Yeomen of the Guard, 'while the lady-taster gave to each of the guard a mouthful to eat, of the particular dish he had brought, for fear of poison' (p. 52).

Selection (ii) is from a letter by Sir John Harington written in 1606. 'He that thriveth in a court must put half his honesty under his bonnet; and many do we know that never part that commodity at all, and sleep with it all in a bag' (*Nugae Antiquae*, II, 153). So said Sir John, and he well knew whereof he spoke, nor, on occasion, was he above following the first part of his dictum. Translator of Ariosto's *Orlando Furioso* (1591) and author of the satirical and rather scurrilous *The Metamorphosis of Ajax* [i.e. 'a jakes' or 'privy'] (1596), in which he offered instructions for the building of the first flush-privy, he was a favourite of the Queen and could sign himself 'your highness' saucy godson' (*Nugae Antiquae*, II, 217). As his letter shows, he both loved and feared Elizabeth (he had had some experience of her anger), and his sharp insight into character admirably catches something of the essence of that brilliant, difficult, and complex woman.

Ben Jonson's comments (in his *Conversations with Drummond*, 1619) are less deferential: 'Queen Elizabeth never saw herself after she became old in a true glass. They painted her and sometimes would vermilion her nose. She always, about Christmas evens, set dice that threw sixes or five, and she knew not they were other, to make her win and esteem herself fortunate. That she had a membrana on her which made her uncapable of man, though for her delight she tried many. At the coming over of Monsieur [the Duc d'Alençon], there was a French chirurgeon who took in hand to cut it; yet fear stayed her and his death.' There is some real question about the so-called 'membrana'.

The third selection (iii), from an undated letter of Dr Leonel Sharp's to the Duke of Buckingham, presents Queen Elizabeth at a moment of crisis and triumph: the Spanish Armada has been decisively defeated (following the battle of Gravelines, 28 July 1588), but the Duke of Parma, with a large army in Holland, still appears to threaten an invasion. To bolster morale, the Queen insists upon visiting her troops and arrives by royal barge at Tilbury, a town on the Thames' estuary opposite Gravesend, on 8 August. Next day she reviews her army and delivers a rousing oration (selection (iii)). William Camden (*The Historie of the Princesse Elizabeth* (1630); trans. R. Norton) describes the moment:

> . . . riding about through the ranks of armed men drawn up on both sides her, with a leader's truncheon in her hand, sometimes with a martial pace, another while gently like a woman, incredible it is how much she encouraged the hearts of her captains and soldiers by her presence and speech to them.

The speech is typical of Elizabeth's public utterances, many of which she composed herself. Rhetorically straightforward, she (as often) with an assumed modesty calls attention to her supposed weakness as a mere woman at the same time that she makes her hearers feel that she is more than the equal of any man ('I myself will be your General'), and, in the midst of appealing to their patriotism, she is careful to strike the hardheaded, realistic note by promising her soldiers 'rewards and crowns'. The speech was met with loud shouts of approval. Elizabeth, and it was one of her greatest strengths, knew her people.

Selection (iv), from *The Diary of John Manningham, 1602–1603*, is a quietly moving report of the Queen's death and the subsequent proclamation of James VI of Scotland as her successor. Comparison with another account by Sir Robert Cary, who, though not present at her death, visited the Queen in the final stages of her illness, suggests that Manningham was well informed (see *Memoirs of Robert Cary, Earl of Monmouth* (1759), pp. 136–47). Cary gives a firsthand account of Elizabeth's growing melancholy and depression:

> When I came to Court [about the end of 1602], I found the Queen ill disposed, and she kept her inner lodging; yet she, hearing of my arrival, sent for me. I found her in one of her withdrawing chambers, sitting low upon her cushions. She called me to her; I kissed her hand, and told her it was my chiefest happiness to see her in safety, and in health, which I wished might long continue. She took me by the hand, and wrung it hard, and said, 'No, Robin, I am not well'; and then discoursed with me of her indisposition,

and that her heart had been sad and heavy for ten or twelve days; and in her discourse, she fetched not so few as forty or fifty great sighs. I was grieved at the first to see her in this plight; for in all my lifetime before, I never knew her fetch a sigh but when the Queen of Scots was beheaded. Then [in 1587], upon my knowledge, she shed many tears and sighs, manifesting her innocence, that she never gave consent to the death of that Queen. [It has been suggested that these tears and sighs were more politic than heartfelt.] (*Memoirs*, pp. 136–7.)

Cary's concern for the Queen may have been genuine enough, but he wasted no time in writing to James in Edinburgh, assuring him that he would be the first to bring him word of the Queen's death. This he did, evading the orders of the Privy Council, hoping to curry favour with the new king. The results of his famous ride were shortlived; James, on coming to London, 'deceived my expectation and adhered to those that sought my ruin' (p. 156).

Thomas Dekker (*1603. The Wonderfull Yeare* (1603), ed. F. P. Wilson in *The Plague Pamphlets of Thomas Dekker* (1925), pp. 11–25) offers a somewhat hyperbolical but basically true report of the public sorrow and fear (of possible civil war over the succession) that attended the Queen's death and the immense sense of relief that flooded the country (particularly London) when James of Scotland was, without any civil disturbances, proclaimed king.

Hundreds of complimentary references to Elizabeth ('The Faerie Queene') appeared with monotonous regularity throughout her reign, many of them in the drama (see E. C. Wilson, *England's Eliza*, (1939)). Elizabeth's refusal to marry and produce an heir led Thomas Sackville and Thomas Norton to write *Gorboduc* (1562), the first regular English tragedy, in which, as a gentle hint, they pictured the chaos and civil wars that plague a kingdom when there is no heir apparent. John Lyly, under the character of Cynthia, the moon-goddess, celebrates Elizabeth in *Endymion* (1588), showing how the Queen, with a single smile of favour, can restore Endymion, who has slept for forty years, to youth and beauty (v.iii). And Ben Jonson, again as Cynthia, pays the aged Queen extravagant compliments in *Cynthia's Revels* (1600–1). After the death of Elizabeth, it became possible to represent the Queen under her own name, a licence Thomas Heywood took almost immediate advantage of in the two parts of *If You Know Not Me You Know Nobody* (1604, 1605), recounting her troubles under Queen Mary and her victory over the Spanish Armada; and a little later George Chapman in *The Conspiracy of Charles Duke of Byron* (1608; IV.i) reports at length her spirited and politic reception of Byron when he comes to England as Henry IV's emissary.

For modern assessments of Elizabeth I, see Sir John Neale, *Queen Elizabeth* (1934) and Elizabeth Jenkins, *Elizabeth the Great* (1958); and for another near-contemporary account see Sir Robert Naunton,

Fragmenta Regalia (1641, 2nd edn); for Harington, see Ruth Hughey, *John Harington of Stepney* (1971).

i

A foreigner views Queen Elizabeth

From Paul Hentzner, *Itinerarium* (1612; trans. from the Latin by Richard Bentley for Horace Walpole and privately printed at Strawberry Hill (1757), pp. 47–51; Bentley's translation has been slightly emended by that in W. B. Rye's *England as Seen by Foreigners* (1865), pp. 103–5).

We arrived next at the royal palace of Greenwich,. . . . . . We were admitted. . . . . . into the presence-chamber, hung with rich tapestry, and the floor, after the English fashion, strewed with hay [i.e. rushes], through which the Queen commonly passes in her way to chapel. . . . . . . First went gentlemen, barons, earls, Knights   5 of the Garter, all richly dressed and bareheaded; next came the Lord High Chancellor of England, bearing the seals in a red-silk purse, between two, one of which carried the royal sceptre, the other the sword of state, in a red scabbard studded with golden fleurs-de-lis, the point upwards. Next came the Queen, in the   10 sixty-fifth year of her age, as we were told, very majestic; her face oblong, fair, but wrinkled; her eyes small, yet black and pleasant; her nose a little hooked; her lips narrow and her teeth black (a defect the English seem subject to from their too great use of sugar). She had in her ears two pearls with very rich drops; she   15 wore false hair, and that reddish-yellow; upon her head she had a small crown. . . . . . .; her bosom was uncovered, as all the English ladies have it till they marry; and she had on a necklace of exceeding fine jewels. Her hands were slender, her fingers rather long, and her stature neither tall nor low; her air was stately, her   20 manner of speaking mild and obliging. That day she was dressed in white silk, bordered with pearls of the size of beans, and over it a mantle of black silk shot with silver threads; her train was very long, the end of it borne by a marchioness; instead of a chain, she had an oblong collar of gold and jewels. As she went along in all   25 this state and magnificence, she spoke very graciously, first to one, then to another, whether foreign ministers, or those who attended for different reasons, in English, French, and Italian; for besides

being well skilled in Greek, Latin, and the languages I have
mentioned, she is mistress of Spanish, Scotch, and Dutch.   30
Whoever speaks to her, it is kneeling; now and then she raises
some with her hand.......Wherever she turned her face, as she
was going along, everybody fell down on their knees. The Ladies
of the Court followed next to her, very handsome and well-shaped,
and for the most part dressed in white. She was guarded on each   35
side by the gentlemen pensioners, fifty in number, with gilt
halberds. In the ante-chapel, next the hall where we were,
petitions were presented to her, and she received them most
graciously, which occasioned the acclamation of *God save the
Queen Elizabeth*! She answered it with *I thank you mine good*   40
people.

NOTES

1   *palace of Greenwich* in Kent, on the south bank of the Thames. Elizabeth
    was born there and it was a favourite of hers, especially in summer.
2   *presence-chamber* reception-room in the palace.
3   *hay* The strewing of green rushes on the floors (Hentzner's 'hay' is a slip)
    was common even in the great houses at this time.
5-6 *Knights......Garter* members of the Order of St George, twenty-seven
    in number (including the sovereign), the highest order of knighthood.
7   *seals* i.e. the seals of state of England, France and Ireland, regularly
    entrusted to the Lord Chancellor as a sign of his office. They were used to
    authenticate royal edicts.
9   *sword of state* the symbol of justice.
16 *reddish-yellow* Bentley translated Hentzner's 'crinem fulvum' as meaning
    'red hair'; 'auburn' (Rye's reading) is another possible translation; but
    'reddish-yellow' seems closest to the Latin.
17 *bosom was uncovered* i.e. the bodice was very low cut.
24 *marchioness* wife of a marquis.
30 *Dutch* i.e. probably German.
36 *gentlemen pensioners* body-guard, instituted by Henry VIII, which served
    in the royal palace.
37 *halberds* combinations of spear and battle-axe, mounted on a handle five
    to seven feet long.
40 *mine* Hentzner's German ('mein') probably got the better of the more
    idiomatic English 'my'.

ii

From a letter by Sir John Harington to Robert Markham (1606) (printed in *Nugae Antiquae* (1779), II, 133–41).

......I marvel to think what strange humours do conspire to patch up the natures of some minds. The elements do seem to strive which shall conquer and rise above the other. In good sooth, our late Queen did enfold them all together. I bless her memory for all her goodness to me and my family; and now will I show you what strange temperament she did sometime put forth. Her mind was ofttime like the gentle air that cometh from the westerly point in a summer's morn; 'twas sweet and refreshing to all around her. Her speech did win all affections and her subjects did try to show all love to her commands; for she would say her state did require her to command what she knew her people would willingly do from their own love to her. Herein did she show her wisdom fully; for, Who did choose to lose her confidence? or, Who would withhold a show of love and obedience when their sovereign said it was their own choice and not her compulsion? Surely she did play well her tables to gain obedience thus without constraint; again, she could put forth such alterations, when obedience was lacking, as left no doubtings whose daughter she was. I say this was plain on the Lord Deputy's coming home, when I did come into her presence; she chafed much, walked fastly to and fro, looked with discomposure in her visage; and, I remember, she catched my girdle when I kneeled to her, and swore, 'By God's Son, I am no Queen, that MAN is above me! Who gave him command to come here so soon? I did send him on other business.' It was long before more gracious discourse did fall to my hearing; but I was then put out of my trouble and bid go home. I did not stay to be bidden twice. If all the Irish rebels had been at my heels, I should not have had better speed, for I did now flee from one whom I both loved and feared too. Her Highness was wont to sooth her ruffled temper with reading every morning, when she had been stirred to passion at the Council, or other matters had overthrown her gracious disposition. She did much admire Seneca's wholesome advisings, when the soul's quiet was flown away; and I saw much of her translating thereof. By art and nature together so blended, it was difficult to find her right humour at any time. Her wisest men and best councillors were oft sore troubled to know her will in matters of state: so covertly did she pass her judgement as seemed to leave all to their discreet management; and, when the business did turn to better advantage, she did most cunningly commit the good issue to her own honour and understanding; but, when ought fell out contrary to her will and intent, the Council were in great strait to defend their own acting and not blemish the Queen's

5

10

15

20

25

30

35

40

good judgement. Herein her wise men did oft lack more wisdom; and the Lord Treasurer would oft shed a plenty of tears on any miscarriage, well knowing the difficult part was, not so much to   45
mend the matter itself, as his mistress's humour; and yet he did most share her favour and good will, and to his opinion she would ofttime submit her own pleasure in great matters. She did keep him till late at night in discoursing alone and then call out another at his departure, and try the depth of all around her sometime.   50
Walsingham had his turn, and each displayed their wit in private. On the morrow everyone did come forth in her presence and discourse at large; and, if any had dissembled with her, or stood not well to her advisings before, she did not let it go unheeded and sometimes not unpunished. Sir Christopher Hatton was wont to   55
say the Queen did fish for men's souls and had so sweet a bait that no one could escape her network. In truth, I am sure her speech was such as none could refuse to take delight in when frowardness did not stand in the way. I have seen her smile, soothe with great semblance of good liking to all around, and cause everyone to   60
open his most inward thought to her; when, on a sudden, she would ponder in private on what had passed, write down all their opinions, draw them out as occasion required, and sometime disprove to their faces what had been delivered a month before. Hence she knew everyone's part and by thus fishing, as Hatton   65
said, she caught many poor fish, who little knew what snare was laid for them. . . . . . As I did bear so much love toward her Majesty, I know not well how to stop my tales of her virtues, and sometimes her faults, for '*nemo nascitur sine – ,*' saith the poet; but even her errors did seem great marks of surprising endowments: 70
When she smiled, it was a pure sunshine, that everyone did choose to bask in, if they could; but anon came a storm from a sudden gathering of clouds and the thunder fell in wondrous manner on all alike. . . . . . .

NOTES

4   *enfold* encompass.
9   *affections* dispositions.
15–16 *play well her tables* manage the game well (as in playing backgammon).
18   *whose daughter* i.e. Henry VIII's.
19   *Lord Deputy's coming home* Robert Devereux, second Earl of Essex, was made Lord Deputy of Ireland in 1599 to bring the Irish rebels to heel. He failed and returned to England against the Queen's orders later in the same year; he was placed under house arrest for several months. Harington had accompanied Essex to Ireland. In a letter to Dr John Still (*Nugae Antiquae*, II, 150), Harington reports that the Queen greeted him with 'What, did the fool bring you too? Go back to your business.'

23   *MAN* i.e. Essex. In 1601, Essex made an abortive attempt at rebellion, for which he was tried and executed. Harington was not implicated.

32–3 *Seneca's wholesome advisings* i.e. Seneca's *Epistulae Morales*. Many years before (1567), Elizabeth had presented Harington with a translation of one of the epistles done by her own hand.

34   *art* learning, nurture.

37   *covertly* indirectly, by implication.

39   *commit* consign.

41   *Council* the Queen's Privy Council.

42   *strait* difficulty, dilemma.
     blemish i.e. appear to impugn.

43   *more wisdom* greater wisdom (? than the queen).

44   *Lord Treasurer* William Cecil, Lord Burghley, greatly loved and admired by the Queen who, rightly, valued his judgement in all affairs of state.

49   *call out* summon (to her presence).

50   *sometime* at one time or another.

51   *Walsingham* Sir Francis Walsingham, Secretary of State, a fanatical Protestant, notorious for his espionage system.
     wit intellectual acumen.

54   *advisings before* i.e. the Queen's opinions expressed in private on the previous evening to the individual councillors.

55   *Hatton* Lord High Chancellor, fiercely loyal to the queen (probably in love with her), taciturn, but famous for his dancing.

57   *network* here apparently used for 'fishing-net', a meaning not given in *OED*.

59   *soothe* encourage, humour.

65   *part* ability, capacity (usually in plural).

69   *nemo nascitur sine* – no one is born without (faults). The 'poet' referred to is Horace (*Satires*, I.iii.68): 'nam vitiis nemo sine nascitur'.

iii

Elizabeth heartens her troops at Tilbury, 1588

From a letter by Dr Leonel Sharp to the Duke of Buckingham (undated) in *Cabala, sive Scrinia Sacra* (2nd edn, 1663), p. 373.

My loving people, we have been persuaded by some that are careful of our safety to take heed how we commit ourself to armed multitudes, for fear of treachery. But, I assure you, I do not desire to live to distrust my faithful and loving people. Let tyrants fear; I have always so behaved myself that, under God, I have placed my   5 chiefest strength and safeguard in the loyal hearts and good will of my subjects. And therefore I am come amongst you, as you see, at this time, not for my recreation and disport, but being resolved, in the midst and heat of the battle, to live or die amongst you all; to lay down for my God, and for my kingdom, and for my people, my   10 honour and my blood, even in the dust. I know I have the body but of a weak and feeble woman, but I have the heart and stomach of a king, and of a king of England too, and think foul scorn that Parma or Spain, or any prince of Europe, should dare to invade the borders of my realm; to which, rather than any dishonour shall   15 grow by me, I myself will take up arms, I myself will be your General, Judge, and Rewarder of every one of your virtues in the field. I know, already for your forwardness, you have deserved rewards and crowns; and we do assure you, in the word of a prince, they shall be duly paid you. In the mean time, my Lieutenant-   20 General shall be in my stead, than whom never prince commanded a more noble or worthy subject; not doubting but by your obedience to my General, by your concord in the camp, and your valour in the field, we shall shortly have a famous victory over those enemies of my God, of my kingdoms, and of my people.   25

NOTES

18   *forwardness* readiness, eagerness.
20–1 *Lieutenant-General* Robert Dudley, Earl of Leicester, one of Elizabeth's early favourites. See p. 102.

iv

The Queen is dead! Long live the King!

From *The Diary of John Manningham of the Middle Temple, 1602–1603* (Harleian MS 5353 in the British Library; see an edition by R. P. Sorlien, 1976).

March 23 [1602, i.e. 1603 n.s.]. I dined with Dr Parry in the Privy Chamber, and understood by him, the Bishop of Chichester, the Dean of Canterbury, the Dean of Windsor, &c. that her Majesty hath been by fits troubled with melancholy some three or four months, but for this fortnight extreme oppressed with it, in so 5 much that she refused to eat anything, to receive any physic, or admit any rest in bed, till within these two or three days. She hath been in a manner speechless for two days, very pensive and silent; since Shrovetide's sitting some times with her eye fixed upon one object many hours together; yet she always had her perfect senses 10 and memory, and yesterday signified by the lifting up of her hand and eyes to heaven, a sign which Dr Parry entreated of her, that she believed that faith which she hath caused to be professed, and looked faithfully to be saved by Christ's merits and mercy only and no other means. She took great delight in hearing prayers, would 15 often at the name of Jesus lift up her hands and eyes to heaven. She would not hear the Archbishop speak of hope of her longer life, but, when he prayed or spake of heaven and those joys, she would hug his hand, &c. It seems she might have lived if she would have used means, but she would not be persuaded, and princes 20 must not be forced. Her physicians said she had a body of a firm and perfect constitution, likely to have lived many years. A royal majesty is no privilege against death.

March 24. This morning about three at clock her Majesty departed this life, mildly like a lamb, easily like a ripe apple from 25 the tree, *cum leve quadam febre, absque gemitu.* Dr Parry told me he was present and sent his prayers before her soul, and I doubt not but she is amongst the royal saints in heaven in eternal joys. About ten at clock the Council and divers noblemen, having been a while in consultation, proclaimed James the Sixth, King of Scots, 30 the King of England, France, and Ireland, beginning at Whitehall gates, where Sir Robert Cecil read the proclamation, which he carried in his hand and after read again at Cheapside. . . . . . .

There was a diligent watch and ward kept at every gate and street, day and night, by householders, to prevent garboils: which 35 God be thanked were more feared than perceived. The proclamation was heard with great expectation and silent joy, no great shouting. I think the sorrow for her Majesty's departure was so deep in many hearts they could not so suddenly show any great

joy, though it could not be less than exceeding great for the 40
succession of so worthy a King. And at night they showed it by
bonfires and ringing. No tumult, no contradiction, no disorder in
the City; every man went about his business as readily, as
peaceably, as securely as though there had been no change nor any
news ever heard of competitors....... The people is full of 45
expectation and great hope of his worthiness, of our nation's
future greatness; everyone promises himself a share in some
famous action to be hereafter performed for his prince and
country. They assure themselves of the continuance of our church
government and doctrine....... But all long to see our new 50
king......

April 13....... The Queen nominated our King for her
successor; for being demanded whom she would have succeed, her
answer was there should no rascals sit in her seat. 'Who then?' 'A
king', said she. 'What king?' 'Of Scots', said she, 'for he hath best 55
right, and in the name of God let him have it.'

NOTES

1 *Dr Parry* Henry Parry, rector of Sundridge and Chevening, later Bishop
   of Worcester.
1–2 *Privy Chamber* in the palace at Richmond, to which the Queen had gone
   in late January.
2–3 *Bishop of Chichester......Windsor* Anthony Watson, Thomas Nevile,
   Giles Thompson (Chaplain to the Queen).
9 *Shrovetide's* i.e. the time of Shrovetide (Quinquagesima Sunday and the
   two following days before the beginning of Lent).
13 *that faith* i.e. the Anglican communion.
14 *saved......only* the Protestant doctrine of salvation through 'faith
   alone as opposed to the Catholic doctrine of 'faith' and 'good works'.
17 *Archbishop* John Whitgift, Archbishop of Canterbury.
25 *ripe apple* Manningham is probably thinking of the well-known passage
   in Cicero's *De Senectute*, xix.
26 *cum......gemitu* with a slight fever and without a groan.
31–2 *Whitehall gates* Whitehall was the royal palace in Westminster; the gates,
   the Holbein and King Street Gates.
33 *Cheapside* the Old Market Place of the City of London.
34 *ward* guard.
35 *garboils* brawls, disturbances.
45 *competitors* According to Thomas Wilson (*The State of England, 1600* in
   Camden Miscellany, XVI (1936)) there were twelve competitors (including
   James VI) who 'gape[d] for the death of that good old Princess the now
   Queen'. Principal among them, according to Wilson, were James of
   Scotland, the Earls of Huntington and Derby, Lord Beauchamp and Lady
   Arabella Stuart.
52–6 Manningham's account differs from that of Sir Robert Cary, who writes
   (*Memoirs* (1759), pp. 140–1): 'On Wednesday, the 23rd of March, she grew

speechless. That afternoon, by signs, she called for her Council, and by putting her hand to her head, when the King of Scots was named to succeed her, they all knew he was the man she desired should reign after her.' Another account (manuscript) combines the two versions, placing Manningham's on 23 March and Cary's on 24 March (see *Somers Tracts*, ed. Sir Walter Scott (1809), I, 247).

King James

Son of the Catholic and ill-fated Mary Queen of Scots and the weak and dissolute Henry Stuart, Lord Darnley, James Stuart, who became James VI of Scotland at the age of one and then James I of England some thirty-six years later, has been described as 'one of the most complicated neurotics ever to come to the English throne' (G. P. V. Akrigg, *Jacobean Pageant, or The Court of King James I* (1962), p. 6). His threat-ridden and tumultuous youth alone would have been enough to explain why. He prided himself upon being a man of learning (to which he had some real pretensions) and his reign (1603–25), unentangled with continental wars, earned him the title, which he much valued, of *rex pacificus*. But partly because he was a 'foreigner', though a staunch Protestant, and partly because of his withdrawn and touchy personality, he never achieved the kind of love and admiration from his English subjects that Elizabeth had so royally borne, and he sowed the seeds, by his championship of the doctrine of the 'divine right of kings', for the harvest reaped by his son, Charles I, in the Civil War some few years later.

The tone of Sir John Harington's letter in the first selection (i) makes an interesting contrast with the tone of his letter about Queen Elizabeth (see selection (ii) in the preceding section). Harington's attitude toward King James is carefully guarded, though he had favoured his succession and, in 1602 (before the Queen's death), had sent to the Scottish King a richly wrought lantern device, with the motto (from the 'good thief' at Golgotha) 'Lord, remember me when thou comest in thy kingdom' – an obvious piece of 'court-craft' and one that presumably led to the interview he here describes. As we read his letter, we feel that Harington, not without reason, is treading very delicately and watching his every word, almost as if he were humouring a spoiled, vain child, an aspect of James's personality that he registers with a wicked nicety. In fairness, of course, we must note that one may well write differently about a dead queen and a living king who holds one's future in his hands; even so, however, the difference in overall tone referred to above remains. Harington trusted Elizabeth, even in her anger; he is at best wary, if not distrustful, of James.

Critical views, contemporary and later, of King James have probably been unduly severe (see Akrigg's defence, pp. 395–6), and it is clear that Lord Howard (see selection (ii)) in his letter to Harington is writing as a member of the old guard, nostalgic for the 'good old days' of the Virgin Queen and 'merry England'. But, in fact, new winds were blowing (economic, political, religious, social and scientific) and Howard's picture of the extreme venality of the new Court is not greatly exaggerated, a Court that was still the arbiter of men and morals:

> Considering duly that a prince's court
> Is like a common fountain, whence should flow

Pure silver drops in general. But if 't chance
Some curs'd example poison't near the head,
Death and diseases through the whole land spread.
(John Webster, *The Duchess of Malfi* (1612–14), I.i.11–15)

Or, as George Chapman, describing Elizabeth's Court in *Bussy D'Ambois* (*c.*1604; I.ii.19–24) earlier put it:

But, as courts should be th'abstracts of their kingdoms
In all the beauty, state, and worth they hold,
So is hers, amply, and by her informed [i.e. given its vital character].
The world is not contracted in a man [i.e. as a microcosm]
With more proportion and expression
Than in her court, her kingdom.

As a cultivated man, who placed great value on his learning, King James patronized the arts, and under his rule Court entertainments (often extravagantly costly) flourished, particularly the masque (see above, p. 72 and below p. 198). An incident, not entirely to James's credit but one that reflects his fondness for such Court entertainment, was reported by Orazio Busino, chaplain to the Venetian ambassador. Attending a performance of Ben Jonson's *Pleasure Reconciled to Virtue* (1618), the masque having come to the final grand dance by the principal masquers (among them the young Prince Charles), Busino comments:

They performed every sort of ballet and dance of every country whatsoever, such as passamezzi, corants, canaries, dances in the Spanish mode, and a hundred other fine gestures devised to tickle the fancy. Last of all they danced the Spanish dance [? pavan], one at a time, each with his lady, and being well nigh tired they began to lag. Whereupon the King, who is naturally choleric, got impatient and shouted aloud, 'Why don't they dance? What did they make me come here for? Devil take you all, dance!' Upon this, the Marquess of Buckingham [one of the masquers], his Majesty's favourite, immediately sprang forward, cutting a score of lofty and very minute capers, with so much grace and agility that he not only appeased the ire of his angry lord, but rendered himself the admiration and delight of everybody. The other masquers, thus encouraged, continued to exhibit their prowess, one after another, with various ladies, also finishing their capers and lifting their goddesses from the ground. We counted thirty-four capers as cut by one cavalier in succession, but none came up to the exquisite manner of the marquess. (Translation, slightly amended, from the *Calendar of Venetian State Papers*, XV (1909), pp. 113–4.)

James also lent his name and patronage to Shakespeare's company, the King's Men, immediately after his accession (see p. 40 for the royal licence), placing that company in an enviable position among its competitors (see above, p. 37). James figures little in the public drama. Ben Jonson and George Chapman may have unwisely glanced at James's character in the original censored version of *Sejanus* (a possible trace remains (III.302–10) in the published text of 1605) and Chapman, later, may have had James in mind in the character of Francis I, King of France, in *Chabot, Admiral of France* (a play of uncertain date and probably not acted until some time after James's death). But the only unquestionable appearance of James on the public stage occurs in Thomas Middleton's anti-Spanish political satire, *A Game at Chess* (1624), in which, in this elaborate chess allegory, he is portrayed as the 'White King' victorious over the machinations of the 'Black King' (Philip IV of Spain) and his minions. Staged by the King's Men at the Globe, the play was immensely popular, with a run of nine consecutive days (Sundays excepted), the first recorded run in English theatre history. The Spanish ambassador was outraged, the authorities closed the Globe for a short period, and Middleton was arrested.

For further information on King James, in addition to Akrigg (referred to above), see S. R. Gardiner, *History of England from the Accession of James I to the Outbreak of the Civil War* (new edn 1893–9), 10 vols.

i

From a letter by Sir John Harington to Sir Amias Paulet (1603/4) (printed in *Nugae Antiquae* (1779), II, 116–20).

My Loving Cousin,

   It behoveth me now to recite my journal, respecting my gracious command of my Sovereign Prince, to come to his closet;......When I came to the presence-chamber and had gotten good place to see the lordly attendants and bowed my knee   5
to the Prince, I was ordered by a special messenger, and that in secret sort, to wait a while in an outward chamber, whence, in near an hour waiting, the same knave led me up a passage and so to a small room, where was good order of paper, ink, and pens put on a board for the Prince's use. Soon upon this, the Prince his   10
Highness did enter, and in much good humour asked, 'If I was cousin to Lord Harington of Exton?' I humbly replied, 'His Majesty did me some honour in enquiring my kin to one whom he had so late honoured and made a Baron'; and, moreover, did add, 'we were both branches of the same tree'. Then he enquired much   15
of learning and showed me his own in such sort as made me remember my examiner at Cambridge aforetime. He sought much to know my advances in philosophy and uttered such profound sentences of Aristotle and such like writers, which I had never read and which some are bold enough to say others do not   20
understand; but this I must pass by. The Prince did now press my reading to him part of a canto in Ariosto, praised my utterance, and said he had been informed of many as to my learning in the time of the Queen. He asked me what I thought pure wit was made of and whom it did best become? Whether a king should not   25
be the best clerk in his own country; and if this land did not entertain good opinion of his learning and good wisdom? His Majesty did much press for my opinion touching the power of Satan in matter of witchcraft and asked me, with much gravity, 'If I did truly understand, why the Devil did work more with ancient   30
women than others?' I did not refrain from a scurvy jest and even said (notwithstanding to whom it was said) that we were taught hereof in scripture, where it is told that the Devil *walketh in dry places*. His Majesty, moreover, was pleased to say much, and favouredly, of my good report for mirth and good conceit; to   35
which I did covertly answer, as not willing a subject should be wiser than his Prince, nor even appear so. More serious discourse did next ensue, wherein I wanted room to continue and sometime room to escape; for the Queen his mother was not forgotten, nor Davison neither. His Highness told me her death was visible in   40
Scotland before it did really happen, being, as he said, spoken of in secret by those whose power of sight presented to them a bloody

head dancing in the air. He then did remark much on this gift and said he had sought out of certain books a sure way to attain knowledge of future chances. Hereat he named many books, 45 which I did not know, nor by whom written, but advised me not to consult some authors which would lead me to evil consultations. I told his Majesty the power of Satan had, I much feared, damaged my bodily frame; but I had not farther will to court his friendship for my soul's hurt. We next discoursed somewhat on religion, 50 when at length he said: 'Now, sir, you have seen my wisdom in some sort, and I have pried into yours. I pray you, do me justice in your report, and, in good season, I will not fail to add to your understanding in such points as I may find you lack amendment'. I made courtesy hereat and withdrew down the passage and out at 55 the gate amidst the many varlets and lordly servants who stood around. Thus you have the history of your neighbour's high chance and entertainment at Court; more of which matter when I come home to my own dwelling and talk these affairs in a corner. I must press to silence hereon, as otherwise all is undone. I did 60 forget to tell that his Majesty much asked concerning my opinion of the new weed tobacco, and said it would, by its use, infuse ill qualities on the brain and that no learned man ought to taste it, and wished it forbidden. . . . . . .

NOTES

2 *recite my journal* report the contents of my diary.
4 *closet* the monarch's private apartment.
   presence-chamber reception-room in the palace
7 *secret sort* stealthy manner.
8 *knave* male servant.
10 *board* table.
13 *enquiring my kin to* asking about my kinship with.
16 *in such sort* in such a way.
17 *examiner* Dr John Still, later Bishop of Bath and Wells.
22 *canto in Ariosto* Harington had translated Ludovico Ariosto's *Orlando Furioso* (published in 1591) under 'orders' from Queen Elizabeth.
26 *clerk* scholar.
29 *witchcraft* James had already published (1597) his *Daemonologie*. In it he had declared his belief in witches and their league with Satan. See below, p. 262.
31 *scurvy* worthless, contemptible.
33 *scripture* Matthew 12:43 and Luke 11:24.
35 *favouredly* favourably.
   mirth . . . . . . conceit gaiety of mind (jocularity) and good understanding.
36 *covertly* indirectly, discreetly.
38 *room to continue* i.e. get a word in edgewise.
39 *room to escape* i.e. avoid having to give an answer.

Queen Mary, Queen of Scotland, beheaded, 8 February 1587, by order of the Council (without Elizabeth's knowledge, though she had earlier signed the death warrant).

40 *Davison* William Davison, undersecretary to Walsingham, who finally procured Elizabeth's signature to Mary's death warrant.

55 *made courtesy* bowed.

56 *varlets* i.e. varlets of the chamber, the King's personal attendants.

60 *press* urge (you).

62 *new weed tobacco* One tradition has it that tobacco was introduced into England from America in 1586 by Sir Francis Drake and Sir Walter Raleigh. King James expressed his abhorrence of the 'new weed' in his *Counterblast to Tobacco* (1604). 'Drinking' (i.e. smoking) tobacco was widely popular in England by this time. James asserts that some gentlemen spend as much as three or four hundred pounds a year on 'this precious stink' and adds: 'And for the vanities committed in this filthy custom, is it not both great vanity and uncleanness that at the table, a place of respect, of cleanliness, of modesty, men should not be ashamed to sit tossing of tobacco pipes and puffing of the smoke of tobacco one to another, making the filthy smoke and stink thereof to exhale athwart the dishes and infect the air, when, very often, men that abhor it are at their repast?' (ed. Edward Arber (1869), pp. 110–11). James followed up his attack by raising the import tax (per pound) from two pence to six shillings and ten pence. The virtues of tobacco, expressed in hyperbolic terms, are celebrated by Sir John Beaumont in a poem called *The Metamorphosis of Tabacco* (1602).

ii

A letter by Thomas Howard, Viscount of Bindon, to Sir John Harington (1611) (printed in *Nugae Antiquae* (1779), II, 271–7).

My Good and Trusty Knight,

If you have good will and good health to perform what I shall commend, you may set forward for Court whenever it suiteth your own conveniency: the King hath often inquired after you, and would readily see and converse again with the 'merry blade', as he 5
hath oft called you, since you was here. I will now premise certain things to be observed by you, toward well gaining our prince's good affection: He doth wondrously covet learned discourse, of which you can furnish out ample means; he doth admire good fashion in clothes, I pray you give good heed hereunto; strange 10
devices oft come into man's conceit; some one regardeth the endowments of the inward sort, wit, valour, or virtue; another hath, perchance, special affection towards outward things, clothes, deportment, and good countenance. I would wish you to be well trimmed; get a new jerkin, well bordered, and not too short; the 15
King saith, he liketh a flowing garment; be sure it be not all of one sort, but diversely coloured, the collar falling somewhat down, and your ruff well stiffened and bushy. We have lately had many gallants who failed in their suits for want of due observance of these matters. The King is nicely heedful of such points, and 20
dwelleth on good looks and handsome accoutrements. Eighteen servants were lately discharged, and many more will be discarded, who are not to his liking in these matters. I wish you to follow my directions, as I wish you to gain all you desire. Robert Carr is now most likely to win the Prince's affection, and doth it wondrously in 25
a little time. The Prince leaneth on his arm, pinches his cheek, smoothes his ruffled garment, and, when he looketh at Carr, directeth discourse to divers others. This young man doth much study all art and device; he hath changed his tailors and tiremen many times, and all to please the Prince, who laugheth at the long 30
grown fashion of our young courtiers, and wisheth for change every day. You must see Carr before you go to the King, as he was with him a boy in Scotland, and knoweth his taste and what pleaseth. In your discourse you must not dwell too long on any one subject, and touch but lightly on religion. Do not of yourself say, 35
'This is good or bad'; but, 'If it were your Majesty's good opinion, I myself should think so and so'. Ask no more questions than what may serve to know the Prince's thought. In private discourse, the King seldom speaketh of any man's temper, discretion, or good virtues; so meddle not at all, but find out a clue to guide you to the 40
heart and most delightful subject of his mind. I will advise one

thing: the roan jennet, whereon the King rideth every day, must not be forgotten to be praised; and the good furniture above all, what lost a great man much notice the other day. A noble did come in suit of a place, and saw the King mounting the roan; delivered his petition, which was heeded and read, but no answer was given. The noble departed, and came to Court the next day, and got no answer again. The Lord Treasurer was then pressed to move the King's pleasure touching the petition. When the King was asked for answer thereto, he said, in some wrath, 'Shall a King give heed to a dirty paper, when a beggar noteth not his gilt stirrups?' Now it fell out that the King had new furniture when the noble saw him in the courtyard, but was overcharged with confusion, and passed by admiring the dressing of the horse. Thus, good knight, our noble failed in his suit. I could relate and offer some other remarks on these matters, but silence and discretion should be linked together like dog and bitch, for of them is gendered security: I am certain it proveth so at this place. You have lived to see the trim of old times, and what passed in the Queen's days: these things are no more the same. Your Queen did talk of her subjects' love and good affections, and in good truth she aimed well; our King talketh of his subjects' fear and subjection, and herein I think he doth well too, as long as it holdeth good. Carr hath all favours, as I told you before: the King teacheth him Latin every morning, and I think some one should teach him English too; for, as he is a Scottish lad, he hath much need of better language. The King doth much covet his presence; the ladies too are not behindhand in their admiration; for I tell you, good knight, this fellow is straight-limbed, well-favoured, strong-shouldered, and smooth-faced, with some sort of cunning and show of modesty; though God wot, he well knoweth when to show his impudence. You are not young, you are not handsome, you are not finely, and yet will you come to Court and think to be well favoured? Why, I say again, good knight, that your learning may somewhat prove worthy hereunto; your Latin and your Greek, your Italian, your Spanish tongues, your wit and discretion, may be well looked unto for a while, as strangers at such a place; but these are not the things men live by nowadays. Will you say the moon shineth all the summer? That the stars are bright jewels fit for Carr's ears? That the roan jennet surpasseth Bucephalus, and is worthy to be bestridden by Alexander? That his eyes are fire, his tail is Berenice's locks, and a few more such fancies worthy your noticing? Your lady is virtuous, and somewhat of a good huswife; has lived in a Court in her time, and I believe you may venture her forth again, but I know those would not quietly rest, were Carr to leer on their wives, as some do perceive, yea, and like it well too they should be so noticed. If any mischance be to be wished, 'tis breaking a leg in the King's presence, for this fellow owes all his

favour to that bout; I think he hath better reason to speak well of
his own horse, than the King's roan jennet. We are almost worn   90
out in our endeavours to keep pace with this fellow in his duty and
labour to gain favour, but all in vain; where it endeth I cannot
guess, but honours are talked of speedily for him. I trust this by my
own son, that no danger may happen from our freedoms. If you
come here, God speed your ploughing at the Court: I know you do   95
it rarely at home. So adieu, my good knight, and I will always write
me

Your truly loving old friend,

T. HOWARD.

NOTES

5   *converse again* See above, p. 190, for Harington's first interview with King
     James.
     'merry blade' pleasant, mirthful fellow.
11   *conceit* fancy, imagination.
     one i.e. man.
14   *countenance* behaviour.
15   *trimmed* dressed.
     jerkin short, usually sleeved, coat, ordinarily worn over the doublet.
18   *ruff* circular neck-wear of linen or muslin, pleated and starched, so that it
     stood out horizontally, sometimes to an absurd degree.
19   *failed......suits* had their petitions refused (with probable play on
     'suit'=garb).
20   *nicely* fastidiously.
24   *Robert Carr* or Ker, was a young Scot, who came to James's notice at a
     tilting at Whitehall (1607) when his horse threw him and broke his leg
     (see below, ll. 87–90). This led to sympathetic visits from James, and by
     the time Howard is writing (1611) Carr had become firmly entrenched as
     James's new favourite. Shortly after Howard wrote (see below, ll. 92–3),
     Carr was made Viscount Rochester (25 March 1611) and later Earl of
     Somerset (4 November 1613). He was later (1616) disgraced (and
     imprisoned in the Tower) as a result of his presumed complicity in the
     scandalous murder of Sir Thomas Overbury (1613), for the most part the
     work of his wife, the notorious Lady Frances (divorced wife of the third
     Earl of Essex).
29   *tiremen* valets, dressers (not in *OED*).
30–1 *long grown fashion* i.e. fashion that had remained in vogue for some time
     past.
33   *with......Scotland* Carr had been one of James's Pages of Honour in
     Scotland but had dropped from his notice until the 'fortunate' tilting
     incident.
39   *temper* character, temperament.
42   *roan jennet* small Spanish horse, dappled, but with one colour prevailing.
     James's attitude toward his horse may remind us of the French Dauphin's
     ecstatic nonsense addressed to his horse in Shakespeare's *Henry V*,
     III.vii.1–68.

43 *furniture* harness trappings.

44 *what* i.e. the failure to mention which.

48 *Lord Treasurer* Robert Cecil, first Earl of Salisbury.

54 *passed by admiring* failed to admire.

59 *trim* fashion, mode.

passed had currency, was acceptable.

63–4 *as long. . . . . .good* i.e. as long as fear and subjection will work.

70 *cunning* ability, cleverness.

73 *not finely* i.e. not the sort of person, physically, to call forth admiration.

74 *well favoured* with a play, perhaps, on 'good-looking'. Cf. l. 69.

78–9 *Will. . . . . .summer?* i.e. ?Will you be willing to talk madly about things of small account? Compare Tilley M1117, M1128.

80 *Bucephalus* Alexander the Great's horse.

82 *Berenice's locks* name of a small northern constellation, near the tail of Leo.

83 *huswife* housewife, one who manages her household with skill and thrift.

86 *leer on* glance lasciviously at.

87 *mischance* See note on l. 24.

89 *bout* match (tilting).

91 *duty* deference (to the King).

94 *freedoms* i.e. the criticisms made of James and the Court. In the wrong hands, this letter could have been very damaging.

95 *God. . . . . .ploughing* God prosper your efforts. Compare George Chapman, *Bussy D'Ambois* (*c.* 1604), I.i.125–6: 'If I may bring up a new fashion,/ And rise in Court with virtue, speed his plough.'

Some other Court matters

The royal Court was a somewhat movable feast. Although its centre was in greater London (the Tower palace in the City; Whitehall, St James's, and Westminster Palaces in Westminster), the sovereign, who was the centre of the Court, also often resided at several other royal residences in the neighbouring counties: Greenwich Palace in Kent, Richmond Palace in Surrey, Windsor Castle in Berkshire, Hampton Court, fifteen miles west of London, and, after 1607, Theobalds, twelve miles north of London in Hertfordshire (see Neville Williams, *The Royal Residences of Great Britain* (1960)). In addition, Elizabeth and James went on 'progresses' (i.e. visits of state) to various parts of the kingdom and were lavishly, sometimes ruinously, entertained at the country estates of the nobility and landed gentry (see selection (ii) below and pp. 102 and 168 above). In effect, then, except in certain administrative matters, where the sovereign was, there was the Court, with all its attendant pageantry and ceremony and its somewhat motley crowd of courtiers and hangers-on.

The Court, containing as it did the seat of power in the persons of the monarch and her or his Privy Council, exercised through a system of appointed officials (including judges) a wide executive control that reached into every corner of the kingdom. It is scarcely surprising, therefore, that, as the royal road to preferment, the Court was a hotbed of intrigue, scandal-mongering, and jockeying for position, increasingly so under King James, in whose reign the moral tone of the Court, relatively controlled under Elizabeth's stricter eye, became more openly, even flagrantly, lax (see selection (ii)) and helped to pave the way, along with other religious and economic causes, for the Puritan revolution of the 1640s. Something of this changed tone is reflected in the popularity, after about 1608, of tragi-comedy, a genre that tended to evade the responsibility of serious moral commitment.

Selection (i), 'A Gallant', from John Earle's *Micro-cosmographie* (1628), might equally well have been entitled 'A Would-be Courtier'. An obvious target, the courtier was fair and rewarding game for the satirist. Celebrating a good courtier as one of the 'twelve wonders of the world', Sir John Davies in an epigram (*Complete Poems*, ed. A. B. Grosart (1876), II, 65) summarizes the common view:

> Long have I liv'd in Court, yet learn'd not all this while,
> To sell poor suitors smoke, not where I hate to smile;
> Superiors to adore, inferiors to despise;
> To fly from such as fall, to follow such as rise;
> To cloak a poor desire under a rich array;
> Not to aspire by vice, though 'twere the quicker way.

See also Sir Thomas Overbury's 'character' of 'A Courtier' (*A Wife* (1614)) and that of 'An Improvident Young Gallant', probably by John

Webster (in the 2nd edn (1615) of the same collection). The courtier/gallant figures prominently in the drama. Shakespeare gives us two sharply critical vignettes: the perfumed and dandified young lord who comes to demand Hotspur's prisoners for the King (*I Henry IV*, I.iii.29–69) and the preciously fashionable Osric in *Hamlet* (v.ii.81–194). Other satirical treatments of the courtier may be found in such characters as Ben Jonson's Fastidious Brisk (*Every Man out of His Humour*, 1599), Hedon (*Cynthia's Revels*, 1600–1), and Sir Diaphanous Silkworm (*The Magnetic Lady*, 1632) and Thomas Middleton's Curvetto, an 'old courtier' (*Blurt, Master-Constable*, 1601–2).

In the second selection (ii), Sir John Harington, in a letter of 1606, reports on, with an obviously disapproving eye, the bacchanalian four-day entertainment offered to King James and his brother-in-law, Christian IV of Denmark, by Robert Cecil, son of Lord Burghley and the first Earl of Salisbury (created 1605), at his estate of Theobalds in Hertfordshire. His account is both amusing and revealing. General drunkenness seems to have been the order of the day (and night), with 'heavy-headed revel east and west' (*Hamlet*, I.iv.17), and the fiasco of the masquelike show of the visit of the Queen of Sheba to Solomon, as rather gleefully told by Harington (not to be confused with another welcoming entertainment composed by Ben Jonson), tells its own sorry tale. Though a good deal of the costs of the visit to Theobalds would have been borne by Cecil as host, the public cost of this twenty-seven-day royal visit was immense and not unrepresentative of the extravagance of James's Court. On a second short visit by Christian in 1614, James is reported to have lavished fifty thousand pounds of ambiguously acquired public funds (see accounts of these two visits in John Nichols, *The Progresses of King James the First* (1828), II, 53–94; III, 13–18).

A scene in John Fletcher's *The Humorous Lieutenant* (*c*.1619), II.iii, gives a lively and nasty picture of a Court bawd busily at work plying her flesh-traffic. The setting may be ancient Greece or Asia Minor (a common device to avoid any charge of direct contemporary allusion), but the situation dramatized would have been familiar enough to anyone associated with contemporary English Court life. Leucippe, Fletcher's bawd, might almost be a portrait of Mistress Anne Turner, the notorious procuress (and poisoner), who figured so centrally in the celebrated Overbury murder trial, but there were many others who might equally well have sat for the portrait. Shakespeare has left us a memorably unpleasant scene (*Pericles*, IV.ii), which describes in graphic detail (some of it perhaps recalled by Fletcher) what happens when Marina, the heroine, falls into the clutches of a bawd and her pander, prime examples of what Pandarus (*Troilus and Cressida*, v.x.51) dubs 'Brethren and sisters of the hold-door trade'; and Thomas Dekker adds to the rogues' gallery in *II Honest Whore* (about 1604–5; III.iii, IV.iii) with the unsavoury characters of Mistress Horseleech and her pander, Bots.

For an intimate glimpse into the sexual mores of this period, see A. L. Rowse, *Simon Forman: Sex and Society in Shakespeare's Age* (1974).

i

From John Earle, *Micro-cosmographie, or, A Peece of the World Discovered* (1628), no. 18.

A Gallant

Is one that was born and shaped for his clothes; and if Adam had not fall'n, had lived to no purpose. He gratulates therefore the first sin and fig leaves that were an occasion of bravery. His first care is his dress, the next his body, and in the uniting of these two lies his soul and its faculties. He observes London trulier than the termers,   5
and his business is the street, the stage, the Court, and those places where a proper man is best shown. If he be qualified in gaming extraordinary, he is so much the more gentle and complete, and he learns the best oaths for the purpose. These are a great part of his discourse, and he is as curious in their newness as the fashion. His   10
other talk is ladies and such pretty things, or some jest at a play. His picktooth bears a great part of his discourse, so does his body, the upper parts whereof are as starched as his linen and perchance use the same laundress. He has learned to ruffle his face from his boot and takes great delight in his walk to hear his spurs gingle.   15
Though his life pass somewhat slidingly, yet he seems very careful of the time, for he is still drawing his watch out of his pocket and spends part of his hours in numb'ring them. He is one never serious but with his tailor, when he is in conspiracy for the next device. He is furnished [with] his jests, as some wanderer with   20
sermons, some three for all congregations, one especially against the scholar, a man to him much ridiculous, whom he knows by no other definition, but a silly fellow in black. He is a kind of walking mercer's shop, and shows you one stuff today and another tomorrow, an ornament to the rooms he comes in, as the fair bed   25
and hangings be; and is merely rateable accordingly, fifty or an hundred pound as his suit is. His main ambition is to get a knighthood, and then an old lady, which if he be happy in, he fills the stage and a coach so much longer. Otherwise, himself and his clothes grow stale together, and he is buried commonly ere he dies   30
in the jail or the country.

NOTES

1–2   *Adam......fall'n* Adam and Eve after the Fall, because they then knew shame, covered their genitals with figleaves.
2   *gratulates* welcomes with joy.
3   *bravery* fine clothes.
4–5   *lies......faculties* i.e. the rational faculty of his soul is lacking.
5   *termers* law students, who attended the Inns of Court and Chancery during term-times.

6 *business is* i.e. spends all his time in or at.

7 *proper* admirable, complete.

7–8 *qualified......extraordinary* i.e. especially expert in games of chance (dice, cards, etc.).

8 *gentle* gentlemanlike.

10 *as the fashion* as (he is) in following the latest fashion in clothes.

12 *picktooth* toothpick.

14 *use......laundress* i.e. his laundress is also his mistress.

14–15 *learned......boot* i.e. he imitates the creases in his leather boots by frowning threateningly to impress people.

16 *slidingly* carelessly, wastefully (not in *OED*).

17 *watch* Pocket-watches were relatively new and a kind of status symbol.

19–20 *next device* newest fashion in clothes or ornamentation.

20–1 *as some......congregations* parenthetical.

24 *mercer's shop* shop belonging to a dealer in fabrics.

26 *hangings* i.e. bed-hangings.
   rateable proportionable; i.e. his value as a man is no more than that of a piece of furniture.

28–9 *fills the stage* i.e. by sitting on it to show off his clothes.

ii

Bacchanalian revels

From a letter by Sir John Harington to Master Secretary Barlow (1606)
(printed in *Nugae Antiquae* (1779), II, 126–30).

......I came here [to Theobalds, the estate of Robert Cecil, first
Earl of Salisbury] a day or two before the Danish king came, and
from the day he did come until this hour I have been well-nigh
overwhelmed with carousal and sports of all kinds. The sports
began each day in such manner and such sort as well-nigh   5
persuaded me of Mahomet's paradise. We had women, and indeed
wine too, of such plenty as would have astonished each sober
beholder. Our feasts were magnificent, and the two royal guests
did most lovingly embrace each other at table. I think the Dane
hath strangely wrought on our good English nobles; for those   10
whom I never could get to taste good liquor now follow the
fashion and wallow in beastly delights. The ladies abandon their
sobriety and are seen to roll about in intoxication. In good sooth,
the Parliament did kindly to provide his Majesty so seasonably
with money, for there hath been no lack of good living: shows,   15
sights, and banquetings from morn to eve.
One day a great feast was held, and, after dinner, the
representation of Solomon his Temple and the coming of the
Queen of Sheba was made, or (as I may better say) was meant to
have been made, before their Majesties, by the device of the Earl 20
of Salisbury and others. But, alas! as all earthly things do fail to
poor mortals in enjoyment, so did prove our presentment hereof.
The Lady who did play the Queen's part did carry most precious
gifts to both their Majesties; but, forgetting the steps arising to the
canopy, overset her caskets into his Danish Majesty's lap, and fell 25
at his feet, though I rather think it was in his face. Much was the
hurry and confusion; cloths and napkins were at hand to make all
clean. His Majesty [of Denmark] then got up and would dance
with the Queen of Sheba, but he fell down and humbled himself
before her, and was carried to an inner chamber and laid on a bed   30
of state, which was not a little defiled with the presents of the
Queen which had been bestowed on his garments, such as wine,
cream, jelly, beverage, cakes, spices, and other good matters. The
entertainment and show went forward, and most of the presenters
went backward or fell down, wine did so occupy their upper   35
chambers. Now did appear, in rich dress, Hope, Faith, and
Charity. Hope did assay to speak, but wine rendered her
endeavours so feeble that she withdrew, and hoped the King
[James] would excuse her brevity. Faith was then all alone, for I
am certain she was not joined with good works, and left the Court   40

in a staggering condition. Charity came to the King's feet, and seemed to cover the multitude of sins her sisters had committed; in some sort she made obeisance and brought gifts, but said she would return home again, as there was no gift which heaven had not already given his Majesty. She then returned to Hope and 45 Faith, who were both sick and spewing in the lower hall. Next came Victory, in bright armour, and presented a rich sword to the King, who did not accept it, but put it by with his hand; and, by a strange medley of versification, did endeavour to make suit to the King. But Victory did not triumph long, for, after much 50 lamentable utterance, she was led away like a silly captive and laid to sleep in the outer steps of the antechamber. Now did Peace make entry and strive to get foremost to the King; but I grieve to tell how great wrath she did discover unto those of her attendants, and, much contrary to her semblance, most rudely made war with 55 her olive branch, and laid on the pates of those who did oppose her coming.

I have much marvelled at these strange pageantries, and they do bring to my remembrance what passed of this sort in our Queen's days (of which I was sometime an humble presenter and assistant), 60 but I ne'er did see such lack of good order, discretion, and sobriety as I have now done. I have passed much time in seeing the royal sports of hunting and hawking, where the manners were such as made me devise the beasts were pursuing the sober creation, and not man in quest of exercise or food....... 65

NOTES

2 *Danish king* Christian IV, King of Denmark and Norway, and brother of Queen Anne, consort of James I.

4–5 *sports......day* The royal visit to Theobalds lasted four days.

6 *Mahomet's paradise* The Mahometan paradise was pictured as one of sensual delights.

had women ?prostitutes were furnished.

8 *royal guests* i.e. James and Christian.

9–12 *the Dane......delights* The Danes (and Germans) were notorious in England for heavy drinking; compare Thomas Nashe, *Pierce Penilesse* (1592; ed. McKerrow, I, 180) and *Hamlet*, I.iv.8–22.

14–15 *Parliament......money* Parliament had recently granted subsidies to James of nearly four hundred thousand pounds for his household expenses.

18–19 *representation......Sheba* This production seems to have been more in the nature of a pageant-show than a formal masque; no text has survived. Sheba's visit to Solomon is described in I Kings 10:1–13. The choice of Solomon was obviously intended as a compliment to James, who greatly valued himself on his 'wisdom'.

20 *by the device* through the invention or contrivance.

25 *canopy* dais with a canopy, on which the two monarchs sat in state.
29 *fell down* i.e. he was drunk.
37 *did assay* attempted.
40 *good works* playing on the Roman Catholic doctrine of salvation through Faith and Good Works.
48 *put it by* pushed it aside. James had a psychological fear of weapons, not without reason considering his early history.
49 *medley of versification* i.e. Victory spoke in verse, apparently badly to Harington's trained ear. Compare 'lamentable utterance', l. 51.
52 *Peace* another compliment to James, who liked to be known as *rex pacificus*.
56 *laid. . . . . .pates* levelled blows (with her olive branch) at the heads.
63 *manners* modes of behaviour.
64 *devise* observe (to myself) that.
     sober creation i.e. man (with his rational faculty).

5 London: life and sights

London, says Donald Lupton, 'is grown so great, I am almost afraid to meddle with her. She's certainly a great world, there are so many little worlds in her; she is the great beehive of Christendom, I am sure of England......I may call her a gallimaufry of all sciences, arts, and trades' (*London and the Countrey Carbonadoed and Quartred into Severall Characters* (1632), pp. 1–2). Despite his awe, however, Lupton manages to 'meddle', furnishing us with twenty-four 'characters', frequently satirical and sometimes mildly witty (see selection (vi)), describing London locales and institutions and relating them to the life of his times (e.g. the Tower, St Paul's Cathedral, London Bridge, the New and Old Exchange, Cheapside, Bridewell and Newgate Prisons, Paris Garden, Bedlam, the playhouses, the fencing and dancing schools). To these he adds twelve 'characters' of different aspects of country life (see above, p. 150). Never reprinted, except in occasional selections, Lupton's little book deserves to be more widely known.

A distinction must be made between what is loosely called London and the City of London. The City proper, except for what was called Farringdon Ward Without, one of the twenty-six wards into which the City was divided for administrative purposes, lay within the bounds of what had been the ancient City walls, which John Stow (*A Survay of London* (edn of 1603), ed. C. L. Kingsford (1908), I, 10) tells us were a little over two miles in circumference. Over the centuries, however, a number of 'suburbs without the walls' (Stow, II, 69–124) had become inextricably attached to the City as an integral part of greater London, most notably the City of Westminster, on the north bank of the Thames immediately to the west, and the Borough of Southwark on the south bank (known as the Bankside), the site of many of London's principal theatres and of Paris Garden (see above, pp. 51 and 168). Southwark was joined to the City by London Bridge (see selection (i)).

It has been estimated (A. J. Cook, *The Privileged Playgoers of Shakespeare's London* (1981), pp. 93–4) that greater London had a population of about 250,000 in 1603, an increase of about 70,000 since 1576. As the centre of trade, in a fast-growing mercantile economy, London attracted hordes of young men and women dedicated to improving their country status, both financially and socially; it also attracted, like bees to the honey-pot, large numbers of undesirables (rogues, vagabonds, prostitutes, pickpockets, 'cony-catchers' – confidence men (and women) of all shades and varieties) who made their living by preying on an all-too-gullible public. (See the following section on 'The underworld in town and country'.)

As the home of the royal Court and the Inns of Court ('the third university'; see above, p. 152), London was *arbiter elegantiarum*, setting the fashions, too often extravagantly, in dress and social behaviour, and creating an atmosphere in which social climbing was inevitably the name of the game. As might be expected, all these various elements contributed to serious overcrowding (particularly in the City) and to dangerously insanitary living conditions (see the section on 'The plague', p. 333). Moreover, London streets, with some few exceptions (e.g. Fleet, Newgate, Cornhill, Lombard, Aldersgate, Bishopsgate, and Holborn) were narrow and sometimes unpaved, often stinking (from the common kennel or sewer for refuse and garbage that ran down the middle of each street), and frequently choked with horsemen, carts, and coaches. It was, then, an exciting metropolis, packed with all levels of society, full of local colour, and teeming with energy, but, except for the comparatively well-to-do who made up only about fifteen per cent of the populace (Cook, p. 94), London could be a hard and bitter place in which to live.

The following selections, very inadequately of course, attempt to catch, in one way or another, something of the 'great beehive', its daily life and some few of the 'sights' that Londoners took for granted but which attracted visitors from all parts of the country and abroad. Further illustrations of London life, as I have noted above, may also be found in a number of selections in other parts of this collection, particularly in the first extended section on the theatre. For a foreigner's sharp-eyed and often detailed account of London and its manners as viewed in 1598, see Paul Hentzner's *Itinerarium* (1612; edn, with translation, of 1757).

Selection (i), 'London Bridge' (from Fynes Moryson's *Itinerary*, 1617), requires no special comment, except to note that old London Bridge was demolished and replaced in 1824 slightly further upstream. Another of London's principal sights, the Tower, is discussed by Stow (*A Survay of London* (1603), I, 44–59) with attention to its early history and present state, and Hentzner (pp. 37–40) describes its contents in considerable detail.

Selection (ii) is from Luke Hutton's *The Blacke Dogge of Newgate* (?1596). Hutton, who had experienced at firsthand the terrors of Newgate Prison, offers an exposé of the criminal malfeasance practised by sergeants (Black Dogs), petty officers responsible for arresting supposed offenders and haling them off to jail (see also John Earle's 'character' of 'A Sergeant or Catchpole' in *Micro-cosmographie* (1628), no. 36, and another, probably by Thomas Dekker, in Sir Thomas Overbury's *His Wife*, ninth impression (1616)). John Taylor the Water Poet (*The Vertue of a Jayle* in *Works*, 1630, pp. 130–1) rattles off a list of eighteen jails in greater London, the best known, apart from Newgate (for felons and debtors), being the Bread Street and Poultry Counters (debtors), Bridewell (a house of correction for prostitutes and 'idle knaves'), Ludgate (debtors and bankrupts), the Fleet (offenders in the courts of Chancery and Starchamber), the Clink (religious offenders), the Marshalsea (debtors) and the Tower (important political prisoners).

For those with some money prison life could be made tolerable by fee-payments to the head keeper and by various financial exactions and extortions to lesser officials, but for poor prisoners, depending upon the relative humanity or inhumanity of the keeper, life could quickly resemble the 'Hell' of which Hutton speaks (see 'characters' of 'A Prison' and 'A Prisoner', probably by Thomas Dekker, in Sir Thomas Overbury's *His Wife* (ninth impression, 1616) and, in general, C. Dobb, 'London's Prisons', *Shakespeare Survey*, XVII (1964), 87–100).

Prison scenes figure frequently in the contemporary drama, particularly in English history plays, where the principal members of the losing faction are thrown into prison, the Tower or some other castle dungeon (e.g. Marlowe's *Edward II* (1591–3) or Shakespeare's *Richard III* and *Richard II*), and a good deal of the action in Shakespeare's *Measure for Measure* takes place in a 'Vienna' prison. Thomas Dekker has a lively scene in Bridewell in *II Honest Whore* (1604–5), V.ii, and Jonson, Chapman and Marston's *Eastward Ho!* (1605; V.v) concludes with a humorous scene in one of the Counters.

The third selection (iii), from Thomas Dekker and John Webster's *Northward Ho!* (1607), describes a visit to Bedlam (Bethlehem) Hospital, the London madhouse. Bedlam was considered one of the 'sights', and visits such as this, to witness the mad antics of the inmates, were a common pastime, one that sadly continued into the second half of the eighteenth century. The present scene may be compared with a similar scene (superior, but too long for inclusion here) in Dekker and Webster's *Westward Ho!* (1604), V.ii, and with the comic subplot of Thomas Middleton and William Rowley's *The Changeling* (1622), which is laid in a madhouse. Although madness was thus often treated in contemporary drama as a potential source for comic humour (the presumed madness of Malvolio in Shakespeare's *Twelfth Night* may serve as a further example) or grotesquerie (the Masque of Madmen in John Webster's *The Duchess of Malfi* (1612–14), IV.ii, which, however, acts as a powerful foil to the heavily morbid tragic atmosphere surrounding the Duchess' death), dramatists also found in madness a source of moving tragic expression in such memorable characters as Hieronimo and Isabella (Thomas Kyd, *The Spanish Tragedy* (c.1587)), Shakespeare's Titus Andronicus, Hamlet, Ophelia, and Lear, Ferdinand (Webster, *The Duchess of Malfi*), D'Amville (Cyril Tourneur, *The Atheist's Tragedy* (1607–11)), and Sir Giles Overreach (Philip Massinger, *A New Way to Pay Old Debts* (1621–5)).

Selection (iv), from Thomas Dekker's *The Guls Horne-booke* (1609), presents a vividly satirical picture of *à la mode* behaviour by would-be gallants in a London ordinary. Dining (around noon) and supping out were fashionable, indeed necessary for most non-family men, and an ordinary or tavern, to be distinguished from an inn, which provided both food and lodging (see Fynes Moryson's high praise of English inns compared to their European counterparts in his *Itinerary* (1617), bk. III, chap. 3), was a common meeting place where men of various social levels could mingle with or entertain their friends and pass the time in eating, drinking, card-playing, and dicing (see an extended dicing scene in Thomas Heywood's *The Wise Woman of Hogsdon* (c.1604), I.i). As

John Earle, in his 'character' of a Tavern (*Micro-cosmographie*, 1628, no. 12), says: 'It is a broacher of more news than hogsheads and more jests than news, which are sucked up here by some spongy brain, and from thence squeezed into a comedy......It is the busy man's recreation, the idle man's business, the Inns a'Court man's entertainment, the scholar's kindness, and the citizen's courtesy.' And the dramatist, Francis Beaumont, particularly celebrates the Mermaid Tavern (in Bread Street) in his 'Letter to Ben Jonson' as a centre of wit and good fellowship:

> ......What things have we seen
> Done at the Mermaid! heard words that have been
> So nimble and so full of subtle flame,
> As if that everyone from whom they came
> Had meant to put his whole wit in a jest,
> And had resolv'd to live a fool the rest
> Of his dull life......

Jonson himself composed a series of twenty-four 'Leges Convivales', which were posted in the Apollo Room of the Devil Tavern (Fleet Street), another of his favourite haunts. See 'Food and drink', selection (ii), p. 120.

But ordinaries and taverns were also sometimes little better than bawdy-houses and were haunted by sharpers bent on fleecing unwary visitors (see, for example, a tale in Robert Greene's *A Notable Discovery of Coosnage* (1591), ed. G. B. Harrison (1923), pp. 17–31). Tavern scenes abound, particularly in City comedy, although the most famous are those at the Boar's Head Tavern, in Shakespeare's *I* and *II Henry IV*, where Falstaff and his cronies (including Prince Hal) hung out. For other examples, see Ben Jonson, *Every Man in His Humour* (1599; rev. *c*.1612), III.i–ii and *Every Man out of His Humour* (1599), III.vi; George Chapman, *May-Day* (1601–9), I.ii; Thomas Middleton, *Michaelmas Term* (1604–6), II.i; Jonson, Chapman, and Marston, *Eastward Ho!* (1605), III.iii; Beaumont and Fletcher, *The Captain* (1609–12), IV.ii.

The fifth selection (v), from Thomas Dekker's *The Dead Tearme* (1608), describes Paul's Walk, 'the land's epitome......the lesser isle [with the inevitable pun on 'aisle'] of Great Britain' (John Earle, *Microcosmographie* (1628)), the central aisle or nave of St Paul's Cathedral and a daily meeting place for people of all kinds and social levels, including a wide variety of criminal elements. In his *Guls Horne-booke* (1609), Dekker devotes a chapter (IV) to explaining 'How a gallant should behave himself in Paul's Walks', either to display his new suit to best advantage or to 'take sanctuary' in the sacred precincts, where, till nightfall, he was for the time safe from his clamouring creditors; and Samuel Rowlands (*The Letting of Humours Blood in the Head-Vaine* (1600), Satire I) gives us a verse portrait of a needy would-be gallant who haunts Paul's and the Royal Exchange (another meeting place), telling tall tales and spreading false rumours. Here 'bills', advertising servants for hire, lodgings or new books, were posted, lawyers conducted business (some of it in the interests of their clients), brokers (called 'gull-gropers') drove usurious bargains with young heirs for ready cash, and pickpockets and cozeners of all stripes flourished, the former even invading the choir itself during services and at sermon times.

As one might expect, dramatists found Paul's Walk a tempting locale for scenes in City comedy. Ben Jonson (*Every Man out of His Humour* (1599), III.i–vi) uses it for an excellent scene in which Shift ('a threadbare shark') inveigles Sogliardo, a country clown, who has just purchased his gentility, to accept him as his instructor in the art of 'drinking' (i.e. smoking) tobacco. Thomas Middleton also sets two scenes here in *Michaelmas Term* (1604–6; I.i) and *Your Five Gallants* (1604–7; IV.vi), the title-characters in the latter giving a kind of cross-section of the criminal elements who plied their trade in the Walk: Frippery, the broker-gallant, Primero, the bawd-gallant, Goldstone, the cheating-gallant, Pursenet, the pocket-gallant, and Tailby, the whore-gallant. See also, 'The underworld in town and country', selection (iv) from Ben Jonson's *The Alchemist* (1612).

The last selection (vi), a 'character' from Donald Lupton's *London and the Countrey Carbonadoed* (1632), attempts a witty treatment of what was in fact a serious problem – the necessary removal of animal and human excrement from the streets and homes of London to combat disease and stench. Each ward in the City and its suburbs had its officially appointed scavengers (the City ward of Bishopsgate had seven, the borough ward of Southwark, six). Despite their efforts, however, walking in the crowded streets was a hazardous business and pedestrians, to protect their clothes from kennel splatterings, would try to 'take the wall' (i.e. to walk as closely as possible to the houses which abutted directly on the street). Needless to say, 'taking the wall' sometimes led to fisticuffs or armed combat, conferring not only comparative safety but social prestige as John Donne's 'fondling motley humorist' (*Satire I*) well knew:

> Now we are in the street. He first of all
> Improvidently proud creeps to the wall,
> And so imprison'd, and hemm'd in by me,
> Sells for a little state his liberty.

Ben Jonson affords us an intimately lurid view of sanitary conditions in London in his scatological poem 'The Famous Voyage'.

i

London Bridge

From Fynes Moryson, *An Itinerary* (1617), bk. II, third part, chap. 2.

The Bridge at London is worthily to be numb'red among the miracles of the world, if men respect the building and foundation, laid artificially and stately over an ebbing and flowing water, upon twenty-one piles of stone, with twenty arches, under which barks may pass, the lowest foundation being (as they say) packs of wool, 5 most durable against the force of the water, and not to be repaired but upon great fall of the waters and by artificial turning or stopping the recourse of them. Or if men respect the houses built upon the bridge, as great and high as those of the firm land, so as a man cannot know that he passeth a bridge, but would judge 10 himself to be in the street, save that the houses on both sides are combined in the top, making the passage somewhat dark, and that in some few open places the river of Thames may be seen on both sides.

NOTES

1   *Bridge at London* This was the only stone bridge spanning the Thames. Crossing from bank to bank was otherwise by small boats which were rowed by 'water-men', of whom a large number haunted both sides of the river and did not enjoy a very savoury reputation. John Stow (*A Survay of London*, edn of 1603; ed. C. L. Kingsford (1908), I, 21–6) describes the vicissitudes and alterations that London Bridge had undergone since it was first constructed in 1209 (being thirty-three years in the building) Moryson does not mention the tower-gates, on either end of the bridge, on which the heads of traitors were exhibited on spikes above the gates (see Stow, p. 60). The German traveller Paul Hentzner (*Itinerarium* (1612, edn of 1757), p. 3) reports that he counted more than thirty such heads in 1598.

3   *artificially* skilfully.

4   *arches* sixty feet high, thirty feet broad, and twenty feet apart (Stow, p. 26).

7   *fall* lowering (of the water level).

7–8 *artificial......stopping* Stow (p. 23) records that while the bridge was originally being built that 'the river for the time was turned another way about by a trench cast for that purpose.'

10   *passeth* crosseth over.

12   *combined......top* To gain a little more floor-space in houses fronting directly on the street, builders often constructed them so that each storey, above the ground floor, projected a foot or more beyond the storey below. In the comparatively narrow quarters of the bridge, the houses on either side apparently converged so that they were essentially joined at the top.

ii

Newgate Prison and rogue officials

From Luke Hutton, *The Blacke Dogge of Newgate* (?1596), sig. C3 r–v.
Hutton was executed as a criminal in 1598. At the end of his rather
pitiful little pamphlet, Hutton describes the criminal dealings of two
sergeants, whom, for fear of reprisals, he calls 'H. S.' and 'E. H.'. Among
other examples, he tells the following story:

Not long since, at a tilting upon triumph on the crownation day,
many good subjects with joy assembled the place of triumph, as
well rejoicing to see the Queen's most excellent Majesty, as also to
see the tilting performed by sundry noble and right honourable
personages. Amongst the rest, there comes a woman with six   5
pounds in her purse, which the cutpurse met withal, she as it
seemed having more mind on the pleasures of the present day and
time than she had of her purse.

The jousts ended for that day, the woman, thinking all had
been well, takes her way homeward with a friend of hers; yet, by the   10
way, this good woman must needs drink with her friend a pint of
wine. But here was the mischief: when the wine was to be paid for,
the woman missed her purse, and, looking on the strings, with a
cold heart she might perceive her purse was cut away. Her friend
to comfort her bade her take no thought, for he knew a man   15
would help her to her purse again; 'And', saith he, 'we will
presently go to him, for I know where he dwells.'

The woman thanked her friend for his courteous offer, and
away they go to E. H. his house, where they found him, to whom
they brake the matter wholly how it was, desiring his help.   20
Presently he had them in the wind and bade them welcome,
promising that, if they would content him for his pains, he would
do her good, asking her what she would willingly bestow to have
her money again. At the first word, she offered him forty shillings.
All this was well, and they agree to meet the next day about   25
Whitehall, where they shall have answer to their content. And so,
after they had drunk a quart of wine at the tavern, for that night
they parted.

The next day, according to promise, they met, and this E. H.
had in his company a man, who, he said, was a constable; but   30
whether he said truly or no I will not say. But to the matter: they
appoint the woman to go to a friend's house hard by, and she
should hear more anon. Away went she, as they had appointed
her, and away go they to look for cutpurses.

I warrant you, they sought not long, but here they met with a   35
cutpurse, whom they take by the sleeve; and there they meet with
another as good a cutpurse as the former; and so they take at the

least a dozen cutpurses. Which, when they have done, the cony-catcher begins to rail mightily, swearing they shall some of them be hanged; but to prison they shall all go, unless this money be had again, showing a warrant, or a piece of paper at the least, which is sufficient to bear the cony-catcher harmless, as he sayeth.   40

Now the cutpurses, though they be all clear of this matter, yet they begin to quake for fear, offering, rather than they will go to prison, they will make up the money, so that E. H. will promise to give it them again when the cutpurse shall be known who cut the purse indeed. This motion the cony-catcher liketh indifferently; and so of those dozen of cutpurses he taketh of some more and of some less, that the sum is largely made up; which done, they are all discharged. Marry, they must have some twenty shillings overplus for their pains and kindness showed to the cutpurses; all which is granted.   45, 50

To be short, no cutpurse scaped their hands but he paid a share, so that there was gathered the first day at the least ten pounds amongst cutpurses; and the next day this E. H. met with the cutpurse who cut the purse indeed, of whom he took the money, with the vantage, and let him go without answering the matter. And to conclude, the woman had four pound of her money again, and so the matter was no more spoken of.   55

NOTES

1   *tilting* jousting on horseback with a lance.
   upon triumph with splendour and public spectacle.
   crownation coronation (variant form). Queen Elizabeth was crowned 15 January 1559.

2   *assembled the place* This transitive use of 'assemble' is unrecorded in *OED*; 'at' or 'in' has probably been omitted.

13   *strings* Purses were attached to the girdle or belt by cords or leather thongs.

19   *E. H. his* i.e. E. H.'s.

20   *brake* broke.

21   *had......wind* perceived (scented) the situation.

22   *pains* labour.

24   *At......word* at once.

25-6 *about Whitehall* in the vicinity of Whitehall, the royal palace just to the south of Charing Cross.

30   *constable* officer of the peace.

36   *take......sleeve* i.e. arrest.

38-9 *cony-catcher* i.e. ironically the sergeant, E. H.; usually applied to the various criminals (cutpurses, for example) who preyed on the citizens.

42   *bear......harmless* i.e. render the sergeant safe from prosecution for false arrest.

43   *clear......matter* innocent of this particular offence.
47   *liketh indifferently* accepteth with indifference (since he has no intention
       of returning the cutpurses' money).
49   *that* so that.
57   *with the vantage* with (a little) more.
57–58 *without......matter* i.e. without being arrested for his theft.

iii

A visit to Bedlam

From Thomas Dekker and John Webster, *Northward Ho!* (1607), IV.iii.

Enter BELLAMONT, MAYBERRY, GREENSHIELD, PHILIP,
LEVERPOOL, CHARTLEY, *all booted*

[The scene opens with some badinage, in which Bellamont
suggests that, on their projected journey to Ware, a town about
twenty miles north of London, they should 'practise jests one
against another' and that the one who is most embarrassed by the
jest played on him should 'bear the charge of the whole journey'.]

BELLAMONT. Stay, yonder's the Dolphin without Bishopsgate,
    where our horses are at rack and manger, and we are going past
    it. Come, cross over. And what place is this?

MAYBERRY. Bedlam, is't not?

BELLAMONT. Where the madmen are: I never was amongst them.   5
    As you love me, gentlemen, let's see what Greeks are within.

GREENSHIELD. We shall stay too long.

BELLAMONT. Not a whit; Ware will stay for our coming, I warrant
    you. Come, a spurt and away! Let's be mad once in our days.
    This is the door.   [*He knocks*]   10

Enter FULLMOON

MAYBERRY. Save you, sir! May we see some a' your mad folks? Do
    you keep 'em?

FULLMOON. Yes.

BELLAMONT. Pray bestow your name, sir, upon us.

FULLMOON. My name is Fullmoon.   15

BELLAMONT. You well deserve this office, good Master Fullmoon.
    And what madcaps have you in your house?

Enter the MUSICIAN

FULLMOON. Divers.

MAYBERRY. God's so, see, see! What's he walkes yonder? Is he
    mad?   20

FULLMOON. That's a musician; yes, he's besides himself.

BELLAMONT. A musician! How fell he mad, for God's sake?

FULLMOON. For love of an Italian dwarf.

BELLAMONT. Has he been in Italy then?

FULLMOON. Yes, and speaks, they say, all manner of languages.   25

Enter the BAWD

OMNES. God's so, look, look! What's she?

BELLAMONT. The dancing bear: a pretty well-favoured little woman.

FULLMOON. They say, but I know not, that she was a bawd, and was frightened out of her wits by fire.   30

BELLAMONT. May we talk with 'em, Master Fullmoon?

FULLMOON. Yes, and you will. I must look about, for I have unruly tenants.   *Exit*

BELLAMONT. What have you in this paper, honest friend?

[*Exit* MUSICIAN]

GREENSHIELD. Is this he has all manner of languages, yet speaks   35
none?

BAWD. How do you, Sir Andrew? Will you send for some aqua-vitae for me? I have had no drink never since the last great rain that fell.

BELLAMONT. No? that's a lie.   40

BAWD. Nay, by gad, then you lie, for all y'are Sir Andrew. I was a dapper rogue in Portingal voyage, not an inch broad at the heel, and yet thus high; I scorned, I can tell you, to be drunk with rain water then, sir, in those golden and silver days. I had sweet bits then, Sir Andrew. How do you, good brother   45
Timothy?

BELLAMONT. You have been in much trouble since that voyage?

BAWD. Never in Bridewell, I protest, as I'm a virgin; for I could never abide that Bridewell, I protest. I was once sick, and I took my water in a basket, and carried it to a doctor's.   50

PHILIP. In a basket!

BAWD. Yes, sir: you arrant fool, there was a urinal in it.

PHILIP. I cry you mercy.

BAWD. The doctor told me I was with child. How many lords, knights, gentlemen, citizens, and others promised me to be   55
godfathers to that child! 'Twas not God's will: the prentices made a riot upon my glass windows the Shrove Tuesday following and I miscarried.

OMNES. O, do not weep!

BAWD. I ha' cause to weep: I trust gentlewomen their diet   60
sometimes a fortnight; lend gentlemen holland shirts, and they
sweat 'em out at tennis; and no restitution, and no restitution.
But I'll take a new order: I will have but six stewed prunes in a
dish and some of Mother Wall's cakes; for my best customers
are tailors.   65

OMNES. Tailors! ha, ha!

BAWD. Ay, tailors: give me your London prentice; your country
gentlemen are grown too politic.

BELLAMONT. But what say you to such young gentlemen as these
are?   70

BAWD. Foh! they, as soon as they come to their lands, get up to
London, and, like squibs that run upon lines, they keep a-
spitting of fire and cracking till they ha' spent all; and when my
squib is out, what says his punk? Foh, he stinks!

Enter the MUSICIAN
[*The* BAWD *sings.*]

Methought this other night, I saw a pretty sight,   75
    Which pleased me much:
A comely country maid, not squeamish nor afraid
    To let gentlemen touch.
I sold her maidenhead once, and I sold her
        maidenhead twice,
    And I sold it last to an alderman of York;   80
And then I had sold it thrice.

MUSICIAN. You sing scurvily.

BAWD. Marry muff, sing thou better, for I'll go sleep my old sleeps.
Exit

BELLAMONT. What are you a-doing, my friend?

MUSICIAN. Pricking, pricking.   85

BELLAMONT. What do you mean by pricking?

MUSICIAN. A gentleman-like quality.

BELLAMONT. This fellow is somewhat prouder and sullener than
the other.

MAYBERRY. O, so be most of your musicians.   90

MUSICIAN. Are my teeth rotten?

OMNES. No, sir.

MUSICIAN. Then I am no comfit-maker nor vintner: I do not get
  wenches in my drink. [*To* BELLAMONT] Are you a musician?

BELLAMONT. Yes.   95

MUSICIAN. We'll be sworn brothers then, look you sweet rogue.

GREENSHIELD. God's so, now I think upon't, a jest is crept into my
  head. Steal away, if you love me.

                        Exeunt [*all but* BELLAMONT *and* MUSICIAN]

                            MUSICIAN *sings*

MUSICIAN. Was ever any merchant's band set better I set it. Walk,
  I'm a-cold: this white satin is too thin unless it be cut, for then   100
  the sun enters. Can you speak Italian too? *Sapete Italiano?*

BELLAMONT. *Un poco.*

MUSICIAN. 'Sblood, if it be in you, I'll poke it out of you. *Un poco!*
  Come march; lie here with me but till the fall of the leaf, and if
  you have but *poco Italiano* in you, I'll fill you full of more *poco.* 105
  March!

BELLAMONT. Come on.   *Exeunt*

[Greenshield's 'jest', later in the scene, is to have Bellamont taken
into custody by Fullmoon, as a 'madman'; the 'jest' is happily
resolved and the whole group sets off for Ware, Bellamont
promising further 'jests' of his own.]

                               NOTES

1   *Dolphin* tavern on the east side of Bishopsgate Street Without, one of the
     old City gates, between Aldgate and Aldersgate, in the north-east part of
     London.
2   *rack and manger* openwork frame (placed above) for hay and straw; and
     box or trough (placed below) for other kinds of feed.
4   *Bedlam* (or Bethlehem, Bethlem) Hospital, where the inmates were
     imprisoned and to some extent cared for. A visit to Bedlam was a favourite
     pastime.
6   *Greeks* (slang) questionable characters (literally, sharpers, cheaters,
     persons of loose morality).
9   *spurt* short space of time.
     Let's be mad Let's frolic (with play on associating with 'madmen').
     Bellamont and Mayberry are both middle-aged.
11   *Save* i.e. God save.
12   *keep* i.e. act as a keeper of Bedlam.
16   *deserve this office* playing on the belief that madness is aggravated at the
     time of a full moon.

17   *madcaps* frolicsome fellows (used here for the play on 'mad').
19   *God's so* exclamation, meaning uncertain (related to 'catso' and 'gadso').
26   *OMNES.* all (speaking together).
27   *dancing bear* The allusion is probably to a well-known performing bear.
       well-favoured good-looking.
30   *fire* probably some oblique reference to venereal disease.
37   *Sir Andrew* The Bawd's mind is confused; she here addresses Bellamont.
       In l. 46 she calls someone else 'Timothy'.
37–8 *aqua-vitae* strong drink (e.g. brandy); literally, 'water of life'.
38   *no......never* intensive double negative.
41   *by gad* softened form of 'by God'.
42   *Portingal voyage* expedition, led by Sir Francis Drake and Sir John Norris,
       against Spain on behalf of Portugal in 1589.
48   *Bridewell* prison (formerly a palace) for bawds, rogues and prostitutes, at
       the Thames end of Fleet Ditch.
56–7 *prentices......Shrove Tuesday* Shrove Tuesday, the last day before the
       beginning of Lent, was a festival holiday on which the City apprentices
       used up excessive energy by, traditionally, wrecking bawdy-houses.
60–1 *trust......fortnight* i.e. so that the gentlewomen could secretly give
       birth to illegitimate children.
61   *holland* fine linen fabric. One is reminded of Mistress Quickly's complaint
       against Falstaff (*I Henry IV*, III.iii.67–74; *II Henry IV*, II.i.1–165).
62   *no restitution* i.e. they never pay their debts.
63   *stewed prunes* a dainty regularly associated with bawdy-houses.
64   *Mother Wall's cakes* Mother Wall resided in Abchurch Lane and was
       known for her pies or pasties.
66   *Tailors! ha, ha!* Proverbially, it took three (or nine) tailors to make up one
       man (Tilley T23).
68   *politic* shrewd, cautious.
72   *squibs......lines* connected fireworks strung on a cord.
83   *Marry muff* exclamation, implying you are talking nonsense.
       old accustomed.
85   *Pricking* (1) writing down notes ('pricks') as in 'prick-song'; (2) smarting,
       grieving (probably with sexual implications; note 'gentleman-like quality'
       in l. 87).
87   *quality* occupation, accomplishment.
93   *comfit-maker* maker of sweetmeats, candies (which could rot the teeth).
       vintner wine seller (the English added sugar to wines).
93–4 *get wenches* beget girls (it was considered more 'manly' to beget sons).
99   *Was......it* If any merchant's neck-band was ever better arranged ('set')
       (than mine), I must have set it.
100   *cut* ornamentally slashed (with insets).
101   *Sapete Italiano?* Do you know Italian?
102   *Un poco* a little.
103   *'Sblood* (By) God's blood.
       poke used for the play on *poco*.

iv

How a young gallant should behave himself in an ordinary

From Thomas Dekker, *The Guls Horne-booke* (1609), chap. V (pp. 22–7).

First having diligently enquired out an ordinary of the largest reckoning whither most of your courtly gallants do resort, let it be your use to repair thither some half-hour after eleven, for then you shall find most of your fashion-mongers planted in the room waiting for meat. Ride thither upon your galloway-nag or your   5
Spanish jennet a swift ambling pace in your hose and doublet, gilt rapier and poniard bestowed in their places and your French lackey carrying your cloak and running before you; or rather in a coach, for that will both hide you from the basilisk-eyes of your creditors and outrun a whole kennel of bitter-mouthed sergeants.   10
    Being arrived in the room, salute not any but those of your acquaintance; walk up and down by the rest as scornfully and as carelessly as a gentleman-usher. Select some friend (having first thrown off your cloak) to walk up and down the room with you. Let him be suited if you can worse by far than yourself: he will be a   15
foil to you, and this will be a means to publish your clothes better than Paul's, a tennis-court, or a playhouse. Discourse as loud as you can, no matter to what purpose; if you but make a noise and laugh in fashion, and have a good sour face to promise quarrelling, you shall be much observed. If you be a soldier, talk how often you   20
have been in action – as, the Portingal Voyage, Cales Voyage, the Island Voyage, besides some eight or nine employments in Ireland and the Low Countries......And that will be an excellent occasion to publish your languages if you have them. If not, get some fragments of French or small parcels of Italian to fling about   25
the table. But beware how you speak any Latin there; your ordinary most commonly hath no more to do with Latin than a desperate town of garrison hath.
    If you be a courtier, discourse of the obtaining of suits, of your mistress's favours, etc.; make enquiry if any gentleman at board   30
have any suit, to get which he would use the good means of a great man's interest with the King; and withal (if you have not so much grace left in you as to blush) that you are (thanks to your stars) in mighty credit, though in your own conscience you know and are guilty to yourself that you dare not (but only upon the privileges of   35
handsome clothes) presume to peep into the Presence......
    If you be a poet and come into the ordinary (though it can be no great glory to be an ordinary poet) order yourself thus: observe no man, doff not cap to that gentleman today at dinner to whom not two nights since you were beholden for a supper; but after a   40
turn or two in the room take occasion (pulling out your gloves) to

have some epigram or satire or sonnet fastened in one of them that
may (as it were unwittingly to you) offer itself to the gentlemen.
They will presently desire it, but without much conjuration from
them and a pretty kind of counterfeit loathness in yourself do not   45
read it. And though it be none of your own, swear you made it.
Marry, if you chance to get into your hands any witty thing of
another man's that is somewhat better, I would counsel you then,
if demand be made who composed it, you may say, 'Faith, a
learned gentleman, a very worthy friend'; and this seeming to lay it   50
on another man will be counted either modesty in you or a sign
that you are not ambitious of praise, or else that you dare not take
it upon you for fear of the sharpness it carries with it. Besides, it
will add much to your fame to let your tongue walk faster than
your teeth though you be never so hungry and, rather than you   55
should sit like a dumb coxcomb, to repeat by heart either some
verses of your own or of any other man's, stretching even very
good lines upon the rack of censure; though it be against all law,
honesty, or conscience, it may chance save you the price of your
ordinary and beget you other supplements. Marry, I would further   60
entreat our poet to be in league with the mistress of the ordinary
because from her, upon condition that he will but rhyme knights
and young gentlemen to her house and maintain the table in good
fooling, he may easily make up his mouth at her cost *gratis* . . . . . .

Before the meat come smoking to the board our gallant must   65
draw out his tobacco-box, the ladle for the cold snuff into the
nostril, the tongs and prining-iron: all which artillery may be of
gold and silver (if he can reach to the price of it); it will be a
reasonable useful pawn at all times when the current of his money
falls out to run low. And here you must observe to know in what   70
state tobacco is in town better than the merchants, and to
discourse of the pothecaries where it is to be sold and to be able to
speak of their wines as readily as the pothecary himself reading the
barbarous hand of a doctor. Then let him show his several tricks in
taking it, as the whiff, the ring, etc. For these are complements   75
that gain gentlemen no mean respect and for which indeed they
are more worthily noted, I ensure you, than for any skill that they
have in learning . . . . . .

You may rise in dinner-time to ask for a close-stool, protesting
to all the gentlemen that it costs you a hundred pound a year in   80
physic besides the annual pension which your wife allows her
doctor. And (if you please) you may (as your great French lord
doth) invite some special friend of yours from the table to hold
discourse with you as you sit in that withdrawing-chamber; from
whence being returned again to the board, you shall sharpen the   85
wits of all the eating gallants about you, and do them great
pleasure, to ask what pamphlets or poems a man might think
fittest to wipe his tail with (marry, this talk will be somewhat foul

if you carry not a strong perfume about you) and, in propounding
this question, you may abuse the works of any man, deprave his   90
writings that you cannot equal, and purchase to yourself in time
the terrible name of a severe critic – nay, and be one of the College
if you'll be liberal enough, and when your turn comes pay for their
suppers.

After dinner, every man as his business leads him – some to   95
dice, some to drabs, some to plays, some to take up friends in the
Court, some to take up money in the City, some to lend testers in
Paul's, others to borrow crowns upon the Exchange......

NOTES

1–2 *ordinary......reckoning* most expensive eating-house. Any significant
     distinction between 'ordinary' and 'tavern' seems impossible to make,
     though Dekker devotes separate chapters to them.

5   *galloway-nag* small-sized horse, originally peculiar to Galloway in
     Scotland.

6   *Spanish jennet* small Spanish horse.

6–7 *gilt rapier* rapier with a gilded hilt.

7   *poniard* dagger.

7–8 *French lackey* French footman (a French lackey was considered
     fashionable).

9   *basilisk-eyes* The eye of the basilisk (a fabulous monster) was considered
     deadly.

10   *sergeants* See selection (ii).

13   *gentleman-usher* gentleman acting as usher to a person of (supposedly)
     higher rank.

15–16 *be a foil* i.e. show you off to advantage.

17   *Paul's* See selection (v).
     tennis-court Tennis, quite different from modern tennis, was at this time
     an indoor sport and tennis-courts were a gathering-place for 'fashionable'
     spectators.

19   *to promise quarrelling* to give the appearance that you were of a naturally
     quarrelsome disposition.

21   *Portingal Voyage* military expedition, under Drake and Norris, sent to
     Portugal in 1589.
     Cales Voyage Cales (Cadiz) was sacked by Lord Howard and the Earl of
     Essex in 1596.

22   *Island Voyage* expedition against the Azores in 1597.

23   *Low Countries* Netherlands.

28   *desperate......garrison* i.e. town of which the garrison is under siege.

29   *suits* petitions for favours to the Court.

36   *Presence* presence-chamber at Court, where the sovereign or nobility
     might be approached with suits of various kinds.

38   *ordinary poet* (1) run-of-the-mill poet; (2) poet who exercises his talent in
     an ordinary.

39   *doff not* do not remove.

43   *unwittingly* emendation for 'vomittingly' in 1609 text.
52–3   *you dare......with it* i.e. you are afraid to acknowledge it as yours
        because of its possibly libellous nature.
54–5   *tongue......teeth* i.e. talk more than you eat.
58   *rack* literally, machine used in torture by which the body was stretched
        causing dislocation of the joints.
64   *make......mouth* i.e. feed himself.
        gratis for nothing.
65   *board* table (often boards set on trestles).
66   *ladle* here used for a 'small spoon'.
        cold snuff i.e. the snuffing up of powdered tobacco which has not been
        ignited ('cold').
67   *tongs* pipe-tongs for placing tobacco in the bowl.
        prining iron (probably an error for 'priming-iron') (1) ?instrument for
        tamping the tobacco down into the bowl of the pipe; (2) ?wire instrument
        for cleaning out the pipe-stem.
72   *pothecaries* apothecaries.
73   *wines* emendation for 'wiues' in 1609 text. 'Wines' may be taken to refer
        to the various medicinal waters prepared by 'pothecaries'.
74   *barbarous......doctor* Doctors' prescriptions, then as now, were known
        for their illegibility, the Latin abbreviations (carelessly written) being
        incomprehensible to the layman.
75   *whiff......ring* unexplained; perhaps expelling smoke through the
        nostrils and blowing smoke-rings.
        complements accomplishments.
79   *close-stool* chamber pot enclosed in a stool or box.
92   *College* group of critics, perhaps associated with Ben Jonson, who
        pontificated on poetry.
96   *drabs* prostitutes.
97   *testers* sixpences.
98   *Exchange* The New Exchange, like Paul's Walk, was a common place of
        resort for gallants.

V

Paul's Walk

From Thomas Dekker, *The Dead Tearme* (1608), ed. A. B. Grosart, *Prose Works*, IV, 49–52. [The speaker is supposedly the ruined and truncated steeple of St Paul's, originally 260 feet high, destroyed by fire in 1561 and never rebuilt.]

For whereas I was at first consecrated to a mystical and religious purpose (the ceremonies of which are daily observed in the better part of me, for my heart is even to this hour an altar upon which are offered the sacrifices of holy prayers for men's sins), yet are some limbs of my venerable body abused and put to profane,   5 horrid, and servile customs: no marvel though my head rot, when the body is so full of diseases; no marvel if the Divine Executioner cut me off by the shoulders, when in my bosom is so much horrible and close treason practised against the King of the whole world.   10

For, albeit, though I never yet came down all my stairs to be an ocular witness-bearer of what I speak and what is (sometimes spoke openly and sometimes spoke in private) committed in my walks, yet doth the daily sound and echo of much knavish villainy strike up into mine ear. What whispering is there in term times,   15 how by some sleight to cheat the poor country clients of his full purse that is stuck under his girdle! What plots are laid to furnish young gallants with ready money (which is shared afterwards at a tavern), thereby to disfurnish him of his patrimony! What buying up of oaths out of the hands of Knights of the Post, who for a few   20 shillings do daily sell their souls! What laying of heads is there together and sifting of the brain, still and anon, as it grows towards eleven of the clock (even amongst those that wear gilt rapiers by their sides), where for that noon they may shift from Duke Humphrey and be furnished with a dinner at some meaner   25 man's table! What damnable bargains of unmerciful brokery, and of unmeasurable usury, are there clapped up! What swearing is there, yea, what swaggering, what facing and outfacing! What shuffling, what shouldering, what justling, what jeering, what biting of thumbs to beget quarrels, what holding up of fingers to   30 remember drunken meetings, what braving with feathers, what bearding with mustachoes, what casting open of cloaks to publish new clothes, what muffling in cloaks to hide broken elbows, so that when I hear such trampling up and down, such spitting, such hawking, and such humming (every man's lips making a noise, yet   35 not a word to be understood), I verily believe that I am the Tower of Babel newly to be builded up, but presently despair of ever being finished, because there is in me such a confusion of languages!

For at one time, in one and the same rank, yea, foot by foot and elbow by elbow, shall you see walking the knight, the gull, the 40 gallant, the upstart, the gentleman, the clown, the captain, the apple-squire, the lawyer, the usurer, the citizen, the bankrout, the scholar, the beggar, the doctor, the idiot, the ruffian, the cheater, the puritan, the cut-throat, the high-man, the low-man, the true-man, and the thief: of all trades and professions some, of all 45 countries some. And thus doth my middle aisle show like the Mediterranean Sea, in which as well the merchant hoists up sails to purchase wealth honestly, as the rover to light upon prize unjustly. Thus, whilst devotion kneels at her prayers, doth profanation walk under her nose in contempt of religion...... 50

NOTES

2   *ceremonies* Dekker notes that divine service is observed twice every day in the choir throughout the year.

15   *term times* four set periods when the law courts were in session. Dekker earlier (pp. 21–37) describes the tremendous bustle and activity during such 'terms' in Westminster compared to the dearth of life and livelihood during the so-called 'vacations'.

16   *country clients* country folk who come to London to seek legal advice.

20   *Knights of the Post* men who got their living by giving false evidence for a fee. 'Post'=?whipping-post.

22   *still and anon* continuously.

23–4   *those......rapiers* impoverished gallants or sharpers dressed to resemble gallants.

25   *Duke Humphrey* 'To dine with Duke Humphrey' meant to go without dinner. The tomb of Sir John Beauchamp, curiously known as Duke Humphrey's tomb, stood in the middle aisle.

27   *clapped up* agreed upon.

28   *facing and outfacing* boasting and impudence.

29   *shuffling* pushing, huddling.
    jeering scoffing.

30   *biting of thumbs* provocative, probably obscene, gesture, as in *Romeo and Juliet*, I.i.42–3.

30–1   *holding......meetings* ?gesture to remind someone of a drinking appointment.

31   *braving* showing off, ostentation, or, perhaps, threatening.

32   *bearding with mustachoes* insolent defiance with moustaches (with play on 'bearding').

33   *broken elbows* i.e. sleeves with holes in the elbows.

35   *hawking* clearing the throat noisily.

36–7   *Tower of Babel* See Genesis 11:1–9.

40   *gull* credulous young man, dupe.

41   *clown* country labourer.

42   *apple-squire* pimp or male bawd.
    bankrout bankrupt (variant form).

44   *high-man, the low-man* Literally, loaded dice; here used figuratively for practitioners of the 'cheating law' who used such dice.

44–5 *true-man* honest man (used for the jingle).

47   *Mediterranean Sea* The middle aisle was known as 'Mediterraneo' or the 'Mediterranean Isle (*or* Aisle)'.
      merchant trading vessel.

48   *rover* pirate ship.

vi

Sanitation in London

From Donald Lupton, *London and the Countrey Carbonadoed and Quartred into Severall Characters* (1632), pp. 94–6.

Scavengers and Goldfinders
These two keep all clean, the one the streets, the other the backsides, but they are seldom clean themselves: the one, like the hangman, doth his work all by day; the other, like a thief, doeth theirs in the night. The goldfinders hold the sense of smelling the 5
least of use, and do not much care for touching the business they have in hand. They both carry their burdens out into the fields; yet sometimes the Thames carries away their loads. They are something like the trade of the barbers, for both do rid away superfluous excrements. The barber's profession is held chief, 10
because that deals with the head and face, but these with the excrements of the posteriorums. The barber's trade and these have both very strong smells, but the goldfinder's is the greatest for strength; the other's is safest and sweetest. The barber useth washing when he is done to cleanse all, and so do these. The 15
barber useth a looking-glass that men may see how he hath done his work, and these use a candle. They are all necessary in the City: as our faces would be foul without the barber, so our streets without the scavenger, and our backsides without the goldfinder. The scavenger seems not to be so great an officer as the 20
goldfinder, for he deals with the excrements chiefly of beasts, but this latter of his own species. Well, had they been sweeter fellows, I would have stood longer on them, but they may answer, they keep all clean, and do that work which scarce anyone but themselves would meddle withal. 25

NOTES

Title *Goldfinders* so dubbed ironically or perhaps because they might find a piece of gold in the pursuance of their office.
7 *fields* i.e. where their 'burdens' might be converted into dunghills and used as manure.
10 *excrements* i.e. hair (in the case of barbers).
12 *posteriorums* posteriors.
13 *smells* (for barbers) either because their clientele was generally unwashed or because they used perfumed waters.
17 *candle* i.e. because the goldfinders worked at night (see l. 5).
19 *backsides* privies.

6 The underworld in town and country

The underworld of Elizabethan–Jacobean England was dangerously well populated, both in the cities (particularly London) and in the countryside. The harsh economic conditions under which some 90 per cent of the population subsisted were a natural breeding-ground for criminal elements, and, if we may accept the numerous contemporary accounts of their felonious activities, they were highly successful in pillaging the public despite the various acts passed by Parliament to control such 'rogues and vagabonds'.

The threat posed by these criminal groups (they were well organized within a hierarchical system both in town and country) produced two early 'discoveries': John Awdely's *The Fraternitye of Vacabondes* (1575; originally published in 1565, an edition of which only a single title page survives) and Thomas Harman's *A Caveat or Warening for Common Cursetors Vulgarly Called Vagabones* (1567) (both ed. by E. Viles and F. J. Furnivall, 1869); see selection (i) and illustration 22. Among the 'fraternity', Awdely distinguishes more than twenty different types of beggars and vagabonds, each with his or her own name and special field of expertise. For example:

> An *Abraham Man* is he that walketh bare-armed and bare-legged, and feigneth himself mad, and carrieth a pack of wool, or a stick with bacon on it, or suchlike toy, and nameth himself 'Poor Tom'. [Edgar in Shakespeare's *Lear* disguises himself as an Abraham Man or Bedlam Beggar under the name 'Poor Tom'.]
>
> A *Prigman* goeth with a stick in his hand like an idle person. His property [special function] is to steal clothes off the hedge, which they call 'storing of the Rogeman' [?furnishing the receiver with stolen goods]; or else filch poultry, carrying them to the alehouse, which they call the 'Bousing Inn [*or* Ken]'; and there sit playing at cards and dice till that is spent which they have so filched. [Harman calls him 'A Hooker or Angler' (chap. III); as Autolycus (*Winter's Tale*, IV.iii.23–4) assures us: 'My traffic is sheets; when the kite builds, look to lesser linen.']
>
> An *Upright Man* is one that goeth with a truncheon or a staff, which staff they call a 'Filtchman'. This man is of so much authority that, meeting with any of his profession, he may call them to account and command a share or 'snap' unto himself of all that they have gained by their trade [thieving] in one month. . . . . . . He may also command any of their women, which they call 'Doxies', to serve his turn. He hath the chief place at any market walk and other assemblies, and is not of any to be controlled.

Awdely's and Harman's books were followed in the 1590s by Robert

Greene's 'Cony-Catching' pamphlets and in the earlier seventeenth century by similar exposés from Samuel Rowlands (*Greenes Ghost Haunting Conie-Catchers* (1602)), Thomas Dekker (see selection (ii)), and Thomas Middleton (*The Blacke Booke* (1604)).

Harman modelled his work on Awdely's, borrowing freely but greatly expanding Awdley's rather sketchy material from firsthand material (as selection (i) proves). He in turn was plagiarized by later writers (particularly Dekker), though honest William Harrison's account of 'thieves and caterpillars in the commonwealth' in his *Description of England* (bk. II, chap. 10, edn of 1587) is careful to acknowledge its debt. Unlike Greene and his imitators, Awdley and Harman tend to deal with the crews of roaming beggars who operated for the most part in the countryside rather than in London, although there is a good deal of overlapping between the urban and country 'fraternities', and Awdely anticipates the 'City' trend by appending three unusually detailed (for him) portraits of London cozeners ('A Courtesy Man', 'A Cheater or Fingerer', 'A Ring Faller'), which, like Harman's 'A Counterfeit Crank' (selection (i)), look forward to Greene's portraits and anecdotes.

In his dedication, Harman discusses the rise 'of all these rowsey [? disorderly, uncouth], ragged rabblement of rakehells', noting that though such beggars had long existed in England they were formerly less organized 'and then nothing given so much to pilfering, picking, and spoiling', and that 'their language, which they term "Peddler's French" or "Canting", began but within these thirty years, little above' (p. 23). Along with a short 'canting' glossary, Harman offers some examples of dialogue between an Upright Man and a Rogue: for example (p. 85), 'I couched a hogshead in a skypper this darkmans' (i.e. 'I laid me down to sleep in a barn this night'); or, 'I cut it is quyer bouse. I boused a flagge the last darkmans' (i.e. 'I say it is a small and naughty drink. I drank a groat [four pence] there the last night').

Some distinction was recognized between the groups of rogues and vagabonds and their City cousins, the 'cony-catchers', and the wandering bands of gypsies or 'Egyptians' (sometimes called 'Moon-men'; see selection (ii)), although in many ways their behaviour seems indistinguishable.

William Harrison (see above) describes the kinds of punishment meted out to these various denizens of the underworld:

> The rogue being apprehended,......if he happen to be convicted for a vagabond,......he is then immediately adjudged to be grievously whipped and burned through the gristle of the right ear with an hot iron of the compass of an inch about, as a manifestation of his wicked life,......[but the punishment is waived if some substantial citizen] will be bound in recognisance to retain him in his service for one whole year. If he be taken the second time, and proved to have forsaken his said service, he shall then be whipped again, bored likewise through the other ear, and

set to service; from whence if he depart before a year be expired, and happen afterward to be attached [arrested] again, he is condemned to suffer pains of death as a fellon (except before excepted) without benefit of clergy or sanctuary, as by the statute [of 1572] doth appear.

In two of Robert Greene's pamphlets (*A Notable Discovery of Coosnage* (1591) and *The Second Part of Conny-catching* (1592)), Greene details the art or 'law' proper to each specialized group of the fraternity of thieves and confidence-men: High law (robbing on the highways), Sacking law (lechery, through bawd and pander), Cheating law (play with false dice), Cross-biting law (cozenage by whores), Cony-catching law (cozenage by cards), Versing law (cozenage with false gold; compare Awdely's 'A Ring Faller'), Figging law (cutting of purses by 'nips' and picking of pockets by 'foists'), Barnard's law (drunken cozenage by cards), Black Art law (picking of locks), Curbing law (hooking at windows), Vincent's law (cozenage at bowls), Prigging law (horse stealing), and Lifting law (stealing of parcels of goods or merchandise). Each 'law' boasted its own special cant or argot, though there was a good deal of cross-fertilizing between the various 'laws' in terms of their activities.

Selection (iii), from a letter by William Fleetwood, Recorder of London 1569–91, to Lord Burghley, describes a raid on a school for pickpockets reminiscent of Fagin's little establishment in Dickens' *Oliver Twist*. Greene (*The Second Part of Conny-catching*, ed. G. B. Harrison (1923), pp. 35–6) also speaks of a 'hall' where the 'fraternity or brotherhood' of nips and foists met to 'confer of weighty matters, touching their workmanship', and he later (pp. 47–9) describes how a 'Diver' (comparable to a 'Courber' or 'Hooker', who pulls 'out of a window any loose linen cloth, apparel, or else any other household stuff [which] they in their art call snappings') 'puts in at the window some little figging boy, who plays his part notably, and perhaps the youth is so well instructed that he is a scholar in the Black Art and can pick a lock, if it be not too cross-warded, and deliver to the Diver what snappings he finds in the chamber.'

Dramatists found the underworld of town and country a useful source for characters and sometimes for plot situations. Selection (iv), for example, from the opening scene of Ben Jonson's *The Alchemist* (1612), sets up the cozening plot-line through the falling out (an omen) of Subtle, Face and Dol Common, three denizens of London's underworld, the 'venter tripartite' as they call themselves, as they quarrel over precedence in the 'game' of who is the most successful sharper (see the section on 'Alchemy' for another selection from *The Alchemist*, showing Subtle in his role as cheating alchemist and Face as his assistant or 'lungs'). City comedy was a natural habitat for cheats and sharpers of all shades (see introductory note to 'London: life and sights' for other examples).

As we noted above, Shakespeare draws on vagabond and beggar lore for Edgar's disguise in *Lear* and for the character of Autolycus, that 'snapper up of unconsider'd trifles' (*Winter's Tale*, IV.iii.26), who, apart from his role as Prigman or Hooker, combines the functions of Irish Toyle or Swigman (peddler) and pickpocket ('nip' or 'foist'). Beaumont and Fletcher employ a band of beggars as a plot device in *Beggars' Bush* (written before 1616; see particularly II.i and III.i) and Richard Brome sets much of *The Jovial Crew, or the Merry Beggars* (1641) in a romanticized beggars' rendezvous supported by the beneficent old Squire Oldrents. Brome's play, especially, makes heavy use of canting language ('Peddler's French'), and Thomas Dekker exploits his detailed knowledge of such argot (see *Lanthorne and Candle-Light*, 1608, chap. I) in *The Roaring Girl, or Moll Cutpurse* (1604–10; V.i).

For further information, see James A. S. McPeek, *The Black Book of Knaves and Unthrifts: In Shakespeare and Other Renaissance Authors* (1969).

i

A counterfeit crank

From Thomas Harman, *A Caveat or Warening for Common Cursetors Vulgarly Called Vagabones* (1567), ed. E. Viles and F. J. Furnivall (1869), pp. 51–6.

Upon All-hall'n-day in the morning last *anno domini* 1566, or my book was half printed, I mean the first impression, there came early in the morning a counterfeit crank under my lodging at the Whitefriars, within the cloister, in a little yard or court, whereabouts lay two or three great ladies, being without the 5
liberties of London, whereby he hoped for the greater gain. This crank there lamentably lamenting and pitifully crying to be relieved, declared to divers there his painful and miserable disease. I being risen and not half ready, heard his doleful words and rueful mournings, hearing him name the falling sickness, thought 10
assuredly to myself that he was a deep dissembler. So, coming out at a sudden, and beholding his ugly and irksome attire, his loathsome and horrible countenance, it made me in a marvellous perplexity what to think of him, whether it were feigned or truth. For after this manner went he: he was naked from the waist 15
upward, saving he had a old jerkin of leather patched, and that was loose about him, that all his body lay out bare; a filthy foul cloth he ware on his head, being cut for the purpose, having a narrow place to put out his face, with a beaver made to truss up his beard, and a string that tied the same down close about his neck; with an old 20
felt hat which he still carried in his hand to receive the charity and devotion of the people, for that would he hold out from him; having his face, from the eyes downward, all smeared with fresh blood, as though he had new fallen, and been tormented with his painful pangs – his jerkin being all berayed with dirt and mire, and 25
his hat and hosen, as though he had wallowed in the mire; surely the sight was monstrous and terrible. I called him unto me, and demanded of him what he ailed. 'Ah, good master', quoth he, 'I have the grievous and painful disease called the falling sickness.' 'Why', quoth I, 'how cometh thy jerkin, hose, and hat so berayed 30
with dirt and mire, and thy skin also?' 'Ah, good master, I fell down on the backside here in the foul lane hard by the waterside; and there I lay almost all night, and have bled almost all the blood out in my body.' It rained that morning very fast; and while I was thus talking with him, a honest poor woman that dwelt thereby 35
brought him a fair linen cloth, and bid him wipe his face therewith; and there being a tub standing full of rain water, offered to give him some in a dish that he might make himself clean: he refuseth the same. 'Why dost thou so?' quoth I. 'Ah, sir',

saith he, 'if I should wash myself, I should fall to bleeding afresh   40
again, and then I should not stop myself.' These words made me
the more to suspect him.

Then I asked of him where he was born, what his name was,
how long he had this disease, and what time he had been here
about London, and in what place. 'Sir', said he, 'I was born at   45
Leicester, my name is Nicholas Genings, and I have had this
falling sickness eight years, and I can get no remedy for the same;
for I have it by kind, my father had it and my friends before me;
and I have been these two years here about London, and a year and
a half in Beth'lem.' 'Why, wast thou out of thy wits?' quoth I.   50
'Yea, sir, that I was.' 'What is the keeper's name of the house?'
'His name is', quoth he, 'John Smith.' 'Then', quoth I, 'he must
understand of thy disease; if thou haddest the same for the time
thou wast there, he knoweth it well.' 'Yea, not only he, but all the
house beside', quoth this crank, 'for I came thence but within this   55
fortnight.'

I had stand so long reasoning the matter with him that I was a-
cold, and went into my chamber and made me ready, and
commanded my servant to repair to Beth'lem, and bring me true
word from the keeper there whether any such man hath been with   60
him as a prisoner having the disease aforesaid, and gave him a note
of his name and the keeper's also. My servant, returning to my
lodging, did assure me that neither was there ever any such man
there, neither yet any keeper of any such name; but he that was
there keeper, he sent me his name in writing, affirming that he   65
letteth no man depart from him unless he be fet away by his
friends, and that none that came from him beggeth about the city.
Then I sent for the printer of this book, and shewed him of this
dissembling crank, and how I had sent to Beth'lem to understand
the truth, and what answer I received again, requiring him that I   70
might have some servant of his to watch him faithfully that day,
that I might understand trustily to what place he would repair at
night unto, and thither I promised to go myself to see their order,
and that I would have him to associate me thither. He gladly
granted to my request, and sent two boys, that both diligently and   75
vigilantly accomplished the charge given them, and found the
same crank about the Temple, whereabout the most part of the
day he begged, unless it were about twelve of the clock he went on
the backside of Clement's Inn without Temple Bar, there is a lane
that goeth into the fields; there he renewed his face again with   80
fresh blood, which he carried about him in a bladder, and daubed
on fresh dirt upon his jerkin, hat, and hosen. And so came back
again unto the Temple, and sometime to the waterside, and
begged of all that passed by. The boys beheld how some gave
groats, some sixpence, some gave more; for he looked so ugly and   85
irksomely, that everyone pitied his miserable case that beheld him.

To be short, there he passed all the day till night approached; and when it began to be somewhat dark, he went to the waterside and took a sculler, and was set over the water into Saint George's Fields, contrary to my expectation; for I had thought he would have gone into Holborn or to Saint Giles-in-the-Field. But these boys, with Argus' and lynx's eyes, set sure watch upon him, and the one took a boat and followed him and the other went back to tell his master.

The boy that so followed him by water had no money to pay for his boat hire, but laid his penner and his inkhorn to gage for a penny; and by that time the boy was set over, his master, with all celerity, had taken a boat and followed him apace. Now had they still a sight of the crank, which crossed over the fields towards Newington, and thither he went, and by that time they came thither it was very dark. The printer had there no acquaintance, neither any kind of weapon about him, neither knew he how far the crank would go, because he then suspected that they dogged him of purpose. He there stayed him, and called for the constable, which came forth diligently to enquire what the matter was. This zealous printer charged this officer with him as a malefactor and a dissembling vagabond. The constable would have laid him all night in the cage that stood in the street. 'Nay', saith this pitiful printer, 'I pray you have him into your house, for this is like to be a cold night, and he is naked: you keep a victualling-house; let him be well cherished this night, for he is well hable to pay for the same. I know well his gains hath been great to-day, and your house is a sufficient prison for the time, and we will there search him.' The constable agreed thereunto: they had him in, and caused him to wash himself; that done, they demanded what money he had about him. Saith this crank, 'So God help me, I have but twelve pence', and plucked out the same of a little purse. 'Why, have you no more?' quoth they. 'No', saith this crank, 'as God shall save my soul at the day of judgment.' 'We must see more', quoth they, and began to strip him. Then he plucked out another purse, wherein was forty pence. 'Tush', saith this printer, 'I must see more'. Saith this crank, 'I pray God I be damned both body and soul if I have any more.' 'No', saith this printer, 'thou false knave, here is my boy that did watch thee all this day, and saw when such men gave thee pieces of six pence, groats, and other money; and yet thou hast shewed us none but small money.' When this crank heard this, and the boy vowing it to his face, he relented and plucked out another purse, wherein was eight shillings and odd money; so had they in the whole that he had begged that day thirteen shillings threepence halfpenny. Then they stripped him stark naked, and as many as saw him said they never saw handsomer man, with a yellow flaxen beard, and fair skinned, without any spot or grief. Then the good wife of the

house fet her goodman's old cloak, and caused the same to be cast
about him, because the sight should not abash her shamefast   135
maidens, neither loathe her squeamish sight.

Thus he set down at the chimney's end, and called for a pot of
beer, and drank off a quart at a draught, and called for another,
and so the third, that one had been sufficient for any reasonable
man, the drink was so strong; I myself, the next morning, tasted   140
thereof. But let the reader judge what and how much he would
have drunk and he had been out of fear. Then when they had thus
wrung water out of flint in spoiling him of his evil-gotten goods,
his passing pence, and fleeting trash, the printer with this officer
were in jolly jollity, and devised to search a barn for some Rogues   145
and Upright Men, a quarter of a mile from the house, that stood
alone in the fields, and went out about their business, leaving this
crank alone with his wife and maidens. This crafty crank, espying
all gone, requested the good wife that he might go out on the
backside to make water, and to exonerate his paunch. She bade him   150
draw the latch of the door and go out, neither thinking or
mistrusting he would have gone away naked. But, to conclude,
when he was out, he cast away the cloak, and, as naked as ever he
was born, he ran away, that he could never be heard of again. Now
the next morning betimes, I went unto Newington, to understand   155
what was done, because I had word or it was day that there my
printer was. And at my coming thither, I heard the whole
circumstance, as I above have written; and I, seeing the matter so
fall out, took order with the chief of the parish that this thirteen
shillings and threepence halfpenny might the next day be equally   160
distributed, by their good discretions, to the poverty of the same
parish, and so it was done.

NOTES

1   *All-hall'n-day* All-Saints'-day, November 1.
     or before.
3   *counterfeit crank* rogue who feigned sickness to win pity and gain money.
4   *Whitefriars* A precinct of London lying between the Thames and Fleet
     Street, adjacent on the west to the Inner Temple. Later known as Alsatia,
     it retained the right of sanctuary into the early eighteenth century and by
     Harman's time had become the haunt of prostitutes and other
     disreputable characters.
6   *liberties* districts subject to the municipal authorities.
9   *half ready* i.e. only partly dressed.
10   *falling sickness* epilepsy.
12   *irksome* disgusting, loathsome.
16   *jerkin* close-fitting coat.
18   *ware* wore.

19   *beaver* ?some sort of scarf. The usual sense ('the lower portion of the face-guard of a helmet') does not seem to apply.

26   *hosen* trousers of some kind, judging by Harman's woodcut, made up of rags knotted together.

32   *backside* back yard, or, possibly, posteriors.

48   *by kind* i.e. by heredity.

50   *Beth'lem* Bedlam (from Bethlehem), the hospital for the insane, located just outside Bishopsgate.

57   *stand* stood (variant form of past participle).

66   *fet* fetched.

70   *again* in return.

72–3 *to......unto* duplicated preposition, common in Elizabethan usage.

77   *Temple* i.e. the Inner Temple, one of the Inns of Court.

79   *Clement's Inn* one of the Inns of Chancery, associated with the Inner Temple.
      Temple Bar gate marking the boundary of the City of London at the west end of Fleet Street.

85   *groats* silver coins worth four pence.

89   *sculler* sculling-boat.

89–90 *Saint George's Fields* open space on the south side of the Thames between Southwark and Lambeth.

91   *Holborn* one of London's main thoroughfares, running west from Newgate Street to Drury Lane.
      Saint Giles-in-the-Field district at the west end of Holborn, named from a former lepers' hospital, surrounding St Giles' parish church; here criminals on the way to Tyburn for execution were given a bowl of wine.

92   *Argus'* In mythology, Argus was supposed to have a hundred eyes.

96   *penner* case for pens, carried at the girdle, with an inkhorn.

97   *that time* i.e. the time that.

100   *Newington* suburb of London, on the south side of the Thames, south of Southwark.

106   *charged......him* i.e. made a charge against him to this officer.

108   *pitiful* compassionate.

110   *victualling-house* inn, tavern.

111   *hable* able (variant form).

117   *of* from.

133   *grief* blemish, sore.

135   *shamefast* bashful, modest.

136   *loathe* excite disgust in.

139   *that* supply 'even though'.

144   *passing......trash* transient pennies and impermanent rubbish (contemptuous terms for 'money').

145–6 *Rogues and Upright Men* two other classes in the 'Fraternity of Vagabonds' (see Harman, chaps. II and IV respectively).

150   *exonerate* evacuate.

151   *draw* pull open.

154   *that* so that. In a later edition (1573), Harman reports that the printer encountered Nicholas Genings again and turned him over to the law; he was punished but finally released 'on that condition he would prove an honest man'.

155   *betimes* early.

161   *poverty* needy poor.

Moonmen or gypsies

From Thomas Dekker, *Lanthorne and Candle-Light* (1608), chap. VIII, 'Moonmen'.

A Moonman signifies in English a 'madman', because the moon hath greatest domination (above any other planet) over the bodies of frantic persons. But these Moonmen, whose images are now to be carved, are neither absolute mad nor yet perfectly in their wits. Their name they borrow from the moon, because, as the moon is   5
never in one shape two nights together, but wanders up and down heaven like an antic, so these changeable-stuff companions never tarry one day in a place, but are the only, and the only base, runagates upon earth.......
 They are a people more scattered than Jews, and more hated: 10
beggarly in apparel, barbarous in condition, beastly in behaviour, and bloody if they meet advantage. A man that sees them would swear they had all the yellow jaundice, or that they were tawny Moors' bastards, for no red-ochre-man carries a face of a more filthy complexion; yet are they not born so, neither has the sun   15
burnt them so; but they are painted so;......By a by-name they are called Gypsies; they call themselves Egyptians; others in mockery call them Moonmen.......Look what difference there is between a civil citizen of Dublin and a wild Irish kern, so much difference there is between one of these counterfeit Egyptians and   20
a true English beggar. An English Rogue is just of the same livery.
 They are commonly an army about fourscore strong, yet they never march with all their bags and baggages together, but (like boothalers) they forage up and down countries, four, five, or six in a company. As the Switzer has his wench and his cock with him   25
when he goes to the wars, so these vagabonds have their harlots, with a number of little children following at their heels, which young brood of beggars are sometimes carried (like so many green geese alive to a market) in pairs of panniers or in dossers like fresh fish from Rye that comes on horseback (if they be but infants). But   30
if they can straddle once, then as well the she-rogues as the he-rogues are horsed, seven or eight upon one jade, strongly pinioned and strangely tied together.
 One shire alone and no more is sure still at one time to have these Egyptian lice swarming within it, for like flocks of wild   35
geese, they will evermore fly one after another; let them be scattered worse than the quarters of a traitor are after he's hanged, drawn, and quartered, yet they have a trick (like water cut with a sword) to come together instantly and easily again. And this is their policy: which way soever the foremost ranks lead, they stick   40

up small boughs in several places, to every village where they pass, which serve as ensigns to waft on the rest.

Their apparel is odd and fantastic, though it be never so full of rents. The men wear scarfs of calico, or any other base stuff, hanging their bodies like morris-dancers with bells and other toys to entice the country people to flock about them,...... The women as ridiculously attire themselves, and (like one that plays the Rogue on a stage) wear rags and patched filthy mantles uppermost, when the under garments are handsome and in fashion.......[No farmyard animals are safe from them, and] The bloody tragedies of all these are only acted by the women, who, carrying long knives or skenes under their mantles, do thus play their parts. The stage is some large heath, or a fir-bush common, far from any houses, upon which, casting themselves into a ring, they enclose the murdered till the massacre be finished. If any passenger come by and, wond'ring to see such a conjuring circle kept by hellhounds, demand what spirits they raise there, one of the murderers steps to him, poisons him with sweet words, and shifts him off with this lie: that one of the women is fallen in labour. But if any mad Hamlet, hearing this, smell villainy and rush in by violence to see what the tawny devils are doing, then they excuse the fact, lay the blame on those that are the actors, and perhaps (if they see no remedy) deliver them to an officer to be had to punishment; but by the way a rescue is surely laid and very valiantly (though very villainously) do they fetch them off and guard them.

The cabins where these land-pirates lodge in the night are the out-barns of farmers and husbandmen (in some poor village or other), who dare not deny them for fear they should ere morning have their thatched houses burning about their ears;...... These barns are the beds of incests, whoredoms, adulteries, and of all other black and deadly-damned impieties; here grows the cursed Tree of Bastardy that is so fruitful; here are written the Books of all Blasphemies, Swearings, and Curses, that are so dreadful to be read. Yet the simple country people will come running out of their houses to gaze upon them, whilst in the meantime one steals into the next room and brings away whatsoever he can lay hold on.

Upon days of pastime and liberty, they spread themselves in small companies amongst the villages; and, when young maids and bachelors (yea, sometimes old doting fools that should be beaten to this world of villainies and forewarn others) do flock about them, they then profess skill in palmistry and, forsooth, can tell fortunes, which for the most part are infallibly true by reason that they work upon rules which are grounded upon certainty; for one of them will tell you that you shall shortly have some evil luck fall upon you, and, within half-an-hour after, you shall find your pocket picked or your purse cut.

NOTES

7 *antic* grotesque character (clown or mountebank).
   changeable-stuff continually altering in appearance (like shot silk), inconstant.

8 *the only* beyond comparison.

9 *runagates* wanderers, vagabonds.

12 *if......advantage* if favourable opportunity offers itself.

14 *red-ochre-man* reddleman, one who sells red ochre.

16 *by-name* nickname.

17 *Egyptians* Gypsies were popularly believed to have originated in Egypt. Antony's heart has 'become the bellows and the fan / To cool a gypsy's lust' (*Antony and Cleopatra*, I.i.9–10).

19 *kern* foot-soldier, drawn from the poorer classes among the 'wild Irish'.

21 *Rogue* Harman (chaps. IV and V) distinguishes between 'A Rogue' and 'A wild Rogue', the latter 'is he that is born a Rogue: he is more subtle and more given by nature to all kind of knavery than the other'.
   livery faction, following (as the gypsies).

24 *boothalers* marauding, pillaging soldiers.

25 *Switzer* native of Switzerland.

28–9 *green geese* young geese, goslings.

29 *pairs of panniers* baskets, slung on either side of a horse, etc.
   dossers same as 'panniers'.

33 *strangely* oddly.

38 *drawn* dragged at a horse's tail, or on a hurdle, to the place of execution, or ?disembowelled.

44 *calico* cotton cloth, probably from the East.

45 *morris-dancers* See pp. 102–7.

48 *stage* Note the extended theatrical metaphor, from ll. 51–6, frequent in writers like Greene, Dekker and Middleton, a reflection of their interest in the theatre.

52 *skenes* knives or daggers.

60 *mad Hamlet* This reference suggests the contemporary emphasis placed on Hamlet's 'madness' as it was played up on the stage. Something of the 'violence' of his action is suggested, in the 'bad quarto' of *Hamlet* (1603), by the Queen's description (IV.i) of his behaviour in the 'closet scene' (III.iv): 'But then he throws and tosses me about, / As one forgetting that I was his mother.' Dekker's reference may, of course, be a reminiscence of the lost non-Shakespearean *Hamlet* (by Thomas Kyd?).

73 *Books* It is not clear exactly what 'Books' Dekker refers to; perhaps he means published accounts of witch trials (see below, pp. 263–71). If so, 'written' (l. 73) must be taken in the sense of 'planned' or 'plotted'. Or, perhaps, he is referring to 'that kind of conjurations, which are contained in such books, which I call the Devil's School' (King James, *Daemonologie* (1597), bk. I, chap. 5).

80 *beaten to* experienced in.

iii

A school for pickpockets

From a letter to Lord Burghley by William Fleetwood, Recorder of London, 7 July 1585 (in Thomas Wright, *Queen Elizabeth and Her Times* (1838), II, 245–51).

The same day, my Lord Mayor being absent about the goods of the Spaniards and also all my Lords the Justices of the benches being also away, we few that were there did spend the same day about the searching out of sundry that were receptors of felons, where we found a great many as well in London, Westminster, 5 Southwark, as in all other places about the same. Amongst our travels this one matter tumbled out by the way, that one Wotton, a gentleman born and sometime a merchant man of good credit, who falling by time into decay, kept an alehouse at Smart's Quay, near Billingsgate, and after, for some misdemeanour being put 10 down, he reared up a new trade of life, and in the same house he procured all the cutpurses about this city to repair to his same house. There was a schoolhouse set up to learn young boys to cut purses. There were hung up two devices, the one was a pocket, the other was a purse. The pocket had in it certain counters and was 15 hung about with hawkes' bells, and over the top did hang a little sacring bell; and he that could take out a counter without any noise was allowed to be a public foister, and he that could take a piece of silver out of the purse, without the noise of any of the bells, he was adjudged a judicial nipper. *Nota*, that a foister is a 20 pickpocket and a nipper is termed a pickpurse or a cutpurse.
. . . . . .
   [Fleetwood adds a '*Memorandum*'.] That in Wotton's house, at Smart's Quay, are written in a table divers posies, and amongst the rest one is thus: 'Si spie, sporte; si non spie, tunc steale.' Another 25 is thus: 'Si spie, si non spie, foyste, nyppe, lyfte, shave, and spare not.' *Note*, that *foyste* is to cut a pocket, *nyppe* is to cut a purse, *lyfte* is to rob a shop or a gentleman's chamber, *shave* is to filch a cloak, a sword, or a silver spoon, or such like, that is negligently looked unto. 30

NOTES

4   *receptors of felons* individuals who sheltered criminals.
5–6 *Westminster, Southwark* Westminster, the borough immediately west of
     the City of London on the north bank of the Thames; Southwark, the
     borough on the south bank (the Bankside) directly opposite the City, to

which it was connected by London Bridge. Both were known as the resort of criminals.

9–10 *Smart's Quay, near Billingsgate* Billingsgate was the principal of the old water-gates of the City, just east of London Bridge. Smart's Quay is east of London Bridge in Billingsgate Ward.

15 *counters* imitation coins (of brass, etc.).

16 *hawkes' bells* small spherical bells ordinarily attached to the legs of hawks (falcons).

17 *sacring bell* small bell rung to summon parishioners to morning prayer or to mark the point in the Communion Service when the congregation should go up to communicate.

18 *public foister* pickpocket worthy to perform in public.

20 *judicial nipper* cutpurse of sound judgement.

24 *posies* short mottoes, usually inscribed in a ring or on a knife.

25–7 *Si spie......not* i.e. 'If spotted, pretend to be amusing yourself, if not spotted, then steal' and 'Whether, spotted or not, foist, nip, lift, shave, and spare not.' Fleetwood then defines the terms.

iv

When thieves fall out......

From Ben Jonson, *The Alchemist* (1612), I.i.

[*Enter*] FACE, SUBTLE, DOL COMMON

[FACE.] Believe't, I will.

SUBTLE.   Thy worst. I fart at thee.

DOL. Ha' you your wits? Why, gentlemen! for love – ......
FACE. [*To* SUBTLE] You most notorious whelp, you insolent
    slave,
    Dare you do this?

SUBTLE.   Yes, faith, yes, faith.

FACE.   Why! who
    Am I, my mongrel? Who am I?

SUBTLE.   I'll tell you,   5
    Since you know not yourself –

FACE.   Speak lower, rogue.

SUBTLE. Yes. You were once (time's not long past) the good,
    Honest, plain, livery-three-pound-thrum, that kept
    Your master's worship's house, here, in the Friars,
    For the vacations –

FACE.   Will you be so loud?   10

SUBTLE. Since, by my means, translated suburb-Captain.

FACE. By your means, Doctor Dog?

SUBTLE.   Within man's memory,
    All this I speak of.

FACE.   Why, I pray you, have I
    Been countenanc'd by you? Or you, by me?
    Do but collect, sir, where I met you first.   15

SUBTLE. I do not hear well.

FACE.   Not of this, I think it.
    But I shall put you in mind, sir: at Pie Corner,
    Taking your meal of steam in from cooks' stalls,
    Where, like the father of hunger, you did walk
    Piteously costive, with your pinch'd-horn nose,   20
    And your complexion, of the Roman wash,
    Stuck full of black and melancholic worms,
    Like poulder-corns shot at th'Artillery-yard.

SUBTLE. I wish you could advance your voice, a little.

FACE. When you went pinn'd up in the several rags 25
    Yo'had rak'd and pick'd from dunghills before day;
    Your feet in mouldy slippers, for your kibes;
    A felt of rug, and a thin threaden cloak
    That scarce would cover your no-buttocks –

SUBTLE.   So, sir!

FACE. When all your alchemy, and your algebra, 30
    Your minerals, vegetals, and animals,
    Your conjuring, coz'ning, and your dozen trades,
    Could not relieve your corps with so much linen
    Would make you tinder but to see a fire,
    I ga' you count'nance, credit for your coals, 35
    Your stills, your glasses, your materials,
    Built you a furnace, drew you customers,
    Advanc'd all your black arts; lent you, beside,
    A house to practise in –

SUBTLE.   Your master's house!

FACE. Where you have studied the more thriving skill 40
    Of bawdry since.

SUBTLE.   Yes, in your master's house.......

FACE. You might talk softlier, rascal.

SUBTLE.   No, you scarab,
    I'll thunder you in pieces. I will teach you
    How to beware, to tempt a Fury again
    That carries tempest in his hand and voice. 45

FACE. The place has made you valiant.

SUBTLE.   No, your clothes!
    Thou vermin, have I ta'en thee out of dung,
    So poor, so wretched, when no living thing
    Would keep thee company but a spider, or worse?
    Rais'd thee from brooms and dust and wat'ring pots? 50
    Sublim'd thee, and exalted thee, and fix'd thee
    I'the third region, call'd our state of grace?......
    Put thee in words and fashion? Made thee fit
    For more than ordinary fellowships?
    Giv'n thee thy oaths, thy quarrelling dimensions? 55
    Thy rules, to cheat at horse-race, cock-pit, cards,
    Dice, or whatever gallant tincture else?
    Made thee a second in mine own great art?
    And have I this for thank? Do you rebel?
    Do you fly out, i'the projection? 60

Would you be gone now?

DOL.   Gentlemen, what mean you?
  Will you mar all?

SUBTLE.   Slave, thou hadst had no name –

DOL. Will you undo yourselves with civil war? . . . . . .

FACE. I shall turn desperate, if you grow thus loud.

SUBTLE. And hang thyself, I care not.

FACE.   Hang thee, collier,   65
  And all thy pots and pans, in picture, I will,
  Since thou hast mov'd me –

DOL. [*Aside*]   O, this'll o'erthrow all.

FACE. Write thee up bawd in Paul's; have all thy tricks
  Of coz'ning with a hollow coal, dust, scrapings,
  Searching for things lost with a sieve and shears,   70
  Erecting figures in your rows of houses,
  And taking in of shadows with a glass,
  Told in red letters; and a face cut for thee,
  Worse than Gamaliel Ratsey's.

DOL.   Are you sound?
  Ha' you your senses, masters?

FACE.   I will have   75
  A book, but barely reckoning thy impostures,
  Shall prove a true philosophers' stone to printers.

SUBTLE. Away, you trencher-rascal!

FACE.   Out, you dog-leech,
  The vomit of all prisons – . . . . . .

DOL.   O me!   80
  We are ruin'd! Lost! Ha' you no more regard
  To your reputations? Where's your judgment? 'Slight,
  Have yet some care of me, o' your republic—

FACE. Away this brach! I'll bring thee, rogue, within
  The statute of sorcery, *tricesimo tertio*   85
  Of Harry the Eight; ay, and (perhaps) thy neck
  Within a noose, for laund'ring gold and barbing it.

DOL. You'll bring your head within a cockscomb, will you?

  She catcheth out FACE *his sword, and breaks* SUBTLE's *glass*

  And you, sir, with your menstrue, gather it up!
  'Sdeath, you abominable pair of stinkards,   90

Leave off your barking and grow one again,
Or, by the light that shines, I'll cut your throats!......

FACE.   'Tis his fault,
He ever murmurs, and objects his pains,
And says the weight of all lies upon him.   95

SUBTLE. Why, so it does.

DOL.   How does it? Do not we
Sustain our parts?

SUBTLE.   Yes, but they are not equal.

DOL. Why, if your part exceed today, I hope
Ours may, tomorrow, match it.

SUBTLE.   Ay, they *may*.

DOL. 'May', murmuring mastiff? Ay, and do. Death on me!   100
Help me to thrattle him.

SUBTLE.   Dorothy, Mistress Dorothy!
'Ods precious, I'll do anything. What do you mean?......

FACE. 'Slid, prove today, who shall shark best.

SUBTLE.   Agreed.

DOL. Yes, and work close and friendly.

SUBTLE.   'Slight, the knot
Shall grow stronger for this breach with me.......   105

NOTES

1   The scene opens in the midst of a quarrel between the three rogues, who
     for some weeks had successfully conducted a series of cheating operations.
8   *livery-three-pound-thrum* meanly and raggedly dressed servant, earning
     three pounds a year.
9   *Friars* Blackfriars, where Face's master (Lovewit) lived.
10   *For* during.
     vacations i.e. when the law courts were not in session.
11   *suburb-Captain* i.e. one who haunted the suburbs of the City pretending
     to be a military man.
14   *countenanc'd* favoured, patronized.
15   *collect* recollect.
16   *I think it* I am sure.
17   *Pie Corner* in Smithfield, known for the cooks' shops there located.
20   *costive* constipated.
     pinch'd-horn nose thin nose like a shoehorn.
21   *complexion* face.

of. . . . . . wash ?swarthy from the use of face lotions used to cure acne.

22   *black. . . . . . worms* i.e. acne or blackheads.

23   *poulder-corns* powder-corns (variant form), grains of powder.
     Artillery-yard in Bishopsgate, where the City Train-bands practised.

24   *advance your voice* speak louder (ironic).

26   *Yo'had* you had.

27   *kibes* ulcerated chilblains, especially on the heel.

28   *felt of rug* hat of rough woollen material.
     thin threaden cloak light cloak made of linen threads, ?threadbare cloak.

31   *minerals. . . . . . animals* terms for materials (except 'algebra') employed
     by an alchemist (Subtle). See 'Alchemy', pp. 303–12 below.

33   *corps* body.

34   *tinder* charred linen, used to catch the spark struck from a flint to kindle a
     fire.
     but even.

35   *ga'* gave.

35–7 *coals. . . . . . furnace* more alchemical paraphernalia.

38   *black arts* magic (see 'conjuring', l. 32); also 'lock-picking' in thieves'
     language.

40–1 *skill of bawdry* i.e. he has turned the house into a brothel.

42   *scarab* dung beetle, which was believed to be generated in manure (see l.
     47).

50   *brooms. . . . . . pots* i.e. the proper business of a servant.

51   *Sublim'd. . . . . . exalted* terms employed in the purifying of materials used
     in alchemy.

52   *third region* highest and purest plane of the universe.

53   *Put. . . . . . words* taught you (fashionable) language.

54   *fellowships* companions.

55   *quarrelling dimensions* rules governing the proper conduct in picking a
     quarrel.

57   *gallant tincture* quality belonging to a gallant.

59   *thank* i.e. thanks.

60   *projection* the moment when the alchemical process is coming to
     perfection in the production of the 'philosophers' stone'.

68   *Write. . . . . . Paul's* Hang up a bill in Paul's Walk exposing you as a bawd
     or pander.

69   *hollow coal* By placing a little silver or gold in a hollowed-out coal, the
     alchemist could pretend to have produced it by his 'art'.

70   *sieve and shears* device, like a divining rod, which was supposed to point
     of itself, after some incantation, to the missing object (or thief).

71   *Erecting figures* casting horoscopes.
     houses signs of the zodiac. See 'Astrology', pp. 296–302 below.

72   *taking. . . . . . glass* seeing figures in a crystal ball.

73   *red letters* Red was used for special emphasis in printing.
     a face cut a woodcut made in your likeness.

74   *Gamaliel Ratsey's* Ratsey was a notorious highwayman, who wore an ugly
     mask when plying his trade.
     sound sane.

77   *prove. . . . . . stone* i.e. be worth its weight in gold.

78   *trencher-rascal* one who scraped trenchers (wooden platters) for a living.

83   *republic* loosely used for 'common interests'.

84   *brach* bitch dog.

85   *tricesimo tertio* thirty-third (year). The statute of 1541 made the 'multiplying' of gold or silver illegal.

86   *Eight* eighth (variant form).

87   *laund'ring......barbing it* washing gold coins in acid and clipping them.

88   *bring......cockscomb* i.e. make a fool of yourself.

89   *menstrue* solvent, contained in the 'glass' Dol has just smashed.

90   *stinkards* stinking fellows.

92   *I'll......throats* Dol Common (her name suggests her profession) is the only one of the three rogues with any 'guts'.

94   *objects his pains* adduces all his efforts (on their behalf).

101   *thrattle* throttle (variant form).

102   *'Ods precious* (by) God's precious (blood or body).

103   *'Slid* (by) God's eyelid.

       shark prey, swindle.

104   *'Slight* (by) God's light.

105   *with me* i.e. so far as I am concerned.

7 Church and State: the religious climate

When Elizabeth came to the throne in 1558, the Church of England, as it had been instituted by Henry VIII and Edward VI between 1536 and 1553, had ceased to exist. It had been swept aside by Elizabeth's half-sister, Queen Mary, who had zealously restored Roman Catholicism as the official state religion. In order to accomplish this, Mary and her bishops took Draconian measures, persecuting all English Protestants who refused to recant, nearly three hundred being burned publicly at the stake as heretics in Smithfield and in other parts of the country during her short reign (1553–8). Such savage measures and her marriage, without issue, to Philip II of Spain (the resulting Spanish influence was deeply resented) made Queen Mary generally unpopular and produced a climate of opinion sympathetic toward change. The outraged Protestant reaction produced one of the great books of the period, John Foxe's influential and massive polemic, *Actes and Monuments* (1563), commonly referred to as *The Book of Martyrs*, which describes in detail, and with graphic illustrations, the various Marian excesses (see selection (i)).

Queen Elizabeth, although she herself was a somewhat lukewarm Protestant, and her advisers, particularly Sir William Cecil (later Lord Burghley), read the signs of the time and decided, as a step toward national stability, to press for a restoration of the Church of England. The situation, however, was a dangerous one, calling for caution, and in many respects their decision had probably as much to do with temporal politics as with specific religious beliefs. The great bulk of the people, perhaps as much as 70 per cent (including many of the old aristocracy), was wedded at heart to the old Roman persuasion; on the other hand, there was the (then) comparatively small but very vocal group of Protestant extremists who had suffered exile during the Marian persecutions. What has been called the Elizabethan compromise (the *via media*) was the result. Parliament, in 1559, passed two statutes, the Act of Supremacy, declaring Elizabeth to be supreme head of the English church, and the Act of Uniformity, making the use of the 1552 *Book of Common Prayer*, the Bible and Erasmus' *Paraphrases* in English, and the Henrician–Edwardian *Book of Homilies* (1547) mandatory in all churches throughout England. Thus, in an important and far-reaching sense, the Church became an arm of the State.

As with most compromises, the more extreme members of neither party were mollified. English Catholics found the break with Rome and the Pope and the anti-Catholic tone of the *Book of Homilies* (including the twenty additional homilies added by royal order in 1563) completely unacceptable. The root-and-branch Puritan reformers accused the government of half measures, fulminating against the retention of episcopal rule, the wearing of church vestments and the *Book of Common Prayer* as 'rags of Rome'. The *Book of Common Prayer* was especially offensive to Puritan sensibilities because it retained in English translation certain forms and prayers derived from the Roman liturgy and forbade the practice of extemporary prayer. Though the English Catholics posed the principal threat during the first three decades of Elizabeth's long reign (1558–1603), a threat that was diminished after the execution of Mary Queen of Scots (1587) and the defeat of the Spanish Armada (1588), with a brief reappearance under James I in the famous Gunpowder Plot of 1605, it was the continually growing strength of the Puritan groups that in the long run was to pose the greatest threat both to the monarchy and the Church of England. Symptomatic of this shift is the fact that Richard Hooker's justly celebrated defence of the English church, *Of the Lawes of Ecclesiasticall Politie* (1594–7), was directed not so much against the attacks of the Catholic faction as against those of the several Puritan sects (Anabaptists, Brownists, Barrowists, the Family of Love, etc.), evidenced most obviously in the seven Martin Marprelate anti-episcopal tracts (1588–9).

Years later, in 1645, assessing the state of the nation after the outbreak of civil war, James Howell (*Epistolae Ho-Elianae* (1645, 1647, 1650, 1655; ed. Joseph Jacobs, 1892, pp. 485–6) thus laments the rising flood-tide of Puritan ascendancy:

> Who would have thought poor England had been brought to this pass? Could it ever have entered into the imagination of man that the scheme and whole frame of so ancient and well-moulded a government should be so suddenly struck off the hinges, quite out of joint, and tumbled into such a horrid confusion? Who would have held it possible, that to fly from Babylon [Catholicism], we should fall into such a Babel [vociferous Puritan sects]? That to avoid superstition, some people should be brought to belch out such a horrid profaneness as to call the Temples of God, the Tabernacles of Satan, the Lord's Supper, a Two-penny Ordinary [eating house]; to make the Communion Table a Manger, and the Font a Trough to water their horses in; to term the white decent robe of the presbyter [priest], the Whore's Smock; the pipes through which nothing came but anthems and holy hymns, the Devil's Bagpipes; the liturgy of the Church [i.e. Anglican], though extracted most of it out of the sacred text [Bible], called by some another kind of *Alcoran*, by others raw porridge, by some a piece forged in Hell?

Elizabethan policy toward Catholics and Protestant dissenters (i.e. those who refused to conform to the Church of England or subscribe to the Thirty-nine Articles of 1571) was more moderate than Mary's anti-Protestant persecution; nevertheless, during Elizabeth's forty-six-year reign about as many (combining the figures for both groups) were executed as in the five-year period under Mary.

The first selection (i), from John Foxe's *Actes and Monuments*, already referred to, describes the burning, for Protestant heresy, of the Mount family at Colchester in 1557, roughly a year before Elizabeth ascended the throne. Foxe's tone, of course, is as usual violently anti-Catholic, but the gratuitous burning of Rose Allin's hand when the family was taken into custody might excuse almost any excess. Sometimes Foxe colours his narrative with horrifying details. Describing the degrading and burning of John Hullier, a Protestant minister, at Cambridge, again in 1557, he writes: 'His flesh being consumed, his bones stood upright even as if they had been alive. Of the people [who sympathized with him], some took as they could get of him, as pieces of bones. One had his heart, the which was distributed so far as it would go; one took the scalp, and looked for the tongue, but it was consumed except the very root. – One rounded [whispered] him in the ear, and desired him to be constant to the end; at which he spake nothing, but showed a joyful countenance, and so continued both constant and joyful to the end' (p. 2197). The stoicism and joy with which Protestant martyrs met their deaths is a constant theme with Foxe (as in the present selection), and the same demeanour characterizes Catholic martyrs under Elizabeth and James. Doubtless, there is some exaggeration, on both sides, for propaganda purposes, but no one, I think, can read these accounts without feeling a sense of wonder and admiration at the dogged courage and indomitable religious conviction with which men and women, high and low alike, chose, rather than recant their beliefs, to die for their faith. See, also, Foxe's moving description of the burning of Hugh Latimer and Bishop Ridley (1555) and Archbishop Cranmer (1556).

Selection (ii), from 'An Homilie against disobedience and wilfull rebellion', in *Certaine Sermons Or Homilies appointed to be read in Churches* (1623 edn), was first published in 1571 as a direct result of the abortive but threatening pro-Catholic Northern Rebellion of 1569. The six-part homily, basically a political statement, buttressed by religious overtones, lays down the Tudor doctrine of 'divine right' ('The right divine of kings to govern wrong' as Pope later put it), according to which the sovereign was viewed as God's vicegerent, divinely appointed by Him, disobedience against whom must be understood to be wilful disobedience against God. Rebellion against even a bad monarch was equally heinous because God's appointment of a bad monarch was His way of punishing a bad people and, in His own good time, God, never man, would remove a bad ruler. A corollary to this view was the doctrine of degree, the proper subordination, according to rank and class, of individuals in the social hierarchy (sovereign, nobles, gentry, commoners) and in the family (parents, children). As Shakespeare's Ulysses, in one of the classic statements on the importance of degree in a commonwealth (*Troilus and Cressida*, I.iii.101–10), says:

> O, when Degree is shak'd,
> Which is the ladder of all high designs,
> The enterprise is sick. How could communities,
> Degrees in schools, and brotherhood in cities,

Peaceful commerce from dividable [separated] shores,
The primogenity [rights of the eldest-born] and due of birth,
Prerogative of age, crowns, sceptres, laurels,
But by degree stand in authentic place?
Take but degree away, untune that string,
And hark what discord follows.

The *Book of Homilies* was an important religio-political instrument of the Elizabethan–Jacobean establishment. Ministers were required to read one of these sermons every Sunday and Holy Day throughout the year, except when the minister preached a sermon of his own, something many of the clergy were apparently too ill-educated to undertake (see Philip Stubbes (*Second Part of the Anatomie of Abuses* (1583), sigs. K5 r–K7 v), who defends what he calls 'reading ministers' as better than no ministers). Since Sunday church attendance was mandatory by law, the people were well drilled in acceptable doctrine, both religious and temporal, particularly in the cardinal virtue of obedience to God and sovereign, and the influence of the *Book of Homilies* may even be traced in the drama, especially in the English history play (see Alfred Hart, *Shakespeare and the Homilies* (1934); E. M. W. Tillyard, *Shakespeare's History Plays* (1946); and Irving Ribner, *The English History Play in the Age of Shakespeare* (rev. edn, 1965); on the *Homilies* specifically, see J. N. Wall, 'Godly and Fruitful Lessons: The English Bible, Erasmus' *Paraphrases*, and the *Book of Homilies*' in *The Godly Kingdom of Tudor England*, ed. J. E. Booty (1981)).

Selection (iii) illustrates the kinds of official measures directed against what was seen, not without reason, as the continuing Catholic threat to the Elizabethan establishment. It is from George Elliot's account (*A Very True Report*, 1581) of his capture of the Jesuit priest Edmund Campion. Elliot, a former Catholic turned informer and government spy or intelligencer, was sent out to catch another priest by the name of Payne, who had entrusted him with details of a plot to murder Elizabeth and members of her Privy Council, and his capture of Campion was entirely accidental. Campion was a highly intelligent, learned and charming young man, and, even though he had published a book (1581) against the Church of England, prominent people (including Queen Elizabeth) did their best (including three rackings!) to get him to renounce his Catholic faith, but he steadfastly refused and was publicly hanged as a traitor.

Elizabethan–Jacobean drama, not surprisingly, since it was carefully censored and controlled by the Court-appointed Master of the Revels, conforms pretty closely to the establishment line. A well-known example of the Master at work may be seen in the manuscript play of *Sir Thomas More* (*c.*1594–5), on which the then Master, Sir Edmund Tilney, wrote: 'Leave out the insurrection wholly and the cause thereof and begin with Sir Thomas More at the Mayor's sessions, with a report afterwards of his good service done being Shrive of London upon a mutiny against the

Lumbards – only a short report and not otherwise at your own perils.'
This meant cutting about a quarter of the play and, to remedy the
situation, Shakespeare, among others, was called in, to furnish a scene
(147 lines) of More's 'good service done', a scene that most scholars
believe to be in Shakespeare's autograph, and one that clearly reflects the
kind of Tudor doctrine briefly discussed above. A similar influence may
be seen in the treatment of such an unlikely (and unlikable) figure as
King John, who, because of his attempted break with Rome and the
Pope, becomes an early Protestant hero (see John Bale's *King Johan*
(1538; rev. ?1558–62), the anonymous *Troublesome Reign of King John*
(c.1587–91), and Shakespeare's *King John* (1594–6)).

The influence of Tudor (and Stuart) political and religious positions
on the English history play generally has already been noted and is
reflected, for example, though not without ambiguities, in Shakespeare's
two tetralogies from Richard II to Richard III. Rebellion and civil
disobedience are uniformly condemned (see, for example, the anonymous *Life and Death of Jack Straw* (1590–3), Shakespeare's *Henry VI*
(particularly the Jack Cade scenes in Part II) and *Henry IV* plays, George
Chapman's *Byron* plays (1608), and John Ford's *Perkin Warbeck*
(c.1629–34)). And, as we might expect, dramatic treatment of Catholics
(priests, bishops, cardinals, popes) and the more extreme Puritan types
was nearly always unsympathetic, vituperative or comically satiric. The
anti-Catholic bias runs the gamut, for example, in Thomas Dekker's *The
Whore of Babylon* (1606–7), written shortly after the Gunpowder Plot, for
as he tells the reader:

> The general scope of this dramatic poem is to set forth......the
> greatness, magnanimity, constancy, clemency, and other incompa-
> rable virtues of our late Queen. And (on the contrary part) the
> inveterate malice, treasons, machinations, underminings, and
> continual bloody stratagems of the purple Whore of Rome [i.e. the
> Roman Catholic Church], to the taking away of our princes' lives
> and utter extirpation of their kingdoms.

As so often, Shakespeare proves a partial exception. He gives us
generally sympathetic priestly characters like Friar Lawrence in *Romeo
and Juliet* or the Duke, disguised as a priest, in *Measure for Measure*, as
well as his character of the subversive and violent Beaufort, bishop and
cardinal, in *I* and *II Henry VI*, a character that looks forward to John
Webster's portraits of the worldly Machiavellians, Cardinal Monticelso
(later Pope) in *The White Devil* (1609–12) and the Cardinal in *The
Duchess of Malfi* (1612–14), typical Italian prelates in the eyes of a
Jacobean audience.

For satiric treatment of hypocritical Puritan figures, see Shakespeare's
Malvolio (*Twelfth Night*), Ben Jonson's Tribulation Wholesome and
Ananias (*The Alchemist*, 1610), Zeal of the Land Busy (*Bartholomew Fair*,
1614), and Cyril Tourneur's Languebeau Snuffe (*The Atheist's Tragedy*,
1611).

i

The martydom of ten faithful and blessed martyrs, five men and five women, burned at Colchester, 1557

From John Foxe, *Actes and Monuments of These Latter and Perilous Dayes Touching Matters of the Church*, 2nd edn, 1570, pp. 2198–202.

[The following excerpt concentrates on the capture and burning of William Mount, his wife Alice, and his step-daughter Rose Allin, who, according to a priest, Thomas Tye, of Colchester in Essex, 'not only absent themselves from the church, and service of God, but do daily allure many other away from the same, which before did outwardly show signs and tokens of obedience' (p. 2199).]

...... the said Sir Thomas Tye bethought with himself, where the persecuted did resort. For in the beginning of Queen Mary's reign, for a twelvemonth and more he came not to church, but frequented the company of godly men and women, which abstained from the same; and, as they thought, he laboured to   5
keep a good conscience: but the sequel showed him to be a false brother......

When Judasly this wicked priest had thus [by reporting them to Bishop Bonner, Bishop of London] wrought his malice against the people of God, within a while after, the storms began to arise   10
against those poor persecuted, William Mount and his company, whereby they were enforced to hide themselves from the heat thereof. And continuing so a little space, at the last, the 7th day of March, anno 1557, being the first Sunday in Lent, and by two of the clock in the morning, one Master Edmund Tyrrel...... took   15
with him the bailiff of the hundred called William Simuel,
...... with divers other a great number; and besetting the house of the said William Mount round about, called to them at length to open the door; which being done, Master Tyrrel with certain of his company went into the chamber where the said Father Mount   20
and his wife lay, willing them to rise: 'for', said he, 'ye must go with us to Colchester Castle.' Mother Mount, hearing that, being very sick, desired that her daughter might first fetch her some drink......

Then he gave her leave and bade her go. So her daughter, the   25
forenamed Rose Allin, maid, took a stone pot in one hand and a candle in the other, and went to draw drink for her mother; and as she came back again through the house, Tyrrel met her, and willed her to give her father and mother good counsel and to advertise them to be better Catholic people......   30

[Rose refuses and is threatened with burning as a heretic.]
Then that cruel Tyrrel, taking the candle from her, held her wrist, and the burning candle under her hand, burning cross-wise over

the back thereof, so long till the very sinews cracked asunder......In which time of his tyranny, he said often to her,　　35
'Why, whore, wilt thou not cry? Thou young whore, wilt thou not
cry?' etc. Unto which always she answered, that she had no cause
she thanked God, but rather to rejoice. He had (she said) more
cause to weep than she, if he considered the matter well. In the
end, when the sinews (as I said) brake that all the house heard　　40
them, he then thrust her from him violently, and said, 'Ha, strong
whore, thou shameless beast! Thou beastly whore!' etc. with such
like vile words.

But she, quietly suffering his rage for the time, at the last said,
'Sir, have ye done what ye will do?' And he said, 'Yea, and if thou　　45
think it be not well, then mend it.' 'Mend it?' [said Rose,] 'nay,
the Lord mend you, and give you repentance, if it be His will. And
now, if you think it good, begin at the feet, and burn to the head
also. For he that set you a-work shall pay you your wages one day,
I warrant you.' And so she went and carried her mother drink, as　　50
she was commanded......

And this said Rose Allin being prisoner, told a friend of hers
this cruel act of the said Tyrrel......'While my one hand', quoth
she, 'was a-burning, I, having a pot in my other hand, might have
laid him on the face with it, if I had would; for no man held my　　55
hand to let me therein.' 'But, I thank God', quoth she, 'with all my
heart, I did not.'......

And Elizabeth Folkes [another of the Colchester martyrs],
when she had plucked off her petticoat, would have given it to her
mother (which came and kissed her at the stake and exhorted her　　60
to be strong in the Lord); but the wicked there attending would
not suffer her to give it. Therefore, taking the said petticoat in her
hand, she threw it away from her, saying 'Farewell, all the world!
Farewell, faith! Farewell, hope!', and so taking the stake in her
hand, said, 'Welcome love!' etc. Now she being at the stake, and　　65
one of the officers nailing the chain about her, in the striking of
the staple he missed the place and struck her with a great stroke of
the hammer on the shoulder-bone; whereat she suddenly turned
her head, lifting up her eyes to the Lord, and prayed smilingly, and
gave herself to exhorting the people again......　　70

In like manner [as the six martyrs burned in the morning], the
said day [2 August 1557] in the afternoon, was brought forth into
the Castle-yard, to a place appointed for the same, William
Mount, John Johnson, Alice Mount, and Rose Allin aforesaid:
which godly constant persons, after they had made their prayers,　　75
and were joyfully tied to the stakes, calling upon the name of God
and exhorting the people earnestly to fly from idolatry, suffered
their martyrdom with such triumph and joy that the people did no
less shout thereat to see it than at the other that were burned the
same day in the morning.　　80

NOTES

1   *Sir* honorific title given to priests; does not imply knighthood.

4   *frequented . . . . . . women* The implication may be that he was acting as a spy for the government.

8   *Judasly* in the manner of Judas, the betrayer of Christ.

16   *hundred* subdivision of a county or shire, having its own court.

30   *advertise* admonish.

35   *In . . . . . . tyranny* i.e. while he was burning her hand.

40   *brake* broke.

49   *he* i.e. the Devil.

55   *laid* struck.

     had would had desired to.

56   *let* hinder, prevent.

61   *the wicked* the officials.

67   *staple* U-shaped iron bar, used to fasten the chains binding the prisoner to the stake.

77   *idolatry* Intercession to statues of the saints was considered a form of idolatry by the Protestant reformers.

78–9 *people . . . . . . shout* i.e. in pity and sympathy.

ii

An Englishman's duty to God and Sovereign

From 'An Homilie against disobedience and wilfull rebellion', part I, in *Certaine Sermons Or Homilies appointed to be read in Churches* (edn of 1623, pp. 275–82).

As GOD the Creator and Lord of all things appointed his angels and heavenly creatures in all obedience to serve and to honour his majesty, so was it his will that man, his chief creature upon the earth, should live under the obedience of his Creator and Lord; and for that cause, GOD, as soon as He had created man, gave unto him a certain precept and law, which he (being yet in the state of innocency, and remaining in Paradise) should observe as a pledge and token of his due and bounden obedience, with denunciation of death if he did transgress and break the said law and commandment. And as GOD would have man to be his obedient subject, so did He make all earthly creatures subject unto man, who kept their due obedience unto man so long as man remained in his obedience unto GOD; in the which obedience if man had continued still, there had been no poverty, no diseases, no sickness, no death, nor other miseries wherewith mankind is now infinitely and most miserably afflicted and oppressed . . . . . . For as long as in this first kingdom the subjects continued in due obedience to GOD their king, so long did GOD embrace all his subjects with his love, favour, and grace, which to enjoy is perfect felicity, whereby it is evident that obedience is the principal virtue of all virtues, and indeed the very root of all virtues and the cause of all felicity. But as all felicity and blessedness should have continued with the continuance of obedience, so with the breach of obedience, and breaking in of rebellion, all vices and miseries did withal break in and overwhelm the world. The first author of which rebellion, the root of all vices and mother of all mischiefs, was Lucifer, first GOD's most excellent creature and most bounden subject, who, by rebelling against the majesty of GOD, of the brightest and most glorious angel, is become the blackest and most foulest fiend and devil; and from the height of Heaven is fallen into the pit and bottom of Hell.

Here you may see the first author and founder of rebellion and the reward thereof; here you may see the grand captain and father of rebels; who, persuading the following of his rebellion against GOD their Creator and Lord unto our first parents Adam and Eve, brought them in high displeasure with GOD, wrought their exile and banishment out of Paradise, a place of all pleasure and goodness, into this wretched earth and vale of misery . . . . . .

Thus do you see that neither Heaven nor Paradise could suffer

any rebellion in them, neither be places for any rebels to remain   40
in. Thus became rebellion, as you see, both the first and the
greatest and the very foot of all other sins, and the first and
principal cause both of all worldly and bodily miseries, sorrows,
diseases, sicknesses, and deaths, and, which is infinitely worse than
all these,......the very cause of death and damnation eternal   45
also. After this breach of obedience to GOD,......GOD forthwith,
by laws given unto mankind, repaired again the rule and order of
obedience thus by rebellion overthrown, and besides the obedience
due unto his majesty, He not only ordained that, in families and
households, the wife should be obedient unto her husband, the   50
children unto their parents, the servants unto their masters, but
also, when mankind increased and spread itself more largely over
the world, He by his holy word did constitute and ordain in cities
and countries several and special governors and rulers, unto whom
the residue of his people should be obedient......   55

By these two places of the Holy Scriptures [Romans 13:1-7; I
Peter 2:13-18], it is most evident that kings, queens, and other
princes (for he speaketh of authority and power be it in men or
women) are ordained of GOD, are to be obeyed and honoured of
their subjects; that such subjects, as are disobedient or rebellious   60
against their princes, disobey GOD and procure their own
damnation; that the government of princes is a great blessing of
GOD, given for the commonwealth, specially of the good and
godly; for the comfort and cherishing of whom GOD giveth and
setteth up princes, and, on the contrary part, to the fear and for   65
the punishment of the evil and wicked. Finally, that if servants
ought to obey their masters, not only being gentle, but such as be
froward, as well and much more ought subjects to be obedient, not
only to their good and courteous but also to their sharp and
rigorous princes. It cometh therefore neither of chance and   70
fortune (as they term it), nor of the ambition of mortal men and
women climbing up of their own accord to dominion, that there
be kings, queens, princes, and other governors over men being
their subjects, but all kings, queens, and other governors are
specially appointed by the ordinance of GOD......Unto the   75
which similitude of heavenly government, the nearer and nearer
that an earthly prince doth come in his regiment the greater
blessing of GOD's mercy is he unto that country and people over
whom he reigneth, and the further and further that an earthly
prince doth swerve from the example of the heavenly government   80
the greater plague is he of GOD's wrath, and punishment by GOD's
justice, unto that country and people over whom GOD for their sins
hath placed such a prince and governor......

What shall subjects do then? Shall they obey valiant, stout,
wise, and good princes and contemn, disobey, and rebel against   85
children being their princes, or against undiscreet and evil

governors? God forbid: for first, what a perilous thing were it to commit unto the subjects the judgment which prince is wise and godly and his government good, and which is otherwise, as though the foot must judge of the head: an enterprise very heinous, and must needs breed rebellion...... And who are most ready to the greatest mischiefs but the worst men?......What an unworthy matter were it then to make the naughtiest subjects, and most inclined to rebellion and all evil, judges over their princes, over their government, and over their councillors to determine which of them be good or tolerable and which be evil and so intolerable...... 90

95

Here you can see that GOD placeth as well evil princes as good, and for what cause he doth both......If we will have an evil prince (when GOD shall send such a one) taken away and a good in his place, let us take away our wickedness which provoketh GOD to place such a one over us, and GOD will either displace him, or of an evil prince make him a good prince, so that we first will change our evil into good...... 100

What shall we say of those subjects? May we call them by the name of subjects, who neither be thankful nor make any prayer to GOD for so gracious a sovereign, but also themselves take armour wickedly, assemble companies and bands of rebels, to break the public peace so long continued and to make, not war, but rebellion to endanger the person of such a gracious sovereign, to hazard the estate of their country (for whose defence they should be ready to spend their lives), and, being Englishmen, to rob, spoil, destroy, and burn in England Englishmen, to kill and murder their own neighbours and kinsfolk, their own countrymen, to do all evil and mischief, yea, and more too than foreign enemies would or could do?...... 105

110

115

NOTES

6   *precept and law* Genesis 2:17.

17   *first kingdom* i.e. God's rule over the angels and man and man's rule over the 'creatures' in the Garden of Eden.

20   *obedience......virtue* Note the continual stress laid on obedience as the cardinal virtue. In the third part of this homily its opposite, disobedience or rebellion, is described as the source of the Seven Deadly Sins: pride, envy, wrath, covetousness, sloth, gluttony, and lechery (p. 293).

26   *mother* i.e. rebellion.

27   *Lucifer* The name means 'light bearer' (Latin), another name for Satan.

30   *most foulest* The double superlative was not uncommon in Elizabethan usage.

38   *vale* valley.

42   *foot* basis.

56–62 *By these . . . . . . damnation* The real point to which the whole homily has
been leading: the sanctity and divinely appointed status of the sovereign
(see ll. 70–5), against whom rebellion must be considered as a crime
against God.

59 *women* inserted with special reference to Queen Elizabeth.

63 *commonwealth* public welfare.

68 *froward* evilly disposed.

68–70 *ought subjects . . . . . . princes* an important part of Tudor doctrine: no
rebellion against a bad sovereign; see ll. 85ff. A bad sovereign was sent as a
punishment by God to a wicked people and would be removed by God in
His own good time.

76 *similitude . . . . . . government* i.e. kings are sometimes referred to as 'gods'
in the Bible.

77 *regiment* rule.

85 *contemn* despise.

85–6 *rebel . . . . . . children* Child monarchs were thought of as dangerous to a
kingdom because of the power struggles that tended to prevail among
different factions during their minority. Shakespeare illustrates the danger
in *I Henry VI*; and compare *Richard III*, II.iii.11: 'Woe to that land that's
govern'd by a child!' (proverbial, Tilley W600).

90 *foot . . . . . . head* i.e. the lowest judge of the highest (proverbial, Tilley
F562).

93 *naughtiest* most wicked.

105 *those subjects* reference to the unsuccessful rebellion of the Duke of
Norfolk and the Northern Earls in favour of Mary Queen of Scots in 1569,
an event that led to the publication of this homily in 1571.

107 *take armour* i.e. arm themselves.

112–16 *being Englishmen . . . . . . do* Sounds the dreaded theme of civil war,
further developed in the third part of this homily, where war is described
as 'the greatest of these worldly mischiefs; but of all wars, civil war is the
worst' (p. 295).

iii

The capture of the Jesuit priest, Edmund Campion

From George Elliot, *A Very True Report of the Apprehension and Taking of that Arch Papist Edmond Campion, The Pope his Right Hand* (1581), sigs. B2 r–C2 r.

[George Elliot, an Ordinary Yeoman of the Queen's Chamber, and David Jenkins, a Messenger of the Queen's Chamber, the former originally of Roman Catholic sympathies but turned informer, set out in July of 1581, armed with a royal warrant, to 'take and apprehend. . . . . . all priests, Jesuits, and such like seditious persons as in our journey we should meet withal.' Recalling his earlier association with Thomas Cooper, a Roman Catholic, Elliot decided to visit his old 'friend', who was then serving as cook in the household of Master Yates, an ardent Catholic, who lived in Lyford, Berkshire. They arrived purposely on a Sunday morning (16 July).]

Where, without the gates of the same house, we espied one of the servants of the house, who most likely seemed, by reason of his lying aloof, to be as if it were a Scout Watcher, that they within might accomplish their secret matters more safely. I called the said servant, and enquired of him for the said Thomas Cooper, the 5 cook. Who answered, that he could not well tell whether he were within or not. I prayed him that he would friend me so much as to see, and told him my name.

The said servant did so (it seemed) for the cook came forth presently unto us where we sate still upon horseback. And after a 10 few such speeches, as betwixt friend and friend when they have been long asunder, were passed, still sitting upon our horses, I told him that I had longed to see him, and that I was then travelling into Derbyshire to see my friends and came so far out of my way to see him. And said I, 'Now I have seen you, my mind is well 15 satisfied, and so fare you well!' 'No,' saith he, 'that shall you not do before dinner.' I made the matter very earnest to be gone; and he, more earnest and importune to stay me. (But in truth I was as willing to stay as he to have me.)

And so, perforce, there was no remedy but stay we must. And 20 having lighted from horseback, and being by him brought into the house, and so into the buttery, and there caused to drink, presently after, the said cook came and whispered with me and asked, whether my friend (meaning the said Jenkins) were within the Church or not? Therein meaning, whether he were a Papist or no? 25 To which I answered, 'He was not; but yet,' said I, 'he is a very honest man, and one that wisheth well that way.' Then said the cook to me, 'Will you go up?' By which speech, I knew he would bring me to a Mass. And I answered him and said, 'Yea, for God's

sake, that let me do; for seeing I must needs tarry, let me take 30
something with me that is good.'

And so we left Jenkins in the buttery, and I was brought by the
cook through the hall, the dining parlour, and two or three other
odd rooms, and then into a fair large chamber, where there was, at
the same instant, one priest, called Satwell, saying Mass, two other 35
priests kneeling by, whereof one was Campion and the other
called Peters *alias* Collington, three nuns, and thirty-seven other
people. When Satwell had finished his Mass, then Campion he
invested himself to say Mass, and so he did; and at the end thereof
made holy bread and delivered it to the people there, to every one 40
some, together with holy water, whereof he gave me part
also......[Campion then preached a sermon 'nigh an hour
long'.]

At the end of which sermon I gat down unto the said Jenkins
so soon as I could......And so we departed with as convenient 45
expedition as we might and came to one Master Fettiplace, a
Justice of Peace in the said country, whom we made privy of our
doings therein, and required him that, according to the tenor of
our commission, he would take sufficient power and go with us
thither. Whereupon the said Justice of Peace, within one quarter 50
of an hour, put himself in a readiness, with forty or fifty men very
well weaponed, who went, in great haste together, with the said
Master Fettiplace and us, to the said Master Yates his house.

Where, at our coming upon the sudden, being abouts one of
the clock in the afternoon of the same day, before we knocked at 55
the gates which was then (as before it was continually accustomed
to be) fast shut (the house being moated round about, within
which moat was a great store of fruit trees and other trees, with
thick hedge rows, so that the danger for fear of losing of the said
Campion and his associates was the more doubted), we beset the 60
house with our men round about without the moat in the best sort
we could devise, and then knocked at the gates and were presently
heard and espied, but kept out by the space of half an hour. In
which time, as it seemeth, they had hidden Campion and the
other two priests in a very secret place within the said 65
house......and then they let us into the house.

Where came presently to our sight Mistress Yates, the good
wife of the house, five gentlemen, one gentlewoman, and three
nuns (the nuns being then disguised in gentlewomen's apparel, not
like unto that they heard Mass in). All which I well remembered 70
to have seen the same morning at the Masses and sermon
aforesaid; yet every one of them a great while denied it......

But knowing certainly that these were but bare excuses,
......I eftsoons put Master Fettiplace in remembrance of our
commission, and so he, myself, and the said Jenkins......went 75
to searching the house, where we found many secret corners......

[The search continues, but Campion and the other two priests are not discovered. Further reinforcements arrive that evening and the next morning, at which time the search is renewed.]

Yet still searching (although in effect clean void of any hope for finding of them), the said David Jenkins, by God's great goodness, espied a certain secret place, which he quickly found to be hollow, and, with a pin of iron which he had in his hand, much like unto a   80
harrow tine, he forthwith did break a hole into the said place; where then presently he perceived the said priests lying all close together upon a bed, of purpose there laid for them; where they had bread, meat, and drink sufficient to have relieved them three or four days together. The said Jenkins then called very loudly and   85
said, 'I have found the traitors!'; and presently company enough was with him, who there saw the said priests (when there was no remedy for them but *nolens volens*) courteously yield themselves......

Of all which matters, news was immediately carried in great   90
haste [by Elliot] to the Lords of the Privy Council, who gave further commission that the said priests and certain other their associates should be brought to the Court under the conduction of myself and the said Jenkins,......

[Campion and the other priests were hanged, drawn, and quartered in a public execution at Tyburn, though by the special mercy of the Queen the disembowelling and quartering were postponed until after they were fully dead from hanging.]

NOTES

 7   *friend* befriend.
17   *dinner* i.e. the midday meal.
20   *perforce* of necessity.
22   *buttery* room where liquor and provisions were stored.
     caused induced.
32 ff. In a side-note, Elliot says defensively: 'Some men blame me for dissembling the matter as I did; but to do my Prince and country service, I hold it lawful to use any reasonable policy. For the field is not always won by strength.' In another side-note to the description of Campion's preaching (here omitted), he adds: 'I had once [i.e. at one point in the proceedings] my commission in my hand to have dealt with them myself alone in the chamber. If I had, I pray you judge what had happened unto me.'
39   *invested* put on liturgical vestments.
40   *made holy bread* blessed ordinary leavened bread (distributed by the priest after the Eucharist to those who had not communicated).
41   *holy water* water blessed by a priest.
44   *gat* got.

47   *country* county.
48   *tenor* import, effect.
54   *abouts* about (genitival form).
60   *doubted* feared.
68–9 *three nuns* According to a side-note, one nun, happily, later escaped 'in
      country maid's apparel'. A following side-note adds: 'Mistress Yates
      proffered us a good sum of money to have given over our search.' Possibly
      true, or a grace note to recommend Elliot's incorruptibility!
74   *eftsoons* again.
79   *secret place* 'Priest's holes' as they were called were often to be found in
      the houses of Roman Catholic adherents.
81   *harrow tine* spike of a harrow (heavy, spiked wooden frame for dragging
      over ploughed land).
88   *nolens volens* willy-nilly (i.e. whether you will or not).

8 The supernatural

Witchcraft and magic

Whatever we may think today of the barbarities performed on thousands of usually innocent victims in the name of religion and morality, the 'fact' of witchcraft ('an art serving for the working of wonders, by the assistance of the Devil, so far as God shall permit,' as Sir Robert Filmer defined it in *An Advertisement to the Jury-Men of England Touching Witches* (1653)) was generally accepted by many of the best minds of the sixteenth and seventeenth centuries. James I, though not perhaps one of the best minds, was for many years a firm believer in witchcraft and, while still James VI of Scotland, had published a treatise called *Daemonologie, in Forme of a Dialogue* (1597). In it, partly as a result of personal experience in the trial of the so-called North Berwick Witches in 1590 (one of whom had 'declared unto him the very words which passed between [him] and his Queen at Upslo in Norway the first night of his marriage', *Newes from Scotland* (1591), ed. G. B. Harrison, p. 15), he asserted the threatening existence of witches and their diabolical powers, a view which, to his credit, he had, by 1618, pretty much renounced. His book was in part an answer to Reginald Scot's *The Discoverie of Witchcraft* (1584), a work in which Scot, though not denying Satan's powers, had dared to show himself deeply sceptical of the whole concept of witches and witchcraft. His definition of the typical 'witch' is justly famous (*The Discoverie*, bk. I, chap. 3):

> One sort of such as are said to be witches are women which be commonly old, lame, blear-eyed, pale, foul, and full of wrinkles; poor, sullen, superstitious, and papists; or such as know no religion: in whose drowsy minds the Devil hath gotten a fine seat; so as what mischief, mischance, calamity, or slaughter is brought to pass they are easily persuaded the same is done by themselves;......whereby they take upon them, yea, and sometimes think, that they can do such things as are beyond the ability of human nature.......Thus in process of time they [her neighbours] have all displeased her and she hath wished evil luck unto them all; perhaps with curses and imprecations made in form [i.e. according to diabolical formulae]. Doubtless (at length) some of her neighbours die or fall sick, or some of their children are visited with diseases......, which by ignorant parents are supposed to be the vengeance of witches......whereas indeed evil humours [morbid bodily fluids] and not strange words, witches, or spirits are the causes of such diseases. Also some of their cattle perish, either by disease or mischance.......The witch......, seeing things sometimes come to pass according to

her wishes, curses, and incantations, being called before a Justice,......confesseth that she (as a goddess) hath brought such things to pass.......Another sort of witches there are which be absolutely cozeners [cheats, imposters].

When King James came to rule England, he is reputed to have had Scot's *Discoverie* burned by the public hangman.

The witch trials of the time make sad reading, evidence usually being hearsay or wildly circumstantial. Although bad enough, the witchcraft mania in England never reached the proportions or the malignant savagery found on the Continent or in Scotland (see selection (i) from the anonymous *Newes from Scotland*), and torture, there a required part of the trial process, was supposedly prohibited by English law. Nevertheless, hundreds of 'witches' were brought to trial between 1550 and 1700 and all too many were convicted and executed. Fortunate, indeed, were the three accused women of Salmesbury (see selection (ii) from *The Wonderfull Discoverie of Witches in the Countie of Lancaster* (1613)), who happened to encounter a sceptical and humane judge. The accusations of Grace Sowerbutts (she was a girl of about fourteen, the child-informer being a particularly vicious and frequent aspect of witch trials) are little, if any, more outrageous than those that, in many other instances, led to conviction and death. Dr Fian (see selection (i)), a foolish (but brave) young man, may perhaps have dabbled in sorcery, but the charges to which he first confessed, under torture, were ridiculous, and the straight-faced way in which the absurdly comic heifer incident is treated in the report (an incident for which he was 'secretly nominated for a notable conjuror' among the Scottish people) is a significant commentary on the frightening credulity underlying most witch trials.

Witches, of course, along with conjurors, necromancers and devils, indeed the whole range of the supernatural (see the section on 'Ghosts', pp. 272–81), appealed to the dramatic imagination. Shakespeare's Witches (the 'Weird Sisters') in *Macbeth* are the most famous. Compare their 'brew' in IV.i with the supposed boiling and broiling of the dead baby in selection (ii) and with a scene in Thomas Middleton's *The Witch* (1609–16), I.ii, where Hecate, the chief witch, presides over a similar operation. Ben Jonson gives a lively depiction of a band of witches, replete with learned annotation, in the anti-masque to *The Masque of Queens* (1609) (see above, pp. 78–80) and of Maudlin, the Witch of Papplewick, in *The Sad Shepherd* (c. 1637); and Thomas Heywood and Richard Brome devote a play (*The Late Lancashire Witches*, 1634) to a second outbreak of witch-hunting in Lancashire in 1633. But one of the best and most sympathetic dramatic treatments of the subject appears in *The Witch of Edmonton* (1621), a collaboration by John Ford, Thomas Dekker and Samuel Rowley. Based on an account of an actual witch trial at the Old Bailey in London (*The Wonderfull Discoverie of Elizabeth Sawyer, a Witch, Late of Edmonton* by Henry Goodcole (1621)), it illustrates Scot's contention of how a poor and defenceless old woman

(Elizabeth Sawyer) was literally driven into the arms of the Devil by her neighbours' inhumanity.

On a more advanced level of magic, the magician or conjuror may be watched exercising his dangerous pursuits in Marlowe's *Dr Faustus* (*c*.1592), in Robert Greene's more lighthearted *Friar Bacon and Friar Bungay* (1589–92), and in Greene and Henry Chettle's *John of Bordeaux* (1590–4). Shakespeare in *The Tempest*, of course, runs the gamut of the supernatural under the direction of Prospero, a so-called 'white magician' (i.e. one who used his power for beneficent purposes, considered by most authorities, however, as pernicious as a practitioner of 'black magic'). For formal conjuring scenes, see *Dr Faustus* (scene iii) and Shakespeare's *II Henry VI*, I.iv; and for a contemporary real-life magician no figure rewards study more than Dr John Dee (1527–1608), sometimes referred to as 'Queen Elizabeth's Merlin', a brilliant mathematician, astrologer and alchemist (see 'Alchemy', pp. 303–12 below).

Further detailed information on witchcraft, etc., may be found in R. H. Robbins (ed.), *The Encyclopedia of Witchcraft and Demonology* (1959); G. L. Kittredge, *Witchcraft in Old and New England* (1929); K. M. Briggs, *Pale Hecate's Team* (1962); and Wayne Shumaker, *The Occult Sciences in the Renaissance* (1972).

i

A Scottish witch trial

From the anonymous *Newes from Scotland* (1591; ed. G. B. Harrison (1924), pp. 18–29).

As touching. . . . . . Doctor Fian, *alias* John Cunningham, the examination of his acts, since his apprehension, declareth the great subtlety of the Devil and therefore maketh things to appear the more miraculous; for being apprehended by the accusation of the said Geillis Duncane aforesaid, who confessed he was their   5
register, and that there was not one man suffered to come to the Devil's readings but only he. The said Doctor was taken and imprisoned, and used with the accustomed pain provided for those offences, inflicted upon the rest as is aforesaid.

First, by thrawing of his head with a rope, whereat he would   10
confess nothing. Secondly, he was persuaded by fair means to confess his follies, but that would prevail as little. Lastly, he was put to the most severe and cruel pain in the world, called the boots, who, after he had received three strokes, being enquired if he would confess his damnable acts and wicked life, his tongue   15
would not serve him to speak, in respect whereof the rest of the witches willed to search his tongue, under which was found two pins thrust up into the head; whereupon the witches did lay, *Now is the charm stinted*, and showed that those charmed pins were the cause he could not confess anything: then was he immediately   20
released of the boots, brought before the King, his confession was taken, and his own hand willingly set thereunto, which contained as followeth:

First, that at the general meetings of those witches he was always present; that he was clerk to all those that were in   25
subjection to the Devil's service, bearing the name of witches; that alway he did take their oaths for their true service to the Devil; and that he wrote for them such matters as the Devil still pleased to command him.

Item, he confessed that by his witchcraft he did bewitch a   30
gentleman dwelling near to the Saltpans, where the said Doctor kept school, only for being enamoured of a gentlewoman whom he loved himself; by means of which his sorcery, witchcraft, and devilish practices, he caused the said gentleman that once in twenty-four hours he fell into a lunacy and madness, and so   35
continued one whole hour together, and for the verity of the same, he caused the gentleman to be brought before the King's Majesty, ... and being in his Majesty's chamber, suddenly he gave a great scritch and fell into a madness, sometime bending himself and sometime cap'ring so directly up that his head did   40

touch the ceiling, to the great admiration of his Majesty and others then present;......he within an hour came again to himself; when, being demanded of the King's Majesty what he saw or did all that while, answered that he had been in a sound sleep.

Item, the said Doctor did also confess that he had used means 45 sundry times to obtain his purpose and wicked intent of the same gentlewoman, and seeing himself disappointed of his intention, he determined by all ways he might to obtain the same,......

It happened this gentlewoman, being unmarried, had a brother, who went to school with the said Doctor, and, calling his 50 scholar to him, demanded if he did lie with his sister, who answered he did, by means whereof he thought to obtain his purpose; and therefore secretly promised to teach him without stripes so he would obtain for him three hairs of his sister's privities, at such time as he would spy best occasion for it, which 55 the youth promised faithfully to perform and vowed speedily to put it in practice, taking a piece of conjured paper of his master to lap them in when he had gotten them; and thereupon the boy practised nightly to obtain his master's purpose, especially when his sister was asleep. 60

But God who knoweth the secrets of all hearts,......would not suffer the intents of this devilish Doctor to come to that purpose which he supposed it would, and......did so work by the gentlewoman's own means, that in the end the same was discovered and brought to light; for she, being one night asleep 65 and her brother in bed with her, suddenly cried out to her mother, declaring that her brother would not suffer her to sleep; whereupon her mother, having a quick capacity, did vehemently suspect Doctor Fian's intention, by reason she was a witch herself, and therefore presently arose and was very inquisitive of the boy to 70 understand his intent, and, the better to know the same, did beat him with sundry stripes, whereby he discovered the truth unto her.

The mother therefore, being well practised in witchcraft, did think it most convenient to meet with the Doctor in his own art, and thereupon took the paper from the boy, wherein he should 75 have put the same hairs, and went to a young heifer which never had borne calf nor gone to the bull, and, with a pair of shears, clipped off three hairs from the udder of the cow and wrapped them in the same paper, which she again delivered to the boy; then willing him to give the same to his said master, which he 80 immediately did.

The schoolmaster so soon as he had received them, thinking them indeed to be the maid's hairs, went straight and wrought his art upon them. But the Doctor had no sooner done his intent to them, but presently the heifer or cow, whose hairs they were 85 indeed, came unto the door of the church, wherein the schoolmaster was, into the which the heifer went and made

towards the schoolmaster, leaping and dancing upon him, and
following him forth of the church and to what place soever he went,
to the great admiration of all the townsmen of Salt pans,...... 90

[After signing a confession, Fian was jailed and appeared very
repentant, crying 'Avoid, Satan, avoid!'. That same night he
escaped, but was shortly recaptured and brought before King
James and members of his Council, where he utterly denied his
earlier confession.]

Whereupon the King's Majesty, perceiving his stubborn
willfulness, conceived and imagined that in the time of his absence
he had entered into new conference and league with the Devil his
master, and that he had been again newly marked, for the which
he was narrowly searched, but it could not in any wise be found; yet 95
for more trial of him to make him confess he was commanded to
have a most strange torment, which was done in the manner
following.

His nails upon all his fingers were riven and pulled off with an
instrument called in Scottish a *turkas*, which in England we call a 100
pair of pincers, and under every nail there was thrust in two
needles over even up to the heads. At all which torments
notwithstanding, the Doctor never shrunk any whit, neither would
he then confess it the sooner for all the tortures inflicted upon
him. 105

Then was he with all convenient speed, by commandment,
conveyed again to the torment of the boots, wherein he continued
a long time, and did abide so many blows in them that his legs
were crushed and beaten together as small as might be, and the
bones and flesh so bruised that the blood and marrow spouted 110
forth in great abundance, whereby they were made unserviceable
forever. And notwithstanding all these grievous pains and cruel
torments, he would not confess anything, so deeply had the Devil
entered into his heart, that he utterly denied all that which he had
before avouched, and would say nothing thereunto but this: that 115
what he had done and said before was only done and said for fear of
pains which he had endured......

......the said Doctor Fian was soon after arraigned,
condemned, and adjudged by the law to die and then to be burned
according to the law of that land, provided in that behalf. 120
Whereupon he was put into a cart, and being first strangled, he
was immediately put into a great fire being ready provided for that
purpose, and there burned in the Castle Hill of Edinburgh on a
Saturday in the end of January last past, 1591.

NOTES

5   *Geillis Duncane* or Gilly Duncan. Charged as a witch, she implicated many others in her confession, among them Fian.

6   *register* official clerk (see l. 25).

7   *Devil's readings* meetings of the witches, at which the 'art' of witchcraft was taught.

8   *pain* torture.

10   *thrawing* wringing, twisting (by drawing the rope tighter and tighter).

11   *fair means* ?equitable methods; ?apparently attractive methods.

13–14   *the boots* The so-called 'Spanish boot' was an instrument designed, through tightening, gradually to crush the foot and lower leg. Striking the boot increased the agony by forcing the wedges to tighten the vice.

17   *willed* desired. Whoever did the searching, witches or torturers, probably placed the pins in Fian's tongue in the process.

18   *into the head* i.e. all the way in.
       lay ?allege. perhaps an error for 'say'.

19   *charm stinted* magic spell broken or brought to an end.

31   *the Saltpans* Fian lived in a village called Saltpans in Lothian. Perhaps here used for 'salt-pans' = shallow depressions near the sea in which sea-water evaporated, leaving salt.

33   *by. . . . . . which* through.

36   *for. . . . . . same* Fian's action, if indeed it was his, seems to suggest that he was trying to advertise his magic powers. Presumably all he meant was to show that the 'gentleman' was mad, hence unsuitable for the 'gentlewoman'.

39   *great scritch* loud screech.

41   *admiration* wonder.

51   *did lie with* i.e. shared a bed with, a necessary practice in some families where houseroom was scant.

53–4   *teach. . . . . . stripes* i.e. instruct him without resorting to beating.

54   *of* from.

57   *conjured paper* paper subjected to magic conjurations.

68   *quick capacity* lively wit.

86   *church* Fian probably conducted his school in the church.

94   *newly marked* The 'Devil's mark' (often nothing more than a simple mole or natural blemish) was considered 'presumptive proof' of an individual's pact with the Devil.

102   *over* ?again and again.

119   *burned* Witches were hanged, rarely burned, under English law.

ii

An accuser accused

From Thomas Potts, *The Wonderfull Discoverie of Witches in the Countie of Lancaster* (1613), ed. G. B. Harrison (1929), pp. 86–103.

The said Grace Sowerbutts upon her oath saith, That for the space of some years now last past she hath been haunted and vexed with some women, who have used to come to her; which women, she saith, were Jennet Bierley, this informer's grandmother; Ellen Bierley, wife to Henry Bierley; Jane Southworth, late the wife of John Southworth; and one Old Doewife, all of Salmesbury aforesaid. And she saith, That now lately those four women did violently draw her by the hair of the head and laid her on the top of a haymow in Henry Bierley's barn. And she saith further, That not long after Jennet Bierley did meet this examinate near unto the place where she dwelleth, and first appeared in her own likeness, and after in the likeness of a black dog, and as [she] did go over a stile, she picked her off; howbeit, she saith she had no hurt then,......[Grace finally confided in her father, though] before that time she never told anybody thereof; and being examined why she did not, she saith, she could not speak thereof, though she desired so to do. And she further saith, That upon Saturday, being the fourth of this instant April, she, going toward Salmesbury boat to meet her mother, coming from Preston, she saw Jennet Bierley, who met [her] at a place called 'The Two Brigs', first in her own shape, and afterwards in the likeness of a black dog with two legs, which dog went close by the left side of [her] till they came to a pit of water, and then the dog spake and persuaded [her] to drown herself there, saying, it was a fair and an easy death. Whereupon [she] thought there came one to her in a white sheet and carried her away from the said pit, upon the coming whereof the black dog departed away; and shortly after the white thing departed also. And after [she] had gone further on her way, about the length of two or three fields, the black dog did meet her again and, going on her left side, as aforesaid, did carry her into a barn of one Hugh Walshman, near thereby, and laid her upon the barn-floor, and covered [her] with straw on her body and hay on her head, and the dog itself lay on the top of the straw; but how long the dog lay there [she] cannot tell,......for......her speech and senses were taken from her.......[Grace was found and carried into Walshman's house and taken home by her parents; on the way] she saith, That at the place......called 'The Two Brigs', Jennet Bierley and Ellen Bierley did appear unto her in their own shapes; whereupon [she] fell down, and after was not able to speak or go till the Friday following.......And she further saith, That, a good while before all this, [she] did go with Jennet Bierley, her grandmother, and Ellen Bierley, her aunt, at the bidding of her grandmother, to the house of one Thomas Walshman......And coming thither in the night, when all the household was abed, the doors being shut, Jennet Bierley did open them,......and Jennet Bierley went into the chamber where Walshman and his wife lay, and from thence brought a little child,......and after Jennet Bierley had set her down by the fire,......she did thrust a nail into the navel of the child, and afterwards did take a pen and put it in at the said place, and did suck there a good space, and afterwards laid the child in bed again.......[The child died shortly after.] And after the death of the child, the next night after the burial thereof, Jennet Bierley and Ellen Bierley, taking this examinate with them, went to Salmesbury church, and there did take up the child; and Jennet did carry it out of the churchyard in her arms, and then did put it in her lap and carried it home to her own house; and having it there did boil some thereof in a pot, and some did broil on the coals, of both which Jennet and Ellen did eat, and would have had this examinate and one Grace Bierley, daughter of Ellen, to have eaten with them, but they refused so to do. And afterwards Jennet and Ellen did seeth the bones of the child in a pot, and with the fat that came out of the bones, they said they would anoint themselves, that thereby they might sometimes change themselves into other shapes. And after all this being done, they said they would lay the bones again in the grave the next night following.......And being further sworn and examined, she deposeth and saith, That about half a year ago, Jennet Bierley, Ellen Bierley, Jane Southworth, and [she], who went by the appointment of Jennet, her grandmother, did meet at a place called Red Bank, upon the north side of the water of Ribble, every Thursday and Sunday at night by the space of a fortnight; and at the waterside there came unto them,......four black things, going upright, and yet not like men in the face, which four did carry the three women and [her] over the water; and when they came to the said Red Bank, they found something there which they did eat.......And after they [but not Grace] had eaten, the three women and [she] danced, every one of them with one of the black things aforesaid, and after their dancing the black things did pull down the three women, and did abuse their bodies, as [she] thinketh, for she saith, that the black thing that was with her did abuse her body. [Grace continues with more 'outrages' committed upon her by Jane Southworth.]

And being further examined touching her being at Red Bank, she saith, That the three women......were carried back again over Ribble by the same black things that carried them thither; and saith, That at their meeting in the Red Bank there did come

45

50

55

60

65

70

75

80

85

also divers other women, and did meet them there, some old, some young, which [she] thinketh did dwell upon the north side of Ribble, because she saw them not come over the water; but [she] knew none of them, neither did she see them eat or dance, or do 90 anything else that the rest did, saving that they were there and looked on.......

[Sir Edward Bromley, the King's Justice in charge of the trial, became suspicious of Grace Sowerbutt's story, and, after considerable questioning of both the girl and the witnesses, 'one witness accusing another', got her to admit that her charges were entirely false and that 'one Master Thompson, which she taketh to be Master Christopher Southworth [a seminary priest], to whom she was sent to learn her prayers, did persuade, counsel, and advise her to deal as formerly hath been said against her grandmother, aunt, and Southworth's wife.' The priest is declared to have acted out of revenge because the three women charged had once been 'obstinate papists' but had left the Romish religion and had become members of the Anglican communion.]

NOTES

2   *years......past* years before this present time of speaking.
6   *Old Doewife* Presumably already dead, since she is not mentioned again.
     Salmesbury i.e. Salesbury, a small town in Lancashire, near Preston on the west coast and on the river Ribble.
9   *haymow* Here probably 'hayloft'.
12   *likeness......dog* An example of so-called 'metamorphosis', a common charge against witches. Curiously missing in Grace's account is any mention of the 'familiar' or 'imp' (a dog, cat, rabbit, etc.) through whom the witch was believed to carry out her criminal designs.
13   *picked* plucked.
18   *instant* present.
19   *boat* ?ferry.
21   *Brigs* bridges.
24   *fair* synonym for 'easy'.
25–6 *one......sheet* Obviously intended to represent some kind of angelic intervention.
33   *dog......straw* With implication of diabolic sexual intercourse.
40   *go* walk.
50   *pen* quill-feather.
62   *seeth* boil.
64   *change themselves* More usually this kind of anointing was used to enable the witch to fly through the air.
70   *meet* Such a meeting of witches, a kind of sabbat, was very rare in England (see (i) above, ll. 24–9), but such a meeting had very recently been publicized at Malking Tower close by in Lancashire.
74–5 *did......water* A version of diabolic transvection or the nocturnal flight.

Ghosts, spirits and the fairies

The preceding section on 'Witchcraft and magic' dealt with what may be
called the mediated world of the supernatural in which necromancers
and witches were supposed to work their *maleficia* or evil, under a
contract relationship, through the agency of the Devil, acting, one might
say, as the Devil's middlemen. But as King James (*Daemonologie* (1597);
see selection (ii)) labours to point out, the Devil and his legions of
darkness often practised *maleficia* without the aid of human intermediar-
ies. 'Be sober, be vigilant: because your adversary the Devil, as a roaring
lion, walketh about seeking whom he may devour' (I Peter 5:8).

As Protestants, both Lewes Lavater (see selection (i) from *Of Ghostes
and Spirites Walking by Night* (1572)) and King James denied the
doctrine of purgatory, that halfway-house, where, as the Ghost of
Hamlet's father describes it, the souls of the dead, who had died in a
state of grace, were 'confin'd to fast in fires, / Till the foul crimes done in
my days of nature / Are burnt and purg'd away' (*Hamlet*, I.v.11-13), and
from which such souls, according to Roman Catholic doctrine, were able
to revisit the earth and appear as apparitions (in bodies of thickened air)
to the living. Having banished Purgatory as 'a vain thing' ('Thirty-nine
Articles', 1562, art. 22), the Anglican church and other Protestant
churches were left with the extremes of Heaven and Hell, from which,
they argued, the souls of the dead could not under any circumstances
return. They did not, however, deny the 'reality' of various kinds of
spiritual manifestations but attributed them to good or evil angels, acting
under God's ordinance, who could appear in the forms of the dead or
living to warn, tempt, incite, or punish mankind. As Lavater notes,
however, good angels manifested themselves very seldom 'in these our
days' (l. 82), most apparitions being, in fact, evil angels, emissaries of the
Devil, sent to ensnare men and women, body and soul.

In an age when the new Protestant doctrines were only beginning to
penetrate a popular consciousness nurtured on centuries of Roman
Catholic teaching, it is not surprising that there was a good deal of
confusion in the lay mind about 'ghosts and spirits walking by night'.
Shakespeare's presentation of the Ghost of Hamlet's father may be taken
as a case in point. The Ghost describes himself in Catholic terms as 'thy
father's spirit' (I.v.9), revisiting the earth from the cleansing fires of
Purgatory (I.v.11-13; lines already quoted above), and as one who had
died 'Cut off even in the blossoms of my sin, / Unhous'led, disappointed,
unanel'd' (i.e. without the benefit of the last rites, including confession
and extreme unction; I.v.76-7). On the other hand, although Hamlet's
first reaction on seeing the Ghost ('Be thou a spirit of health, or goblin
damn'd, / Bring with thee airs from heaven, or blasts from hell',
I.iv.40-1; and later I.v.92-3) could be in line with either Catholic or
Protestant theology, his immediate questioning of its authenticity seems,
perhaps, to reflect the newer Protestant view that most such apparitions

should be suspected as evil spirits bound on the Devil's work. Moreover, when Hamlet later describes the realm of death as 'The undiscover'd country, from whose bourn / No traveller returns' (III.i.78–9), he would seem to be denying his assessment of the spirit as 'an honest ghost' (I.v.138), unless, indeed, he accepts the Ghost, in Protestant terms, as a good angel assuming the form of his dead father. None of this ghostly ambiguity worries the average reader or playgoer, but its presence underscores the 'mingl'd yarn' of old and new doctrine that existed in Shakespeare's time and would continue to exist for many years to come.

In the world of the drama, revenge ghosts and other theatrical apparitions (e.g. the three oracular apparitions that warn Macbeth in IV.i or the Ghost of the Friar that comes to warn Bussy in act V of George Chapman's *Bussy D'Ambois* (*c*.1604)), which for a modern audience now demand a measured suspension of disbelief, were stock dramatic devices throughout Elizabethan–Jacobean times and would have been accepted as 'natural' in the climate of opinion then prevailing. The revenge ghost, a useful motivating agent for a sensational plot-line and bloody deeds, was generally associated with Seneca, who in two plays, *Thyestes* and *Octavia* (the latter then usually attributed to him), had made influential use of the device. Indeed, an English translator, Jasper Heywood, even added 'The Sprite of Achilles' bent on revenge to Seneca's *Troas* (1559), presumably on the principle that if Seneca had failed to provide one the less Seneca he! Unlike the Ghost of the elder Hamlet, most of the revenge ghosts that stalk through play after play are presented without much attention to either the problems raised by the unchristian revenge ethic or their origins. They are simply accepted as shades of the dead ranging to 'glut on revenge' (as the Ghost of Gorlois happily puts it in Thomas Hughes's *The Misfortunes of Arthur* (1588)) and crying (like the Ghost of Albanact in W. S.'s *Locrine* (1591–5); III.vi.41, 54), 'Revenge! revenge for blood!' and '*Vindicta, vindicta!*'; or like the Ghost in the pre-Shakespearean (Kydean?) *Hamlet*, which was compared by Thomas Lodge (*Wits Miserie, and the Worlds Madnesse* (1596), p. 56) to one who was 'as pale as the vizard of the ghost which cried so misera[b]ly at the Theatre, like an oyster-wife, *Hamlet, revenge!*'. Something of the huffing rhetorical tone, imitated in part from 'English Seneca', 'let blood line by line and page by page' (Thomas Nashe, 'Preface' to Greene's *Menaphon* (1589), ed. McKerrow, III, 315–16), and considered proper to the 'high style' for earlier such ghosts, may be sampled in the following lines spoken by the Ghost of Corineus (a second ghost in *Locrine*, V.iv.21–5):

> The boisterous Boreas thund'reth forth revenge;
> The stony rocks cry out on sharp revenge;
> The thorny bush pronounceth dire revenge.
>
> *Sound the alarm [to battle].*
>
> Now, Corineus, stay and see revenge,
> And feed thy soul with Locrine's overthrow.

It was customary for stage ghosts to materialize as they were at the moment of death (e.g. Banquo in *Macbeth* (III.iv.80), who rises 'With twenty mortal murthers [i.e. wounds] on his crown'); once again, however, the Ghost of the elder Hamlet proves an exception, sporting two costumes, first appearing on the battlements (I.i) armed in 'complete steel', later, again appropriately, in the Queen's closet (III.iv) dressed in his 'night-gown' (i.e. dressing-gown).

Other representative revenge ghosts may be studied in Thomas Kyd's *The Spanish Tragedy* (c.1586–7), in which the Ghost of Don Andrea, escorted and humoured by a personified abstraction called Revenge, presides over nine deaths, 'spectacles to please my soul!'; Shakespeare's *Richard III* (v.iii) and *Julius Caesar* (IV.iii); John Marston's *Antonio's Revenge* (1600–1; III.iff.); Thomas Heywood's *II Iron Age* (1612–13; V.i); George Chapman's *Revenge of Bussy D'Ambois* (c.1612; V.iii, v), a play with an anti-revenge theme; and Thomas Middleton and William Rowley's *The Changeling* (1622; V.i). A notably rare example of an anti-revenge ghost occurs in Cyril Tourneur's *The Atheist's Tragedy* (c.1611; II.vi), when the murdered Montferrers appears to his son, Charlemont, and urges him to 'leave revenge unto the King of kings'.

Finally, King James's fourth class of spirits, the 'Faerie' (see selection (ii) from his *Daemonologie* (1597)), though he had summarily dismissed them as nothing more than illusions of the Devil, continued to thrive in the popular mind and achieved 'a local habitation and a name' through Spenser in *The Faerie Queene* (1590–6) and Shakespeare in Mercutio's Queen Mab speech (*Romeo and Juliet*, I.iv.53–94) and *A Midsummer Night's Dream*. Between them, they drew together the scattered strands of floating fairy lore with such imaginative vitality and 'realism' that their work, especially Shakespeare's, became the source and inspiration for most later treatments of the 'world of Faerie' in English literature. Both Shakespeare and Ben Jonson have some fun with fairy disguise in *The Merry Wives of Windsor* (IV.iv; V.iv, v) and *The Alchemist* (III.v; V.iv).

For further discussion of fairy beliefs in this period, see K. M. Briggs, *The Anatomy of Puck* (1959).

From Lewes [Ludwig] Lavater, *Of Ghostes and Spirites Walking by Night*, trans. R. H. (1572), ed. J. Dover Wilson and Mary Yardley (1929), pp. 53, 71–4, 91, 160–1, 167, 195–6.

Albeit many melancholic, mad, fearful, and weak-sensed men do oftentimes imagine many things which in very deed are not, and are likewise deceived sometime by men or by brute beasts, and moreover mistake things which proceed of natural causes to be bugs and spirits,......yet it is most certain and sure that all   5
those things which appear unto men are not always natural things nor always vain terrors to affray men, but that spirits do often appear and many strange and marvellous things do sundry times chance.......

Some man walketh alone in his house and, behold, a spirit   10
appeareth in his sight; yea, and sometimes the dogs also perceive them and fall down at their masters' feet and will by no means depart fro them, for they are sore afraid themselves too. Some man goeth to bed and layeth him down to rest, and by and by there is some thing pinching him or pulling off the clothes; sometimes it   15
sitteth on him or lieth down in the bed with him, and many times it walketh up and down in the chamber. There have been many times men seen, walking on foot, or riding on horseback, being of a fiery shape, known unto divers men, and such as died not long before. And it hath come to pass likewise that some either slain in   20
the wars, or otherwise dead naturally, have called unto their acquaintance being alive and have been known by their voice.

Many times in the night season there have been certain spirits heard softly going, or spitting, or groaning, who being asked what they were have made answer that they were the souls of this or that   25
man, and that they now endure extreme torments.......And hereby it may be well proved that they were not always priests, or other bold and wicked men, which have feigned themselves to be souls of men deceased, as I have before said, insomuch that even in those men's chambers, when they have been shut, there have   30
appeared such things when they have with a candle diligently searched before whether any thing have lurked in some corner or no. Many use at this day to search and sift every corner of the house before they go to bed that they may sleep more soundly, and yet nevertheless they hear some crying out and making a   35
lamentable noise, etc.

It hath many times chanced that those of the house have verily thought that some body have overthrown the pots, platters, tables, and trenchers, and tumbled them down the stairs, but after it waxed day, they have found all things orderly set in their places   40
again. It is reported that some spirits have thrown the door off

from the hooks and have troubled and set all things in the house out of order, never setting them in their due place again, and that they have marvellously disquieted men with rumbling and making a great noise....... 45

Pioners or diggers for metal do affirm that in many mines there appear strange shapes and spirits, who are appareled like unto other labourers in the pit. These wander up and down in caves and underminings and seem to bestir themselves in all kind of labour,...... They very seldom hurt the labourers (as they say) 50 except they provoke them by laughing and railing at them.......

I heard of a grave and wise man, which was a magistrate in the territory of Tigurie, who affirmed that, as he and his servant went through the pastures in the summer very early, he espied one whom he knew very well wickedly defiling himself with a mare, 55 wherewith, being amazed, he returned back again and knocked at his house whom he supposed he had seen, and there understood for a certainty that he went not one foot out of his chamber that morning. And in case he had not diligently searched out the matter, the good and honest man had surely been cast in prison 60 and put on the rack. I rehearse this history for this end, that judges should be very circumspect in these cases, for the Devil by these means doth oftentimes circumvent the innocent.......

You will say, I hear and understand very well that these things are not men's souls, which continually remain in their appointed 65 places; I pray you then what are they? To conclude in few words: if it be not a vain persuasion proceeding through weakness of the senses, through fear, or some such like cause, or if it be not deceit of men or some natural thing,...... it is either a good or evil angel, or some other forewarning sent by God,...... Angels for 70 the most part take upon them the shapes of men, wherein they appear.......

But it is no difficult matter for the Devil to appear in divers shapes, not only of those which are alive, but also of dead men,......yea, and (which is a less matter) in the form of beasts 75 and birds, etc., as to appear in the likeness of a black dog, a horse, an owl, and also to bring incredible things to pass, it is a thing most manifest.......

We ought, not without great cause, to suspect all spirits and other apparitions. For, albeit God doth use the help and service of 80 good angels for the preservation of his elect, yet notwithstanding in these our days they appear unto us very seldom.

NOTES

5   *bugs* bugbears, hobgoblins.

13   *fro* from.

16   *sitteth*......*with him* a reference to the 'nightmare' or succubus demon
     which was believed to have sexual relations with a man. The male
     equivalent was known as an 'incubus'.

23   *certain spirits* Lavater would not admit that these are the actual souls of
     the dead individuals but good or evil angels that have assumed their forms.

24   *going* walking.

27   *priests* Lavater's Protestant prejudice shows itself.

37–45 Lavater seems to be referring to poltergeists.

46   *Pioners* (i.e. pioneers) miners. Compare Hamlet's reference to the Ghost
     ('this fellow in the cellarage') as 'old mole' and 'worthy pioner' (*Hamlet*,
     I.v.151, 162–3).

53   *Tigurie* Zurich, Switzerland.

61   *rack* instrument of torture on which individuals were 'stretched' and their
     joints dislocated.

73–5 *Devil*......*men* Compare Hamlet's reaction to the Ghost of the elder
     Hamlet (*Hamlet*, I.iv, 40–1; see also I.v.92–3).

79   *not*......*cause* i.e. for very good reasons.

ii

From King James, *Daemonologie, in Forme of a Dialogue* (1597), ed. G. B.
Harrison (1924), pp. 56–75), bk. III, chaps. i–v.

Epistemon. That kind of the devils conversing in the earth may be
divided in four different kinds, whereby he affrayeth and troubleth
the bodies of men. . . . . . . The first is, where spirits troubles some
houses or solitary places. The second, where spirits follows upon
certain persons and at divers hours troubles them. The third, when   5
they enter within them and possess them. The fourth is these kind
of spirits that are called vulgarly the Faerie. Of the three former
kinds ye heard already, how they may artificially be made by
witchcraft to trouble folk. Now it rests to speak of their natural
coming as it were, and not raised by witchcraft. . . . . . . As to the   10
first kind of these spirits, that were called by the ancients by divers
names, ... if they were spirits that haunted some houses by
appearing in divers and horrible forms and making great din, they
were called *Lemures* or *Spectra*. If they appeared in likeness of any
defunct to some friends of his, they were called *umbrae*   15
mortuorum. . . . . . . The cause why they haunt solitary places, it is
by reason that they may affray and brangle the more the faith of
such as them alone haunts such places. . . . . . . On the other part,
when he troubles certain houses that are dwelt in, it is a sure token
either of gross ignorance or of some gross and slanderous sins   20
amongst the inhabitants thereof, which God by that extraordinary
rod punishes.
    Philomathes. But by what way or passage can these spirits enter
in these houses, ... door and window being steeked?
    Epistemon. They will choose the passage for their entress   25
according to the form that they are in at that time. For if they have
assumed a dead body, whereinto they lodge themselves, they can
easily enough open without din any door or window and enter in
thereat. And if they enter as a spirit only, any place where the air
may come in at is large enough an entry for them; for, as I said   30
before, a spirit can occupy no quantity. . . . . . .
    And that the Devil may use as well the ministry of the bodies of
the faithful in these cases, as of the unfaithful, there is no
inconvenient; for his haunting with their bodies after they are
dead can noways defile them in respect of the soul's absence.   35
. . . . . .
    As to the next two kinds, ... I will conjoin them in one,
because as well the causes are alike in the persons that they are
permitted to trouble, as also the ways whereby they may be
remedied and cured.   40
    Philomathes. What kind of persons are they that uses to be so
troubled?

Epistemon. Two kinds in special: either such as being guilty of grievous offences, God punishes by that horrible kind of scourge, or else being persons of the best nature, peradventure, that ye shall find in all the country about them, GOD permits them to be troubled in that sort for the trial of their patience and wakening up of their zeal, for admonishing of the beholders not to trust over much in themselves, since they are made of no better stuff and, peradventure, blotted with no smaller sins......

Philomathes.......which is, I pray you, the end and mark he [the Devil] shoots at in this turn?

Epistemon. It is to obtain one of two things thereby, if he may: the one is the tinsel of their life by inducing them to such perilous places at such time as he either follows or possesses them, which may procure the same.......The other thing that he presses to obtain by troubling of them is the tinsel of their soul by enticing them to mistrust and blaspheme God, either for the intollerableness of their torments, as he assayed to have done with Job, or else for his promising unto them to leave the troubling of them, in case they would so do,......

[James then (bk. III, chap. 3) discusses 'that kind of following spirits called *Incubi* [male] and *Succubi* [female]', who it was claimed had sexual relations with their victims and denies that any monstrous births can result because 'we know spirits hath no seed proper to themselves'.]

Philomathes. Now, I pray you, come on to that fourth kind of spirits.

Epistemon. That fourth kind of spirits, which by the Gentiles was called *Diana* and her wand'ring court, and amongst us was called the Faerie (as I told you) or our good neighbours, was one of the sorts of illusions that was rifest in the time of papistry; for although it was holden odious to prophesy by the Devil, yet whom these kind of spirits carried away, and informed, they were thought to be sonsiest and of best life. To speak of the many vain trattles founded upon that illusion: how there was a King and Queen of Faerie, of such a jolly court and train as they had; how they had a teind and duty, as it were, of all goods; how they naturally rode and went, eat and drank, and did all other actions like natural men and women......

Philomathes. But how can it be then that sundry witches have gone to death with that confession that they have been transported with the Faerie to such a hill, which opening, they went in, and there saw a fair Queen, who being now lighter, gave them a stone that had sundry virtues, which at sundry times hath been produced in judgment?

Epistemon. I say that, even as I said before of that imaginar

ravishing of the spirit forth of the body [as in the case of witches].
For may not the Devil object to their fantasy, their senses being
dulled, and as it were asleep, such hills and houses within them,   85
such glistering courts and trains, and whatsoever such like
wherewith he pleaseth to delude them? And in the meantime,
their bodies being senseless, to convey in their hand any stone or
such like thing, which he makes them to imagine to have received
in such a place?   90

NOTES

1   *Epistemon* Greek for 'the knowledgeable one' (i.e. King James).
     conversing moving about.
2   *affrayeth* scares, frightens.
3   *troubles* Northern form of the plural in -s is common in Scottish usage and
     lingers in sixteenth-century English, for example, occasionally in
     Shakespeare.
7   *the Faerie* collective term for the inhabitants of fairyland, fairy-folk.
8   *artificially* unnaturally, by artifice.
14   *Lemures* spirits of the dead, in Roman mythology.
     Spectra apparitions.
15   *defunct* deceased person.
15–16 *umbrae mortuorum* shades of the dead.
17   *brangle* shake.
20   *gross ignorance* It is not clear whose 'gross ignorance' is referred to – that
     of the inhabitants or of the haunting spirit.
23   *Philomathes.* Greek for 'a lover of learning'.
24   *steeked* locked up.
25   *entress* entrance.
31   *quantity* amount (of space).
32   *ministry* agency.
34   *inconvenient* impropriety, abuse.
35   *in respect of* because of.
51   *mark* target.
54   *tinsel* forfeiture, loss.
54–5 *inducing. . . . . .places* Compare Horatio's fear that the Ghost will lure
     Hamlet to 'the dreadful summit of the cliff', tempting him to cast himself
     over in a fit of madness (*Hamlet*, I.iv.69–74).
58   *mistrust and blaspheme God* Such actions could lead to despair, or the so-
     called 'sin against the Holy Ghost', the unforgivable sin, in which a man,
     like Faustus (in Marlowe's *Dr Faustus*, 1592–3), in the grip of the Devil
     (Mephostophilis), believes that he is so far fallen into sin that it is not in
     God's power to forgive him.
64   *Gentiles* i.e. heathen.
65   *Diana* Roman goddess of the hunt, who was believed to preside over
     nocturnal incantations.
     wand'ring court train of attendants.
66   *good neighbours* James earlier (bk. III, chap. 2) refers to 'this spirit called
     Brownie', who 'haunted divers houses without doing any evil, but doing as

it were necessary turns up and down the house.' Thomas Nashe (*The Terrors of the Night* (1594); ed. McKerrow, I, 347) calls them 'The Robin Goodfellows, elves, fairies, hobgoblins of our latter age', and Shakespeare describes their actions and mischief through Puck (or Robin Goodfellow) in *Midsummer Night's Dream* (II.i.32–57) and Mercutio's Queen Mab speech in *Romeo and Juliet* (I.iv.53–94).

68   *holden* held.

68-9 *whom . . . . . . informed* The fairies were believed to substitute one of their own children for unbaptized infants. The 'fairy' child was known as a 'changeling' and the stolen baby was supposedly brought up ('informed') by the fairy-folk.

70   *sonsiest* most lucky, fortunate.

71   *trattles* idle tales.

72   *train* body of attendants. Compare Titania and Oberon's 'trains' in *Midsummer Night's Dream*.

73   *teind* tithe or tenth part (a form of tax or 'duty').

74   *went* walked.
      eat ate.

79   *lighter* ?more luminous.

80   *virtues* magical powers.

82   *imaginar* imaginary (not in *OED*; perhaps an error for 'imaginary').

84   *object . . . . . . fantasy* present to their imagination.

9 The law: crime and punishment

English law, like American law, which is based on it, if not exactly 'a ass, a idiot' as Dickens' Mr Bumble calls it in a moment of frustration, is an extraordinarily complex system of jurisprudence, full of conflicts and contradictions built up over centuries of practice. Though this may be less true of statute law (the acts of Parliament), it is not a greatly exaggerated characterization of what is called 'common law' (both criminal and civil), also known as 'case law', in which judicial determination depends on precedents furnished by earlier cases often of considerable antiquity. As William Harrison complains (*The Description of England* (1587), bk. II, chap. 9), English laws are 'always so variable and subject to alteration and change that oft in one age divers judgments do pass upon one manner of case,......In such a year of the prince, this opinion was taken for sound law; [such judgments] do answer nothing else, but that the judgment of our lawyers is now altered so that they say far otherwise.'

Later in the same chapter Harrison laments the growing mercenary greed of the legal profession (a note for our own times!):

> For as after the coming of the Normans the nobility had the start, and after them the clergy, so now all the wealth of the land doth flow unto our common lawyers,......which argueth that they wax rich apace and will be richer if their clients become not the more wiser and wary hereafter......The time hath been that our lawyers did sit in Paul's upon stools against the pillars and walls to get clients, but now some of them will not come from their chambers to the Guildhall in London under ten pounds, or twenty nobles at the least. And one being demanded why he made so much of his travel [*or* travail?], answered, that it was but folly for him to go so far when he was assured to get more money by sitting still at home. A friend of mine also had a suit of late of some valure [value] and, to be sure of counsel at his time, he gave unto two lawyers (whose names I forbear to mention) twenty shillings apiece, telling them of the day and hour wherein his matter should be called upon. To be short, they came not unto the bar at all, whereupon he stayed [postponed the case] for that day. On the morrow, after he met them again, increased his former gifts by so much more and told them of the time, but they once again served him as before. In the end, he met them both in the very hall door, and, after some timorous [apprehensive] reprehension of their uncourteous demeanor toward him, he bestowed either three angels or four more upon each of them, whereupon they promised peremptorily [positively] to speak earnestly in his cause. And yet for all this, one of them, having not yet sucked enough, utterly deceived him; the other indeed came in, and, wagging a scroll

which he had in his hand before the judge, he spake not above
three or four words, almost so soon uttered as a 'good morrow',
and so went from the bar. And this was all the poor man gat [got]
for his money and the care his counselors did seem to take of his
cause then standing upon the hazard.

Harrison, of course, paints an extreme picture. Many lawyers doubtless
gave an honest return for their fees and many judges were above bribes
(unlike the Judge in selection (iii)), but the widespread criticisms levelled
at the legal profession throughout the period suggest that sharp (if not
downright dishonest) practice was all too common, a practice which
almost inevitably (as still today) favoured the rich at the expense of the
poor. As Philip Stubbes says (*The Anatomie of Abuses* (1583, 2nd edn; in
F. J. Furnivall's edn, pp. 117–18):

> If you have *argent* [silver], or rather *rubrum unguentum*, I dare
> not say gold but red ointment, to grease them [i.e. lawyers] in the
> fist withal, then your suit shall want no furtherance; but if this
> liquor be wanting, then farewell client;......So long as any of
> this ointment is dropping, they will bear him in hand [make him
> think] his matter is good and just, and all to keep him in ure
> [make him continue his suit] till all be gone; and then they will tell
> him his matter is naught.

Stubbes also attacks the greed and irresponsibility of lawyers in *The
Second Part of the Anatomie of Abuses* (1583, sigs. G3 v–G8 v). Francis
Bacon's admonitory essay 'Of Judicature' (*Essayes* (1625), no. 56) is still
relevant and should be required reading for all would-be judges and
lawyers.

Selection (i), from Harrison's *The Description of England* (1587),
offers an unpleasantly vivid account of the different kinds of punishment,
under law, then practised in England. Executions were regularly carried
out publicly and were considered as a corrective warning (if not officially
entertainment) for the people who witnessed them. Henry Machyn, in
his *Diary* for 1550–63, records some twenty-five such public executions
(most of them multiple) at Tyburn for those years alone. Treason, except
for members of the nobility, was punished with hanging, drawing, and
quartering, and traitors' heads were displayed on spikes above the south
entrance of London Bridge. If all this strikes us today as brutal and
barbarous, it may perhaps chasten our feelings of superiority if we recall
the recent official Nazi atrocities and the present widespread practice of
torture in, for example, certain South American countries. The beast is
still just under the skin.

The second selection (ii), from Robert Southwell's *An Humble
Supplication to Her Majestie* (1595; written 1591), is part of his
impassioned plea for some mitigation of the government's cruel
treatment of Catholics, particularly seminary priests and Jesuits
(Southwell was a Jesuit), as sternly set out in a proclamation ('By the

Queen') published in 1591, organizing and strengthening policies already in effect (see 'Church and State', selection (iii)). Southwell's account of the unspeakable tortures to which Catholic priests were subjected in an effort to force them to renounce their religious allegiance to the Pope, or to extort a confession (often implicating others) of complicity in plots against the Elizabethan Protestant establishment, is, of course, horrifying on any terms, but the times were dangerous and the tortures used no more nauseatingly inhumane than those employed by Catholics against Protestants in Queen Mary's reign (see 'Church and State', selection (i)) or by the Spanish Inquisition. Very shortly after completing his *Supplication*, Southwell was arrested, underwent some of the tortures he so vividly describes, and was executed as a traitor. He is now best remembered for his beautiful little poem 'The Burning Babe'.

Selection (iii), a scene from Thomas Lodge and Robert Greene's *A Looking-Glass for London and England* (1587–91), is concerned with the growing dangers posed by the practice of usury and its relation to legal malpractice. A dressed-up form of the older moral interlude, *A Looking-Glass* dramatizes, in the setting of the profligate city of Nineveh, a whole catalogue of sins and sinners (pride, adultery, incest, riotous living, usury, bribery, corruption, etc.), using them as warning examples (a lookingglass) for London and England, the lesson in each episode being driven home by the prophets Hosea or Jonah.

The problem raised by usury (i.e. the taking of interest on money or goods loaned) was a very controversial question in Elizabethan–Jacobean England. The important statute of 1571, though it declared that 'all usury, being forbidden by the law of God is sin and detestable', nevertheless allowed a maximum interest rate of ten pounds in the hundred. Most churchmen and some civilians, however, still believed any usury to be a damnable sin against God and nature (see, for example, Thomas Wilson's *A Discourse upon Usury* (1572) or, as Thomas Dekker put it (*Work for Armourers* (1609), ed. A. B. Grosart, IV, 131–2): 'Usury was the first that ever taught Money to commit incest with Gold and Silver, her nearest kinsmen.' The endless arguments pro (economic) and con (religious and moral) are much too complex to discuss here (see R. H. Tawney's useful Introduction to his edition (1925) of Wilson's tract and Francis Bacon's 'Of Usury' in *Essayes* (1625; no. 41)), and the law, even though the penalties were considerably lighter under the Elizabethan statute (1571) than those laid down by the earlier Henrician statute, tended to turn a blind eye to infringements, especially if the 'usurer' (often a well-to-do merchant) used various forms of bribery and subversion.

The scene is probably the work of Lodge, since the episode is based closely on a passage in Lodge's earlier pamphlet, *An Alarum against Usury* (1584; in *Works*, Hunterian Club edn (1883), I, 36–7). The Usurer's treatment of Thrasybulus and Alcon and later bribing of the Judge and Lawyer are probably not much exaggerated, as we may infer from other recorded cases. The play ends in an orgy of repentance under the didactic eye of Jonah, and the Usurer restores the property of Thrasybulus and Alcon, though the Judge and Lawyer are simply forgotten after their single scene.

Not surprisingly, the figure of the usurer, described by Nicholas Breton in his 'character' of 'An Usurer' (*The Good and the Bad*, 1616) as 'a kind of canker that, with the teeth of interest, eats the hearts of the poor, and a venomous fly that sucks out the blood of any flesh that he lights on', became a favourite target for many later dramatists, particularly in City comedy. Perhaps best known are Marlowe's Barabas (*The Jew of Malta*, 1589–90), Shakespeare's Shylock (*The Merchant of Venice*, 1597), Security (in Marston, Jonson, Chapman's *Eastward Ho!*, 1605), Harry Dampit (in Middleton's *A Trick to Catch the Old One*, 1604–7), Morecraft (in Beaumont and Fletcher's *The Scornful Lady*, 1613–16), and Sir Giles Overreach (in Massinger's *A New Way to Pay Old Debts*, 1621–5).

Lawyers too, of course, come in for their share of satire and criticism. *Ignoramus* (1615), a Cambridge Latin comedy by George Ruggle, has a rascally lawyer as its central character and satirizes the legal jargon of what was called law-French and law-Latin, widely used in the law courts and in legal documents. Memorable courtroom scenes occur in Shakespeare's *The Merchant of Venice* (IV.i) and *The Winter's Tale* (III.ii); John Webster's *The White Devil* (1609–12; III.ii), *The Devil's Law Case* (1609–12; IV.i–ii), and *Appius and Virginia* (after 1608; IV.i); George Chapman's *The Tragedy of Charles Duke of Byron* (1608; V.ii) and *Chabot* (date uncertain; III.ii, V.ii); Nathan Field and Philip Massinger's *The Fatal Dowry* (1616–19; I.ii, V.ii); John Fletcher and Philip Massinger's *The Spanish Curate* (1622; III.iii); and Ben Jonson's *Volpone* (1606; IV.ii), a scene in which Jonson gives us a brilliantly devastating portrait of the lawyer Voltore (vulture) as he subverts justice with a dazzling display of sophistry.

For further comment on the lawyer as a figure in literary satire (including the drama), see E. F. J. Tucker, *Intruder into Eden: Representations of the Common Lawyer in English Literature 1350–1750* (1984).

i

Of sundry kinds of punishment appointed for offenders

From William Harrison, *The Description of England*, bk. II, chap. 11 (in 1587 edn of Holinshed's *Chronicles*).

In cases of felony, manslaughter, robbery, murder, rape, piracy, and such capital crimes as are not reputed for treason or hurt of the estate, our sentence pronounced upon the offender is, to hang till he be dead. For of other punishments used in other countries we have no knowledge or use; and yet so few grievous crimes   5
committed with us as elsewhere in the world. To use torment also or question by pain and torture in these common cases with us is greatly abhorred, sith we are found always to be such as despise death, and yet abhor to be tormented, choosing rather frankly to open our minds than to yield our bodies unto such servile halings   10
and tearings as are used in other countries. And this is one cause wherefore our condemned persons do go so cheerfully to their deaths; for our nation is free, stout, haughty, prodigal of life and blood, as Sir Thomas Smith saith, lib. 2, cap. 25, *De Republica*, and therefore cannot in any wise digest to be used as villains and   15
slaves, in suffering continually beating, servitude, and servile torments. No, our gaolers are guilty of felony, by an old law of the land, if they torment any prisoner committed to their custody for the revealing of his complices.

The greatest and most grievous punishment used in England   20
for such as offend against the State is drawing from the prison to the place of execution upon an hurdle or sled, where they are hanged till they be half dead, and then taken down, and quartered alive; after that, their members and bowels are cut from their bodies, and thrown into a fire, provided near hand and within   25
their own sight, even for the same purpose.

Sometimes, if the trespass be not the more heinous, they are suffered to hang till they be quite dead. And whensover any of the nobility are convicted of high treason by their peers, that is to say, equals (for an inquest of yeomen passeth not upon them, but only   30
of the lords of parliament), this manner of their death is converted into the loss of their heads only, notwithstanding that the sentence do run after the former order. In trial of cases concerning treason, felony, or any other grievous crime not confessed, the party accused doth yield, if he be a noble man, to be tried by an inquest   35
(as I have said) and his peers; if a gentleman, by gentlemen; and an inferior, by God and by the country, to wit, the yeomanry (for combat or battle is not greatly in use), and, being condemned of felony, manslaughter, etc., he is eftsoons hanged by the neck till he be dead, and then cut down and buried. But if he be convicted   40

of wilful murder, done either upon pretended malice or in any
notable robbery, he is either hanged alive in chains near the place
where the fact was committed (or else, upon compassion taken,
first strangled with a rope), and so continueth till his bones
consume to nothing. We have use neither of the wheel nor of the   45
bar, as in other countries; but, when wilful manslaughter is
perpetrated, beside hanging, the offender hath his right hand
commonly stricken off before or near unto the place where the act
was done, after which he is led forth to the place of execution, and
there put to death according to the law......   50
    If a woman poison her husband, she is burned alive; if the
servant kill his master, he is to be executed for petty treason; he
that poisoneth a man is to be boiled to death in water or lead,
although the party die not of the practice; in cases of murder, all
the accessories are to suffer pains of death accordingly. Perjury is   55
punished by the pillory, burning in the forehead with the letter P,
the rewalting of the trees growing upon the grounds of the
offenders, and loss of all his moveables. Many trespasses also are
punished by the cutting off of one or both ears from the head of
the offender, as the utterance of seditious words against the   60
magistrates, fraymakers, petty robbers, etc. Rogues are burned
through the ears; carriers of sheep out of the land, by the loss of
their hands; such as kill by poison are either boiled or scalded to
death in lead for seething water. Heretics are burned quick;
harlots and their mates, by carting, ducking, and doing of open   65
penance in sheets in churches and market steads, are often put to
rebuke. Howbeit, as this is counted with some either as no
punishment at all to speak of, or but little regarded of the
offenders, so I would wish adultery and fornication to have some
sharper law. For what great smart is it to be turned out of an hot   70
sheet into a cold, or after a little washing in the water to be let
loose again unto their former trades? Howbeit the dragging of
some of them over the Thames between Lambeth and Westminster at the tail of a boat is a punishment that most terrifieth them
which are condemned thereto; but this is inflicted upon them by   75
none other than the Knight Marshall, and that within the compass
of his jurisdiction and limits only......
    Witches are hanged, or sometimes burned; but thieves are
hanged (as I said before) generally on the gibbet or gallows, saving
in Halifax, where they are beheaded after a strange manner, and   80
whereof I find this report. There is and hath been of ancient time
a law, or rather a custom, at Halifax, that whosoever does commit
any felony, and is taken with the same, or confess the fact upon
examination, if it be valued by four constables to amount to the
sum of thirteenpence-halfpenny, he is forthwith beheaded upon   85
one of the next market days (which fall usually upon the Tuesdays,
Thursdays, and Saturdays), or else upon the same day that he is so

convicted, if market be then holden. The engine wherewith the
execution is done is a square block of wood of the length of four
foot and a half, which doth ride up and down in a slot, rabbet, or 90
regal, between two pieces of timber, that are framed and set
upright, of five yards in height. In the nether end of the sliding
block is an axe, keyed or fastened with an iron into the wood,
which being drawn up to the top of the frame is there fastened by
a wooden pin (with a notch made into the same, after the manner 95
of a Samson's post), unto the middest of which pin also there is a
long rope fastened that cometh down among the people, so that,
when the offender hath made his confession and hath laid his neck
over the nethermost block, every man there present doth either
take hold of the rope (or putteth forth his arm so near to the same 100
as he can get, in token that he is willing to see true justice
executed), and, pulling out the pin in this manner, the head-block
wherein the axe is fastened doth fall down with such a violence
that, if the neck of the transgressor were so big as that of a bull, it
should be cut in sunder at a stroke and roll from the body by a 105
huge distance. If it be so that the offender be apprehended for an
ox, oxen, sheep, kine, horse, or any such cattle, the self beast or
other of the same kind shall have the end of the rope tied
somewhere unto them, so that they, being driven, do draw out the
pin, whereby the offender is executed...... 110

Rogues and vagabonds are often stocked and whipped; scolds
are ducked upon cucking-stools in the water. Such felons as stand
mute, and speak not at their arraignment, are pressed to death by
huge weights laid upon a board, that lieth over their breast, and a
sharp stone under their backs; and these commonly held their 115
peace, thereby to save their goods unto their wives and children,
which, if they were condemned, should be confiscated to the
prince. Thieves that are saved by their books and clergy, for the
first offence, if they have stolen nothing else but oxen, sheep,
money, or such like, which be no open robberies, as by the 120
highway side, or assailing of any man's house in the night, without
putting him in fear of his life, or breaking up his walls or doors,
are burned in the left hand, upon the brawn of the thumb, with a
hot iron, so that, if they be apprehended again, that mark
bewrayeth them to have been arraigned of felony before, whereby 125
they are sure at that time to have no mercy......

NOTES

3 *estate* administration of the government.
5 *yet* despite (this fact).
10 *halings* haulings, violent draggings.

14   *De Republica* i.e. *De Republica Anglorum. The Maner of Governement of England* (1583).

19   *complices* accomplices.

24   *members* i.e. privy members.

30   *inquest* jury.
      yeomen landholders below the rank of gentlemen.

30–1 *only of* only (an inquest or jury) of.

33   *after* according to.

38   *combat* i.e. trial by combat. Compare Shakespeare, *II Henry VI*, II.iii.59–105.

39   *eftsoons* soon afterwards.

41   *pretended* intended.

45   *wheel* contrivance, resembling a wheel, used in various ways as an instrument of torture.

46   *bar* iron bar used for breaking felons on the wheel.

54   *the party* i.e. the person poisoned.

57   *rewalting* tearing down.

61   *fraymakers* creators of disturbances.

64   *quick* alive.

66   *steads* places.

73–4 *between......Westminster* i.e. from the south bank to the north bank.

75–6 *by......than* by no one except.

76   *Knight Marshall* officer of the royal household, who had judicial cognizance of transgressions committed within a twelve-mile radius of the royal palace.

80   *Halifax* town in Yorkshire.

88   *engine* machine, a forerunner of the French guillotine.

90–1 *rabbet or regal* synonyms for 'groove'.

92   *nether* lower.

96   *Samson's post* kind of mousetrap.

112   *cucking-stools* chairs in which the offenders were exposed to the jeers of the spectators or were ducked in pond or river.

112–13 *stand mute* i.e. will not plead 'Guilty' or 'Not guilty'. The Press-yard in old Newgate Prison was the original scene of this barbarous form of torture. Harrison seems to have overlooked this when he claims (ll. 6–11) that English law 'abhorred' torture. See, also, selection (ii).

118   *books and clergy* By pleading 'benefit of clergy' (by this time simply the rights accorded to one who could read his so-called 'neck-verse' in Latin, usually the opening of the fifty-first psalm), the death sentence for some felonies could be evaded for first offenders. Ben Jonson, for example, by pleading his 'clergy' in a case of 'manslaughter' (the death of Gabriel Spencer in a duel), was burned in the thumb and escaped the death penalty, though his goods were confiscated.

121–2 *without putting him* i.e. so long as he didn't put him.

125   *bewrayeth* betrayeth.

ii

The treatment of Catholic priests under Elizabeth

From Robert Southwell, *An Humble Supplication to Her Majestie* (1595; ed. R. C. Bald (1953), pp. 33–4). [Southwell replies to the charge in the Queen's proclamation of 1591 that Catholic priests had admitted that they 'would take part with any army of the Pope against our realm'.]

......it is a most unlikely thing, unless it were pressed out of some frail tongue by force of torture, that was rather willing to say what they seemed to require than to abide the hell of so intollerable torments......It is not enough to confess we are priests, for that is seldom denied; but we must be urged upon the 5
torture with other odious interrogatories far from our knowledge, much farther from our action. We are compelled to accuse those whom our conscience assureth us to be innocent, and to cause their overthrows by our confession, to whose souls we were pastors, and they the fosterers of our bodies; and if we do not, 10
because without untruth or injury we cannot answer, we are so unmercifully tormented that our deaths, though as full of pangs as hanging, drawing, and unbowelling quick can make them, are unto us rather remedies than further revenges, more releasing than increasing our miseries. Some are hanged by the hands eight or 15
nine or twelve hours together, till not only their wits, but even their senses, fail them; and when the soul, weary of so painful an harbour, is ready to depart, they apply cruel comforts, and revive us, only to martyr us with more deaths; for eftsoons they hang us up in the same manner,......Some are whipped naked so long 20
and with such excess that our enemies, unwilling to give constancy her right name, said that no man without the help of the Devil could with such undauntedness suffer so much. Some, beside their tortures, have been forced to lie continually booted and cloathed many weeks together, pined in their diet, consumed with vermin, 25
and almost stifled with stench. Some have been watched and kept from sleep till they were past the use of reason, and then examined upon the advantage, when they could scarcely give accompt of their own names. Some have been tortured in such parts as is almost a torture to Christian ears to hear it; let it then be judged 30
what it was to chaste and modest men to endure it, the shame being no less offensive to their minds than the pain (though most excessive) to their bodies. Divers have been thrown into unsavoury and dark dungeons, and brought so near starving, that some for famine have licked the very moisture off the walls;......What 35
unsufferable agonies we have been put to upon the rack, it is not possible to express, the feeling so far exceedeth all speech. Some with instruments have been rolled up together like a ball and so

crushed that the blood sprouted out at divers parts of their
bodies......It is not possible to keep any reckoning of the   40
ordinary punishments of Bridewell, now made the common
purgatory of priests and Catholics, as grinding in the mill, being
beaten like slaves, and other outrageous usages. For to these are
we forced at the discretion of such as, being to all other despised
underlings, take a felicity in laying their commandements and   45
showing their authority upon us, to whom every warder, porter,
and jailor is an unresisted lord.

NOTES

6   *interrogatories* questions.

10   *they......bodies* i.e. Catholic sympathizers, who had given them refuge
and sustenance. See 'Church and State', selection (iii).

13   *hanging......unbowelling* See above, selection (i), ll. 20–6. This was the
punishment accorded condemned traitors, except for members of the
nobility, who were beheaded.
    quick alive.

25   *pined......diet* made feeble from lack of food.

26   *watched* kept under close observation.

28   *upon the advantage* i.e. taking advantage of their state of mind (from loss
of sleep).
    accompt account (variant form).

39   *sprouted* shot forth.

41   *Bridewell* house of correction, usually for prostitutes and 'idle knaves'.
The Clink was more usually used for religious prisoners. See a scene in
Bridewell in Thomas Dekker's *II Honest Whore* (1604–5), v.ii.

44   *other* others.

45   *commandements* (quadrisyllabic) commandments, orders (variant form).

iii

From Thomas Lodge and Robert Greene, *A Looking-Glass for London and England* (written 1587–91, published 1594), lines 290–403 (in Malone Society Reprints, ed. W. W. Greg, 1932).

Enter the USURER, *a young Gentleman* [THRASYBULUS], *and a poor man* [ALCON]

USURER. Come on, I am every day troubled with these needy companions. What news with you? What wind brings you hither?

THRASYBULUS. Sir, I hope, how far soever you make it off, you remember too well for me, that this is the day wherein I should 5 pay you money that I took up of you alate in a commodity.

ALCON. And, sir, sir-reverence of your manhood and gentry, I have brought home such money as you lent me.

USURER. You, young gentleman, is my money ready?

THRASYBULUS. Truly, sir, this time was so short, the commodity so 10 bad, and the promise of friends so broken, that I could not provide it against the day; wherefore I am come to entreat you to stand my friend and to favour me with a longer time, and I will make you sufficient consideration.

USURER. Is the wind in that door? If thou hast my money, so it is; I 15 will not defer a day, an hour, a minute, but take the forfeit of the bond.

THRASYBULUS. I pray you sir, consider that my loss was great by the commodity I took up. You know, sir, I borrowed of you forty pounds, whereof I had ten pounds in money and thirty 20 pounds in lute-strings, which when I came to sell again, I could get but five pounds for them; so had I, sir, but fifteen pounds for my forty. In consideration of this ill bargain, I pray you, sir, give me a month longer.

USURER. I answered thee afore, not a minute. What have I to do 25 how thy bargain proved? I have thy hand set to my book that thou received'st forty pounds of me in money.

THRASYBULUS. Ay, sir, it was your device that, to colour the statute, but your conscience knows what I had.

ALCON. Friend, thou speakest Hebrew to him when thou talkest to 30 him of conscience, for he hath as much conscience about the forfeit of an obligation as my blind mare, God bless her, hath over a manger of oats.

THRASYBULUS. Then there is no favour, sir?

USURER. Come tomorrow to me, and see how I will use thee. 35

THRASYBULUS. No, covetous caterpillar, know that I have made extreme shift rather than I would fall into the hands of such a ravening panther; and therefore here is thy money and deliver me the recognizance of my lands.

USURER. [*Aside.*] What a spite is this – hath sped of his crowns! If 40 he had missed but one half hour, what a goodly farm had I gotten for forty pounds! Well, 'tis my cursed fortune. O, have I no shift to make him forfeit his recognizance?

THRASYBULUS. Come, sir, will you dispatch and tell your money?
Strikes four a'clock

USURER. [*Aside.*] Stay, what is this a'clock? Four; let me see – 'to 45 be paid between the hours of three and four in the afternoon'. This goes right for me. – You, sir, hear you not the clock, and have you not a counterpane of your obligation? The hour is past; it was to be paid between three and four; and now the clock hath strucken four. I will receive none; I'll stand to the 50 forfeit of the recognizance.

THRASYBULUS. Why, sir, I hope you do but jest; why, 'tis but four, and will you for a minute sake take forfeit of my bond? If it were so, sir, I was here before four.

USURER. Why didst thou not tender thy money then? If I offer thee 55 injury, take the law of me; complain to the judge. I will receive no money.

ALCON. Well, sir, I hope you will stand my good master for my cow. I borrowed thirty shillings on her, and for that I have paid you eighteen pence a week, and for her meat you have had her 60 milk; and I tell you, sir, she gives a goodly sup. Now, sir, here is your money.

USURER. Hang, beggarly knave! Comest to me for a cow? Did I not bind her bought and sold for a penny? And was not thy day to have paid yesterday? Thou gett'st no cow at my hand. 65

ALCON. No cow, sir! alas, that word 'no cow' goes as cold to my heart as a draught of small drink in a frosty morning. No cow, sir! why, alas, alas, Master Usurer, what shall become of me, my wife, and my poor child?

USURER. Thou gett'st no cow of me, knave; I cannot stand prating 70 with you, I must be gone.

ALCON. Nay, but hear you, Master Usurer: 'no cow', why, sir, here's your thirty shillings. I have paid you eighteen pence a week, and therefore there is reason I should have my cow.

USURER. What pratest thou? Have I not answered thee thy day is   75
broken?

ALCON. Why, sir, alas, my cow is a commonwealth to me: for first,
sir, she allows me, my wife, and son for to banquet our selves
withal – butter, cheese, whey, curds, cream, sod-milk, raw-
milk, sour-milk, sweet-milk, and butter-milk: besides, sir, she   80
saved me every year a penny in almanacs, for she was as good to
me as a prognostication; if she had but set up her tail and have
galloped about the mead, my little boy was able to say, 'O,
father, there will be a storm'; her very tail was a calendar to me:
and now to lose my cow! Alas, Master Usurer, take pity upon   85
me.

USURER. I have other matters to talk on; farewell, fellows.

THRASYBULUS. Why, but, thou covetous churl, wilt thou not
receive thy money and deliver me my recognizance?

USURER. I'll deliver thee none; if I have wronged thee, seek thy   90
mends at the law.   [Exit]

THRASYBULUS. And so I will, insatiable peasant.

ALCON. And, sir, rather than I will put up this word 'no cow', I will
lay my wife's best gown to pawn. I tell you, sir, when the slave
uttered this word 'no cow', it struck to my heart, for my wife   95
shall never have one so fit for her turn again; for indeed, sir, she
is a woman that hath her twiddling-strings broke.

THRASYBULUS. What meanest thou by that, fellow?

ALCON. Marry, sir, sir-reverence of your manhood, she breaks
wind behind; and indeed, sir, when she sat milking of her cow   100
and let a fart, my other cows would start at the noise and kick
down the milk, and away; but this cow, sir, the gentlest cow!
my wife might blow whilst she burst. And having such good
conditions, shall the Usurer come upon me with 'no cow'? Nay,
sir, before I pocket up this word 'no cow', my wife's gown goes   105
to the lawyer. Why, alas, sir, 'tis as ill a word to me as 'no
crown' to a king.

THRASYBULUS. Well, fellow, go with me and I'll help thee to a
lawyer.

ALCON. Marry, and I will, sir. 'No cow!' well, the world goes hard.   110
                                                                    Exeunt

[In a later scene, we witness the ministrations of the 'law'. Their
lawyer (Signor Mizaldo) assures Thrasybulus and Alcon that their
cases against the Usurer are 'evident', but, after both he and the
Judge accept bribes from the Usurer, their cases are decided in
favour of the Usurer.]

NOTES

2   *companions* fellows (used pejoratively).

4–5 *how.......me* i.e. however much you may pretend not to know why I am here, you remember it all too well to suit me.

6   *alate* lately.

      commodity goods sold on credit by a usurer to a needy person, who immediately raised some cash by reselling them at a lower price (often to the usurer himself).

7   *sir-reverence of* with all respect for (?ironic).

14   *consideration* compensation (above the original money owed).

15   *Is......door?* Is this the direction things are taking?

      so it is i.e. that's acceptable.

28–9 *colour the statute* give the appearance of conforming to the limitations of the statute on usury (1571) by which the lender could not exceed 10 per cent in interest.

32   *obligation* written contract or bond under seal containing a penalty with a condition annexed.

36–7 *made extreme shift* taken extreme measures.

39   *recognizance* obligation, statute bond (see l. 32).

48   *counterpane* duplicate copy.

53   *minute sake* uninflected genitive.

      If even though.

58–9 *stand......cow* play the part of a good man so far as my cow is concerned.

60   *for* in lieu of.

61   *sup* mouthful.

64   *bind......penny* i.e. according to the condition of the bond, the terms of the bargain and sale.

66   *word* phrase.

67   *small drink* weak beer.

70   *prating* chattering.

77   *commonwealth* source of general well-being.

78–9 *for......withal* to feast (used ironically?) ourselves therewith.

79   *sod-milk* boiled milk.

81   *a penny* either the price of an almanac (often titled 'An Almanac or Prognostication' for a given year) or = some money.

84   *calendar* indication or sign (apparently peculiar to Lodge in this sense; see *OED*).

87   *fellows* Compare 'companions' l. 2.

88   *churl* low-bred miser.

91   *mends* amends, reparations.

97   *twiddling-strings* vulgar expression for the *sphincter ani*.

99   *Marry* mild oath, 'by the Virgin Mary'.

101 *my other cows* i.e. other cows he had had before this one.

103–4 *good conditions* satisfactory state of affairs.

10 Old science and new philosophy

Astrology

Two main branches of astrology must be distinguished: Natural Astrology (concerned with the movement of the heavenly bodies and natural phenomena such as tides, eclipses, etc.), the forerunner of modern astronomy; and Judicial Astrology (concerned with predicting the influence of the stars on human affairs). The former was generally recognized as a 'science'. Judicial astrology, however, though of very ancient origins, fell under attack by the Italian humanist, Pico della Mirandola, as early as 1495 and later polemics both for and against appeared on the Continent and in England throughout the Renaissance and later (see Don C. Allen, *The Star-Crossed Renaissance* (1941) and Wayne Shumaker, *The Occult Sciences in the Renaissance* (1972)), and a form of judicial astrology is still practised even today. Pico set the tone of later attacks, calling judicial astrology 'a cheat of mercenary liars, prohibited by both civil and church law, preserved by human curiosity, mocked by philosophers, cultivated by itinerant hawkers, and suspect to the best and most prudent men' (Shumaker, p. 18). Strong words, but like numerous succeeding 'discoveries' of alleged fraud, they had little effect on the popular (and sometimes learned) belief in the 'science' of prognostication by horoscopes or 'figure casting'. Queen Elizabeth had her personal astrologer, Dr John Dee, an eminent mathematician and Hermetic philosopher, who, for example, forecast the most propitious day for her coronation (Peter J. French, *John Dee: The World of an Elizabethan Magus* (1972), p. 6), and horoscopes were regularly cast at the birth of an heir by high and low alike. Edward VI's horoscope predicted his death in his fifty-fifth year (he died in his sixteenth; the horoscope, later published, was allegedly doctored to fit the facts) and, several hundred years after, two horoscopes were cast for Edward VII.

The technical details of judicial astrology cannot be discussed here (see Shumaker), but one particularly damaging 'aspect' of the practice (even today) may be noticed. Horoscopes, since the time of Ptolemy (second century AD), have been based on a purely arbitrary zodiac invented by Ptolemy himself, which even then, as he knew, failed to allow for the precession of the equinoxes, i.e. 'the zodiacal band changes its position relative to a given point on the ecliptic by one sign in about 2,000 years' (Shumaker, p. 15). Thus, 'the influence of the imaginary Aries is still supposed to flow from the position already mostly occupied by Aquarius and soon to be wholly occupied by it.' As Shumaker adds: 'This gross fiction underlies every horoscope cast from Ptolemy's time to our own.'

The selection, from John Melton's *Astrologaster* (1620), presents a no-

nonsense case against a particular (but representative) quack, 'Doctor *P. C.*', who practises, on an all-too-gullible public, not only 'sacred astrology, divine astrology, the Art of Arts, the Science of Sciences' (p. 11), but the mysteries of medicine, alchemy and magic. Unlike most other treatises on the subject, *pro* and *con*, Melton writes in an easy colloquial (sometimes literary) style aimed at the ordinary reader, and the portrait he gives us of 'Master Doctor' magisterially seated at his table waiting for unwary victims is memorable. See, also, Philip Stubbes (*The Second Part of the Anatomie of Abuses* (1583; sigs. H5 v–I8 r)), who, after a long diatribe against astronomers and astrologers, 'star tooters [gazers]' as he calls them, says: 'I neither condemn astronomy, nor astrology, nor yet the makers of prognostications or almanacs for the year. But I condemn the abuse of them both' (sig. I7 r), and Francis Bacon ('Of Prophecies', in *Essayes* (1625; no. 35)).

A scene (II.ii) in Philip Massinger's *The City Madam* (1632) nicely exposes the self-seeking subterfuges of the judicial astrologer in the character of Stargaze, who, like Dr *P. C.*, is a quack-of-all trades. Massinger's satire, however, is two-pronged: judicial astrology is turned to ridicule through the presumption and pretence of the loquacious Stargaze, with his stream of 'learned' jargon aimed more at obfuscation than meaning; and the social climbing and merely mercenary motives of arranged marriages are sharply criticized.

Shakespeare, somewhat ambiguously perhaps, uses an apparently credulous belief in judicial astrology to characterize Gloucester in *King Lear* (I.ii.118–33) and assigns its summary dismissal to the villain Edmund:

> This is the excellent foppery of the world, that when we are sick in fortune – often the surfeits of our own behavior – we make guilty of our disasters the sun, the moon, and stars, as if we were villains on necessity, fools by heavenly compulsion, knaves, thieves, and treachers by spherical predominance; drunkards, liars, and adulterers by an enforc'd obedience to planetary influence; and all that we are evil in, by a divine thrusting on. An admirable evasion of whoremaster man, to lay his goatish disposition on the charge of a star! My father compounded with my mother under the Dragon's tail, and my nativity was under Ursa Major, so that it follows, I am rough and lecherous. Fut, I should have been that I am, had the maidenl'est star in the firmament twickled on my bastardizing.

On the other hand, John Webster in *The Duchess of Malfi* (1612–14; II.iii) employs a horoscope cast for the Duchess's first child by her secret husband, Antonio, as a serious plot device. Ironically, though the irony seems unintentional, this is the only one of her children by Antonio still alive at the end of the play, despite the fact that the 'nativity' had forecast a short life and violent death. A gang of four rogue astrologers is used to complicate the plot in John Fletcher's *The Bloody Brother*

(1616–24); a similar character figures in Thomas Tomkis's *Albumazer* (1615), an academic Cambridge comedy strongly influenced by Jonson's *Alchemist* (1610); and the shady practices of what were called 'wise women', a kind of poor man's surrogate for the astrologer, many of whom flourished in and around London and in the countryside, preying on the illiterate, are neatly exposed by Thomas Heywood in *The Wise Woman of Hogsdon* (c.1604).

From John Melton, *Astrologaster, or, The Figure-Caster* (1620), pp. 4–8 (see a facsimile reprint in Augustan Reprint Society, no. 174x (1975)). [Melton imagines himself walking in a garden where he encounters 'some twenty women that came talking and walking down an alley' followed by an 'ancient man'. He asks the 'ancient man' where all these chattering women were bound.]

'Son', said he,......'these women your eyes did lately take notice of are creatures so ignorantly obstinate that neither the mild entreaty of a friend can persuade them from their follies, nor the bad report of an enemy dissuade them from their perverseness. The party to whom they come is a bird, of whose kind I think 5 there are but few living, for he professeth himself to be a Wise-man; and the cause of their coming is to be resolved either of money, silver spoons, rings, gowns, plate, or linen they have lost; some, to know how many children they shall have; some, how many husbands, and which shall love them best; others, about 10 other business; but, in general, all of them to know something which indeed at the last comes to nothing. And I myself (like a holiday fool) have been there at the least half a score times, only to give my money away to be laughed at......
'For going to the Cross one Sunday morning to hear a sermon, 15 some *Mercurian* and nimble-finger'd pickpocket, that had more mind of my purse than the preacher, gelt it of sixteen pound; so that I went home lighter by two stone than I went out. After I had fretted much, and to no purpose, I used all the means I could to recover my loss, as by seeing the Keepers of Newgate, who know 20 which of that law are appointed to filch in every part of the City; yet still I came home a greater loser than I went out; for always being in hope to find that which I lost, I lost more by bribing one knave to discover another. At the last, it was my bad fortune to meet with an old woman, that put a greater confidence in the 25 Jews' *Cabals* and *Talmud*, the *Shepherds' Kalendar*, and books of Palmistry than any part of the Bible, who advised me to repair to Doctor *P. C.* in Moorfields,......so giving this old piece of superstition a tester for her news, I instantly went to Master Doctor, who, perceiving me to be one that loved gold well 30 (because age most commonly is covetous), thought the better to work upon me, as he did; for his Doctorship had the art to hold me in hand three weeks, in which time he made the sixteen pounds I lost twenty; and when all came to a period, he told me that he had laboured hard for me and, at the last, by his no small 35 industry and pains, had found out the thief that had my money, but he was fled into the Low Countries, because there were many warrants out to apprehend him for many thefts and burglaries he

had committed; and if it pleased me to take shipping and sail
thither, I should be sure to find him at the *Labour in Vain* in   40
Bredau......Yet howsoever I may doubt, nay, truly resolve
myself, that he hath palpably cheated me, yet it was impossible to
find him a liar, except I meant to take more pains about it than it
was worth. Therefore, as patiently as I am able, I am going home
again, purposing hereafter to take heed of two pickpockets: the   45
one, the diver that met with me in Paul's Churchyard; the other,
the Doctor in Moorfields that robb'd me as well as the first, who in
my mind hath deserved, for his artificial cheating, the pillory, as
well as the other did the gallows for stealing......'

[Melton decides to visit Master Doctor in disguise in order to
expose him.]

Therefore, on a morning which was as calm as I could wish my   50
thoughts now were, I put on a suit of coarse northern dozens, with
all accoutrements that were most suitable to that homeliness, and
with all expedition went to Master Doctor; and, hastily knocking
at his worship's door, there came running down the stairs with a
nimble dexterity (the little *Mephistopheles*) his boy, demanding   55
with whom I would speak; to whom, in a broad Somerset
language, I answered, 'With Master Doctor, upon an urgent
business'. Upon the delivery of this message, this young spirit, like
exhaled dew, nimbly flew away from me, who upon an instant, like
a flash of lightning, was in my bosom again before I could perceive   60
him; and then, without any more interrogatories, marshalled me
up into his master's study, who sat in this manner following:
Before a square table, covered with a green carpet, on which lay
a huge book in folio, wide open, full of strange characters, such as
the Egyptians and Chaldeans were never guilty of; not far from   65
that a silver wand, a surplice, a watering pot, with all the
superstitious or rather feigned instruments of his cozening art.
And to put a fairer colour on his black and foul science, on his
head he had a four-cornered cap, on his back a fair gown (but
made of a strange fashion); in his right hand he held an astrolabe,   70
in his left, a mathematical glass. At the first view, there was no
man that came to him (if he were of any fashion) could offer him
for his advice less than a Jacobus, and the meanest half a piece,
although he, peradventure, rather than have nothing, would be
contented with a brace of two-pences.   75

[With the humility proper to his disguise, Melton pretends to have
lost a 'chain of gold of three hundred links', tips with a gold angel,
and is treated to an 'oration' by Master Doctor laying out his
expertise in magic, astrology and medicine. Melton then treats
Master Doctor (pp. 15–80) to a detailed refutation, point by point,
of all the supposed tenets of astrology.]

NOTES

6–7 *Wise-man* one skilled in hidden arts, magic, witchcraft, astrology, etc.

7 *to be......of* to be informed about.

13 *holiday fool* simpleton, who, on a holiday occasion, spends his money foolishly. Cf. Shakespeare, *The Tempest*, II.ii.29–30.

15 *Cross* Paul's Cross, in St Paul's Churchyard, at which open-air sermons were delivered.

16 *Mercurian* one under the protection of Mercury, the Roman god and patron of thieves and traders. Autolycus, the rogue in *The Winter's Tale*, was 'litter'd under Mercury' (IV.iii.25).

17 *gelt* castrated (i.e. by a 'nip', one who cut purses).

18 *two stone* Melton considers a 'stone' weight to be eight pounds (more usually fourteen pounds); probable play on 'stone'=testicle.

20 *Keepers of Newgate* warders of Newgate, a principal London prison. Melton characterizes them as 'knaves' (l. 24). See 'London: life and sights', (ii).

21 *law* i.e. figging law, the fraternity of pickpockets (see introductory note to 'The underworld in town and country', p. 226).

26 *Cabals* the unwritten tradition (the 'cabbala') supposedly handed down from Moses to post-biblical Rabbis.
    Talmud the body of Jewish civil and traditionary law (AD 200–408); like the 'cabbala' associated with mysterious 'learning'.
    Shepherds' Kalendar i.e. *The Kalender of Shepherdes*, a popular fifteenth-century French manual (three English translations), containing astrological, moral, and medical information and lurid woodcuts. Not to be confused with Spenser's *The Shepheardes Calendar* (1579).

28 *Doctor P. C.* probably a reference to a real individual with these initials, who practised his 'art' in Moorfields, a district directly north of the old London city walls.

29 *tester* silver coin worth sixpence.

32–3 *hold......hand* keep me in expectation.

40 *Labour in Vain* an inn (an invented name to suggest the futility of his pursuit).

41 *Bredau* Breda, city in northern Brabant, Netherlands.

43 *find* prove.

46 *diver* pickpocket.

48 *artificial* artfully cunning (with play on Master Doctor's 'art').
    pillory wooden framework, with two movable boards having holes through which the head and hands of an offender were thrust, while he (or she) stood undergoing the taunts of the public for a stated number of hours.

51 *dozens* kind of coarse woollen cloth.

55 *little Mephistopheles* i.e. small devil. Melton is probably thinking of Marlowe's *Dr Faustus*, making an analogy between Master Doctor and Faustus as conjurors. He refers to the play on p. 31.

57 *language* dialect.

59 *exhaled dew* dew evaporating.

63 *carpet* table covering.

64 *book in folio* volume in folio format, roughly $7\frac{1}{2}$ by $12\frac{1}{2}$ in.

65 *Egyptians and Chaldeans* often referred to as the founders of magic and astrology.

66 *surplice* loose vestment of white linen (meant to suggest Master Doctor's 'purity'?).

watering pot vase representing the zodiacal constellation Aquarius (one of the twelve signs of the zodiac, a central concept in astrology).

70   *astrolabe* instrument for taking altitudes in both natural and judicial astrology.

71   *mathematical glass* perhaps a magic mirror or crystal, or simply an optic glass or telescope. Master Doctor claims to be able to see what is going on throughout the world by looking into it (pp. 10–11).

73   *Jacobus* gold coin, first minted under James I, worth twenty to twenty-four shillings; also known as a 'sovereign'.

half a piece ?gold coin, worth about ten shillings, equivalent to an 'angel'.

Alchemy

As in the case of astrology, alchemy must be viewed from two levels. The first was mystical or philosphical alchemy, a complicated amalgam of 'natural' and 'demonic' magic, Hermetic mysteries, neo-Platonism and Christianity, through which a magus, like, for example, Shakespeare's Prospero or the celebrated Dr John Dee, sought to understand and master the secrets not only of the natural world of created things (the 'book of the creatures') but the supernatural world of spirits. Hence grew Dee's famous, if controversial, angelic visions, which were reported to him through his medium, Edward Kelley, who is generally thought to have duped Dee by playing on his credulity and profound religious faith (see Peter J. French, *John Dee: The World of an Elizabethan Magus* (1972)). The second level, chemical alchemy, is what is usually thought of when we speak of alchemy today, and it may, in its concern with physical experiments, though not in its theory, be considered the forerunner of modern chemistry. The ultimate aim of the chemical alchemist was the production of the Elixir or the Philosophers' Stone, the 'medicine of men and metals' and a 'sovereign cure for all ills' (see Wayne Shumaker, *The Occult Sciences in the Renaissance* (1972), pp. 178, 193). Thus, we might say, health and wealth were the alchemist's goals, but it was the second, his claim to be able to transmute base metals into gold or silver, through the operation of the Philosophers' Stone, that most appealed to innate human greed (though the alchemist himself was supposed to be above such self-serving motives) and led to the emergence of the quack alchemist who, like the quack astrologer, fleeced a gullible public.

The first well-known English exposé of the rogue alchemist is, of course, Chaucer's 'Canon's Yeoman's Tale' in *The Canterbury Tales*. The Yeoman, the Canon's laboratory assistant, reveals, with a great deal of technical detail, the mercenary chicanery that motivates his master's supposed search for 'the stone', and several hundred years later little has changed as Thomas Nashe complains (*Have with You to Saffron-Walden* (1596), ed. McKerrow, III, 52): 'Whether you call his fire purgatory or no, the fire of alchumy hath wrought such a purgation or purgatory in a great number of men's purses in England that it hath clean fired them out of all they have.' And John Donne, though admitting that occasional useful by-products might result from the search for the Philosophers' Stone, denies the whole concept:

> O! 'tis imposture all;
> And as no chemic yet th'Elixir got,
>   But glorifies his pregnant pot,
>   If by the way to him befall
> Some odoriferous thing, or med'cinal,
>   So lovers dream a rich and long delight,
>   But get a winter-seeming summer's night.
>
> ('Loves Alchymie')

Aside from Chaucer's satiric tale, the best-known literary 'discovery' of alchemy is Ben Jonson's play, *The Alchemist* (1610; see the following selection). Three rogues, Subtle, Face and Dol Common, the 'venter tripartite' as they call themselves, run the whole gamut of cheating devices, practising not only alchemy (on which Jonson lays the principal emphasis in the Sir Epicure Mammon and Tribulation/Ananias episodes) but judicial astrology (the Drugger episodes), demonology (the Dapper episodes, in which Dol plays the role of the Fairy Queen), marriage broking and procurement and the techniques of 'quarrelling' by the book. Jonson again attacks alchemy in his masque, *Mercury Vindicated from the Alchemists at Court* (1616); and Robert Burton, author of *The Anatomy of Melancholy* (1621), under Jonson's banner, devotes several scenes (IV.i, iv; V.iii) of his Latin academic comedy, *Philosophaster* (1617), translated Paul Jordan-Smith (1931), to exposing the mercenary basis of chemical alchemy.

From Ben Jonson, *The Alchemist* (1610), II.iii. [Subtle, the Alchemist, is supposedly about to produce the Philosophers' Stone for one of his dupes, Sir Epicure Mammon. Sir Epicure, with the sceptical Surly, has arrived full of greedy, grandiose, and 'golden' dreams.]

[*Enter*] SUBTLE

MAMMON. Good morrow, Father.

SUBTLE. Gentle son, good morrow,
And, to your friend, there. What is he, is with you?

MAMMON. An heretic, that I did bring along,
In hope, sir, to convert him.

SUBTLE. Son, I doubt
Yo'are covetous, that thus you meet your time   5
I' the just point: prevent your day, at morning.
This argues something, worthy of a fear
Of importune and carnal appetite.
Take heed, you do not cause the blessing leave you,
With your ungovern'd haste. I should be sorry,   10
To see my labours, now, e'en at perfection,
Got by long watching, and large patience,
Not prosper, where my love, and zeal hath plac'd 'hem.
Which (heaven I call to witness, with yourself,
To whom, I have pour'd my thoughts) in my ends,   15
Have looked no way, but unto public good,
To pious uses, and dear charity,
Now grown a prodigy with men. Wherein
If you, my son, should now prevaricate,
And, to your own particular lusts, employ   20
So great, and catholic a bliss: be sure,
A curse will follow, yea, and overtake
Your subtle, and most secret ways.

MAMMON. I know, sir,
You shall not need to fear me. I but come,
To ha' you confute this gentleman.

SURLY. Who is,   25
Indeed, sir, somewhat costive of belief
Toward your stone: would not be gull'd.

SUBTLE. Well, son,
All that I can convince in, is this,
The work is done: bright Sol is in his robe.
We have a med'cine of the triple soul,   30

    The glorified spirit. Thanks to be heaven,
    And make us worthy of it. Eulenspiegel!

FACE. [*Within*]
    Anon, sir.

SUBTLE.   Look well to the register,
    And let your heat, still, lessen by degrees,
    To the aludels.

FACE. [*Within*]   Yes, sir.

SUBTLE.   Did you look   35
    O' the bolt's-head yet?

FACE. [*Within*]   Which, on D, sir?

SUBTLE.   Ay.
    What's the complexion?

FACE. [*Within*]   Whitish.

SUBTLE.   Infuse vinegar,
    To draw his volatile substance, and his tincture:
    And let the water in glass E be filtered,
    And put into the gripe's egg. Lute him well;   40
    And leave him clos'd in *balneo.*

FACE. [*Within*]   I will, sir.

SURLY. What a brave language here is? Next to canting?

SUBTLE. I have another work you never saw, son,
    That, three days since, pass'd the philosophers' wheel,
    In the lent heat of Athanor, and's become   45
    Sulphur o' nature.

MAMMON.   But 'tis for me?

SUBTLE.   What need you?
    You have enough in that is perfect.

MAMMON.   O, but –

SUBTLE. Why, this is covetise!

MAMMON.   No, I assure you,
    I shall employ it all, in pious uses,
    Founding of colleges, and grammar schools,   50
    Marrying young virgins, building hospitals,
    And now, and then, a church.

                [*Enter* FACE]

SUBTLE.   How now?

FACE.   Sir, please you,

Shall I not change the filter?

SUBTLE.   Marry, yes.
        And bring me the complexion of glass B...... [*Exit* FACE]

[The bandying of 'terms of art' continues and Subtle, with Face's
assistance, mulcts the delighted Sir Epicure of some more money,
though Subtle generously says:]

SUBTLE. This needs not. But that you will have it, so,   55
        To see conclusions of all. For two
        Of our inferior works, are at fixation.
        A third is in ascension. Go your ways.
        Ha' you set the oil of Luna in kemia?

FACE. Yes, sir.

SUBTLE.   And the philosophers' vinegar?

FACE.   Ay.   [*Exit* FACE]   60

SURLY. We shall have a salad.

MAMMON.   When do you make projection?

SUBTLE. Son, be not hasty, I exalt our med'cine,
        By hanging him in *balneo vaporoso*;
        And giving him solution; then congeal him;
        And then dissolve him; then again congeal him;   65
        For look, how oft I iterate the work,
        So many times, I add unto his virtue.
        As, if at first, one ounce convert a hundred,
        After his second loose, he'll turn a thousand;
        His third solution, ten; his fourth, a hundred.   70
        After his fifth, a thousand thousand ounces
        Of any imperfect metal, into pure
        Silver, or gold, in all examinations,
        As good as any of the natural mine.
        Get you your stuff here, against afternoon,   75
        Your brass, your pewter, and your andirons.

MAMMON. Not those of iron?

SUBTLE.   Yes, you may bring them, too.
        We'll change all metals.

SURLY.   I believe you, in that.

MAMMON. Then I may send my spits?

SUBTLE.   Yes, and your racks.

SURLY. And dripping pans, and pot-hangers, and hooks?   80
        Shall he not?

SUBTLE. If he please.

SURLY. To be an ass.

SUBTLE. How, sir!

MAMMON. This gent'man, you must bear withal.
I told you, he had no faith.

SURLY. And little hope, sir,
But, much less charity, should I gull myself.

SUBTLE. Why, what have you observ'd, sir, in our art, 85
Seems so impossible?

SURLY. But your whole work, no more.
That you should hatch gold in a furnace, sir,
As they do eggs in Egypt!

SUBTLE. Sir, do you
Believe that eggs are hatch'd so?

SURLY. If I should?

SUBTLE. Why, I think that the greater miracle. 90
No egg, but differs from a chicken, more,
Than metals in themselves.

SURLY. That cannot be.
The egg's ordain'd by nature, to that end:
And is a chicken in *potentia*.

SUBTLE. The same we say of lead, and other metals, 95
Which would be gold, if they had time.

MAMMON. And that
Our art doth further.

SUBTLE. Ay, for 'twere absurd
To think that nature, in the earth, bred gold
Perfect, i' the instant. Something went before.
There must be remote matter.

SURLY. Ay, what is that? 100

SUBTLE. Marry, we say –

MAMMON. Ay, now it heats: stand, Father.
Pound him to dust –

SUBTLE. It is, of the one part,
A humid exhalation, which we call
Materia liquida, or the unctuous water;
On th' other part, a certain crass, and viscous 105
Portion of earth; both which, concorporate,

Do make the elementary matter of gold:
Which is not, yet, *propria materia*,
But common to all metals, and all stones.
For, where it is forsaken of that moisture   110
And hath more dryness, it becomes a stone;
Where it retains more of the humid fatness,
It turns to sulphur, or to quicksilver,
Who are the parents of all other metals.
Nor can this remote matter, suddenly,   115
Progress so from extreme, unto extreme,
As to grow gold, and leap o'er all the means.
Nature doth, first, beget th' imperfect; then
Proceeds she to the perfect. Of that airy,
And oily water, mercury is engender'd;   120
Sulphur o' the fat and earthy part: the one
(Which is the last) supplying the place of male,
The other of the female, in all metals.
Some do believe hermaphrodeity,
That both do act, and suffer. But, these two   125
Make the rest ductile, malleable, extensive.
And, even in gold, they are; for we do find
Seeds of them, by our fire, and gold in them:
And can produce the species of each metal
More perfect thence, than nature doth in earth.   130
Beside, who doth not see, in daily practice,
Art can beget bees, hornets, beetles, wasps,
Out of the carcasses and dung of creatures;
Yea, scorpions of an herb, being rightly plac'd:
And these are living creatures, far more perfect,   135
And excellent, than metals.

MAMMON.   Well said, Father!
Nay, if he take you in hand, sir, with an argument,
He'll bray you in a mortar.

SURLY.   Pray you, sir, stay.
Rather, than I'll be bray'd, sir, I'll believe,
That alchemy is a pretty kind of game,   140
Somewhat like tricks o' the cards, to cheat a man,
With charming.

SUBTLE.   Sir?

SURLY.   What else are all your terms,
Whereupon no one o' your writers 'grees with other?
Of your elixir, your *lac virginis*,
Your stone, your med'cine, and your chrysosperm,   145
Your sal, your sulphur, and your mercury,
Your oil of height, your tree of life, your blood,

Your marcasite, your tutie, your magnesia,
Your toad, your crow, your dragon, and your panther,
Your sun, your moon, your firmament, your adrop,   150
Your lato, azoch, zernich, chibrit, autarit,
And then, your red man, and your white woman,
With all your broths, your menstrues, and materials,
Of piss and eggshells, women's terms, man's blood,
Hair o' the head, burnt clouts, chalk, merds, and clay,   155
Poulder of bones, scalings of iron, glass,
And worlds of other strange ingredients,
Would burst a man to name?

SUBTLE.   And all these, nam'd
  Intending but one thing: which art our writers
  Us'd to obscure their art.

MAMMON.   Sir, so I told him,   160
  Because the simple idiot should not learn it,
  And make it vulgar.

SUBTLE.   Was not all the knowledge
  Of the Egyptians writ in mystic symbols?
  Speak not the Scriptures, oft, in parables?
  Are not the choicest fables of the poets,   165
  That were the fountains, and first springs of wisdom,
  Wrapp'd in perplexed allegories?

MAMMON.   I urg'd that,
  And clear'd to him, that Sisyphus was damn'd
  To roll the ceaseless stone, only, because
  He would have made ours common. Who is this?   170
                  DOL *is seen.*

SUBTLE. God's precious – What do you mean? Go in, good lady,
  Let me entreat you. Where's this varlet?

                    [*Enter* FACE]

FACE.   Sir?

SUBTLE. You very knave! Do you use me thus?

FACE.   Wherein, sir?

SUBTLE. Go in, and see, you traitor. Go.   [*Exit* FACE]

MAMMON.   Who is it, sir?

SUBTLE. Nothing, sir. Nothing.

MAMMON.   What's the matter? Good, sir!   175
  I have not seen you thus distemper'd. Who is 't?

SUBTLE. All arts have still had, sir, their adversaries,

                    FACE *returns*

  But ours the most ignorant......

NOTES

1   *Father* Alchemists laid great stress on the necessity for a priest-like purity of life and motivation, an aspect of the profession the rogue Subtle continually dwells on.

3   *heretic* unbeliever (in alchemy).

5   *meet your time* This is the day for 'projection', i.e. the final production of the 'Philosophers' Stone' (see introductory note).

18   *prodigy with* i.e. something almost unknown among.

23   *subtle* Subtle, really describing himself, plays on his assumed name.

26   *costive* reluctant (literally 'constipated').

27   *gull'd* cheated.

29   *Sol . . . . . . robe* explained as: The essence of gold ('Sol'[=the Sun] was the astrological sign for gold) is ascendant, ready to work projection. It is impossible here to explain the flood of alchemical jargon with which Subtle lets loose during the remainder of the scene; in fact, to do so misses, in one sense, the point of Subtle's performance, which is merely to mystify and impress Surly, the 'heretic'. Those interested may consult the excellent notes in Alvin B. Kernan's edition of the play (*The Yale Ben Jonson*, 1974). As we might expect from Jonson, the use of the various terms is technically accurate.

31   *glorified spirit* i.e. the 'Elixir', a presumably liquidized form of the Philosophers' Stone.

32   *Eulenspiegel* (Owlglass), the name of a rogue hero in a popular German jest book. As a name for Face, it is meant to sound impressive.

33   *Anon* i.e. I will come at once.

35   *aludels* open-ended pots made to fit together.

36   *bolt's-head* long-necked round flask.

40   *gripe's egg* pot shaped like a griffin's egg.
     Lute enclose in clay (to ensure slow heating).

41   *in balneo* in a sand- or water-bath (also to ensure slow heating). Compare l. 63.

42   *Next to canting* the next best thing to talking thieves' jargon (see introductory note to 'The underworld in town and country').

43   *work* experimental project.

45   *lent* slow.

47   *in that is* in what is (already).

48   *covetise* covetousness, greed.

49   *pious uses* Nicolas Flamel, a medieval alchemist, is reported to have 'founded or endowed fourteen hospitals . . . . . . built three chapels, and . . . . . . made gifts to seven churches from his profits' (Shumaker, p. 163).

66   *iterate* repeat.

69   *loose* i.e. dissolving.

73   *in all examinations* under all tests.

82   *gent'man* gentleman.

88   *eggs in Egypt* Eggs in Egypt were often hatched in incubators.

94   *chicken in potentia* i.e. a chicken is potentially a chicken even in the egg (Aristotelian). Jonson's argument in ll. 90–167 is heavily indebted to Martin Delrio's *Disquisitiones Magicae* (1599–1600).

101   *it heats* the contest grows warm.
      stand i.e. stand firm.

124   *hermaphrodeity* having the characteristics of both male and female.
138   *bray* pulverize.
154   *terms* menstrual discharges.
155   *merds* ordures.
156   *Poulder* powder (variant form).
160   *obscure their art* i.e. to keep the art of alchemy from being understood by the 'profane vulgar', the uninitiate and ignorant. All the 'occult sciences' used the same argument.
168   *clear'd* explained.
       Sisyphus Greek mythological figure, who for his sins, was forever condemned, in the underworld, to roll a boulder up a steep hill. As soon as he reached the top, the boulder slipped from his grasp and he was forced to repeat the task. This 'fable of the poets' illustrates the mysterious wisdom hidden in 'perplexed allegories'.
170   SD DOL *is seen.* This apparently accidental appearance of Dol Common, a confederate of Subtle and Face, is part of a carefully laid plan to lure Sir Epicure into making improper advances to Doll, disguised as a Lord's daughter. Subtle arranges to catch them together (IV.v), pretends great moral indignation at Sir Epicure's 'impurity', and evades the necessity of producing the 'stone' by engineering the destruction of the 'great experiment' (*'A great crack and noise within.'*).

Man as metaphor or master of the world

The two following selections present man's relation to the world of nature in radically different terms, though both agree, if in different ways, on the potential greatness and centrality of man. One is the view of man inherited from the Middle Ages and early Renaissance, splendid but essentially static; the other, a view of the New Man, modern man, in some respects less imaginatively appealing, but dynamically active in mining the 'rich storehouse [of nature], for the glory of the Creator and the relief of man's estate' (Francis Bacon, *The Advancement of Learning* (1605), in *Works*, ed. James Spedding, III (1859), 294).

In the first selection (i), from Sir Walter Raleigh's *History of the World* (1614), man is seen, by analogy, as a little world (microcosm) which reflects, through a series of intimate interrelationships, all aspects, both physical and spiritual, of the great world or universe (macrocosm). This view of man as microcosm of the macrocosm goes back in its essentials to the Greeks and represents a kind of interpenetration of mind and matter that offered writers a vast treasury of allusion and metaphor. As John Donne put it: 'I am a little world made cunningly / Of elements and an angelic sprite' (*Holy Sonnets*, V). Or as Pico della Mirandola had earlier said: 'It is a commonplace of the schools that man is a little world, in which we may discern a body mingled of earthy elements, and ethereal breath, and the vegetable life of plants, and the senses of the lower animals, and reason, and the intelligence of angels, and a likeness of God.'

In the course of his magnificent humanist tribute to man as 'the measure of all things', one that should be read with Hamlet's famous lines on 'What a piece of work is a man' (II.ii.303–8), Raleigh brings together most of the accepted doctrines or 'scientific' schemata which were popularly believed to relate man and the rest of created nature: the Great Chain of Being, in which man occupied a central position between the Angels and the Beasts, but linked to both; the medical/psychological theory of the Four Humours (see 'Medicine, psychology and disease' (i)); astral influence as interpreted through the workings of the Ptolemaic (earth-centred) hypothesis of the universe; and the metaphysical doctrine of correspondence with its assumption of the underlying unity of all things, the one in the many and the many in the one (see E. M. W. Tillyard, *The Elizabethan World Picture* (1946)).

Selection (ii) is extracted from Francis Bacon's *Novum Organum* (1620), bk. I. In a series of 182 'aphorisms', Bacon there lays out his empirical method for achieving a triumphal 'entrance' into what he calls 'the kingdom of man' (bk. I, lxviii), a kingdom not to be confused with the kingdom of God, and undertakes to expose the several generic frailties of the human mind (the 'Idols of the Mind') that have in past ages deprived man of the full enjoyment or understanding of the limitless and unplumbed resources of the material world. Thus Bacon sounds the modern ideal of progress. Unlike Raleigh, he sees man, not so much as an integral, if static, part of nature, but as a comparatively separate entity, who, through the right exercise of reason, can become the master of the physical universe and the benefactor of mankind. In Bacon, then, we begin to see the emergence of the New Man, who, though he may give a deferential nod to theology and religion ('I humbly pray that things human may not interfere with things divine'), can immediately after remark, 'And now having said my prayers, I turn to man' (Preface to *Instauratio Magna*, 1620, in *Works*, IV (1860), 20; see Basil Willey, *Seventeenth Century Background* (1934)).

Though Bacon is now most often read for his *Essayes, or Counsels, Civil and Morall* (1597-1625), he was a man of deep and various learning, one who claimed to 'take all knowledge to be my province' (letter to Burghley, *c.*1591), and his scientific/philosophical works (mostly, like the *Novum Organum*, in Latin, the international language) were widely read and influential both in England and Europe. He was, of course, not alone, and earlier signs of movement in the sciences were already afoot – from Copernicus' heliocentric hypothesis of the universe announced in 1541 (toward which Bacon remained strangely ambivalent) to Galileo's and Kepler's work in astronomy and physics, William Gilbert's study of magnetic fields and William Harvey's discovery of the circulation of the blood. But Bacon was a principal spokesman for the 'New Philosophy', and it was his conception of an institution devoted solely to natural science (the 'House of Solomon' in *The New Atlantis*, 1627) that was an important incentive to the foundation of the Royal Society in 1660.

Important and basic changes in thought are difficult to assimilate and this was especially true as a result of the several attacks being launched against the old and time-honoured Ptolemaic earth-centred system by Copernicus, Galileo and Kepler, a general knowledge of which only seems to have begun to penetrate English consciousness in the opening years of the seventeenth century, arousing in many people a sense of insecurity and bewilderment. Man might not be, after all, the centre of the centre (a common term for the Earth), and if not, what then could man believe? John Donne (*The First Anniversarie* (1611), ll. 205-14) voices some of this uneasiness:

> The New Philosophy calls all in doubt;
> The element of Fire is quite put out;
> The Sun is lost, and th'Earth, and no man's wit
> Can well direct him where to look for it.
> And freely men confess that this world's spent,
> When in the planets and the firmament
> They seek so many new; they see that this
> Is crumbled out again t'his atomies.
> 'Tis all in pieces, all coherence gone;
> All just supply, and all relation.

And that omnivorous reader Robert Burton (*The Anatomy of Melancholy*

(1621), 'Digression of Air', ed. A. R. Shilleto, from 6th edn 1651–2, 1896, II, 66) fills out the chorus of confusion:

In the mean time the world is tossed in a blanket amongst them; they hoise the Earth up and down like a ball, make it stand and go at their pleasures. One saith the Sun stands, another he moves; a third comes in, taking them all at rebound, and lest there should any paradox be wanting, he [Fabricious] finds certain clouds and spots in the Sun by the help of glasses, which multiply (saith Kepler) a thing seen a thousand times bigger *in plano* [at its own level], and makes it come 32 times nearer to the eye of the beholder.

i

That man is (as it were) a little world

From Sir Walter Raleigh, *The History of the World* (1614), bk. I, chap. 2, section 5.

Man, thus compounded and formed by God, was an abstract or model, or brief story of the universal......And whereas God created three sorts of living natures, to wit, angelical, rational, and brutal; giving to angels an intellectual, and to beasts a sensual nature, he vouchsafed unto man both the intellectual of angels, the 5 sensitive of beasts, and the proper rational belonging unto man,......and because in the little frame of man's body there is a representation of the universal, and (by allusion) a kind of participation of all the parts thereof, therefore was man called *microcosmos*, or the little world......for out of earth and dust was 10 formed the flesh of man, and therefore heavy and lumpish; the bones of his body we may compare to the hard rocks and stones, and therefore strong and durable;......His blood, which disperseth itself by the branches of veins through all the body, may be resembled to those waters which are carried by brooks and 15 rivers over all the earth; his breath to the air; his natural heat to the enclosed warmth which the earth hath in itself, which, stirred up by the heat of the sun, assisteth nature in the speedier procreation of those varieties which the earth bringeth forth; our radical moisture, oil, or balsamum (whereon the natural heat 20 feedeth and is maintained) is resembled to the fat and fertility of the earth; the hairs of man's body, which adorns or overshadows it, to the grass, which covereth the upper face or skin of the earth; our generative power, to nature, which produceth all things; our determinations, to the light, wandering, and unstable clouds, 25 carried every where with uncertain winds; our eyes, to the light of the sun and moon; and the beauty of our youth, to the flowers of the spring, which, either in a very short time, or with the sun's heat, dry up and wither away, or the fierce puffs of wind blow them from the stalks; the thoughts of our mind, to the motion of 30 angels; and our pure understanding (formerly called *mens*, and that which always looketh upwards), to those intellectual natures which are always present with God; and, lastly, our immortal souls (while they are righteous) are by God himself beautified with the title of his own image and similitude......In this also is the little world 35 of man compared, and made more like the universal (man being the measure of all things......), that the four complexions resemble the four elements, and the seven ages of man the seven planets; whereof our infancy is compared to the Moon, in which we seem only to live and grow, as plants; the second age to 40

Mercury, wherein we are taught and instructed; our third age to
Venus, the days of love, desire, and vanity; the fourth to the Sun,
the strong, flourishing, and beautiful age of man's life; the fifth to
Mars, in which we seek honour and victory, and in which our
thoughts travel to ambitious ends; the sixth age is ascribed to   45
Jupiter, in which we begin to take account of our times, judge of
ourselves, and grow to the perfection of our understanding; the last
and seventh to Saturn, wherein our days are sad and overcast, and
in which we find by dear and lamentable experience, and by the
loss which can never be repaired, that of all our vain passions and   50
affections past, the sorrow only abideth: our attendants are
sicknesses and variable infirmities; and by how much the more we
are accompanied with plenty, by so much the more greedily is our
end desired, whom when time hath made unsociable to others, we
become a burden to ourselves: being of no other use than to hold   55
the riches we have from our successors.

NOTES

1-2 *abstract or model* Raleigh's whole discussion turns on the Greek idea of
     man as being in himself a 'little world', a microcosm of the great world or
     'macrocosm' (see ll. 9–10), which included not only the earth but the
     whole planetary system as described in the Ptolemaic (geo-centric)
     system.

3   *three......natures* See 'The Four Humours and other related matters',
     selection (ii), note on ll. 4–18, for a discussion of the Great Chain of Being
     to which Raleigh is here alluding.
     to wit that is.

4-5 *an intellectual......nature* Angels, by intellection, could 'know'
     intuitively without the necessity (as in man) of going through the process
     of logical reasoning.

5-7 *vouchsafed......man* Raleigh here differs from the usual account,
     which gave man a 'tripartite soul': rational, sensitive and vegetal (the last
     two of which he shared with the beasts and plant life).

10   *earth and dust* Compare Genesis 2:7.

16   *natural heat* body temperature.

20   *radical moisture* the humour or moisture naturally inherent in all plants
     and animals; 'oil' (essential oils, necessary to life in man and plants) and
     'balsamum' (preservative essence, conceived by Paracelsus to exist in all
     organic bodies) are here used as equal to 'radical moisture'.

25   *determinations* decisions, conclusions.

30   *motion* apprehension. Compare *Hamlet* II.ii.306: 'how like an angel in
     apprehension, how like a god!' (see below, ll. 31–3). The whole speech is
     relevant to a number of Raleigh's comments.

31   *pure understanding* the faculty of comprehending and reasoning, our
     right reason (as it was before being clouded by the Fall).
     mens intellectual faculty.

32   *looketh upwards* i.e. with the 'eyes of the mind'.

34–5 *title......image* Thus man is a microcosm of God.
37 *four complexions* the four humours (see 'Medicine, psychology and disease', selection (i), p. 327).
38 *four elements* earth, water, air, fire.
    seven ages of man There are many treatments of the several periods of man's life (the number of ages may differ); the most famous statement is that of Jaques in *As You Like It* (II.vii.139–66).
38–9 *seven planets* as arranged in the Ptolemaic system: (above the spheres of the four elements, Earth as the centre) Moon, Mercury, Venus, Sun, Mars, Jupiter and Saturn (followed, in ascending order, by the Circle of the Fixed Stars, the Crystalline Sphere, the Primum Mobile, or First Mover, and the Empyrean, or Highest Heaven).
45 *travel* probably here with the sense of 'travail' (=labour, work).
52 *variable* diverse, various; changeable, fluctuating.

ii

'The entrance into the kingdom of man' and the Idols of the Mind

From Francis Bacon, *Novum Organum* (1620), the second part of *Instauratio Magna* (1620), as translated from the Latin original in *The Works of Francis Bacon*, ed. J. Spedding, R. L. Ellis, D. D. Heath, IV (1860), bk. I, Aphorisms xix–lxii.

xix. There are and can be only two ways of searching into and discovering truth. The one flies from the senses and particulars to the most general axioms, and from these principles, the truth of which it takes for settled and immoveable, proceeds to judgment and to the discovery of middle axioms. And this way is now in fashion. The other derives axioms from the senses and particulars, rising by a gradual and unbroken ascent, so that it arrives at the most general axioms last of all. This is the true way, but as yet untried.

xxv. The axioms now in use, having been suggested by a scanty and manipular experience and a few particulars of most general occurrence, are made for the most part just large enough to fit and take these in: and therefore it is no wonder if they do not lead to new particulars. And if some opposite instance, not observed or not known before, chance to come in the way, the axiom is rescued and preserved by some frivolous distinction; whereas the truer course would be to correct the axiom itself.

xxvi. The conclusions of human reason as ordinarily applied in matter of nature, I call for the sake of distinction *Anticipations of Nature* (as a thing rash or premature). That reason which is elicited from facts by a just and methodical process, I call *Interpretation of Nature*.

xxxviii. The idols and false notions which are now in possession of the human understanding, and have taken deep root therein, not only so beset men's minds that truth can hardly find entrance, but even after entrance obtained, they will again in the very instauration of the sciences meet and trouble us, unless men being forewarned of the danger fortify themselves as far as may be against their assaults.

xxxix. There are four classes of Idols which beset men's minds. To these for distinction's sake I have assigned names – calling the first class *Idols of the Tribe*; the second, *Idols of the Cave*; the third, *Idols of the Market-place*; the fourth, *Idols of the Theatre*.

xl. The formation of ideas and axioms by true induction is no doubt the proper remedy to be applied for the keeping off and clearing away of idols......

xli. The *Idols of the Tribe* have their foundation in human nature itself, and in the tribe or race of men. For it is a false assertion that the sense of man is the measure of things. On the contrary, all perceptions, as well of the sense as of the mind, are 40 according to the measure of the individual and not according to the measure of the universe. And the human understanding is like a false mirror, which, receiving rays irregularly, distorts and discolours the nature of things by mingling its own nature with it.

xlii. The *Idols of the Cave* are the idols of the individual man. 45 For every one (besides the errors common to human nature in general) has a cave or den of his own, which refracts and discolours the light of nature; owing either to his own proper and peculiar nature; or to his education and conversation with others; or to the reading of books, and the authority of those whom he esteems and 50 admires; or to the difference of impressions, accordingly as they take place in a mind preoccupied and predisposed or in a mind indifferent and settled; or the like. So that the spirit of man (according as it is meted out to different individuals) is in fact a thing variable and full of perturbation, and governed as it were by 55 chance. Whence it was well observed by Heraclitus that men look for sciences in their own lesser worlds, and not in the greater or common world.

xliii. There are also idols formed by the intercourse and association of men with each other, which I call *Idols of the* 60 *Market-place*, on account of the commerce and consort of men there. For it is by discourse that men associate; and words are imposed according to the apprehension of the vulgar. And therefore the ill and unfit choice of words wonderfully obstructs the understanding. Nor do the definitions or explanations 65 wherewith in some things learned men are wont to guard and defend themselves, by any means set the matter right. But words plainly force and overrule the understanding, and throw all into confusion, and lead men away into numberless empty controversies and idle fancies. 70

xliv. Lastly, there are idols which have immigrated into men's minds from the various dogmas of philosophies, and also from wrong laws of demonstration. These I call *Idols of the Theatre*; because in my judgment all the received systems are but so many stage-plays, representing worlds of their own creation after an 75 unreal and scenic fashion. Nor is it only of the systems now in vogue, or only of the ancient sects and philosophies, that I speak: for many more plays of the same kind may yet be composed and in like artificial manner set forth, seeing that errors the most widely different have nevertheless causes for the most part alike. Neither 80 again do I mean this only of entire systems, but also of many principles and axioms in science, which by tradition, credulity, and negligence have come to be received......

xlv. The human understanding is of its own nature prone to suppose the existence of more order and regularity in the world 85 than it finds. And though there be many things in nature which are singular and unmatched, yet it devises for them parallels and conjugates and relatives which do not exist. Hence the fiction that all celestial bodies move in perfect circles; spirals and dragons being (except in name) utterly rejected. Hence too the element of Fire with its orb is brought in, to make up the square with the other three which the sense perceives. Hence also the ratio of density of the so-called elements is arbitrarily fixed at ten to one. And so on of other dreams. And these fancies affect not dogmas only, but simple notions also.

l. But by far the greatest hindrance and aberration of the human understanding proceeds from the dullness, incompetency, and deceptions of the sense; in that things which strike the sense outweigh things which do not immediately strike it, though they be more important......Hence all the working of the spirits inclosed in tangible bodies lies hid and unobserved of men. So also all the more subtle changes of form in the parts of coarser substances (which they commonly call alteration, though it is in truth local motion through exceedingly small spaces) is in like manner unobserved. And yet unless these two things just mentioned be searched out and brought to light, nothing great can be achieved in nature, as far as the production of works is concerned......

li. The human understanding is of its own nature prone to abstractions and gives a substance and reality to things which are fleeting. But to resolve nature into abstractions is less to our purpose than to dissect her into parts;......

lv. There is one principal and as it were radical distinction between different minds, in respect of philosophy and the sciences; which is this: that some minds are stronger and apter to mark the differences of things, others to mark their resemblances. The steady and acute mind can fix its contemplations and dwell and fasten on the subtlest distinctions; the lofty and discursive mind recognizes and puts together the finest and most general resemblances. Both kinds however easily err in excess, by catching the one at gradations the other at shadows.

lix. But the *Idols of the Market-place* are the most troublesome of all: idols which have crept into the understanding through the alliances of words and names. For men believe that their reason governs words; but it is also true that words react on the understanding; and this it is that has rendered philosophy and the sciences sophistical and inactive......

lx. The idols imposed by words on the understanding are of two kinds. They are either names of things which do not exist,......or they are names of things which exist, but yet confused and ill-defined, and hastily and irregularly derived from realities......

90

95

100

105

110

115

120

125

130

lxi. But the *Idols of the Theatre* are not innate, nor do they steal into the understanding secretly, but are plainly impressed and received into the mind from the play-books of philosophical   135
systems and the perverted rules of demonstration.

lxii. . . . . . And in the plays of this philosophical theatre you may observe the same thing which is found in the theatre of the poets, that stories invented for the stage are more compact and elegant, and more as one would wish them to be, than true stories   140
out of history. . . . . .

NOTES

8   *the true way* i.e. by induction through the experimental or empirical method as opposed to deduction (i.e. arguing from logical propositions to other propositions without testing such principles or laws ('axioms') against physical facts established by experiments). Bacon's claim that such an inductive method was 'as yet untried' (ll. 8–9) sounds like nonsense (Aristotle defines the inductive method), but Bacon is here talking about a rigorously controlled, machine-like method, 'rising by a gradual and unbroken assent' (l. 7), that arrives only at a law or principle after *all* the evidence has been taken into account. If we understand the true 'causes', we can then anticipate the final 'effects'.

11   *manipular* that which has been manipulated (hence made to fit the axiom).

13–14   *they. . . . . .particulars* One of Bacon's continual complaints is that the deductive method employed by scholastic philosophy simply spun on itself and produced no new insight into the physical world of nature that might be used to improve man's lot in this life. This insistence on practical utility became one of the foundations of later scientific research.

23   *idols* false mental images or conceptions.

27   *instauration* renovation, renewal. Compare the title of Bacon's projected but uncompleted work, *Instauratio Magna* ('The Great Renovation or Restoration'), of which the *Novum Organum* ('The New Organon [a system of rules or principles of demonstration or investigation]') was a part.

47   *refracts* deflects.

48   *proper and peculiar* distinctive and unique.

49   *conversation* living together with, intercourse.

53   *indifferent* evenly balanced.

54   *meted* measured.

56   *Heraclitus* Greek philosopher (fifth century BC), who believed, as represented in the so-called element of fire, that Becoming (eternal flux or change), not Being, was the sole actuality.

63   *apprehension. . . . . .vulgar* understanding of the common, uneducated man.

72   *dogmas* opinions, tenets (of particular philosophical systems).

73   *wrong. . . . . .demonstration* proofs usually arrived at through faulty application of the rules of logic.

79   *artificial* contrived (as opposed to 'natural').

84–6 *The human......finds* Bacon is here referring in part to the sorts of neatly arranged patterns and detailed interrelationships between man and nature that are illustrated in selection (i) above.

88 *relatives* things standing in some relation to one another.

89 *move......circles* so, according to Aristotle; not, according to Ptolemy.
spirals spiral curves or coils.
dragons not explained. The usual terms for 'spirals and dragons' would be 'eccentrics and epi-cycles'.

90–1 *element......orb* In the Ptolemaic system (earth-centred), fire as one of the four elements (earth, water, air, fire) occupied an 'orb' above the 'orb' of air.

91 *make......square* complete the pattern.

100 *spirits* subtle or intangible elements or principles in material things.

103 *alteration* change in character or appearance.

104 *local......spaces* i.e. particles (or atoms) in motion.

113–14 *one principal......minds* In what follows Bacon sets up a distinction between the analytical mind proper to the scientist and seeker of truth and the synthesizing mind which sees the world in terms of metaphor, the one in the many and the many in the one. As a scientist Bacon has little use for the second type (e.g. the poet) and the implicit attack on metaphor resonates strongly in Thomas Hobbes (*Leviathan* (1651), pt. I, chap. 8) and John Locke (*Essay Concerning Human Understanding* (1690), chap. 11, 'The difference of wit and judgment').

119 *finest* subtlest, most esoteric.

139–41 *stories......history* May be taken as an oblique criticism of the history plays written by Shakespeare and his contemporaries in which the 'truth of history' was improved upon for didactic, aesthetic and structural reasons.

11 Medicine, psychology and disease

The Four Humours and other related matters

As the essential basis of what we now call the Elizabethan–Jacobean faculty psychology, the doctrine of the Four Humours figured prominently in contemporary attempts to explain the various behavioural characteristics or personal temperaments that so obviously existed among individual men and women – in other words, to account for what became known as his or her 'humour'. Some knowledge of this physiological/psychological doctrine is necessary for an understanding of almost everything written during this period, particularly so in the drama, where the presentation of character was inevitably strongly influenced by humour theories.

Deriving principally from the writings of Galen (AD c.130–c.200), and, except for Paracelsus, widely accepted by medical men and scientists, though with adaptations and embroideries, the doctrine of the Four Humours (sanguine, choleric, phlegmatic, and melancholy) was used to explain both the physical characteristics of men and women and their temperamental, psychological make-up or 'complexion'. Robert Burton, in his famous compendium of contemporary medical and scientific lore called *The Anatomy of Melancholy* (1621, revised and augmented in five later editions), defines a 'humour' as 'a liquid or fluent part of the body, comprehended in it, for the preservation of it; and is either innate or born with us, or adventitious and acquisite' (ed. A. R. Shilleto, from 6th edn, 1651–2 (1896), I, 169). The special characteristics associated with each of the four humours may be found in selection (i), from *The Englishmans Doctor, or The Schoole of Salerne* (1608, translated by Sir John Harington from the medieval Latin text). The preponderance of one of the humours in the body determined a person's 'humour'. A 'balanced humour' was very rare, though perhaps Shakespeare intends us to see such a humour in Horatio in *Hamlet*, who is not 'passion's slave' (III.ii.72), or in Brutus in *Julius Caesar* ('the elements / So mix'd in him that Nature might stand up / And say to all the world, "This was a man!"' (v.v.73–5). Each humour could become 'sick' or 'adusted' (i.e. too hot and dry), a state that could lead to eccentric or violent behaviour, particularly serious in the choleric or melancholy humour and producing different forms of melancholy madness, one of the principal topics of Burton's *Anatomy*, together with its possible causes and cures. Moreover, a person's 'humour' could change under the pressures of life and age; thus Hamlet, at one time a supposedly sanguine humour as befitted a prince, falls prey to melancholy and many of the attributes of the melancholic as described by Burton (I, 442–51):

>. . . . . .these symptoms [are] infinite,. . . . . .*for scarce is there one of a thousand that dotes alike,. . . . . .Fear* and *Sorrow*, which, as

they are frequent causes, so, if they persever [persevere] long,......they are most assured signs, inseparable companions, and characters of melancholy......*Suspicion* and *jealousy* are general symptoms: they are commonly distrustful, timorous, apt to mistake and amplify, *facilè irascibiles* [easily angered], testy, pettish, peevish, and ready to snarl upon every small occasion......*Inconstant* they are in all their actions, vertiginous, restless, unapt to resolve of any business, they will and will not,......Now prodigal, and then covetous, they do, and by-and-by repent them of that which they have done, so that both ways they are troubled, whether they do or do not, want or have, hit or miss,......erected and dejected in an instant; animated to undertake, and upon a word spoken again discouraged. Extreme passionate,......and what they desire, they do most furiously seek:......prone to revenge, soon troubled, and most violent in all their imaginations, not affable in speech, or apt to vulgar [common] compliment, but surly, dull, sad, austere......neglect habit [clothing], etc......and yet of a deep reach [mental capacity], excellent apprehension, judicious, wise, and witty: for I am of that nobleman's mind, *Melancholy advanceth men's conceits* [mental capacities] *more than any humour whatsoever*, improves their meditations more than any strong drink or sack [strong wine].

The most desirable and fortunate of the humours were sanguine and choleric, and both were associated with rulers and noblemen, the choleric being especially proper to great warriors (e.g. Marlowe's Tamburlaine or Shakespeare's Hotspur in *I Henry IV*). The worst and most unlucky of the humours was melancholy; while the phlegmatic humour was considered as essentially feminine, being governed by the Moon and the planet Venus. Robert Greene (*Mamillia, Part II*, (1593), ed. A. B. Grosart, *Works*, II, 221) thus contrasts the choleric and phlegmatic humours:

For Socrates, Plato, yea and Aristotle himself,......assigned this as a particular quality appertaining to womankind, namely, to be fickle and inconstant, alleging this astronomical reason, that *Luna* [Moon], a feminine and mutable planet, hath such predominant power in the constitution of their complexion, because they be phlegmatic, that of necessity they must be fickle, mutable, and inconstant; whereas choler, wherewith men do abound, is contrary, and therefore by consequence stable, firm, and without change.

As Shakespeare's Cleopatra, after the death of Antony, proudly says (*Antony and Cleopatra*, V.ii.238–41):

......I have nothing
Of woman in me; now from head to foot

> I am marble constant; now the fleeting moon
> No planet is of mine.

As the verses in selection (i) show (see the notes), each of the four humours was considered to be under particular planetary influence and was associated with the four elements (earth, water, air and fire), the different seasons of the year and the several 'ages' of man (see Jaques on the 'seven ages' in *As You Like It*, II.vii.139–66).

As we have observed, the theory of the humours inevitably influenced the general presentation of character both in and out of the drama, but Ben Jonson, inspired perhaps by George Chapman's *An Humorous Day's Mirth* (1597), applied it with a special twist to comedy, evolving what has become known as the 'comedy of humours' (*Every Man in His Humour*, 1598; *Every Man out of His Humour*, 1599; and *Cynthia's Revels*, 1601). He specifically defines the genre in his 'Induction' to *Every Man out*, where he distinguishes between dramatic characters that represent a genuine psychological humour (e.g. Kitely, a 'jealous humour' in *Every Man in*, or Morose, the man who can't abide any noise, in *Epicoene*, 1609) as opposed to an affected or assumed humour (e.g. Master Stephen and Master Matthew in *Every Man in*). A detailed account of the humour theory and its application to the drama may be found in L. B. Campbell, *Shakespeare's Tragic Heroes: Slaves of Passion* (1930), section II, and J. W. Draper, *The Humors and Shakespeare's Characters* (1944).

Selection (ii), from Timothy Bright's *A Treatise of Melancholie* (1586), discusses in medical/religious terms the threefold nature of man: body, spirit, and soul (see ll. 59–67). The spirit, not like the soul immortal, is defined by Burton (I, 170) as 'a most subtile vapour, which is expressed [exuded] from the *blood* and the instrument of the soul, to perform all his actions; a common tie or *medium* betwixt the body and the soul, as some will have it.' Although usually thought of as three different spirits (natural, vital and animal; see the notes), Bright prefers to consider these as manifestations of a single spirit, which he here describes as 'a true-love knot to couple heaven and earth [i.e. soul and body]' and later as a 'subtile instrument' (p. 45), a description that seems to be echoed in John Donne's famous lines in 'The Extasie' (ll. 61–4):

> As our blood labours to beget
>   Spirits, as like souls as it can,
> Because such fingers need to knit
>   That subtile knot, which makes us man.

i

From *The Englishmans Doctor, or The Schoole of Salerne* (1608), translated from the medieval Latin text by Sir John Harington.

Four humours reign within our bodies wholly,
And these compared to four elements:
The *Sanguine, Choler, Phlegm,* and *Melancholy*:
The latter two are heavy, dull of sense;
Th'other two are more jovial, quick, and jolly,   5
And may be likened thus without offence.
Like air both warm and moist is *Sanguine* clear;
Like fire doth *Choler* hot and dry appear;
Like water cold and moist is *Phlegmatic*;
The *Melancholy* cold, dry earth is like.   10

*   *   *

Complexions cannot virtue breed or vice,
Yet may they unto both give inclination.
The *Sanguine* gamesome is, and nothing nice;
Love[s] wine and women and all recreation;
Likes pleasant tales and news, plays, cards, and dice;   15
Fit for all company and every fashion;
Though bold, not apt take offence, not ireful,
But bountiful and kind, and looking cheerful;
Inclining to be fat and prone to laughter,
Loves mirth and music, cares not what comes after.   20

*   *   *

Sharp *Choler* is an humour most pernicious,
All violent and fierce and full of fire,
Of quick conceit, and therewithal ambitious;
Their thoughts to greater fortunes still aspire;
Proud, bountiful enough, yet oft malicious;   25
A right bold speaker and as bold a liar;
On little cause to anger great inclined;
Much eating still, yet ever looking pined:
In younger years they use to grow apace,
In elder hairy on their breast and face.   30

*   *   *

The *Phlegmatic* are most of no great growth,
Inclining to be rather fat and square;
Given much unto their ease, to rest and sloth;

Content in knowledge to take little share;
To put themselves to any pain most loth,   35
So dead their spirits, so dull their senses are:
Still either sitting, like to folk that dream,
Or else still spitting to avoid the phlegm.
One quality doth yet these harms repair,
That for the most part *Phlegmatic* are fair.   40

*   *   *

The *Melancholy* from the rest do vary,
Both sport and ease and company refusing;
Exceeding studious, ever solitary;
Inclining pensive still to be, and musing;
A secret hate to others apt to carry: 45
Most constant in his choice, though long a-chusing;
Extreme in love sometime, yet seldom lustful;
Suspicious in his nature and mistrustful:
A wary wit, a hand much given to sparing,
A heavy look, a spirit little daring.   50

NOTES

2   *four elements* i.e. earth, water, air, and fire. See ll. 7–10.

5   *jovial* mirthful, convivial. The sanguine humour was under the influence of the planet Jupiter or Jove (hence 'jovial').
     quick lively.

7   *warm and moist* the special qualities associated with the element of air and, by transference, with the sanguine humour. For fire, water, and earth, see ll. 8–10.

11   *Complexions* A person's 'complexion', both bodily and mental, was determined by the relative proportions of the four humours in his or her physical make-up. If, as usual, one humour predominated (such as sanguine), that person would be of a sanguine humour or complexion.

13   *Sanguine* As the name implies, the humour associated with the blood; also linked to the element of air, the planet Jupiter, the liver and the periods of youth and spring.

16   *every fashion* This suggests that a sanguine humour is something of a clothes-horse, given to following all the latest fashions.

20   *cares......after* i.e. lives for the moment.

21   *Choler* the humour associated with the liver and yellow bile; also linked with the element of fire, the Sun and Mars (hence 'martial') and the periods of manhood and summer.

23   *quick conceit* lively intelligence or imagination.

28   *Much eating still* always eating a great deal.
     pined wasted by hunger, emaciated.

31   *Phlegmatic* the basically feminine humour (all women were considered to be phlegmatic, as were artists) associated with the phlegm and liver; also

linked to the element of water, the Moon and Venus, and the periods of childhood and winter.

no great growth i.e. short (compare 'square', l. 32).

35   *pain* effort.

38   *avoid* void, eject.

40   *fair* in colouring and hair, light as opposed to dark.

41   *Melancholy* the humour associated with black bile, and the liver and spleen; also linked with the element of earth, the planet Saturn (hence 'saturnine'), and the periods of old age and winter.

44   *pensive* plunged in thought (= 'musing').

49   *A wary wit* one whose mind is continually on guard against deception.

ii

How melancholy worketh fearful passions in the mind

From Timothy Bright, *A Treatise of Melancholie* (1586), chap. 9, pp. 33–8.

Before I declare unto you how this humour afflicteth the mind, first it shall be necessary for you to understand what the familiarity is betwixt mind and body; how it affecteth it, and how it is affected of it again. You know God first created all things subject to the course of times and corruption of the Earth, after that He had   5
distinguished the confused mass of things into the heavens and the four elements. This Earth He had endued with a fecundity of infinite seeds of all things, which He commanded it, as a mother, to bring forth, and, as it is most agreeable to their nature, to entertain with nourishment that which it had borne and brought   10
forth; whereby, when He had all the furniture of this inferior world, of these creatures some He fixed there still and maintaineth the seeds till the end of all things and that determinate time which He hath ordained for the emptying of those seeds of creatures, which He first endued the Earth withal. Other some, that is to say   15
the animals, He drew wholly from the Earth at the beginning and planted seed in them only, and food from other creatures: as beasts, and man in respect of his body. The difference only this: that likely it is man's body was made of purer mould, as a most precious tabernacle and temple, wherein the image of God should   20
afterward be enshrined, and being formed, as it were, by God's proper hand received a greater dignity of beauty and proportion, and stature erect, thereby to be put in mind whither to direct the religious service of his Creator.

    This tabernacle thus wrought, as the gross part yielded a mass   25
for the proportion to be framed of, so had it by the blessing of God, before inspired, a spiritual thing of greater excellency than the red earth, which offered itself to the eye only. This is that which philosophers call the spirit, which spirit so prepareth that work to the receiving of the soul, that, with more agreement, the   30
soul and body have grown into acquaintance, and is ordained of God, as it were, a true-love knot to couple heaven and earth together; yea, a more divine nature than the heavens with a base clod of earth, which otherwise would never have grown into society; and hath such indifferent affection unto both that it is   35
both equally affected and communicateth the body and corporal things with the mind, and spiritual and intelligible things after a sort with the body......This spirit is the chief instrument, and immediate, whereby the soul bestoweth the exercises of her faculty in her body, that passeth to and fro in a moment, nothing in   40

swiftness and nimbleness being comparable thereunto, which
when it is depraved by any occasion, either rising from the body or
by other means, then becometh it an instrument unhandsome for
performance of such actions as require the use thereof; and so the
mind seemeth to be blameworthy, wherein it is blameless; and 45
fault of certain actions imputed thereunto, wherein the body and
this spirit are rather to be charged, things corporal and earthly: the
one, in substance, and the other in respect of that mixture
wherewith the Lord tempered the whole mass in the beginning...... 50

Now, although these spirits rise from earthly creatures, yet are
they more excellent than earth, or the earthy parts of those natures
from which they are drawn, and rise from that divine influence of
life and are not of themselves earthy; neither yet comparable in
pureness and excellency unto that breath of life wherewith the 55
Lord made Adam a living soul, which proceeded not from any
creature that He had before made, as the life of beasts and trees,
but immediately from Himself, representing in some part the
character of his image. So then these three we have in our nature
to consider distinct for the clearer understanding of that I am to 60
entreat of: the body of earth; the spirit from virtue of that Spirit
which did, as it were, hatch that great egg of Chaos; and the soul
inspired from God, a nature eternal and divine, not fettered with
the body, as certain philosophers have taken it, but handfasted
therewith by that golden clasp of the spirit, whereby one (till the 65
predestinate time be expired and the body become unmeet for so
pure a spouse) joyeth at and taketh liking of the other.

NOTES

1   *this humour* i.e. melancholy; here used to mean both the humour itself
    and the disease known as melancholy.

2   *familiarity* intimate intercourse.

3   *it affecteth it* the melancholy humour influences the mind.

3-4 *how......again* how the melancholy humour is in turn influenced by
    the mind.

4-18 *God first created......body* Bright's account of the creation is the usual
    amalgam of the biblical story in Genesis and the neo-Platonic conception
    of the Great Chain of Being, which, as Pope put it, 'with God began' (i.e.
    God – pure actuality; angels – pure intellect; man – reason; animals –
    sense; plants – growth; inanimate matter – mere being). God created
    either by 'fiat' (let there be') or by emanation (the nature of good (i.e.
    God) is naturally diffusive), and in creating He created all possible forms
    (the Platonic doctrine of plenitude, i.e. 'infinite seeds', l. 8), each link in
    the descending chain being connected to the link above and below (the
    Aristotelian doctrine of continuity, a continuity that was broken with the
    Fall of Man). This is, of course, a simplification of a very involved and
    complicated concept (see A. O. Lovejoy, *The Great Chain of Being*, 1961).

8   *seeds of all things* i.e. *rationes seminales*, the seeds, implanted by God, from

which all things are generated as by universal causes (see W. C. Curry, *Shakespeare's Philosophical Patterns* (1959), 2nd edn, pp. 38–9). See *Macbeth*, IV.i.59, 'nature's germains'.

11 *furniture* furnishing.

11–12 *inferior world* the Earth.

12–14 *some He . . . . . . creatures* Bright seems to be referring, not very clearly, to the belief that God, in creating all possible forms at the time of creation (plenitude), arranged to have certain 'seeds' reserved and only to be made operative at his own 'determinate time'. 'creatures' = all created things, either animate or inanimate.

19 *man's . . . . . . mould* Such a view would accord with man's position in the Great Chain, 'a creature of middle nature betwixt Angels and Beasts' (Bright, p. 30).

23 *stature erect* That man walked upright, unlike the beasts, with his head pointed at heaven, was taken as another characteristic distinguishing him from the rest of the animal creation.

25 *gross part* i.e. the body.

27 *before inspired* earlier breathed in.

29 *the spirit* not to be confused with the soul, also 'inspired' by God. Bright, unlike most authorities, writes of a single 'spirit' (pp. 46–7), but three kinds were usually distinguished: natural, vital and animal. The 'natural' were produced in the liver; the 'vital' were produced in the heart from the natural spirits; and the 'animal' 'formed of the *vital*, brought up to the brain, and diffused by the nerves, to the subordinate members, give sense and motion to them all' (Robert Burton, *The Anatomy of Melancholy*, ed. A. R. Shilleto (1896), I, 170).

30 *work* i.e. the body.

32 *true-love knot* complicated, ornamental knot symbolic of true love. See introductory note.

35 *indifferent* impartial, neutral.

37 *intelligible* capable of being apprehended only by the understanding (not by the senses).

37–8 *after a sort* in a certain way.

39–40 *soul . . . . . . body* Bright (pp. 42–4) discusses the soul as having 'one universal and simple faculty', but the usual view postulated three distinct faculties: vegetal, the nutritive, generational faculty, which, in the chain of being, it shares with plants and beasts; sensible, relating to the 'inward senses' (common sense, phantasy, memory) and the 'outward senses' (touch, hearing, smell, taste, sight), which it shares with the beasts; and rational, with its two 'powers' (understanding and will), which is the special prerogative of man and links him, in the chain, with the faculty of intellection [knowing without the need of logical reasoning], the distinguishing attribute of the angels (see Burton, I, 176–92). Man was thus usually thought of as possessing a 'tripartite soul'.

51 *spirits . . . . . . creatures* i.e. the spirits were generated through the nourishment furnished to man by the flora and fauna ('earthly creatures').

59 *character* stamp, imprint.

62 *egg of Chaos* Compare Genesis 1:2 (Geneva, 1560): 'And the earth was without form and void, and darkness was upon the deep, and the Spirit of God moved upon the waters.'

64 *handfasted* spiritually betrothed, joined.

67 *spouse* i.e. the soul.

The plague

Now that we live in a society threatened by AIDS, it has become easier for us to understand the terror which mention of the plague, or pestilence, aroused in the hearts of sixteenth- and seventeenth-century Englishmen. Until the Great Fire of 1666, London was never wholly free from it, a certain number of plague deaths being a more or less accepted fact each month. This was bad enough, but the real horror began (see selection (i)) when the number of plague deaths reached epidemic proportions, as happened, for example, in 1563, 1570, 1592-4, 1603, 1609 and 1625. In the 1603 epidemic alone, from December 1602 to 22 December 1603, 35,104 persons died of the plague in London and its environs, roughly one-sixth out of a population of about 250,000 (see F. P. Wilson, *The Plague in Shakespeare's London* (1927), pp. 114-15).

Four causes of the plague were widely bandied about: (1) God's punishment for a wicked people; (2) corrupt air; (3) certain conjunctions of the stars and planetary aspects; (4) the individual's natural bodily constitution (Wilson, pp. 3-7). Of these, one, corrupt air, had some relevance to the spread of pneumonic plague, a rarer form, which was infectious and spread by coughing; none of them was relevant, in any significant way, so far as bubonic plague was concerned. Indeed, it was not until the end of the nineteenth century that the real cause was discovered – rat fleas, which carried the disease from their dead hosts, black house rats, and were driven in turn to prey on human hosts. Ironically, though cities like London were heavily infested by rats and though other animals (like dogs and cats, which were slaughtered by the hundreds) were suspected of spreading the disease, rats seem to have escaped special notice, either on the Continent, where the plague also flourished, or in England (Wilson, p. 36). Again ironically, in view of the frenzied attempts that were made to avoid contact with plague victims, bubonic plague, unlike the pneumonic form, is now recognized as non-infectious in itself. The agent of transmission was the rat flea.

A graphic and uncomfortably detailed discussion of the plague, its supposed causes and questionable cures, may be found in William Bullein's *A Dialogue......against the Fever Pestilence* (1564, rev. edn 1578, ed. M. W. and A. H. Bullen, *EETS*, 1887). Bullein spares his reader nothing, as, for example, in his description of the bodily symptoms of the typical plague victim:

> They which are smitten with this stroke or plague are not so open in the spirits as in other sicknesses are, but strait winded [short of breath]; they do swoon and vomit yellow choler [bile], swelled in the stomach with much pain, breaking forth with stinking sweat; the extreme parts very cold, but the internal parts boiling with heat and burning; no rest; blood distilling from the nose, urine somewhat watery and sometime thick with stink, sometime of colour yellow, sometime black; scalding [inflammation] of the

tongue; ordure most stinking; with red eyen [eyes], corrupted
mouth, with blackness, quick pulse and deep but weak, headache,
altered voice, loss of memory, sometime with raging in strong
people. (p. 38)

Bullein then continues with equally lurid descriptions of the plague sores
(or bubos) and advocates, along with a bewildering collection of
medicines, the letting of blood, purging and lancing. One wonders
which was more lethal, the treatment or the disease!

Knowing almost nothing of the real cause of the plague, the
authorities were hampered in dealing with the overwhelming problems
that an epidemic presented. So-called 'Plague-orders' were issued,
officers of various kinds (searchers, warders, nurses, dog- and rat-
catchers, etc.) were appointed, and infected houses were marked with a
red cross and their inhabitants supposedly isolated. Finally, a Pesthouse,
for those stricken by the plague, was erected (1594) outside the City, but
of very limited capacity (Wilson, pp. 74–84). Despite all efforts, however,
when an epidemic struck, chaos reigned, and something of the terror of
such times is powerfully realized in selection (i) from Thomas Dekker's
1603. The Wonderfull Yeare (1603).

Dekker, to whom six pamphlets on the plague, ranging in date from
1603 to 1630, have been attributed, subscribed to the belief that the
plague was a judgement of God:

> Our heavenly parts are plaguey sick,
> And there such leperous spots do stick,
> That God in anger fills his hand
> With vengeance, throwing it on this land.
>
> (*Newes from Graves-ende* (1604), sig. D1 v)

And he considers the 1603 plague epidemic as a kind of purge:

> For since his Maiden-Servant's gone [i.e. Elizabeth],
> And his new Viceroy fills the throne,
> Heaven means to give him (as his bride)
> A nation new and purified. (*Ibid.*, sig. D3 r)

But this fatalistic view does not prevent Dekker from experiencing to the
full 'The Horror of a plague, the Hell', and he writes with a sense of
humane pity for the anguish and fear that surround him from high and
low alike. He is, however, highly critical of those, mostly the well-to-do,
who flocked out of the City 'to save yourselves, and in that flight undo
others' (*A Rod for Run-awayes* (1625), sig. B2 v), thus spreading the
infection (see selection (i), ll. 49ff.) and removing potential financial
support from the City authorities.

On the other hand, John Taylor the Water Poet (*The Fearefull
Summer: or Londons Calamitie, the Countryes Discurtesie*, 1625) is
particularly harsh in his criticism of 'those beastly, barbarous, cruel
Country Cannibals' who would lend no aid of any kind to those fleeing
the 1625 plague raging in London (an attitude also noted by Dekker in
selection (i)).

Selection (ii), from Gervase Markham's *The English Hus-wife* (1615), details a few of the many different means used as safeguards against, or treatments for, the plague. Fighting as they were in the dark, reputable physicians, like Thomas Lodge, (see his *A Treatise of the Plague*, 1603) did what they could, but quacks flourished, each with his own special nostrums, and turned the public misery to their gain.

Theatres, not surprisingly, were considered as breeding grounds for the plague and, when plague deaths exceeded thirty, or even fewer, a week, they were often closed for various periods of time. Theatres were closed in 1592–4, except for two brief intervals; again for almost a year in 1603–4, and for about six months in 1625. Such long inhibitions worked great hardship on the players, forcing them to make provincial tours. Even this expedient was not always open to them; many towns would refuse to receive them for fear of infection. The visitation of the actors to Elsinore in *Hamlet*, though they were forced on the road for a different reason, may be seen as analogous. See the anonymous *Stage Players Complaint in A pleasant Dialogue betweene Cane of the* Fortune *and Reed of the* Friers (1641; in *The Old Book Collector's Miscellany*, ed. C. Hindley (1873), III).

i

From Thomas Dekker, *1603. The Wonderfull Yeare* (1603) (text based on edn by F. P. Wilson in *The Plague Pamphlets of Thomas Dekker* (1925), pp. 27–31).

What an unmatchable torment were it for a man to be barred up every night in a vast, silent charnel-house?......Were not this an infernal prison? Would not the strongest-hearted man (beset with such a ghastly horror) look wild? and run mad? and die? And even such a formidable shape did the diseased City appear in: for he   5 that durst (in the dead hour of gloomy midnight) have been so valiant as to have walked through the still and melancholy streets, what think you should have been his music? Surely, the loud groans of raving sick men, the struggling pangs of souls departing. In every house grief striking up an alarum, servants crying out for   10 masters, wives for husbands, parents for children, children for their mothers. Here, he should have met some frantically running to knock up sextons; there, others fearfully sweating with coffins to steal forth dead bodies, lest the fatal handwriting of death should seal up their doors. And to make this dismal consort more   15 full, round about him bells heavily tolling in one place and ringing out in another. The dreadfulness of such an hour is inutterable: let us go further......
  And in this manner do the tedious minutes of the night stretch out the sorrows of ten thousand. It is now day, let us look forth   20 and try what consolation rises with the sun: not any, not any! For before the jewel of the morning be fully set in silver, a hundred hungry graves stand gaping, and every one of them (as at a breakfast) hath swallowed down ten or eleven lifeless carcasses; before dinner, in the same gulf are twice so many more devoured;   25 and before the sun takes his rest those numbers are doubled. Threescore that not many hours before had every one several lodgings very delicately furnished are now thrust all together into one close room: a little noisome room, not fully ten foot square. Doth not this strike coldly to the heart of a worldly miser? To   30 some the very sound of death's name is in stead of a passing-bell. What shall become of such a coward being told that the selfsame body of his, which now is so pampered with superfluous fare, so perfumed and bathed in odoriferous waters, and so gaily apparelled in variety of fashions, must one day be thrown (like   35 stinking carrion) into a rank and rotten grave, where his goodly eyes, that did once shoot forth such amorous glances, must be eaten out of his head; his locks that hang wantonly dangling, trodden in dirt under foot: this doubtless (like thunder) must needs strike him into the earth. But (wretched man!) when thou shalt see   40 and be assured (by tokens sent thee from heaven) that tomorrow

thou must be tumbled into a muck-pit and suffer thy body to be bruised and pressed with threescore dead men, lying slovenly upon thee, and thou to be undermost of all! yea, and perhaps half of that number were thine enemies! (and see how they may be revenged, for the worms that breed out of their putrifying carcasses shall crawl in huge swarms from them and quite devour thee), what agonies will this strange news drive thee into?

If thou art in love with thyself, this cannot choose but possess thee with frenzy. But thou art gotten safe (out of the civil city, Calamity) to thy parks and palaces in the country, lading thy asses and thy mules with thy gold (thy god!), thy plate and thy jewels; and the fruits of thy womb thriftily growing up but in one only son (the young landlord of all thy careful labours), him also hast thou rescued from the arrows of infection. Now is thy soul jocund and thy senses merry. But open thine eyes, thou fool! and behold that darling of thine eye (thy son) turned suddenly into a lump of clay; the hand of pestilence hath smote him even under thy wing. Now dost thou rent thine hair, blaspheme thy Creator, cursest thy creation, and basely descendest into brutish and unmanly passions, threat'ning in despite of Death and his plague to maintain the memory of thy child in the everlasting breast of marble: a tomb must now defend him from tempests. And for that purpose the sweaty hind (that digs the rent he pays thee out of the entrails of the earth), he is sent for to convey forth that burden of thy sorrow. But note how thy pride is disdained: that weatherbeaten, sunburnt drudge, that not a month since fawned upon thy worship like a spaniel and, like a bondslave, would have stooped lower than thy feet, does now stop his nose at thy presence and is ready to set his mastiff as high as thy throat to drive thee from his door. All thy gold and silver cannot hire one of those (whom before thou didst scorn) to carry the dead body to his last home. The country round about thee shun thee as a basilisk, and therefore to London (from whose arms thou cowardly fledst away) post upon post must be galloping to fetch from thence those that may perform that funeral office. But there are they so full of grave-matters of their own that they have no leisure to attend thine. Doth not this cut thy very heartstrings in sunder? If that do not, the shutting up of this tragical act I am sure will: for thou must be enforced with thine own hands to wind up that blasted flower of youth in the last linen that ever he shall wear; upon thine own shoulders must thou bear part of him, thy amazed servant the other; with thine own hands must thou dig his grave, not in the church or common place of burial (thou hast not favour, for all thy riches, to be so happy), but in thine orchard or in the proud walks of thy garden, wringing thy palsy-shaken hands instead of bells (most miserable father!), must thou search him out a sepulchre.

NOTES

2   *charnel-house* house or vault in which the bones of the dead were piled up in order to make room for new burials in the churchyard.

10   *alarum* mechanism which sounds the alarm as a warning of danger.

13   *sextons* church officers, whose business it was to bury the dead.

14   *fatal......death* A red cross, about fourteen inches long and broad, was painted in oil colours upon infected houses, and a paper was fastened on the lintel with the inscription 'Lord have mercy upon us!' (Wilson). This placed the house off bounds and was intended to isolate the inhabitants. Compare *Romeo and Juliet*, v.iii, where Friar John is trapped in such a house.

22–6   *a hundred......doubled* See introductory note.

29   *noisome* ill-smelling, stinking.

30   *worldly miser* one proud of his wealth and possessions (with play on 'miser' = wretch).

31   *passing-bell* bell rung, for a fee, at the death of a person.

41   *tokens* i.e. the sores which were a sign of the bubonic plague.

42   *muck-pit* literally, cesspool.

43   *slovenly* in a careless, untidy manner.

50   *thou......safe* See introductory note. Lovewit, in Ben Jonson's *The Alchemist* (1610), is typical of those who left the City during plague times, a well-to-do gentleman. The plague fell most heavily on the poor, who of necessity lived in overcrowded, unsanitary, indeed filthy, conditions.

53   *thriftily* worthily, handsomely.

59   *rent* rend, tear.

64   *hind* farm servant.

73   *basilisk* fabulous reptile, whose breath and eyes were supposed to be fatal.

74   *post* post-rider, carrying express letters.

78   *heartstrings* according to early ideas of anatomy, the tendons or nerves supposed to brace the heart.

82   *servant* Unlike the hind above, the household servant had already been exposed to the infection.

ii

How to avoid or treat the plague

From Gervase Markham, *The English Hus-wife* (1615), bk. II of *Country Contentments*, pp. 8–9.

To preserve your body from the infection of the plague, you shall take a quarter of old ale, and after it hath risen upon the fire and hath been scummed, you shall put thereinto of *aristolochia longa*, of angelica, and of celandine, of each half an handful, and boil them well therein; then strain the drink through a clean cloth, and   5
dissolve therein a dram of the best mithridate; as much ivory finely powdered and searced, and six spoonful of dragon-water; then put it in a close glass; and every morning fasting take five spoonful thereof, and after bite and chaw in your mouth the dried root of angelica, or smell, as on a nosegay, to the tasselled end of a ship   10
rope, and they will surely preserve you from infection.

But if you be infected with the plague, and feel the assured signs thereof, as pain in the head, drought, burning, weakness of stomach and such like: then you shall take a dram of the best mithridate, and dissolve it in three or four spoonful of dragon-   15
water, and immediately drink it off, and then with hot cloths or bricks, made extreme hot and laid to the soles of your feet, after [you] have been wrapt in woollen cloths, compel the sick party to sweat, which if he do, keep him moderately therein till the sore begin to rise; then to the same apply a live pigeon cut in two parts,   20
or else a plaster made of the yolk of an egg, honey, herb of grace chopped exceeding small, and wheat flour, which in very short space will not only ripen, but also break the same without any other incision; then after it hath run a day or two, you shall apply a plaster of melilot unto it till it be whole.   25

NOTES

2 *quarter* Markham here means a 'quart'.
3 *aristolochia longa* birthwort (also called 'heartwort').
4 *angelica* i.e. *herba angelica*, considered helpful in warding off the plague.
   celandine swallowwort (plant with yellow flowers, producing a thick yellow juice).
6 *dram* one eighth of an ounce.
   mithridate compound of many ingredients considered a universal remedy against infectious diseases.
   as much i.e. a dram.
7 *searced* strained through a sieve.
   dragon-water medicinal preparation (?made from dragonwort).

8   *close glass* stoppered glass container.
      fasting i.e. before breakfast.
9   *chaw* chew.
20   *live* i.e. freshly killed.
21   *herb of grace* rue.
25   *melilot* i.e. *melilotus* or yellow melilot, the dried flowers of which were used in making poultices (plasters).

12 At sea: sea-fights, discovery, trade, colonization

The sixteenth century marked the beginning of England's emergence as a great naval power, both military and commercial. The indefatigable Richard Hakluyt, who, in addition to being the compiler of his great collection, *The Principall Navigations, Voyages and Discoveries of the English Nation* (1589; 2nd edn, 3 vols., 1598–1600; references throughout to the Everyman edn (1907), 8 vols.), was also a consultant on naval affairs, writes with justifiable pride ('Epistle Dedicatorie', 1589, p. 344) that, though Englishmen had formerly been 'full of activity, stirrers abroad, and searchers of the remote parts of the world', under the inspiration of Elizabeth's 'peerless government,' they 'have excelled all nations and people of the earth':

> For which of the kings of this land before her Majesty had their banners ever seen in the Caspian Sea? Which of them hath ever dealt with the Emperor of Persia,......and obtained for her merchants large and loving privileges? who ever saw before this regiment [reign] an English ledger [ambassador] in the stately porch of the Grand Signor at Constantinople? Who ever found English consuls and agents at Tripolis in Syria, at Aleppo, at Babylon, at Balsera, and, which is more, who ever heard of Englishmen at Goa before now? What English ships did heretofore ever anchor in the mighty river of Plate? Pass and repass the unpassable (in former opinion) Strait of Magellan, range along the coast of Chili, Peru, and all the backside of Nova Hispania, further than a Christian ever passed, traverse the mighty breadth of the South Sea,......double the famous Cape of Bona Speranza [Cape of Good Hope], arrive at the isle of Santa Helena, and last of all return home richly laden with the commodities of China, as the subjects of this now flourishing monarchy have done?......Is it not as strange that the born naturals [natives] of Japan and the Philippinas are here to be seen, agreeing with our climate, speaking our language, and informing us of the state of their eastern habitations?

It is perhaps forgivable that Hakluyt, in the fresh flush of England's new consciousness of its destiny, says nothing here (except through place names) of the earlier exploits of the Italian, Spanish, Portuguese, and Dutch in matters of discovery and trade.

Behind many of the English voyages, lay the abortive hope of discovering a North-West or North-East Passage across the North Polar regions as a short-cut to trading in China (Cathay), thus obviating the costly, dangerous and time-consuming necessity of approaching the coast of Asia by sailing around the southern tips of Africa and India or South America. In 1553, discouraged by the general failure to discover a North-West Passage, the Company of Merchant Adventurers (later known as the Muscovy Company), under the direction of Sebastian Cabot, sent a small expedition (three ships, the largest of 160 tons, accompanied by three pinnaces) to search for a north-east arctic route under Sir Hugh Willoughby. It failed, of course, in its primary objective (Sir Hugh and his crew being frozen to death off Lapland), but one of the other captains, Richard Chancellor, landing with his men, penetrated into Russia as far south as Moscow and laid the foundations for what became a flourishing trade with the Muscovites (see the accounts in Hakluyt, I, 232-333).

The lengthy instructions (Hakluyt, I, 232-41) issued by Cabot for this expedition are revealing, in part for their hardheaded business sense. For example: complete obedience to those in authority (internecine quarrelling among the members of an expedition had too often been, and would continue to be, a cause of failure); mariners' liveries to be worn only on special occasions in order to impress the natives; special care and attention to be given to the sick and wounded (mortality on such expeditions was very high under the hard conditions prevailing); disclosure of their religion forbidden and careful observance of the laws and rites of the country visited; any native lured aboard to be treated with courtesy but, if possible, to be made drunk so that 'you shall know the secrets of his heart'; no expression of contempt, derisive laughter, etc., to be directed at local inhabitants; discovery of the commodities they most need and what they have to trade with in return, particularly what metals may be found in that country; visits to local rulers always in strength, never being separated from one's weapons for fear of ambush; diligent watch kept on board against attacks from swimmers intent on acquiring human meat for cannibalistic appetites.

An East India Company, similar in intent to the Muscovy Company, was finally incorporated in 1599, after several earlier voyages had revealed the rich commercial possibilities. See A. L. Rowse, *The Expansion of Elizabethan England* (1955), for a lively discussion of all these matters.

Many famous names have come ringing down the years: Francis Drake (see selection (iii)), Thomas Cavendish (each of whom circled the globe, 1577-80 and 1586-88), John Hawkins (see selection (ii)), Martin Frobisher, Richard Grenville (see selection iv), Walter Raleigh, John Smith (see selection (v)), Henry Hudson. All of them were brave, tough and, according to their lights, honourable men, heroic figures in the eyes of the nation, then and later, a slightly romantic view that must not be allowed to obscure the fact that, in modern terms, most of them were also little better than pirates who roamed the seven seas in search of booty, sacking, plundering and slave-trading whenever opportunity offered. Historically considered, however, they were no worse than their European contemporaries; in fact, the record suggests that they were comparatively more humane, men of their word, and often welcomed by the various 'barbarous' peoples who had suffered under the cruel rigours of Spanish and Portuguese conquest.

Selection (i), from Thomas Nashe's *Lenten Stuffe* (1599), suggests how hard and dangerous the ordinary sailor's life in such 'voyages of purchase or reprisals' most often was. Under Nashe's usual hyperbole lies a sober core of reality gathered from his reading of Hakluyt's *Principall Navigations*, other European accounts and word of mouth from some of the veteran sailors whom he must have encountered at Yarmouth, a fishing town, to which he had retreated to avoid prosecution for his part in a controversial play (now lost) called *The Isle of Dogs* (1597).

The second selection (ii) is excerpted from John (later Sir John) Hawkins' description of his third 'troublesome voyage' (1567–8) to the West Indies by way of Guinea, where he had seized between four and five hundred negroes, which he sold as slaves to the Spaniards in the West Indies. If the privations suffered by the crews in such expeditions were severe, as Nashe records, what must conditions have been like for the shanghaied negroes, shackled and jammed into the holds of small ships (the *Jesus of Lubeck*, by far the largest, was only 700 tons, and this was large by contemporary English standards)? Two passages from an account of one of Hawkins' earlier voyages (1564) are uncomfortably suggestive. Putting in at St Dominica ('an island of the cannibals') for water, Hawkins found none but rain-water 'and such as fell from the hills, and remained as a puddle in the dale, whereof we filled for our negroes' (Hakluyt, VII, 20). Later, he addressed a special plea to a Spanish official 'to have licence for the sale of certain lean and sick negroes, which he had in his ship, like to die upon his hands if he kept them ten days, having little or no refreshing for them, whereas other men having them, they would recover well enough' (Hakluyt, VII, 25–6).

Hawkins as slaver (and he had plenty of company, English and European) may properly shock us today and the fact that slave labour was not allowed in England does not soften, in a sense indeed darkens, the picture. But we must, nevertheless, temper our reaction to Hawkins and his contemporaries and remember that the idea of slavery as an institution was then widely accepted (Sir Thomas More, for example, countenanced it in his *Utopia* (1516)), that the Spanish and others employed galley-slaves, that English participation in the slave trade continued in the British colonies up to 1807, and that slavery flourished in the southern states of the United States until the Emancipation Proclamation of 1863, long after it had been repudiated by Europe.

Selection (iii), from John Speed's *The Historie of Great Britaine* (1623, 2nd edn) recounts events on the second and third days (21, 22 July 1588) of the more than week-long series of sea battles between the English fleet and the Spanish Armada which, with the aid of an army under the Prince of Parma, ready massed in the Netherlands with troop transport vessels, had been despatched by Philip II to invade and subjugate England and restore Catholicism. The mighty Spanish fleet, 'never the like had before sailed upon the ocean sea' (Hakluyt, II, 371), contained 130 ships (64 castle-like galleons, 8 galliasses and galleys, 23 great hulks, etc.), manned by 19,290 soldiers, 8,350 sailors, 2,080 galley-slaves and armed with 2,630 great ordnance; the English had about a hundred comparatively small, light ships, over half not men of war but armed merchant vessels pressed into service. The apparent disparity seemed to be staggering, but with much greater manoeuvrability, superior seamanship, and much more accurate gunnery the English fleet, aided also by the weather, wrought havoc on the heavy, cumbersome, and unwieldly Spanish 'castles'. It was essentially all over by 29 July (the battle off Gravelines) and the 'vincible Armado', as Speed (p. 1204) dubs it, badly mauled and depleted, set out on its disastrous homeward voyage around the north of Scotland, stormy weather wrecking many more ships, with further heavy loss of life. English casualties were very low and not a single ship was lost, 'whereupon it is most apparent that God miraculously preserved the English nation' (Hakluyt, II, 393). Open hostilities with Spain continued into the late 1590s, but the threat to England was never again so dangerous.

Selection (iv), from Sir Walter Raleigh's *Report of the Truth of the fight......Betwixt the* Revenge......*And an Armada of the King of Spaine* (1591), is, in its way, one of the small classics of Elizabethan prose. Its central figure, Sir Richard Grenville, Raleigh's cousin, was, despite (or because of) his stubborn courage, a controversial figure, and Raleigh seems to have written his account 'to soothe and extenuate everybody' (Arber, p. 6). Many saw in him the epitome of English heroism and blamed Lord Thomas Howard, Admiral of the small English fleet of which the *Revenge* was a part, for failing to come back to support Grenville and the *Revenge* (Raleigh admits the possibility that Grenville had acted unwisely (ll. 33–5) and later defends Howard's behaviour); others, though not questioning Grenville's personal bravery, taxed him with extreme foolhardiness and disregard for his men's lives, when, as most accounts suggest, having the opportunity to slip away and join Howard, he chose rather to bull his way alone through the midst of the large Spanish fleet (53 ships). Whatever our view of Grenville, the last fight of the *Revenge* remains as one of the most stirring and memorable moments in the annals of England's naval history – a glorious defeat. A Dutchman, Jan Huyen van Linschoten (*His Discours of Voyages into the East and West Indies,* trans. W. Phillip (1598), fol. 192) purports to record Grenville's dying words (spoken in Spanish, the final ironic touch):

> Here die I, Richard Grenville, with a joyful and quiet mind, for that I have ended my life as a true soldier ought to do that hath fought for his country, queen, religion, and honour; whereby my soul most joyful departeth out of this body and shall always leave behind it an everlasting fame of a valiant and true soldier that hath done his duty as he was bound to do.

The last selection (v), from Captain John Smith's *Generall Historie of Virginia, New-England, and the Summer Isles* (1624; ed. E. Arber, 1895), describes the earlier fortunes of the expedition, of which Smith was a leading member, that founded the Crown colony at Jamestown, Virginia, in 1607, the first successful attempt (see headnote) to establish a permanent English colony in North America. Captain Smith is now most often remembered for his 'romantic' interlude with Pocahontas, daughter of Powhatan, 'Emperor' of the Indian tribes in that region. Captured by the Indians, Smith was about to be clubbed to death by Powhatan's orders, when 'Pocahontas, the king's dearest daughter, when no entreaty could prevail, got his head in her arms and laid her own upon his to save him from death; whereat the Emperor was contented he should live to make him hatchets and her bells, beads, and copper' (Arber, p. 400; the whole incident makes lively reading for the light it throws on Indian behaviour and customs). Smith persuaded Powhatan, through the promise of gifts, to let him return to Jamestown, after which Pocahontas 'ever once in four or five days......brought him so much provision that saved many of their lives that else for all this had starved with hunger' (Arber, p. 401). As one of the few effective members of the original expedition, Smith became President of the Council in 1608, but returned to England a year later. Thereafter he was closely concerned with the settlement of New England, which he first visited in 1614 (see his *Advertisements for the unexperienced Planters of New England, or any where* (1631), in Arber, pp. 917–66). See also, Francis Bacon's 'Of Plantations', in *Essayes* (1625; no. 33).

The Elizabethan fascination with all aspects of seafaring (trade, privateering, discovery, colonization, national defence) inevitably left its mark on the drama, most famously, of course, in Shakespeare's *The Tempest*, a play in which, for many details, he drew directly on three accounts of an expedition under Sir George Somers, which set out from Plymouth for Jamestown in 1609. Somers's flagship, the *Sea Adventure* (its names catches much of the tone of the period), was wrecked on the island of Bermuda ('the still-vex'd Bermoothes', I.ii.229), but the crew (and the newly appointed governor of Virginia, Sir Thomas Gates), 'not a hair perish'd' (I.ii.217), finally arrived at Jamestown almost a year later in two small pinnaces. Shakespeare modelled the character of Caliban (perhaps an anagram of 'cannibal') in part on the Indian aborigines as they were described in these and other accounts. In *The Merchant of Venice*, Shakespeare presents Antonio as a representative of the new rising merchant class, and the risks inherent in mercantile ventures play an important part in complicating the plot, and Thomas Dekker in *The Shoemakers' Holiday* (1599) shows how Simon Eyre's canny purchase, at bargain rates, of a shipload of exotic commodities from Candia (Crete) becomes the cornerstone of Eyre's meteoric rise to Lord Mayor of London.

Naturally the historic defeat of the Spanish Armada caught the attention of popular dramatists like Dekker and Heywood, and the event figures in Dekker's *The Whore of Babylon* (1606–7) and Heywood's *II If You Know Not Me You Know Nobody* (1605). Heywood and William Rowley also devote the whole of Act IV in *Fortune by Land and Sea* (1607–9) to staging a lively sea fight between a pair of English renegade pirates and a 'good' English privateer, the scenes alternating from ship to ship until finally the pirates' ship is boarded and captured.

Among many, a few other miscellaneous reflections of the new sea-age may be noticed in contemporary plays: in *Eastward Ho!* (1605, by Marston, Chapman, and Jonson) the spendthrift Sir Petronel Flash undertakes an abortive trading expedition to Virginia, which ends up wrecked on the Isle of Dogs, a peninsula in the Thames; in *The Travels of the Three English Brothers* (1607, by John Day, William Rowley, and George Wilkins) the various maritime, military, and mercantile adventures of the Sherley brothers (Thomas, Anthony, Robert) in Persia and Turkey are romantically (and exaggeratedly) presented; in *The City Madam* (1632) Philip Massinger complicates his plot by disguising some of his characters as Indian potentates from Virginia; and in *The Memorable Masque* (1613) George Chapman includes a chorus of sun-worshipping Virginian Priests, whose 'robes were tuck'd up before, strange hoods of feathers and scallops about their necks, and on their heads turbants, stuck with several colour'd feathers, spotted with wings of flies of extraordinary bigness, like those of their country.'

In one instance, enthusiasm for the drama even exercised its influence on sailors at sea. In 1607–8, Shakespeare's *Hamlet* (twice) and *Richard II* were performed on board the *Dragon*, a ship belonging to the East India Company commanded by Captain Keeling, 'to keep my people from idleness and unlawful games or sleep' (E. K. Chambers, *William Shakespeare* (1930), II, 334–5).

i

A sailor's life

From Thomas Nashe, *Nashes Lenten Stuffe* (1599), ed. R. B. McKerrow, *Works*, III (1905), 180–1.

Voyages of purchase or reprisals, which are now grown a common traffic, swallow up and consume more sailors and mariners than they breed, and lightly not a slop of a rope-haler they send forth to the Queen's ships but he is first broken to the sea in the herring-man's skiff or cock-boat, where having learned to brook all waters, 5
and drink as he can out of a tarry can, and eat poor John out of swuty platters, when he may get it, without butter or mustard, there is no ho with him, but, once heart'ned thus, he will needs be a man-of-war, or a tobacco-taker, and wear a silver whistle. Some of these for their haughty climbing come home with wooden legs, 10
and some with none, but leave body and all behind. Those that escape to bring news tell of nothing but eating tallow and young blackamores, of five and five a rat in every mess and the shipboy to the tail, of stopping their noses when they drunk stinking water that came out of the pump of the ship, and cutting a greasy buff 15
jerkin in tripes and broiling it for their dinners. Divers Indian adventures have been seasoned with direr mishaps, not having for eight days' space the quantity of a candle's-end among eight score to grease their lips with; and landing in the end to seek food, by the cannibal savages they have been circumvented and forced to 20
yield their bodies to feed them.

NOTES

1   *purchase* pillage, plunder.
3   *lightly* commonly.
      slop i.e. sailor (contemptuously so called from the wide baggy breeches worn by sailors).
      rope-haler one who hales (hauls) on the rigging.
5   *cock-boat* small boat, often towed behind a larger ship.
6   *poor John* salted and dried hake.
7   *swuty* sooty (variant form), dirty.
8   *no ho with* no stopping.
9   *man-of-war* a man-of-war's man or sailor (one who served in an armed ship).
      tobacco-taker tobacco smoker. The context suggests that sailors were heavy smokers.
      silver whistle Mariners, by statute, were allowed to wear a silver whistle for signalling commands.
13   *five and five* i.e. ten (to each rat).
      mess ship's company.

15–16 *buff jerkin* short coat of ox-hide.
16   *tripes* ?long strips (resembling the intestines (='tripes') of an animal).
17   *adventures* i.e. expeditions to the West Indies.

ii

The slave trade

From John Hawkins, 'The third troublesome voyage made with the *Jesus of Lubeck*, the *Minion*, and four other ships, to the parts of Guinea, and the West Indies, in the yeeres 1567 and 1568' (in Richard Hakluyt, *The Principall Navigations, Voyages and Discoveries of the English Nation* (1589; Everyman edn, 1907), VII, 53–5).

The ships departed from Plymouth the second day of October, anno 1567, and had reasonable weather until the seventh day, at which time, forty leagues north from Cape Finisterre, there arose an extreme storm, which continued four days, ... whereupon [having received severe damage] in the same storm we set our course homeward, determining to give over the voyage; but the eleventh day of the same month the wind changed with fair weather, whereby we were animated to follow our enterprise, ... directing our course with the islands of the Canaries, where, according to an order before prescribed, all our ships, before dispersed, met at one of those islands, called Gomera, where we took water and departed from thence the fourth day of November towards the coast of Guinea and arrived at Cape Verde, the eighteenth of November, where we landed 150 men, hoping to obtain some negroes; where we got but few, and those with great hurt and damage to our men, which chiefly proceeded of their envenomed arrows. And, although in the beginning they seemed to be but small hurts, yet there hardly escaped any that had blood drawn on them, but died in strange sort, with their mouths shut, some ten days before they died and after their wounds were whole; . . . . . . From thence we passed the time upon the coast of Guinea, searching with all diligence the rivers from Rio Grande unto Sierra Leone, till the twelfth of January, in which time we had not gotten together 150 negroes . . . . . .

[Discouraged by sickness among his men and the late time of the year, Hawkins decides to return home, first selling off his negroes to the Portuguese at Mina (Guinea) for gold to defray the expenses of the expedition.]

But even in that present instant, there came to us a negro, sent   25
from a king oppressed by other kings his neighbours, desiring our aid, with promise that as many negroes as by these wars might be obtained, as well of his part as of ours, should be at our pleasure. Whereupon we concluded to give aid and sent 120 of our men, which, the fifteenth of January, assaulted a town of the negroes of   30
our ally's adversaries, which had in it 8,000 inhabitants, being very strongly impaled and fenced after their manner; but it was so well defended that our men prevailed not, but lost six men and forty hurt, so that our men sent forthwith to me for more help. Whereupon, considering that the good success of this enterprise   35
might highly further the commodity of our voyage, I went myself and, with the help of the king of our side, assaulted the town, both by land and sea, and very hardly with fire (their houses being covered with dry palm leaves) obtained the town, put the inhabitants to flight, where we took 250 persons, men, women,   40
and children; and by our friend the king of our side there were taken 600 prisoners, whereof we hoped to have had our choice; but the negro (in which nation is seldom or never found truth) meant nothing less; for that night he removed his camp and prisoners, so that we were fain to content us with those few which   45
we had gotten ourselves.

Now had we obtained between four and five hundred negroes, wherewith we thought it somewhat reasonable to seek the coast of the West Indies, and there, for our negroes and other our merchandise, we hoped to obtain whereof to countervail our   50
charges with some gains; whereunto we proceeded with all diligence, furnished our watering, took fuel, and departed the coast of Guinea the third of February, continuing at the sea with a passage more hard than before hath been accustomed till the twenty-seventh day of March, which day we had sight of an island   55
called Dominica, ... From thence we coasted from place to place, making our traffic with the Spaniards as we might, somewhat hardly, because the King [of Spain] had straitly commanded all his governors in those parts by no means to suffer any trade to be made with us. Notwithstanding, we had had   60
reasonable trade and courteous entertainment, ... saving at Capo de la Vela, in a town called Rio de la Hacha (from whence come all the pearls).

The Treasurer, who had the charge there, would by no means agree to any trade or suffer us to take water. He had fortified his   65
town with divers bulwarks in all places where it might be entered,

and furnished himself with an hundred harquebusiers, so that he
thought by famine to have enforced us to have put aland our
negroes; of which purpose he had not greatly failed, unless we had
by force entered the town; which (after we could by no means   70
obtain his favour) we were enforced to do, and so, with two
hundred men, brake in upon their bulwarks and entered the town,
with the loss only of two men of our parts and no hurt done to the
Spaniards, because, after their volley of shot discharged, they all
fled. Thus having the town with some circumstance, as partly by   75
the Spaniards' desire of negroes and partly by friendship of the
Treasurer, we obtained a secret trade; whereupon the Spaniards
resorted to us by night and bought of us to the number of 200
negroes. In all other places where we traded the Spaniards'
inhabitants were glad of us and traded willingly......   80

[After many other adventures and skirmishes with the Spaniards (pp.
55–62), Hawkins sailed back to England, arriving in Cornwall on 25
January 1568.]

NOTES

3 *leagues* a league equals three nautical miles, a nautical mile being 1.15 of a
   statute mile.
19 *with......shut* i.e. with lockjaw.
36 *commodity* profit.
38 *hardly* with great difficulty.
44 *meant nothing less* i.e. had no intention of abiding by his agreement. It
   would be a toss-up whether the negro king's 600 prisoners or Hawkins'
   250 suffered more.
47 *four......negroes* The suffering and deprivation of such captured
   negroes, crammed into six comparatively small ships, must have been
   indescribable; many, of course, died on board before they could be sold.
65 *take water* i.e. fresh water to refurnish the ships' supply.
66 *bulwarks* ramparts, fortifications.
67 *harquebusiers* soldiers who were supplied with harquebuses, large muskets
   having a matchlock operated by a trigger and supported for firing on a
   forked rest.
75 *with some circumstance* with some ado.

iii

The 'Invincible' Spanish Armada

From John Speed, *The Historie of Great Britaine* (1623, 2nd edn), pp. 1201–2.

[The English Admiral, Lord Thomas Howard, believing that the Spanish fleet had been so badly mauled by storms that it could not undertake any further assault that year (1588), holed his fleet up in Plymouth. Suddenly word was brought that the Armada was in the Channel. Taken by surprise, Howard managed, however, to get his fleet out of the harbour and on 20 July first attacked the Spanish fleet.]

[21 July] The next day the two fleets fought within musket shot, where the English Admiral fell most hotly on the Vice-Admiral of Spain; at which present they well perceived their own oversights: their great ships (like castles) powerful to defend, but not offend, to stand, but not to move, and therefore far unfit for fight in those narrow seas; their enemies, nimble, and ready at all sides to annoy them, and as apt to escape harms themselves by being low built and easily shot over. Therefore they gathered themselves close in form of a half-moon and slackened their sails, that their whole fleet might keep together. Notwithstanding, one of their great galleons, wherein was Don Pedro de Valdez, Vasques de Silva, Alonzo de Sayas, and other noblemen, was sore battered by the English shot, in avoiding whereof she fell foul upon another ship and, ere she could be cleared, had her foremast broken off, which so hindered her sail that she was unable to keep way with the fleet, nor they of courage to succour these lords, but left both ship and them in this sudden and unlooked for distress. But night coming on, and she lagging behind, the Lord Admiral, supposing neither men nor mariners to be left within board, and fearing to lose sight of the Spaniards, passed by, ...

[22 July] The next day following, Sir Francis Drake [English Vice-Admiral], espying this lagging galleon, sent forth a pinnace to command them to yield; otherwise his bullets should force them without further favour; but Valdez, to seem valorous, answered, that they were 450 strong, that himself was Don Pedro and stood on his honour, and therefore propounded certain conditions. But the knight sent his reply, that he had not leisure to parley: if he would yield, presently do it; if not, he should well prove that Drake was no dastard. Whereupon, Pedro hearing that it was the *fiery Drake* (ever terrible to the Spaniards) who had him in chase, with forty of his followers, came on board Sir Francis his ship; where, first giving him the congé, he protested that he, and all his, were resolved to die in defence, had they not fallen under his power,

5

10

15

20

25

30

whose valor and felicity was so great that Mars and Neptune
seemed to attend him in his attempts, and whose generous mind   35
towards the vanquished had often been experienced, even of his
greatest foes. Sir Francis, requiting his Spanish compliments with
honourable English courtesies, placed him at his own table and
lodged him in his own cabin. The residue of that company were
sent unto Plymouth, where they remained eighteen months till   40
their ransoms were paid; but Sir Francis his soldiers had well paid
themselves with the spoil of the ship, wherein were 55,000 ducats
in gold, which they shared merrily among them. The same day,
Michael de Oquendo, Admiral to the *Quadron Guipusco*, and
Vice-Admiral to the whole fleet, suffered no less disaster, whose   45
ship, being one of the greatest galleons, fell suddenly on fire, all
the upper part of the ship and most of the persons therein
consumed; howbeit, the gunpowder in the hold was all saved, and
the rest of the scorched Spaniards, with the hulk, brought into
Plymouth, to the great joy of the beholders.   50

[This was just the beginning. Sea battles raged until 29 July, when,
off Gravelines, the Spaniards were so badly mauled that they
abandoned their mission and began their return voyage by way of
the North Sea around the north of Scotland, a disastrous journey
in which they lost many more ships and men through storm,
hunger and thirst. Of the 130 ships that left Spain, only about half
survived the ill-fated expedition.]

NOTES

3   *present* time.
13   *another ship* i.e. Spanish ship.
15   *keep way with* maintain the sailing speed of.
28   *well prove* i.e. have it proved (upon him).
29   *dastard* coward (refusing to risk a fight).
29–30 *fiery Drake* Probably with a play on 'fire-drake'＝a mythical 'fiery
      dragon' or a kind of firework.
31   *Francis his* Francis's.
32   *congé* ceremonial bow.
34   *felicity* good fortune.
     Mars and Neptune Roman god of war and god of the sea, respectively.
35   *attend* lend aid to.
40   *Plymouth* more accurately, Torbay.
42   *ducats* gold coins worth about nine shillings.
49   *hulk* large ship.

iv

The last fight of the *Revenge*

From Sir Walter Raleigh, *A Report of the Truth of the fight about the Iles of the Açores, this last Summer. Betwixt the* Revenge, *one of her Majesties Shippes, And an Armada of the King of Spaine* (1591; ed. E. Arber, 1871, pp. 17–25).

The Lord Thomas Howard, with six of her Majesty's ships, six victuallers of London, the bark *Ralegh*, and two or three pinnaces riding at anchor near unto Flores, one of the westerly islands of the Azores, the last of August in the afternoon, had intelligence by one Captain Middleton, of the approach of the Spanish 5 armada......He had no sooner delivered the news but the fleet was in sight: many of our ships' companies were on shore in the island; some providing ballast for their ships; others filling of water and refreshing themselves from the land with such things as they could either for money or by force recover. By reason whereof, our 10 ships being all pestered and romaging, everything out of order, very light for want of ballast, and that which was most to our disadvantage, the one half part of the men of every ship sick and utterly unserviceable; for in the *Revenge* there were ninety diseased; in the *Bonaventure*, not so many in health as could 15 handle her main sail......

The Spanish fleet, having shrouded their approach by reason of the island, were now so soon at hand, as our ships had scarce time to weigh their anchors, but some of them were driven to let slip their cables and set sail. Sir Richard Grenville was the last 20 weighed, to recover the men that were upon the island, which otherwise had been lost. The Lord Thomas with the rest very hardly recovered the wind, which Sir Richard Grenville not being able to do, was persuaded by the Master and others to cut his main sail, and cast about, and to trust to the sailing of his ship: for the 25 squadron of Seville were on his weather bow. But Sir Richard utterly refused to turn from the enemy, alleging that he would rather choose to die, than to dishonour himself, his country, and her Majesty's ship, persuading his company that he would pass through the two squadrons, in despite of them, and enforce those 30 of Seville to give him way. Which he performed upon divers of the foremost, who, as the mariners term it, sprang their luff and fell under the lee of the *Revenge*. But the other course had been the better, and might right well have been answered in so great an impossibility of prevailing. Notwithstanding out of the greatness 35 of his mind, he could not be persuaded. In the mean while as he attended those which were nearest him, the great *San Philip* being in the wind of him, and coming towards him, becalmed his sails in such sort, as the ship could neither make way nor feel the helm: so huge and high cargued was the Spanish ship, being of a thousand and five hundred tons, who after laid the *Revenge* aboard. When he was thus bereft of his sails, the ships that were under his lee luffing up also laid him aboard: of which the next was the *Admiral of the Biscaines*, a very mighty and puissant ship commanded by Brittan Dona. The said *Philip* carried three tier of ordinance on a side, and eleven pieces in every tier. She shot eight forth right out of her chase, besides those of her stern ports. 40

45

After the *Revenge* was entangled with this *Philip*, four other boarded her; two on her larboard, and two on her starboard. The fight thus beginning at three of the clock in the afternoon continued very terrible all that evening. But the great *San Philip* having received the lower tier of the *Revenge*, discharged with cross-bar shot, shifted herself with all diligence from her sides, utterly misliking her first entertainment. Some say that the ship foundered, but we cannot report it for truth, unless we were assured. The Spanish ships were filled with companies of soldiers, in some two hundred besides the mariners, in some five, in others eight hundred. In ours there were none at all, beside the mariners, but the servants of the commanders and some few voluntary gentlemen only. After many interchanged volleys of great ordinance and small shot, the Spaniards deliberated to enter the *Revenge*, and made divers attempts, hoping to force her by the multitudes of their armed soldiers and musketeers, but were still repulsed again and again, and at all times beaten back into their own ships, or into the seas. In the beginning of the fight, the *George Noble* of London, having received some shot thorough her by the armados, fell under the lee of the *Revenge*, and asked Sir Richard what he would command him, being but one of the victuallers and of small force. Sir Richard bid him save himself, and leave him to his fortune. After the fight had thus, without intermission, continued while the day lasted and some hours of the night, many of our men were slain and hurt, and one of the great galleons of the armada and the *Admiral of the Hulks* both sunk, and in many other of the Spanish ships great slaughter was made...... 50

55

60

65

70

75

But to return to the fight, the Spanish ships which attempted to board the *Revenge*, as they were wounded and beaten off, so always others came in their places, she having never less than two mighty galleons by her sides, and aboard her. So that ere the morning, from three of the clock the day before, there had fifteen several armados assailed her; and all so ill approved their entertainment, as they were, by the break of day, far more willing to hearken to a composition, than hastily to make any more assaults or entries. But as the day increased, so our men decreased: and as the light grew more and more, by so much more grew our discomforts. For 80

85

none appeared in sight but enemies, saving one small ship called
the *Pilgrim*, commanded by Jacob Whiddon, who hovered all
night to see the success; but in the morning, bearing with the
Revenge, was hunted like a hare amongst many ravenous hounds,
but escaped.   90

All the powder of the *Revenge* to the last barrel was now spent,
all her pikes broken, forty of her best men slain, and the most part
of the rest hurt. In the beginning of the fight she had but one
hundred free from sickness, and fourscore and ten sick, laid in
hold upon the ballast: a small troop to man such a ship, and a weak   95
garrison to resist so mighty an army. By those hundred all was
sustained, the volleys, boardings, and ent'rings of fifteen ships of
war, besides those which beat her at large. On the contrary, the
Spanish were always supplied with soldiers brought from every
squadron: all manner of arms and powders at will. Unto ours there   100
remained no comfort at all, no hope, no supply either of ships,
men, or weapons; the masts all beaten overboard, all her tackle cut
asunder, her upper work altogether razed, and in effect evened she
was with the water, but the very foundation or bottom of a ship,
nothing being left overhead either for flight or defence. Sir   105
Richard finding himself in this distress, and unable any longer to
make resistance, having endured in this fifteen hours' fight the
assault of fifteen several armados, all by turns aboard him, and by
estimation eight hundred shot of great artillery, besides many
assaults and entries; and that himself and the ship must needs be   110
possessed by the enemy, who were now all cast in a ring round
about him (the *Revenge* not able to move one way or other, but as
she was moved with the waves and billow of the sea), commanded
the master gunner, whom he knew to be a most resolute man, to
split and sink the ship; that thereby nothing might remain of glory   115
or victory to the Spaniards: seeing in so many hours' fight, and
with so great a navy they were not able to take her, having had
fifteen hours' time, fifteen thousand men, and fifty and three sail
of men-of-war to perform it withal. And persuaded the company,
or as many as he could induce, to yield themselves unto God, and   120
to the mercy of none else; but as they had, like valiant resolute
men, repulsed so many enemies, they should not now shorten the
honour of their nation by prolonging their own lives for a few
hours or a few days. The master gunner readily condescended and
divers others; but the Captain and the Master were of another   125
opinion, and besought Sir Richard to have care of them: alleging
that the Spaniard would be as ready to entertain a composition, as
they were willing to offer the same; and that there being divers
sufficient and valiant men yet living, and whose wounds were not
mortal, they might do their country and prince acceptable service   130
hereafter. And (that where Sir Richard had alleged that the
Spaniards should never glory to have taken one ship of her

Majesty's, seeing that they had so long and so notably defended themselves) they answered, that the ship had six foot water in hold, three shot under water, which were so weakly stopped, as with the first working of the sea, she must needs sink, and was besides so crushed and bruised, as she could never be removed out of the place. 135

And as the matter was thus in dispute, and Sir Richard refusing to hearken to any of those reasons: the Master of the *Revenge* 140 (while the Captain won unto him the greater party) was convoyed aboard the General Don Alfonso Bassan. Who, finding none over hasty to enter the *Revenge* again, doubting lest Sir Richard would have blown them up and himself, and perceiving by the report of the Master of the *Revenge* his dangerous disposition, yielded that 145 all their lives should be saved, the company sent for England, and the better sort to pay such reasonable ransom as their estate would bear, and in the mean season to be free from galley or imprisonment. To this he so much the rather condescended as well, as I have said, for fear of further loss and mischief to 150 themselves, as also for the desire he had to recover Sir Richard Grenville, whom for his notable valour he seemed greatly to honour and admire.

When this answer was returned, and that safety of life was promised, the common sort being now at the end of their peril, 155 the most drew back from Sir Richard and the master gunner, being no hard matter to dissuade men from death to life. The master gunner, finding himself and Sir Richard thus prevented and mastered by the greater number, would have slain himself with a sword, had he not been by force withheld and locked into his 160 cabin. Then the General sent many boats aboard the *Revenge*, and divers of our men, fearing Sir Richard's disposition, stole away aboard the General and other ships. Sir Richard, thus over-matched, was sent unto by Alfonso Bassan to remove out of the *Revenge*, the ship being marvellous unsavoury, filled with blood 165 and bodies of dead and wounded men like a slaughter house. Sir Richard answered that he might do with his body what he list, for he esteemed it not, and as he was carried out of the ship he swounded, and reviving again desired the company to pray for him. The General used Sir Richard with all humanity, and left 170 nothing unattempted that tended to his recovery, highly com-mending his valour and worthiness, and greatly bewailed the danger wherein he was, being unto them a rare spectacle, and a resolution seldom approved, to see one ship turn toward so many enemies, to endure the charge and boarding of so many huge 175 armados, and to resist and repel the assaults and entries of so many soldiers. All which and more is confirmed by a Spanish Captain of the same armada, and a present actor in the fight, who being severed from the rest in a storm, was by the *Lion* of London, a

small ship, taken, and is now prisoner in London...... 180
There were slain and drowned in this fight, well near two thousand of the enemies,...... The *Admiral of the Hulks* and the *Ascention* of Seville were both sunk by the side of the *Revenge*; one other recovered the road of Saint Michels, and sunk also there; a fourth ran herself with the shore to save her men. Sir Richard 185 died, as it is said, the second or third day aboard the General, and was by them greatly bewailed. What became of his body, whether it were buried in the sea or on the land we know not: the comfort that remaineth to his friends is, that he hath ended his life honourably in respect of the reputation won to his nation and 190 country, and of the same to his posterity, and that being dead, he hath not outlived his own honour.

NOTES

2   *victuallers* smaller ships employed to carry provisions for a fleet.
     pinnaces small light vessels, attendant on larger vessels as tenders or scouting ships.
4   *last of August* 31 August 1591.
6   *armada* fleet of ships of war (hence the 'Spanish Armada' of 1588).
10   *recover* obtain.
11   *pestered* encumbered, obstructed.
     romaging having the cargo rearranged.
14   *ninety* out of a total of about two hundred.
19   *let slip* allow the anchor cable to run out, thus losing the anchor.
21   *weighed* raised the anchor to set sail.
24   *cut* unfurl, dress.
25   *cast about* change course.
32   *sprang their luff* brought the ship's head closer to the wind.
33   *under the lee* to leeward.
34   *answered* successful.
40   *high cargued* ?with a forecastle and half-deck.
40-1 *thousand......tons* By contrast the *Revenge*, which had been Sir Francis Drake's flagship against the Spanish Armada in 1588, was a little more than five hundred tons.
41   *after laid......aboard* subsequently ran alongside the *Revenge* (with intent to board her). 1591 edn reads 'afterlaid', but the form is otherwise unknown, though it might perhaps mean 'ran up under her stern' (i.e. behind).
42-3 *luffing up* bringing (the ships) into the wind.
45   *ordinance* ordnance (variant form), i.e. guns, in this case.
49   *larboard......starboard* left side (looking from the stern)......right side.
53   *cross-bar shot* ball with a bar projecting on each side.
58   *none* i.e. soldiers. Other reports differ on this point.
59-60 *voluntary gentlemen* gentlemen volunteers.
61   *deliberated* determined.

67   *armados* i.e. individual Spanish ships.

83   *composition* mutual agreement for the cessation of hostilities.

88   *success* outcome.
      bearing with sailing toward.

92   *pikes* long wooden-shafted weapons, with a pointed head of iron or steel.

98   *beat......large* fired on her from a distance.

103   *upper work* forecastle, etc.

104   *but* only.

118   *fifteen thousand* Hakluyt (*Principall Voyages*, 1598) trims this to 'above ten thousand'.

126   *them* i.e. all the men still surviving.

141   *convoyed* conveyed (variant form).

142   *aboard......Bassan* i.e. on to the ship (the *St Paul*) of the General (or Admiral) of the Spanish fleet, Don Alfonso Bassan.

148   *free from galley* i.e. they would not be forced to serve as galley-slaves in Spanish vessels.

149   *condescended* yielded, agreed.

157   *being* Supply 'it' before 'being'.

163   *aboard the General* i.e. aboard the General's ship.

165   *marvellous* extraordinarily.

169   *swounded* swooned (variant form).

174   *resolution seldom approved* fixed determination not often demonstrated (in a man).

181–2 *two thousand* Hakluyt again reduces 'two' to 'one'.

v

The plantation of Virginia, Jamestown, 1607

From John Smith, *The Generall Historie of Virginia, New-England, and the Summer Isles* (1624), bk. III (ed. E. Arber, 1895, 385–9).

[Virginia, named after Elizabeth, the Virgin Queen, was discovered in 1584 by an English expedition under the command of Philip Amadas and Arthur Barlow. Their glowing report resulted in a colonizing expedition under Sir Richard Grenville (see selection (iv)) in 1585, which deposited 108 settlers on Roanoke, an island off what is now North Carolina. They abandoned the settlement after a year and were brought back to England under the care of Sir Francis Drake. In 1586 Grenville planted another fifty men on Roanoke, who, when visited by a relief expedition in 1587, had disappeared (as did another 115 left there in 1587). After these ill-fated attempts, the project was abandoned until late 1606, when, under royal commission to found a Crown colony, the expedition described below set out and established Jamestown in 1607, the first permanent English colony on the North American mainland.]

Captain Bartholomew Gosnoll, one of the first movers of this plantation, having many years solicited many of his friends, but found small assistants, at last prevailed with some gentlemen, as Captain John Smith, Master Edward-Maria Wingfield, Master Robert Hunt, and divers others, who depended a year upon his   5
projects; but nothing could be effected, till by their great charge and industry, it came to be apprehended by certain of the nobility, gentry, and merchants, so that his Majesty, by his letters patents, gave commission for establishing councils, to direct here, and to govern and to execute there. To effect this was spent another year,   10
and by that, three ships were provided, one of a hundred tons, another of forty, and a pinnace of twenty. The transportation of the company was committed to Captain Christopher Newport, a mariner well practised for the western parts of America. But their orders for government were put in a box, not to be opened, nor the   15
governors known, until they arrived in Virginia.

On the nineteenth of December, 1606, we set sail from Blackwall, but by unprosperous winds were kept six weeks in the sight of England; all which time Master Hunt, our preacher, was so weak and sick that few expected his recovery. Yet although he   20
were but twenty miles from his habitation (the time we were in the Downs), and notwithstanding the stormy weather, nor the scandalous imputations (of some few, little better than atheists, of the greatest rank amongst us) suggested against him, all this could never force from him so much as a seeming desire to leave the   25
business, but preferred the service of God, in so good a voyage,

before any affection to contest with his godless foes, whose disastrous designs (could they have prevailed) had even then overthrown the business, so many discontents did then arise, had he not with the water of patience and his godly exhortations (but 　30 chiefly by his true devoted examples) quenched those flames of envy and dissension.

We watered at the Canaries, we traded with the salvages at Dominica, three weeks we spent in refreshing ourselves amongst these West India Isles......　35

Gone from thence in search of Virginia, the company was not a little discomforted, seeing the mariners had three days passed their reckoning and found no land; so that Captain Ratcliffe (captain of the pinnace) rather desired to bear up the helm to return for England than make further search. But God, the guider of all good 　40 actions, forcing them by an extreme storm to hull all night, did drive them by his providence to their desired port, beyond all their expectations; for never any of them had seen that coast.

The first land they made they called Cape Henry; where thirty of them, recreating themselves on shore, were assaulted by five 　45 salvages, who hurt two of the English very dangerously.

That night was the box opened and the orders read, in which Bartholomew Gosnoll, John Smith, Edward Wingfield, Christopher Newport, John Ratcliffe, John Martin, and George Kendall were named to be the council, and to choose a president amongst 　50 them for a year, who with the council should govern. Matters of moment were to be examined by a jury, but determined by the major part of the council, in which the president had two voices.

Until the thirteenth of May [1607] they sought a place to plant in; then the council was sworn, Master Wingfield was chosen 　55 president, and an oration made, why Captain Smith was not admitted of the council as the rest.

Now falleth every man to work: the council contrive the fort, the rest cut down trees to make place to pitch their tents; some provide clapboard to relade the ships, some make gardens, some 　60 nets, etc. The salvages often visited us kindly. The president's overweening jealousy would admit no exercise at arms, or fortification but the boughs of trees cast together in the form of a half moon by the extraordinary pains and diligence of Captain Kendall......What toil we had with so small a power to guard 　65 our workmen a-days, watch all night, resist our enemies, and effect our business, to relade the ships, cut down trees, and prepare the ground to plant our corn, etc., I refer to the reader's consideration.

Six weeks being spent in this manner, Captain Newport (who was hired only for our transportion) was to return with the ships. 　70 Now Captain Smith, who all this time from their departure from the Canaries was restrained as a prisoner, upon the scandalous suggestions of some of the chief (envying his repute) who feigned he intended to usurp the government, murder the council, and make himself king, that his confederates were dispersed in all the three ships, and that divers of his confederates that revealed it, would affirm it; for this he was committed as a prisoner. Thirteen weeks he remained thus suspected, and by that time the ships should return they pretended out of their commiserations to refer him to the Council in England to receive a check, rather than, by particulating his designs, make him so odious to the world, as to touch his life, or utterly overthrow his reputation. But he so much scorned their charity, and publicly defied the uttermost of their cruelty, he wisely prevented their policies, though he could not suppress their envies; yet so well he demeaned himself in this business, as all the company did see his innocency and his adversaries' malice, and those suborned to accuse him accused his accusers of subornation. Many untruths were alleged against him, but, being so apparently disproved, begat a general hatred in the hearts of the company against such unjust commanders, that the president was adjudged to give him two hundred pounds, so that all he had was seized upon, in part of satisfaction, which Smith presently returned to the store for the general use of the colony.

Many were the mischiefs that daily sprung from their ignorant (yet ambitious) spirits; but the good doctrine and exhortation of our preacher, Master Hunt, reconciled them, and caused Captain Smith to be admitted of the council.

The next day all received the communion, the day following the salvages voluntarily desired peace, and Captain Newport returned for England with news; leaving in Virginia one hundred, the fifteenth of June 1607.

75

80

85

90

95

100

NOTES

3   *small assistants* hardly any helpers or promoters. Smith may mean us to read 'assistance'.

5   *depended* waited in expectation (of success).

6   *charge* expense.

7   *apprehended* taken up, understood.

8   *letters patents* written authority.

18   *Blackwall* eastern suburb of London, on the Thames.

22   *Downs* roadstead off the east coast of Kent.

27   *affection* disposition.

29   *business* i.e. the whole project.

33   *salvages* savages (variant form).

37–8 *passed their reckoning* i.e. they had reckoned to have sighted the mainland (three days before).

39   *bear......helm* put the helm 'up' to bring the vessel into the wind.

41   *hull* drift to the wind with sails furled.

53   *two voices* i.e. two votes in order to break a tie. This arrangement seems to have been usual.

58   *contrive* i.e. draw up plans for.

60   *clapboard* staves to make barrels (for water).
       relade store again (with adequate water supply and other provisions).

62   *overweening jealousy* exaggerated suspicion (of his rivals among the other settlers). The president quickly changed his mind after an attack by the 'salvages', in which a boy was killed and seventeen men wounded.

68   *corn* i.e. wheat.

77–8   *Thirteen weeks* i.e. 24 March to 10 June 1607.

78   *that time* the time that.

79   *commiserations* (pretended) feelings of compassion.

80   *check* reprimand.

81   *particulating* particularizing.

89   *begat* begot.

92   *in part of satisfaction* i.e. as a means of meeting the fine.

97   *admitted . . . . . . council* Shortly after this Smith became president of the council.

13 Epilogue: the Elizabethan stage jig

As one of the few surviving examples of a genuine Elizabethan stage jig, George Attowell's *Frauncis new Jigge* (*c*.1595) may serve as a suitable epilogue to a collection of contemporary selections illustrating the moral, social, religious and economic conditions out of which Elizabethan–Jacobean England grew and flourished. Ephemeral in nature, sometimes with political and satiric overtones, and often apparently rowdy and suggestively bawdy, the stage jig, a mélange of dancing and singing, often (as in the present instance) given some slight dramatic form by a simple plot line, was presented at the end of a play (tragic or comic; see above, p. 56) and was an eagerly awaited and popular part of an afternoon at the theatre.

Stage jigs, comparable in some ways to the farcical 'after-pieces' of the Restoration and the eighteenth and nineteenth centuries, afforded an outlet for pent-up emotions and energies, sometimes with unfortunate results so far as the behaviour of the audience was concerned. For this reason, as well as for possible moral considerations, stage jigs were opposed not only by the usual anti-theatre factions (an official attempt was made to suppress 'jigs at the end of plays' in 1612) but by the best dramatists for more aesthetic reasons. As Thomas Dekker observes (*A Strange Horse-Race* (1613), ed. A. B. Grosart, *Prose Works*, III, 340):

> And, as I have often seen, after the finishing of some worthy tragedy or catastrophe [the fifth act] in the open theatres [i.e. public theatres, like the Fortune or Red Bull] that the scene hath been more black (about a nasty bawdy jig) than the most horrid scene in the play was, the stinkards [the 'groundlings' among the audience] speaking all things, yet no man understanding any thing; a mutiny being amongst them, yet none in danger; no tumult, and yet no quietness; no mischiefs begotten, and yet mischief born; the swiftness of such a torrent, the more it overwhelms, breeding the more pleasure.

Ben Jonson also complains (Induction to *Bartholomew Fair*, 1614) of 'the concupiscence of jigs and dances' as beneath serious comedy. And Shakespeare's Hamlet facetiously accuses Polonius of preferring 'a jig or a tale of bawdry' (III.ii.500) to a good play, though Shakespeare includes a rudimentary form of the stage jig at the end of *II Henry IV*, where a dancer (perhaps William Kemp) speaks a prose epilogue and concludes it with a dance. Both Kemp and the earlier comedian, Richard Tarlton, were particularly famous as 'jig-makers'.

The close association of George Attowell (or Attewell) with 'Frauncis Jigge' was most probably as performer rather than author. He is known only as an actor connected with Lord Strange's Men and perhaps with the Queen's Men from 1590–95. Judged by the comparatively few other extant examples, 'Attowell's Jig', as it is usually called, is fairly typical in its use of dialogue arranged in various ballad stanzas and its vestigial plot, the dancing and singing being accompanied by several commonly known ballad 'tunes' played by the theatre 'music' (pipe and tabor and/or fiddlers). Whether the dialogue was all sung, or partly spoken and partly sung, is not, I believe, now known. Certainly Bess, a boy actor, enters singing a stanza from an earlier traditional ballad (see notes).

The author of 'Attowell's Jig' suggests some slight social criticism: Richard, a farmer, who might have been presented as a country clown in a less sympathetic treatment, is honest and faithful to his wife; Francis, a gentleman, is dissolute, with no respect for the sanctity of marriage. Richard rings true; Francis' repentance is merely *pro forma* till next time. But the moral tone is light and one may suspect that, with its seduction plot evaded only by the time-honoured 'bed trick' (compare Shakespeare's *All's Well That Ends Well* and *Measure for Measure*), it would have qualified as a 'nasty bawdy jig' in the view of the sterner moralists of the period.

For further information, see H. E. Rollins, *A Pepysian Garland* (1922), pp. xiv–xx; C. R. Baskervill, *The Elizabethan Jig* (1929); C. J. Sisson, *Lost Plays of Shakespeare's Age* (1936), chap. III.

George Attowell (*or* Attewell), *Frauncis new Jigge, betweene Frauncis a Gentleman, and Richard a Farmer* (c.1595), broadside in the Pepys Collection, Magdalene College, Cambridge (ed. Hyder E. Rollins in *A Pepysian Garland* (1922), pp. 1–10).

[*Enter*] BESS.
[To the tune of 'Walsingham'.]

1   BESS [*Singing*] As I went to Walsingham,
        To the shrine with speed,
    Met I with a jolly palmer,
        In a pilgrim's weed.

[*Enter* FRANCIS.]

    Now God you save, you jolly palmer!   5
        FRANCIS. Welcome, lady gay!
    Oft have I sued to thee for love.
        BESS. Oft have I said you nay.

2   FRANCIS. My love is fixed. BESS. And so is mine,
        But not on you;   10
    For to my husband whilst I live,
        I will ever be true.

    FRANCIS. I'll give thee gold and rich array.
        BESS. Which I shall buy too dear.
    FRANCIS. Nought shalt thou want; then say not nay.   15
        BESS. Naught would you make me, I fear.

3   What though you be a gentleman,
        And have lands great store?
    I will be chaste, do what you can,
        Though I live ne'er so poor.   20
    FRANCIS. Thy beauty rare hath wounded me,
        And pierc'd my heart.
    BESS. Your foolish love doth trouble me;
        Pray you, sir, depart.

4   FRANCIS. Then tell me, sweet, wilt thou consent   25
        Unto my desire?
    BESS. And if I should, then tell me, sir,
        What is it you require?

    FRANCIS. For to enjoy thee as my love.
        BESS. Sir, you have a wife: 30
    Therefore let your suit have an end.
        FRANCIS. First will I lose my life.

5   All that I have thou shalt command.
    BESS. Then my love you have.
  FRANCIS. Your meaning I well understand.   35
    BESS. I yield to what you crave.
  FRANCIS. But tell me, sweet, when shall I enjoy
    My heart's delight?
  BESS. I prithee, sweetheart, be not coy,
    Even soon at night.   40

6   My husband is rid ten miles from home,
    Money to receive;
In the evening see you come.
    FRANCIS. Till then I take my leave.   *[Exit]*
  BESS. Thus have I rid my hands full well   45
    Of my amorous love,
And my sweet husband will I tell
    How he doth me move.

        Enter RICHARD, *Bess's husband.*
        To the tune of 'The Jewish dance'.

7   RICHARD. Hey, down a down,
    Hey down a down, a down!   50
There is never a lusty farmer
    In all our town
That hath more cause
    To lead a merry life
Than I that am married   55
    To an honest, faithful wife.
  BESS. I thank you, gentle husband,
    You praise me to my face.
  RICHARD. I cry thee mercy, Bessie,
    I knew thee not in place.   60

8   BESS. Believe me, gentle husband,
    If you knew as much as I,
The words that you have spoken,
    You quickly would deny;
For since you went from home,   65
    A suitor I have had,
Who is so far in love with me
    That he is almost mad.
He'll give me gold and silver store,
    And money for to spend,   70
And I have promis'd him therefore
    To be his loving friend.

9   RICHARD. Believe me, gentle wife,
        But this makes me to frown;
    There is no gentleman nor knight,   75
        Nor lord of high renown,
    That shall enjoy thy love, girl,
        Though he were ne'er so good!
    Before he wrong my Bessie so,
        I'll spend on him my blood.   80
    And therefore tell me who it is
        That doth desire thy love.
    BESS. Our neighbour, Master Francis,
        That often did me move;

10 To whom I gave consent   85
        His mind for to fulfill,
    And promis'd him this night
        That he should have his will.
    Nay, do not frown, good Dickie,
        But hear me speak my mind: 90
    For thou shalt see, I'll warrant thee,
        I'll use him in his kind;
    For unto thee I will be true
        So long as I do live;
    I'll never change thee for a new,   95
        Nor once my mind so give.

11 Go you to Mistress Francis,
        And this to her declare,
    And will her with all speed
        To my house to repair,   100
    Where she and I'll devise
        Some pretty knavish wile;
    For I have laid the plot
        Her husband to beguile.
    Make haste, I pray, and tarry not,   105
        For long he will not stay.
    RICHARD. Fear not, I'll tell her such a tale
        Shall make her come away.   [*Exit*]

12 BESS. Now, Bess, bethink thee
        What thou hast to do.   110
    Thy lover will come presently,
        And hardly will he woo.
    I will teach my gentleman
        A trick that he may know
    I am too crafty and too wise   115

To be o'erreached so!
But here he comes now; not a word,
   But fall to work again.   *She sews*

[*Enter* FRANCIS.]

FRANCIS. How now, sweetheart, at work so hard?
   BESS. Ay, sir, I must take pains.   120

13   FRANCIS. But say, my lovely sweeting,
   Thy promise wilt thou keep?
Shall I enjoy thy love,
   This night with me to sleep?
BESS. My husband rid from home,   125
   Here safely may you stay.
FRANCIS. And I have made my wife believe
   I rid another way.
BESS. Go in, good sir, what e'er betide,
   This night and lodge with me.   130
FRANCIS. The happiest night that ever I had!
   Thy friend still will I be.   [*Exit*]

Enter MISTRESS FRANCIS *with* RICHARD.
To the tune of 'Bugle Bow'.

14   WIFE. I thank you, neighbour Richard,
   For bringing me this news.
RICHARD. Nay, thank my wife that loves me so,   135
   And will not you abuse.
WIFE. But see whereas she stands,
   And waiteth our return.
RICHARD. You must go cool your husband's heat,
   That so in love doth burn.   140
BESS. Now, Dickie, welcome home,
   And, mistress, welcome hither.
Grieve not, although you find
   Your husband and I together;
For you shall have your right,   145
   Nor will I wrong you so:
Then change apparel with me straight,
   And unto him do go. [BESS *and* WIFE *exchange clothes*]
WIFE. For this your kind good will
   A thousand thanks I give,   150
And make account I will requite
   This kindness, if I live.
BESS. I hope it shall not need;
   Dick will not serve me so:
I know he loves me not so ill   155
   A-ranging for to go.

RICHARD. No, faith, my lovely Bess;
   First will I lose my life,
Before I'll break my wedlock bonds,
   Or seek to wrong my wife.   [*Exit* WIFE] 160
Now thinks good Master Francis
   He hath thee in his bed,
And makes account he is grafting
   Of horns upon my head.
But softly! stand aside;   165
   Now shall we know his mind,
And how he would have used thee,
   If thou hadst been so kind.   [*They stand to one side*]

Enter MASTER FRANCIS *with his own wife, having a mask*
    before her face, supposing her to be BESS.
    To the tune of 'Go from my window'.

15   FRANCIS. Farewell my joy and heart's delight,
      Till next we meet again.   170
   Thy kindness to requite, for lodging me all night,
      Here's ten pound for thy pain;
   And more to show my love to thee
      Wear this ring for my sake.
   WIFE. Without your gold or fee you shall have more of
      me.   175
      FRANCIS. No doubt of that I make.

16   WIFE. Then let your love continue still.
      FRANCIS. It shall, till life doth end.
   WIFE. Your wife I greatly fear. FRANCIS. For her thou
      need'st not care,
      So I remain thy friend.   180
   WIFE. But you'll suspect me, without cause,
      That I am false to you,
   And then you'll cast me off, and make me but a scoff,
      Since that I prove untrue.

17   FRANCIS. Then never trust man for my sake,   185
      If I prove so unkind.
   [WIFE.] So often have you sworn, sir, since that you were
      born,
      And soon have chang'd your mind.
   [FRANCIS.] Nor wife nor life, nor goods nor lands,
      Shall make me leave my love;   190
   Nor any worldly treasure make me forgo my pleasure,
      Nor once my mind remove.

18   WIFE. But soft a while! Who is yonder? Do you see
          My husband? Out, alas!
       FRANCIS. And yonder is my wife! Now shall we have a
          life!   195
       How cometh this to pass?

    [RICHARD *and* BESS, *disguised as the* WIFE, *come forward.*]

    RICHARD. Come hither gentle Bess. I charge thee, do
          confess
       What makes Master Francis here?
    [WIFE.] Good husband, pardon me! I'll tell the truth to
          thee.
       RICHARD. Then speak and do not fear.   200

19   FRANCIS. Nay, neighbour Richard, hark to me;
          I'll tell the troth to you.
       [BESS.] Nay, tell it unto me, good sir, that I may see
          What you have here to do.
       But you can make no scuse to colour this abuse;   205
          This wrong is too too great.
       RICHARD. Good sir, I take great scorn you should proffer
          me the horn.
       WIFE. Now must I cool this heat.   [*She unmasks*]

20   Nay, neighbour Richard, be content;
          Thou hast no wrong at all.   210
       [*To* FRANCIS] Thy wife hath done thee right, and
          pleasur'd me this night.
       FRANCIS. This frets me to the gall.
       Good wife, forgive me this offence;
          I do repent mine ill.
       WIFE. I thank you with mine heart for playing this kind
          part,   215
          Though sore against your will.

21   Nay, gentle husband, frown not so,
          For you have made amends.
       I think it is good gain to have ten pound for my pain;
          Then let us both be friends.   220
       FRANCIS. Ashamed I am and know not what to say.
          Good wife, forgive this crime.
       Alas, I do repent. WIFE. Tut, I could be content
          To be served so many a time!

22   FRANCIS. Good neighbour Richard, be content;   225
          I'll woo thy wife no more:

I have enough of this. WIFE. Then all forgiven is,
　　I thank thee, Dick, therefore,
And to thy wife I'll give this gold;
　　I hope you'll not say no: 230
Since I have had the pleasure, let her enjoy the treasure.
　　FRANCIS. Good wife, let it be so.

23　　BESS. I thank you, gentle mistress. RICHARD. Faith, and so
　　　　do I.
　　Sir, learn your own wife to know,
And shoot not in the dark for fear you miss the mark.   235
　　BESS. He hath paid for this, I trow.
All women learn of me. FRANCIS. All men by me take
　　heed
　　How you a woman trust.
WIFE. Nay, women trust no men. FRANCIS. And if they
　　do, how then?
　　WIFE. There's few of them prove just.   240

24　　Farewell, neighbour Richard! Farewell honest Bess!
　　I hope we are all friends.
[RICHARD.] [*To* FRANCIS] And if you stay at home, and
　　use not thus to come,
　　Here all our quarrel ends.

FINIS.

George Attowell.

NOTES

[The musical notation for the tunes of 'Walsingham', 'Bugle Bow' and 'Go from my window' may be found in C. L. Simpson, *The British Broadside Ballad and Its Music*, 1966, pp. 741, 74, 259; that for 'The Jewish dance' is unknown, the only reference to it occurring in this jig.]

1–8 These lines (perhaps only 1–4) are in the earlier tradition of a ballad on the pilgrimage to the shrine of Our Lady of Walsingham (see *Bishop Percy's Folio Manuscript*, ed. J. W. Hales and F. J. Furnivall (1868), III, 465–72). The priory at Old Walsingham (in Norfolk) was dissolved in 1538 and the famous image of the Virgin Mary burned.

4 *weed* garment, clothing.

15–16 *Nought......Naught* nothing......immoral, vicious.

39 *coy* modest, shy. This line may be a continuation of Francis' lines, Bess beginning to speak with l. 40 ('coy' is more suitable to Bess).

56 *honest* chaste.

96 *once* ever.

102 *knavish wile* roguish trick.

106 *stay* wait (i.e. he'll be back soon).

108 *come away* i.e. come here.

112 *hardly* pressingly, strongly.

125 *rid* having ridden.

128 *another way* in a direction other than this.

163–4 *grafting......head* A man whose wife was unfaithful to him (a cuckold) was supposed, metaphorically, to sprout horns – a jest the Elizabethans never tired of. Thus Othello (III.iii.284) says 'I have a pain upon my forehead, here.', when he thinks Desdemona has been unfaithful to him with Cassio.

171 *lodging......night* The time scheme is obviously, as so often in Elizabethan–Jacobean drama, very elastic.

172 *for thy pain* in recompense for your trouble.

175–6 Some neat, if rather heavy, irony.

192 *remove* change.

193 *But soft* exclamation to enjoin silence.

199 The Wife, disguised as Bess, pretends to address Richard as her husband. Assigned to Bess in 1595 text.

202 *troth* truth.

203 Bess, disguised as Francis' Wife. Assigned to Wife in 1595 text.

205 *scuse* excuse.
      colour disguise.

207 *proffer......horn* See note on ll. 163–4.

211 *pleasur'd me* given me pleasure (with my husband).

212 *frets......gall* rubs me on a sore spot.

227 *of this* as a result of all that has happened.

243–4 These lines are wrongly given to the Wife in 1595 text. Either Richard (as here) or Bess is possible.

Glossary

The following short glossary, containing more frequently used words or special forms, is intended to supplement the annotation in the explanatory notes, where, to avoid repetition, such words and forms are not always glossed. Modern meanings are not usually included, since the context in which a word appears should make it clear when the modern sense is, or is not, applicable.

a': *prep.* of, on, at, in
after: *prep.* according to; *adv.* afterwards
albeit: *conj.* even though
and: *conj.* if, though
angel: *n.* gold coin worth about ten shillings

because: *conj.* in order that
beside: *adv.* besides, in addition to; opposed to, against
betime: *adv.* in good time; betimes: *adv.* early
but: *conj.* but that; only; if; without

cog: *v.* cheat, deceive, beguile
commodity: *n.* consignment of wares; profit, gain
companion: *n.* base fellow
conceit: *v.* conceive, form an idea or opinion; *n.* conception, thought, intelligence; imagination; imaginative notion, fancy; trick, device.
conversation: *n.* behaviour, manner of life; living together, intercourse
cony: *n.* rabbit; dupe, gull; term of endearment
cony-catcher: *n.* cheat, sharper, swindler
cozen: *v.* cheat, deceive, swindle
cozenage: *n.* deceit, fraud
cozener: *n.* cheat, impostor, sharper, swindler
cunning: *n.* ability, cleverness; *adj.* learned, skilful
cupboard: *n.* sideboard
curious: *adj.* skilful, expert; accurate; fastidious; elegant

device: *n.* excuse, contrivance, trick
doublet: *n.* close-fitting garment, with or without sleeves

effeminate: *adj.* unmanly
eftsoons: *adv.* again, soon afterwards

fact: *n.* deed, act
for: *conj.* because; in order that; *prep.* for the sake of, because of; against
forsooth: *adv.* in truth
furniture: *n.* furnishings, equipment, trappings

go: *v.* walk
goodman (of the house): *n.* husband, head of the household
gripe: *v.* grip, grasp, seize
groat: *n.* silver coin worth four pence
gull: *v.* cheat, swindle, deceive: *n.* dupe, simpleton, country fellow (victim of the 'cony-catcher')

ha': have
handkercher: *n.* handkerchief
hardly: *adv.* with difficulty, scarcely; strongly
'hem: *pron.* them
his: *pron.* its; form of genitive inflection = *'s*
hose, hosen: *n.* long stockings; breeches
howbeit: *conj.* nevertheless
huswife: *n.* housewife

jerkin: *n.* close-fitting short coat

kind: *n.* nature, natural disposition; manner

learn: *v.* teach
let: *v.* hinder, impede; *n.* hindrance, impediment
lewd: *adj.* ill-mannered, naughty, wicked; lascivious; ignorant

marry: *interj.* indeed, why, to be sure (weakened oath, 'by the Virgin Mary')
mate: *n.* fellow (contemptuous)

next: *adj.* nearest (in relationship or place)
nice: *adj.* trifling, fastidious, precise
noble: *n.* gold coin worth between six shillings, eight pence, and ten shillings

or: *conj.* before, sooner than
other: *pron.* others

pain(s): *n.* labour, effort
parts: *n.* abilities, capacities
peradventure: *adv.* perhaps, possibly
perforce: *adv.* of necessity
plate: *n.* silver service dish(es)
present: *adj.* immediate, instant
presently: *adv.* at once, immediately
pretend: *v.* intend, import
prevent: *v.* foresee, anticipate
proper: *adj.* (one's or its) own; admirable, good-looking; complete

quality: *n.* profession, occupation (often with reference to actors); status, rank

quick: *adj.* living, alive, lively; perceptive

quoth: said

ruff: *n.* neckwear of starched linen, standing out all round the neck, worn by both men and women

several: *adj.* different; distinct

shift: *n.* trick, evasive stratagem

shilling: *n.* silver coin worth twelve pence; twenty shillings constituted one pound

simple: *n.* medicinal herb; *adj.* slight, insignificant; witless

sith: *adv., prep., conj.* since

sithence: *adv., prep., conj.* since

sleight: *n.* trick, device

sometime: *adv.* at one time or another

still: *adv.* continually, constantly, always

tester: *n.* silver coin worth six pence

toy: *n.* trifle

vulgar: *adj.* common, popular, ordinary

wist: known

withal: *prep.* with, moreover

wot: know

y'are: you are

Index of plays

Note: bold numbers refer to illustrations.

General Index

Note: page references to plays quoted or cited are not included under author in the General Index; for these, see Index of Plays under play title. Bold numbers refer to illustrations.